Societal values don't [W9-BYS-930] western, my values don't bind others

*The Editor*

RICHARD SWEDBERG is professor of sociology at Cornell University. He is the author of *Max Weber and the Idea of Economic Sociology* and *A Max Weber Dictionary*. He is co-editor (with Neil Smelser) of *The Handbook of Economic Sociology* and (with Mark Granovetter) of *The Sociology of Economic Life*.

★ Purpose Rationality seperate from outcomes
Rationality as its own purpose is uniquely western

- Economic rationality subject to everyone according to economics, inescapable according to economics
  - utility, nonjudgemental, no socially ordained or justiciable purpose

West: Means seperated from ends, Rationality seperate from purpose; value, no goal purpose

# Norton Critical Editions in the History of Ideas

AQUINAS • St. Thomas Aquinas on Politics and Ethics
*translated and edited by Paul E. Sigmund*

DARWIN
*selected and edited by Philip Appleman (Third Edition)*

ERASMUS • The Praise of Folly and Other Writings
*translated and edited by Robert M. Adams*

HERODOTUS • The Histories
*translated by Walter E. Blanco, edited by Walter E. Blanco*
*and Jennifer Tolbert Roberts*

HOBBES • *Leviathan*
*edited by Richard E. Flathman and David Johnston*

LOCKE • The Selected Political Writings of John Locke
*edited by Paul E. Sigmund*

MACHIAVELLI • The Prince
*translated and edited by Robert M. Adams (Second Edition)*

MALTHUS • An Essay on the Principle of Population
*edited by Philip Appleman (Second Edition)*

MARX • The Communist Manifesto
*edited by Frederic L. Bender*

MILL • Mill: The Spirit of the Age, On Liberty,
The Subjection of Women
*edited by Alan Ryan*

MORE • Utopia
*translated and edited by Robert M. Adams (Second Edition)*

NEWMAN • Apologia Pro Vita Sua
*edited by David J. DeLaura*

NEWTON
*selected and edited by I. Bernard Cohen and Richard S. Westfall*

ROUSSEAU • Rousseau's Political Writings
*translated by Julia Conaway Bondanella, edited by Alan Ritter*

ST. PAUL • The Writings of St. Paul
*edited by Wayne A. Meeks and John T. Fitzgerald (Second Edition)*

THOREAU • Walden and Resistance to Civil Government
*edited by William Rossi (Second Edition)*

THUCYDIDES • The Peloponnesian War
*translated by Walter E. Blanco, edited by Walter E. Blanco*
*and Jennifer Tolbert Roberts*

TOCQUEVILLE • Democracy in America
*edited by Isaak Kramnick*

WATSON • The Double Helix: A Personal Account
of the Discovery of the Structure of DNA
*edited by Gunther S. Stent*

WEBER • The Protestant Ethic and the Spirit of Capitalism
*edited by Richard Swedberg*

WOLLSTONECRAFT • A Vindication of the Rights of Woman
*edited by Carol H. Poston (Second Edition)*

A NORTON CRITICAL EDITION

Max Weber

# THE PROTESTANT ETHIC AND THE SPIRIT OF CAPITALISM

## THE TALCOTT PARSONS TRANSLATION
## INTERPRETATIONS

*Edited by*

RICHARD SWEDBERG
**CORNELL UNIVERSITY**

W • W • NORTON & COMPANY • *New York* • *London*

W. W. Norton & Company has been independent since its founding in 1923, when William Warder Norton and Mary D. Herter Norton first published lectures delivered at the People's Institute, the adult education division of New York City's Cooper Union. The firm soon expanded its program beyond the Institute, publishing books by celebrated academics from America and abroad. By mid-century, the two major pillars of Norton's publishing program—trade books and college texts—were firmly established. In the 1950s, the Norton family transferred control of the company to its employees, and today—with a staff of four hundred and a comparable number of trade, college, and professional titles published each year—W. W. Norton & Company stands as the largest and oldest publishing house owned wholly by its employees.

The text of this book is composed in Fairfield Medium with the display set in Bernhard Modern.
Manufacturing by the Courier Companies—Westford division.
Book design by Antonina Krass.
Composition by Binghamton Valley Composition.
Production manager: Eric Pier-Hocking.

Library of Congress Cataloging-in-Publication Data

Weber, Max, 1864-1920.
    [Protestantische Ethik und der Geist des Kapitalismus. English]
    The Protestant ethic and the spirit of capitalism / Max Weber; the Talcott Parsons translation interpretations edited by Richard Swedberg.—1st ed.
    p. cm.—(A Norton critical edition)
    Includes bibliographical references.
    **ISBN 978-0-393-93068-9 (pbk.)**
    1. Capitalism—Religious aspects—Protestant churches.
2. Protestant work ethic.   I. Title.
    BR115.C3W413   2009
    306.6—dc22                                            2008037340

W. W. Norton & Company., Inc., 500 Fifth Avenue, New York,
N. Y. 10110
www.wwnorton.com
W. W. Norton & Company Ltd., Castle House, 75/76 Wells Street, London
W1T 3QT

1   2   3   4   5   6   7   8   9   0

# Contents

# Preface

*The Protestant Ethic and the Spirit of Capitalism* by Max Weber is one of the world's most famous studies in social science, competing for the first place with works such as *Capital* by Karl Marx and *Democracy in America* by Alexis de Tocqueville. What accounts for its fame and why has "the Protestant work ethic" become a common expression in many languages? First of all, there is the bold and counterintuitive thesis in Weber's work: religion helped to create modern capitalism. The story of how the link between religion and capitalism came into being is also constructed in a very dramatic way, with the earnest Protestant believer looking for signs to please God and discovering that hard work and profit making are such signs.

Second, *The Protestant Ethic* addresses and tries to explain why modern people live in a world where two of the most central and cherished values are hard work and profit making, regardless of one's political and religious beliefs. There is finally an additional quality to *The Protestant Ethic* that is harder to put one's finger on but which is nonetheless there. It has to do with its capacity to simultaneously convince and enervate people. From the moment that it was published, Weber's study has led to a stormy debate that is still going on. Its readers either admire the arguments in *The Protestant Ethic* or dislike them.

The ambivalent reception of *The Protestant Ethic* has no doubt thrived on the subtlety of Weber's argument. A quick summary of his work would read as follows. During the sixteenth to nineteenth century in Europe, certain religious ideas emerged that Weber refers to as ascetic Protestantism. These were not only religious; they also helped to strengthen and spread a radically new type of mentality to economic affairs that would radically change the nature of capitalism, as it had been known till then.

While people had earlier approached economic issues in a traditional manner, be it issues relating to the management of their households or interactions in the marketplace, this now came to an end. From now on, a very rational and methodical type of economic mentality appeared. Once this mentality had grown strong, it helped to accelerate Western capitalism into becoming a new and formidable dynamic force that would change the world in profound ways.

While originally there was an explicit link between religion in the form of ascetic Protestantism and the economy, according to Weber, this would soon change. Today, he says, people live in a cosmos in which you have to work hard and reinvest your money or you will go under in the relentless competition that exists. Religion no longer has anything to do with modern, rational capitalism.

The ascetic Protestants, who played a key role in helping this new "spirit of modern, rational capitalism" to come into being, consisted of a small number of people organized in sects or sect-like churches, such as Calvinism, Pietism, Methodism, and various Baptist sects. Their beliefs were similar to Lutheranism, Weber says, in that they all saw man's work on earth as a religious task, something that began with the Reformation and had its roots in Luther's famous translation of the Bible.

But the ascetic Protestants differed from the Lutherans in that they were not traditional in their approach to life. Instead, they were strongly rational and methodical in everything they did, whether it was religious tasks or political and economic tasks. While Luther wanted people to render unto God the things that are God's, and unto Caesar the things that are Caesar's, the approach of the ascetic Protestants was different. They were truly radical and not traditional in spirit; and if the secular lords did not behave in accordance with the Bible, they should not be obeyed.

The ascetic Protestants could be found in countries such as Switzerland, England, the Netherlands, and from the 1600s and onward (but not discussed by Weber in this study), also in the United States. In all of these sects, the great motivating force of ascetic religion somehow also got linked to the force of profit making and the idea that working hard is a way of honoring God. The result was a tremendous social force that made it possible for modern rational capitalism to ideologically emerge as the most important institution in the West, displacing the Church once and for all.

As soon as it was published in 1904–05, *The Protestant Ethic* was criticized; and the debate still goes on today, more than a century later. Why, it was asked, did this new type of modern dynamic capitalism emerge only in the West and not, say, in China or India? Do not these countries have religions that are similar to Protestantism in being rational and disciplined, such as Confucianism, Shintoism, Jainism, and so on? And even if they do not, does not Japan (and today China) show that the modern type of capitalism can also emerge outside the West?

As far as the West itself was concerned, it was wondered, why did just ascetic Protestantism play the key role in ushering in modern capitalism and not, say, Catholicism, Judaism, or Protestantism in general (including Lutheranism)? And anyway, where were Weber's empirical proofs for all of this? More precisely, how do we know that the Calvinists, Baptists, and other ascetic Protestants indeed looked for signs, that they saw successful profit making as one of these signs, and that their methodical and ascetic mentality then spread to other people and helped to create and spread this alleged new "spirit of capitalism"?

Answers have been given to all of these questions, but the debate still continues, as exemplified by the articles that have been included at the end of this volume. The debate has recently been extended to the issue of how to best translate Weber's text into English, French, and other languages. The Norton Critical Edition uses the first and legendary translation from 1930 of American sociologist Talcott Parsons. But it should be noted that this translation has been the focus of much debate (see, especially, the 2005 article by Lawrence Scaff [cited in the Bibliography], for a summary of this debate).

RICHARD SWEDBERG

# Translator's Preface

Max Weber's essay, *Die protestantische Ethik und der Geist des Kapitalismus*, which is here translated, was first published in the *Archiv für Sozialwissenschaft und Sozialpolitik*, Volumes XX and XXI, for 1904–5. It was reprinted in 1920 as the first study in the ambitious series *Gesammelte Aufsätze zur Religionssoziologie*, which was left unfinished by Weber's untimely death in that same year. For the new printing he made considerable changes, and appended both new material and replies to criticism in footnotes. The translation has, however, been made directly from this last edition. Though the volume of footnotes is excessively large, so as to form a serious detriment to the reader's enjoyment, it has not seemed advisable either to omit any of them or to attempt to incorporate them into the text. As it stands it shows most plainly how the problem has grown in Weber's own mind, and it would be a pity to destroy that for the sake of artistic perfection. A careful perusal of the notes is, however, especially recommended to the reader, since a great deal of important material is contained in them. The fact that they are printed separately from the main text should not be allowed to hinder their use. The translation is, as far as is possible, faithful to the text, rather than attempting to achieve any more than ordinary, clear English style. Nothing has been altered, and only a few comments to clarify obscure points and to refer the reader to related parts of Weber's work have been added.

The Introduction, which is placed before the main essay, was written by Weber in 1920 for the whole series on the Sociology of Religion. It has been included in this translation because it gives some of the general background of ideas and problems into which Weber himself meant this particular study to fit. That has seemed particularly desirable since, in the voluminous discussion which has grown up in Germany around Weber's essay, a great deal of misplaced criticism has been due to the failure properly to appreciate the scope and limitations of the study. While it is impossible to appreciate that fully without a thorough study of Weber's sociological work as a whole, this brief introduction should suffice to prevent a great deal of misunderstanding.

The series of which this essay forms a part was, as has been said, left unfinished at Weber's death. The first volume only had been prepared for the press by his own hand. Besides the parts translated here, it contains a short, closely related study, *Die protestantischen Sekten und der Geist des Kapitalismus*; a general introduction to the further studies of particular religions which as a whole he called *Die Wirtschaftsethik der Weltreligionen*; and a long study of Confucianism and Taoism. The second and third volumes, which were published after his death, without the thorough revision which he had contemplated, contain studies of Hinduism and Buddhism and Ancient Judaism. In addition he had done work on other studies, notably of Islam, Early Christianity, and Talmudic Judaism, which were not yet in a condition fit for publication in any form. Nevertheless, enough of the whole series has been preserved to show something of the extraordinary breadth and depth of Weber's grasp of cultural problems. What is here presented to English-speaking readers is only a fragment, but it is a fragment which is in many ways of central significance for Weber's philosophy of history, as well as being of very great and very general interest for the thesis it advances to explain some of the most important aspects of modern culture.

TALCOTT PARSONS
Cambridge, Mass., U.S.A.
*January* 1930

The Text of
# THE PROTESTANT ETHIC AND THE SPIRIT OF CAPITALISM

# Author's Introduction

A product of modern European civilization, studying any problem of universal history, is bound to ask himself to what combination of circumstances the fact should be attributed that in Western civilization, and in Western civilization only, cultural phenomena have appeared which (as we like to think) lie in a line of development having *universal* significance and value.

Only in the West does science exist at a stage of development which we recognize to-day as valid. Empirical knowledge, reflection on problems of the cosmos and of life, philosophical and theological wisdom of the most profound sort, are not confined to it, though in the case of the last the full development of a systematic theology must be credited to Christianity under the influence of Hellenism, since there were only fragments in Islam and in a few Indian sects. In short, knowledge and observation of great refinement have existed elsewhere, above all in India, China, Babylonia, Egypt. But in Babylonia and elsewhere astronomy lacked—which makes its development all the more astounding—the mathematical foundation which it first received from the Greeks. The Indian geometry had no rational proof; that was another product of the Greek intellect, also the creator of mechanics and physics. The Indian natural sciences, though well developed in observation, lacked the method of experiment, which was, apart from beginnings in antiquity, essentially a product of the Renaissance, as was the modern laboratory. Hence medicine, especially in India, though highly developed in empirical technique, lacked a biological and particularly a biochemical foundation. A rational chemistry has been absent from all areas of culture except the West.

The highly developed historical scholarship of China did not have the method of Thucydides. Machiavelli, it is true, had predecessors in India; but all Indian political thought was lacking in a systematic method comparable to that of Aristotle, and, indeed, in the possession of rational concepts. Not all the anticipations in India (School of Mimamsa), nor the extensive codification especially in the Near East, nor all the Indian and other books of law, had the strictly systematic forms of thought, so essential to a rational jurisprudence, of the Roman law and of the Western law under its influence. A structure like the canon law is known only to the West.

A similar statement is true of art. The musical ear of other peoples has probably been even more sensitively developed than our own, certainly not less so. Polyphonic music of various kinds has been widely distributed over the earth. The co-operation of a number of instruments and also the singing of parts have existed elsewhere. All our rational tone intervals have been known and calculated. But rational harmonious music, both counterpoint and harmony, formation of the tone material on the basis of three triads with the harmonic third; our chromatics and enharmonics, not interpreted in terms of space, but, since the Renaissance, of harmony; our orchestra, with its string quartet as a nucleus, and the organization of ensembles of wind instruments; our bass accompaniment; our system of notation, which has made possible the composition and production of modern musical works, and thus their very survival; our sonatas, symphonies, operas; and finally, as means to all these, our fundamental instruments, the organ, piano, violin, etc.; all these things are known only in the Occident, although programme music, tone poetry, alteration of tones and chromatics, have existed in various musical traditions as means of expression.

In architecture, pointed arches have been used elsewhere as a means of decoration, in antiquity and in Asia; presumably the combination of pointed arch and cross-arched vault was not unknown in the Orient. But the rational use of the Gothic vault as a means of distributing pressure and of roofing spaces of all forms, and above all as the constructive principle of great monumental buildings and the foundation of a *style* extending to sculpture and painting, such as that created by our Middle Ages, does not occur elsewhere. The technical basis of our architecture came from the Orient. But the Orient lacked that solution of the problem of the dome and that type of classic rationalization of all art—in painting by the rational utilization of lines and spatial perspective—which the Renaissance created for us. There was printing in China. But a printed literature, designed *only* for print and only possible through it, and, above all, the Press and periodicals, have appeared only in the Occident. Institutions of higher education of all possible types, even some superficially similar to our universities, or at least academies, have existed (China, Islam). But a rational, systematic, and specialized pursuit of science, with trained and specialized personnel, has only existed in the West in a sense at all approaching its present dominant place in our culture. Above all is this true of the trained official, the pillar of both the modern State and of the economic life of the West. He forms a type of which there have heretofore only been suggestions, which have never remotely approached its present importance for the social order. Of course the official, even the specialized official, is a very old constituent of the most various societies. But no country and no age has ever experienced, in the same sense as the modern Occident, the absolute and complete dependence of its whole existence, of the political, technical, and economic conditions of its life, on a specially trained *organization* of officials. The most important functions of the everyday life of society have come to be in the hands of technically, commercially, and above all legally trained government officials.

Organization of political and social groups in feudal classes has been common. But even the feudal state of *rex et regnum*[1] in the Western sense has only been known to our culture. Even more are parliaments of periodically elected representatives, with government by demagogues and party leaders as ministers responsible to the parliaments, peculiar to us, although there have, of course, been parties, in the sense of organizations for exerting influence and gaining control of political power, all over the world. In fact, the State itself, in the sense of a political association with a rational, written constitution, rationally ordained law, and an administration bound to rational rules or laws, administered by trained officials, is known, in this combination of characteristics, only in the Occident, despite all other approaches to it.

And the same is true of the most fateful force in our modern life, capitalism. The impulse to acquisition, pursuit of gain, of money, of the greatest possible amount of money, has in itself nothing to do with capitalism. This impulse exists and has existed among waiters, physicians, coachmen, artists, prostitutes, dishonest officials, soldiers, nobles, crusaders, gamblers, and beggars. One may say that it has been common to all sorts and conditions of men at all times and in all countries of the earth, wherever the objective possibility of it is or has been given. It should be taught in the kindergarten of cultural history that this naïve idea of capitalism must be given up once and for all. Unlimited greed for gain is not in the least identical with capitalism, and is still less its spirit. Capitalism *may* even be identical with the restraint, or at least a rational tempering, of this irrational impulse. But capitalism is identical with the pursuit of profit, and forever *renewed* profit, by means of continuous, rational, capitalistic enterprise. For it must be so: in a wholly capitalistic order of society, an individual capitalistic enterprise which did not take advantage of its opportunities for profit-making would be doomed to extinction.

Let us now define our terms somewhat more carefully than is generally done. We will define a capitalistic economic action as one which rests on the expectation of profit by the utilization of opportunities for exchange, that is on (formally) peaceful chances of profit. Acquisition by force (formally and actually) follows its own particular laws, and it is not expedient, however little one can forbid this, to place it in the same category with action which is, in the last analysis, oriented to profits from exchange.[2] Where capitalistic acquisition is rationally pursued, the corresponding action is adjusted to calculations in terms of capital. This means that the action is adapted to a systematic utilization of goods or personal services as means of acquisition in such a way that, at the close of a business period, the balance of the enterprise in money assets (or, in the case of a continuous enterprise, the periodically estimated money value of assets) exceeds the capital, i.e. the estimated value of the material means of production used for acquisition in exchange. It makes no difference whether it involves a quantity of goods entrusted *in natura* to a travelling merchant, the proceeds of which may consist in other goods *in natura* acquired by trade, or whether it involves a manufacturing enterprise, the assets of which consist of buildings, machinery, cash, raw materials, partly and wholly manufactured goods, which are balanced against liabilities. The important fact is always that a calculation of capital in terms of money is made, whether by modern book-keeping methods or in any other way, however primitive and crude. Everything is done in terms of balances: at the beginning of the enterprise an initial balance, before every individual decision a calculation to ascertain its probable profitableness, and at the end a final balance to ascertain how much profit has been made. For instance, the initial balance of a *commenda*[3] transaction would determine an agreed money value of the assets put into it (so far as they were not in money form already), and a final balance would form the estimate on which to base the distribution of profit and loss at the end. So far as the transactions are rational, calculation underlies every single action of the partners. That a really accurate calculation or estimate may not exist, that the procedure is pure guess-work, or simply traditional and conventional, happens even to-day in every form of capitalistic enterprise where the circumstances do not demand strict accuracy. But these are points affecting only the *degree* of rationality of capitalistic acquisition.

For the purpose of this conception all that matters is that an actual adaptation of economic action to a comparison of money income with money expenses takes place, no matter how primitive the form. Now in this sense capitalism and capitalistic enterprises, even with a considerable rationalization of capitalistic calculation, have existed in all civilized countries of the earth, so far as economic documents permit us to judge. In China, India, Babylon, Egypt, Mediterranean antiquity, and the Middle Ages, as well as in modern times. These were not merely isolated ventures, but economic enterprises which were entirely dependent on the continual renewal of capitalistic undertakings, and even continuous operations. However, trade especially was for a long time not continuous like our own, but consisted essentially in a series of individual undertakings. Only gradually did the activities of even the large merchants acquire an inner cohesion (with branch organizations, etc.). In any case, the capitalistic enterprise and the capitalistic entrepreneur, not only as occasional but as regular entrepreneurs, are very old and were very widespread.

Now, however, the Occident has developed capitalism both to a quantitative extent, and (carrying this quantitative development) in types, forms, and directions which have never existed elsewhere. All over the world there have been merchants, wholesale and retail, local and engaged in foreign trade. Loans of all kinds have been made, and there have been banks with the most various functions, at least comparable to ours of, say, the sixteenth century. Sea loans,[4] *commenda*, and transactions and associations similar to the *Kommanditgesellschaft*,[5] have all been widespread, even as continuous businesses. Whenever money finances of public bodies have existed, moneylenders have appeared, as in Babylon, Hellas, India, China, Rome. They have financed wars and piracy, contracts and building operations of all sorts. In overseas policy they have functioned as colonial entrepreneurs, as planters with slaves, or directly or indirectly forced labour, and have farmed domains, offices, and, above all, taxes. They have financed party leaders in elections and *condottieri*[6] in civil wars. And, finally, they have been speculators in chances for pecuniary gain of all kinds. This kind of entrepreneur, the capitalistic adventurer, has existed everywhere. With the exception of trade and credit and banking transactions, their activities were predominantly of an irrational and speculative character, or directed to acquisition by force, above all the acquisition of booty, whether directly in war or in the form of continuous fiscal booty by exploitation of subjects.

The capitalism of promoters, large-scale speculators, concession hunters, and much modern financial capitalism even in peace time, but, above all, the capitalism especially concerned with exploiting wars, bears this stamp even in modern Western countries, and some, but only some, parts of large-scale international trade are closely related to it, to-day as always.

But in modern times the Occident has developed, in addition to this, a very different form of capitalism which has appeared nowhere else: the rational capitalistic organization of (formally) free labour. Only suggestions of it are found elsewhere. Even the organization of unfree labour reached a considerable degree of rationality only on plantations and to a very limited extent in the *Ergasteria*[7] of antiquity. In the manors, manorial workshops, and domestic industries on estates with serf labour it was probably somewhat less developed. Even real domestic industries with free labour have definitely been proved to have existed in only a few isolated cases outside the Occident. The frequent use of day labourers led in a very few cases—especially State monopolies, which are, however, very different from modern industrial organization—to manufacturing organizations, but never to a rational organization of apprenticeship in the handicrafts like that of our Middle Ages.

Rational industrial organization, attuned to a regular market, and neither to political nor irrationally speculative opportunities for profit, is not, however, the only peculiarity of Western capitalism. The modern rational organization of the capitalistic enterprise would not have been possible without two other important factors in its development: the separation of business from the household, which completely dominates modern economic life, and closely connected with it, rational book-keeping. A spatial separation of places of work from those of residence exists elsewhere, as in the Oriental bazaar and in the *ergasteria* of other cultures. The development of capitalistic associations with their own accounts is also found in the Far East, the Near East, and in antiquity. But compared to the modern independence of business enterprises, those are only small beginnings. The reason for this was particularly that the indispensable requisites for this independence, our rational business book-keeping and our legal separation of corporate from personal property, were entirely lacking, or had only begun to develop.[8] The tendency everywhere else was for acquisitive enterprises to arise as parts of a royal or manorial *household* (of the *oikos*),[9] which is, as Rodbertus has perceived, with all its superficial similarity, a fundamentally different, even opposite, development.

However, all these peculiarities of Western capitalism have derived their significance in the last analysis only from their association with the capitalistic organization of labour. Even what is generally called commercialization, the development of negotiable securities and the rationalization of speculation, the exchanges, etc., is connected with it. For without the rational capitalistic organization of labour, all this, so far as it was possible at all, would have nothing like the same significance, above all for the social structure and all the specific problems of the modern Occident connected with it. Exact calculation—the basis of everything else—is only possible on a basis of free labour.[10]

And just as, or rather because, the world has known no rational organization of labour outside the modern Occident, it has known no rational socialism. Of course, there has been civic economy, a civic food-supply policy, mercantilism and welfare policies of princes, rationing, regulation of economic life, protectionism, and *laissez-faire* theories (as in China). The world has also known socialistic and communistic experiments of various sorts: family, religious, or military communism, State socialism (in Egypt), monopolistic cartels, and consumers' organizations. But although there have everywhere been civic market privileges, companies, guilds, and all sorts of legal differences between town and country, the concept of the citizen has not existed outside the Occident, and that of the bourgeoisie outside the modern Occident. Similarly, the proletariat as a class could not exist, because there was no rational organization of free labour under regular discipline. Class struggles between creditor and debtor classes; landowners and the landless, serfs, or tenants; trading interests and consumers or landlords, have existed everywhere in various combinations. But even the Western mediæval struggles between putters-out and their workers exist elsewhere only in beginnings. The modern conflict of the large-scale industrial entrepreneur and free-wage labourers was entirely lacking. And thus there could be no such problems as those of socialism.

Hence in a universal history of culture the central problem for us is not, in the last analysis, even from a purely economic viewpoint, the development of capitalistic activity as such, differing in different cultures only in form: the adventurer type, or capitalism in trade, war, politics, or administration as sources of gain. It is rather the origin of this sober bourgeois capitalism with its rational organization of free labour. Or in terms of cultural history, the problem is that of the origin of the Western bourgeois class and of its peculiarities, a problem which is certainly closely connected with that of the origin of the capitalistic organization of labour, but is not quite the same thing. For the bourgeois as a class existed prior to the development of the peculiar modern form of capitalism, though, it is true, only in the Western hemisphere.

Now the peculiar modern Western form of capitalism has been, at first sight, strongly influenced by the development of technical possibilities. Its rationality is to-day essentially dependent on the calculability of the most important technical factors. But this means fundamentally that it is dependent on the peculiarities of modern science, especially the natural sciences based on mathematics and exact and rational experiment. On the other hand, the development of these sciences and of the technique resting upon them now receives important stimulation from these capitalistic interests in its practical economic application. It is true that the origin of Western science cannot be attributed to such interests. Calculation, even with decimals, and algebra have been carried on in India, where the decimal system was invented. But it was only made use of by developing capitalism in the West, while in India it led to no modern arithmetic or book-keeping. Neither was the origin of mathematics and mechanics determined by capitalistic interests. But the *technical* utilization of scientific knowledge, so important for the living conditions of the mass of people, was certainly encouraged by economic considerations, which were extremely favourable to it in the Occident. But this encouragement was derived from the peculiarities of the social structure of the Occident. We must hence ask, from *what* parts of that structure was it derived, since not all of them have been of equal importance?

Among those of undoubted importance are the rational structures of law and of administration. For modern rational capitalism has need, not only of the technical means of production, but of a calculable legal system and of administration in terms of formal rules. Without it adventurous and speculative trading capitalism and all sorts of politically determined capitalisms are possible, but no rational enterprise under individual initiative, with fixed capital and certainty of calculations. Such a legal system and such administration have been available for economic activity in a comparative state of legal and formalistic perfection only in the Occident. We must hence inquire where that law came from. Among other circumstances, capitalistic interests have in turn undoubtedly also helped, but by no means alone nor even principally, to prepare the way for the predominance in law and administration of a class of jurists specially trained in rational law. But these interests did not themselves create that law. Quite different forces were at work in this development. And why did not the capitalistic interests do the same in China or India? Why did not the scientific, the artistic, the political, or the economic development there enter upon that path of rationalization which is peculiar to the Occident?

For in all the above cases it is a question of the specific and peculiar rationalism of Western culture. Now by this term very different things may be understood, as the following discussion will repeatedly show. There is, for example, rationalization of mystical contemplation, that is of an attitude which, viewed from other departments of life, is specifically irrational, just as much as there are rationalizations of economic life, of technique, of scientific research, of military training, of law and administration. Furthermore, each one of these fields may be rationalized in terms of very different ultimate values and ends, and what is rational from one point of view may well be irrational from another. Hence rationalizations of the most varied character have existed in various departments of life and in all areas of culture. To characterize their differences from the view-point of cultural history it is necessary to know what departments are rationalized, and in what direction. It is hence our first concern to work out and to explain genetically the special peculiarity of Occidental rationalism, and within this field that of the modern Occidental form. Every such attempt at explanation must, recognizing the fundamental importance of the economic factor, above all take account of the economic conditions. But at the same time the opposite correlation must not be left out of consideration. For though the development of economic rationalism is partly dependent on rational technique and law, it is at the same time determined by the ability and disposition of men to adopt certain types of practical rational conduct. When these types have been obstructed by spiritual obstacles, the development of rational economic conduct has also met serious inner resistance. The magical and religious forces, and the ethical ideas of duty based upon them, have in the past always been among the most important formative influences on conduct. In the studies collected here we shall be concerned with these forces.[11]

Two older essays[12] have been placed at the beginning which attempt, at one important point, to approach the side of the problem which is generally most difficult to grasp: the influence of certain religious ideas on the development of an economic spirit, or the *ethos* of an economic system. In this case we are dealing with the connection of the spirit of modern economic life with the rational ethics of ascetic Protestantism. Thus we treat here only one side of the causal chain. The later studies on the Economic Ethics of the World Religions[13] attempt, in the form of a survey of the relations of the most important religions to economic life and to the social stratification of their environment, to follow out both causal relationships, so far as it is necessary in order to find points of comparison with the Occidental development. For only in this way is it possible to attempt a causal evaluation of those elements of the economic ethics of the Western religions which differentiate them from others, with a hope of attaining even a tolerable degree of approximation. Hence these studies do not claim to be complete analyses of cultures, however brief. On the contrary, in every culture they quite deliberately emphasize the elements in which it differs from Western civilization. They are, hence, definitely oriented to the problems which seem important for the understanding of Western culture from *this* view-point. With our object in view, any other procedure did not seem possible. But to avoid misunderstanding we must here lay special emphasis on the limitation of our purpose.

In another respect the uninitiated at least must be warned against exaggerating the importance of these investigations. The Sinologist, the Indologist, the Semitist, or the Egyptologist, will of course find no facts unknown to him. We only hope that he will find nothing definitely wrong in points that are essential. How far it has been possible to come as near this ideal as a non-specialist is able to do, the author cannot know. It is quite evident that anyone who is forced to rely on translations, and furthermore on the use and evaluation of monumental, documentary, or literary sources, has to rely himself on a specialist literature which is often highly controversial, and the merits of which he is unable to judge accurately. Such a writer must make modest claims for the value of his work. All the more so since the number of available translations of real sources (that is, inscriptions and documents) is, especially for China, still very small in comparison with what exists and is important. From all this follows the definitely provisional character of these studies, and especially of the parts dealing with Asia.[14] Only the specialist is entitled to a final judgment. And, naturally, it is only because expert studies with this special purpose and from this particular view-point have not hitherto been made, that the present ones have been written at all. They are destined to be superseded in a much more important sense than this can be said, as it can be, of all scientific work. But however objectionable it may be, such trespassing on other special fields cannot be avoided in comparative work. But one must take the consequences by resigning oneself to considerable doubts regarding the degree of one's success.

Fashion and the zeal of the *literati*[15] would have us think that the specialist can to-day be spared, or degraded to a position sub-ordinate to that of the seer. Almost all sciences owe something to dilettantes, often very valuable view-points. But dilettantism as a leading principle would be the end of science. He who yearns for seeing should go to the cinema, though it will be offered to him copiously to-day in literary form in the present field of investigation also.[16] Nothing is farther from the intent of these thoroughly serious studies than such an attitude. And, I might add, whoever wants a sermon should go to a conventicle. The question of the relative value of the cultures which are compared here will not receive a single word. It is true that the path of human destiny cannot but appal him who surveys a section of it. But he will do well to keep his small personal commentarie to himself, as one does at the sight of the sea or of majestic mountains, unless he knows himself to be called and gifted to give them expression in artistic or prophetic form. In most other cases the voluminous talk about intuition does nothing but conceal a lack of perspective toward the object, which merits the same judgment as a similar lack of perspective toward men.

Some justification is needed for the fact that ethnographical material has not been utilized to anything like the extent which the value of its contributions naturally demands in any really thorough investigation, especially of Asiatic religions. This limitation has not only been imposed because human powers of work are restricted. This omission has also seemed to be permissible because we are here necessarily dealing with the religious ethics of the classes which were the culture-bearers of their respective countries. We are concerned with the influence which *their* conduct has had. Now it is quite true that this can only be completely known in all its details when the facts from ethnography and folk-lore have been compared with it. Hence we must expressly admit and emphasize that this is a gap to which the ethnographer will legitimately object. I hope to contribute something to the closing of this gap in a systematic study of the Sociology of

Religion.[17] But such an undertaking would have transcended the limits of this investigation with its closely circumscribed purpose. It has been necessary to be content with bringing out the points of comparison with our Occidental religions as well as possible.

Finally, we may make a reference to the *anthropological* side of the problem. When we find again and again that, even in departments of life apparently mutually independent, certain types of rationalization have developed in the Occident, and only there, it would be natural to suspect that the most important reason lay in differences of heredity. The author admits that he is inclined to think the importance of biological heredity very great. But in spite of the notable achievements of anthropological research, I see up to the present no way of exactly or even approximately measuring either the extent or, above all, the form of its influence on the development investigated here. It must be one of the tasks of sociological and historical investigation first to analyse all the influences and causal relationships which can satisfactorily be explained in terms of reactions to environmental conditions. Only then, and when comparative racial neurology and psychology shall have progressed beyond their present and in many ways very promising beginnings, can we hope for even the probability of a satisfactory answer to that problem.[18] In the meantime that condition seems to me not to exist, and an appeal to heredity would therefore involve a premature renunciation of the possibility of knowledge attainable now, and would shift the problem to factors (at present) still unknown.

# Part I
# The Problem

## Chapter 1.
## Religious Affiliation and Social Stratification[1]

A glance at the occupational statistics of any country of mixed religious composition brings to light with remarkable frequency[2] a situation which has several times provoked discussion in the Catholic press and literature,[3] and in Catholic congresses in Germany, namely, the fact that business leaders and owners of capital, as well as the higher grades of skilled labour, and even more the higher technically and commercially trained personnel of modern enterprises, are overwhelmingly Protestant.[4] This is true not only in cases where the difference in religion coincides with one of nationality, and thus of cultural development, as in Eastern Germany between Germans and Poles. The same thing is shown in the figures of religious affiliation almost wherever capitalism, at the time of its great expansion, has had a free hand to alter the social distribution of the population in accordance with its needs, and to determine its occupational structure. The more freedom it has had, the more clearly is the effect shown. It is true that the greater relative participation of Protestants in the ownership of capital,[5] in management, and the upper ranks of labour in great modern industrial and commercial enterprises,[6] may in part be explained in terms of historical circumstances[7] which extend far back into the past, and in which religious affiliation is not a cause of the economic conditions, but to a certain extent appears to be a result of them. Participation in the above economic functions usually involves some previous ownership of capital, and generally an expensive education; often both. These are to-day largely dependent on the possession of inherited wealth, or at least on a certain degree of material well-being. A number of those sections of the old Empire which were most highly developed economically and most favoured by natural resources and situation, in particular a majority of the wealthy towns, went over to Protestantism in the sixteenth century. The results of that circumstance favour the Protestants even to-day in

15

their struggle for economic existence. There arises thus the historical question: why were the districts of highest economic development at the same time particularly favourable to a revolution in the Church? The answer is by no means so simple as one might think.

The emancipation from economic traditionalism appears, no doubt, to be a factor which would greatly strengthen the tendency to doubt the sanctity of the religious tradition, as of all traditional authorities. But it is necessary to note, what has often been forgotten, that the Reformation meant not the elimination of the Church's control over everyday life, but rather the substitution of a new form of control for the previous one. It meant the repudiation of a control which was very lax, at that time scarcely perceptible in practice, and hardly more than formal, in favour of a regulation of the whole of conduct which, penetrating to all departments of private and public life, was infinitely burdensome and earnestly enforced. The rule of the Catholic Church, "punishing the heretic, but indulgent to the sinner", as it was in the past even more than to-day, is now tolerated by peoples of thoroughly modern economic character, and was borne by the richest and economically most advanced peoples on earth at about the turn of the fifteenth century. The rule of Calvinism, on the other hand, as it was enforced in the sixteenth century in Geneva and in Scotland, at the turn of the sixteenth and seventeenth centuries in large parts of the Netherlands, in the seventeenth in New England, and for a time in England itself, would be for us the most absolutely unbearable form of ecclesiastical control of the individual which could possibly exist. That was exactly what large numbers of the old commercial aristocracy of those times, in Geneva as well as in Holland and England, felt about it. And what the reformers complained of in those areas of high economic development was not too much supervision of life on the part of the Church, but too little. Now how does it happen that at that time those countries which were most advanced economically, and within them the rising bourgeois middle classes, not only failed to resist this unexampled tyranny of Puritanism, but even developed a heroism in its defence? For bourgeois classes as such have seldom before and never since displayed heroism. It was "the last of our heroisms", as Carlyle, not without reason, has said.

But further, and especially important: it may be, as has been claimed, that the greater participation of Protestants in the positions of ownership and management in modern economic life may to-day be understood, in part at least, simply as a result of the greater material wealth they have inherited. But there are certain other phenomena which cannot be explained in the same way. Thus, to mention only a few facts: there is a great difference discoverable in Baden, in Bavaria, in Hungary, in the type of higher education which Catholic parents, as opposed to Protestant, give their children. That the percentage of Catholics among the students and graduates of higher educational institutions in general lags behind their proportion of the total population,[8] may, to be sure, be largely explicable in terms of inherited differences of wealth. But among the Catholic graduates themselves the percentage of those graduating from the institutions preparing, in particular, for technical studies and industrial and commercial occupations, but in general from those preparing for middle-class business life, lags still farther behind the percentage of Protestants.[9] On the other hand, Catholics prefer the sort of training which the humanistic Gymnasium affords. That is a circumstance to which the above explanation does not apply, but which, on the contrary, is one reason why so few Catholics are engaged in capitalistic enterprise.

Even more striking is a fact which partly explains the smaller proportion of Catholics among the skilled labourers of modern industry. It is well known that the factory has taken its skilled labour to a large extent from young men in the handicrafts; but this is much more true of Protestant than of Catholic journeymen. Among journeymen, in other words, the Catholics show a stronger propensity to remain in their crafts, that is they more often become master craftsmen, whereas the Protestants are attracted to a larger extent into the factories in order to fill the upper ranks of skilled labour and administrative positions.[10] The explanation of these cases is undoubtedly that the mental and spiritual peculiarities acquired from the environment, here the type of education favoured by the religious atmosphere of the home community and the parental home, have determined the choice of occupation, and through it the professional career.

The smaller participation of Catholics in the modern business life of Germany is all the more striking because it runs counter to a tendency which has been observed at all times[11] including the present. National or religious minorities which are in a position of subordination to a group of rulers are likely, through their voluntary or involuntary exclusion from positions of political influence, to be driven with peculiar force into economic activity. Their ablest members seek to satisfy the desire for recognition of their abilities in this field, since there is no opportunity in the service of the State. This has undoubtedly been true of the Poles in Russia and Eastern Prussia, who have without question been undergoing a more rapid economic advance than in Galicia, where they have been in the ascendant. It has in earlier times been true of the Huguenots in France under Louis XIV, the Non-conformists and Quakers in England, and, last but not least, the Jew for two thousand years. But the Catholics in Germany have shown no striking evidence of such a result of their position. In the past they have, unlike the Protestants, undergone no particularly prominent economic development in the times when they were persecuted or only tolerated, either in Holland or in England. On the other hand, it is a fact that the Protestants (especially certain branches of the movement to be fully discussed later) both as ruling classes and as ruled, both as majority and as minority, have shown a special tendency to develop economic rationalism which cannot be observed to the same extent among Catholics either in the one situation or in the other.[12] Thus the principal explanation of this difference must be sought in the permanent intrinsic character of their religious beliefs, and not only in their temporary external historico-political situations.[13]

It will be our task to investigate these religions with a view to finding out what peculiarities they have or have had which might have resulted in the behaviour we have described. On superficial analysis, and on the basis of certain current impressions, one might be tempted to express the difference by saying that the greater other-worldliness of Catholicism, the ascetic character of its highest ideals, must have brought up its adherents to a greater indifference toward the good things of this world. Such an explanation fits the popular tendency in the judgment of both religions. On the Protestant side it is used as a basis of criticism of those (real or imagined) ascetic ideals of the Catholic way of life, while the Catholics answer with the accusation that materialism results from the secularization of all ideals through Protestantism. One recent writer has attempted to formulate the difference of their attitudes toward economic life in the following manner: "The Catholic is quieter, having less of the acquisitive impulse; he prefers a life of the greatest possible security, even with a smaller income, to a life of risk and excitement, even though it may bring the chance of gaining honour and riches. The proverb says jokingly, 'either eat well or sleep well'. In the present case the Protestant prefers to eat well, the Catholic to sleep undisturbed."[14]

In fact, this desire to eat well may be a correct though incomplete characterization of the motives of many nominal Protestants in Germany at the present time. But things were very different in the past: the English, Dutch, and American Puritans were characterized by the exact opposite of the joy of living, a fact which is indeed, as we shall see, most important for our present study. Moreover, the French Protestants, among others, long retained, and retain to a certain extent up to the present, the characteristics which were impressed upon the Calvinistic Churches everywhere, especially under the cross in the time of the religious struggles. Nevertheless (or was it, perhaps, as we shall ask later, precisely on that account?) it is well known that these characteristics were one of the most important factors in the industrial and capitalistic development of France, and on the small scale permitted them by their persecution remained so. If we may call this seriousness and the strong predominance of religious interests in the whole conduct of life otherworldliness, then the French Calvinists were and still are at least as otherworldly as, for instance, the North German Catholics, to whom their Catholicism is undoubtedly as vital a matter as religion is to any other people in the world. Both differ from the predominant religious trends in their respective countries in much the same way. The Catholics of France are, in their lower ranks, greatly interested in the enjoyment of life, in the upper directly hostile to religion. Similarly, the Protestants of Germany are to-day absorbed in worldly economic life, and their upper ranks are most indifferent to religion.[15] Hardly anything shows so clearly as this parallel that, with such vague ideas as that of the alleged otherworldliness of Catholicism, and the alleged materialistic joy of living of Protestantism, and others like them, nothing can be accomplished for our purpose. In such general terms the distinction does not even adequately fit the facts of to-day, and certainly not of the past. If, however, one wishes to make use of it at all, several other observations present themselves at once which, combined with the above remarks, suggest that the supposed conflict between otherworldliness, asceticism, and ecclesiastical piety on the one side, and participation in capitalistic acquisition on the other, might actually turn out to be an intimate relationship.

As a matter of fact it is surely remarkable, to begin with quite a superficial observation, how large is the number of representatives of the most spiritual forms of Christian piety who have sprung from commercial circles. In particular, very many of the most zealous adherents of Pietism are of this origin. It might be explained as a sort of reaction against mammonism on the part of sensitive natures not adapted to commercial life, and, as in the case of Francis of Assisi, many Pietists have themselves interpreted the process of their conversion in these terms. Similarly, the remarkable circumstance that so many of the greatest capitalistic entrepreneurs—down to Cecil Rhodes—have come from clergymen's families might be explained as a reaction against their ascetic upbringing. But this form of explanation fails where an extraordinary capitalistic business sense is combined in the same persons and groups with the most intensive forms of a piety which penetrates and dominates their whole lives. Such cases are not isolated, but these traits are characteristic of many of the most important Churches and sects in the history of Protestantism. Especially Calvinism, wherever it has appeared,[16] has shown this combination. However little, in the time of the expansion of the Reformation, it (or any other Protestant belief) was bound up with any particular social class, it is characteristic and in a certain sense typical that in French Huguenot Churches monks and business men (merchants, craftsmen) were particularly numerous among the proselytes, especially at the time of the persecution.[17] Even the Spaniards knew that heresy (i.e. the Calvinism of the Dutch) promoted trade, and this coincides with the opinions which Sir William Petty expressed in his discussion of the reasons for the capitalistic development of the Netherlands. Gothein[18] rightly calls the Calvinistic diaspora the seed-bed of capitalistic economy.[19] Even in this case one might consider the decisive factor to be the superiority of the French and Dutch economic cultures from which these communities sprang, or perhaps the immense influence of exile in the breakdown of traditional relationships.[20] But in France the situation was, as we know from Colbert's struggles, the same even in the seventeenth century. Even Austria, not to speak of other countries, directly imported Protestant craftsmen.

But not all the Protestant denominations seem to have had an equally strong influence in this direction. That of Calvinism, even in Germany, was among the strongest, it seems, and the reformed faith[21] more than the others seems to have promoted the development of the spirit of capitalism, in the Wupperthal as well as elsewhere. Much more so than Lutheranism, as comparison both in general and in particular instances, especially in the Wupperthal, seems to prove.[22] For Scotland, Buckle, and among English poets, Keats, have emphasized these same relationships.[23] Even more striking, as it is only necessary to mention, is the connection of a religious way of life with the most intensive development of business acumen among those sects whose otherworldliness is as proverbial as their wealth, especially the Quakers and the Mennonites. The part which the former have played in England and North America fell to the latter in Germany and the Netherlands. That in East Prussia Frederick William I tolerated the Mennonites as indispensable to industry, in spite of their absolute refusal to perform military service, is only one of the numerous well-known cases which illustrates the fact, though, considering the character of that monarch, it is one of the most striking. Finally, that this combination of intense piety with just as strong a development of business acumen, was also characteristic of the Pietists, is common knowledge.[24]

It is only necessary to think of the Rhine country and of Calw. In this purely introductory discussion it is unnecessary to pile up more examples. For these few already all show one thing: that the spirit of hard work, of progress, or whatever else it may be called, the awakening of which one is inclined to ascribe to Protestantism, must not be understood, as there is a tendency to do, as joy of living nor in any other sense as connected with the Enlightenment. The old Protestantism of Luther, Calvin, Knox, Voet, had precious little to do with what to-day is called progress. To whole aspects of modern life which the most extreme religionist would not wish to suppress to-day, it was directly hostile. If any inner relationship between certain expressions of the old Protestant spirit and modern capitalistic culture is to be found, we must attempt to find it, for better or worse not in its alleged more or less materialistic or at least anti-ascetic joy of living, but in its purely religious characteristics. Montesquieu says (*Esprit des Lois*, Book XX, chap. 7) of the English that they "had progressed the farthest of all peoples of the world in three important things: in piety, in commerce, and in freedom". Is it not possible that their commercial superiority and their adaptation to free political institutions are connected in some way with that record of piety which Montesquieu ascribes to them?

A large number of possible relationships, vaguely perceived, occur to us when we put the question in this way. It will now be our task to formulate what occurs to us confusedly as clearly as is possible, considering the inexhaustible diversity to be found in all historical material. But in order to do this it is necessary to leave behind the vague and general concepts with which we have dealt up to this point, and attempt to penetrate into the peculiar characteristics of and the differences between those great worlds of religious thought which have existed historically in the various branches of Christianity.

Before we can proceed to that, however, a few remarks are necessary, first on the peculiarities of the phenomenon of which we are seeking an historical explanation, then concerning the sense in which such an explanation is possible at all within the limits of these investigations.

## Chapter 2. The Spirit of Capitalism

In the title of this study is used the somewhat pretentious phrase, the *spirit* of capitalism. What is to be understood by it? The attempt to give anything like a definition of it brings out certain difficulties which are in the very nature of this type of investigation.

If any object can be found to which this term can be applied with any understandable meaning, it can only be an historical individual, i.e. a complex of elements associated in historical reality which we unite into a conceptual whole from the standpoint of their cultural significance.

Such an historical concept, however, since it refers in its content to a phenomenon significant for its unique individuality, cannot be defined according to the formula *genus proximum, differentia specifica*,[1] but it must be gradually put together out of the individual parts which are taken from historical reality to make it up. Thus the final and definitive concept cannot stand at the beginning of the investigation, but must come at the end. We must, in other words, work out in the course of the discussion, as its most important result, the best conceptual formulation of what we here understand by the spirit of capitalism, that is the best from the point of view which interests us here. This point of view (the one of which we shall speak later) is, further, by no means the only possible one from which the historical phenomena we are investigating can be analysed. Other standpoints would, for this as for every historical phenomenon, yield other characteristics as the essential ones. The result is that it is by no means necessary to understand by the spirit of capitalism only what it will come to mean to *us* for the purposes of our analysis. This is a necessary result of the nature of historical concepts which attempt for their methodological purposes not to grasp historical reality in abstract general formulæ, but in concrete genetic sets of relations which are inevitably of a specifically unique and individual character.[2]

Thus, if we try to determine the object, the analysis and historical explanation of which we are attempting, it cannot be in the form of a conceptual definition, but at least in the beginning only a provisional description of what is here meant by the spirit of capitalism. Such a description is, however, indispensable in order clearly to understand the object of the investigation. For this purpose we turn to a document of that spirit which contains what we are looking for in almost classical purity, and at the same time has the advantage of being free from all direct relationship to religion, being thus, for our purposes, free of preconceptions.

> Remember, that *time* is money. He that can earn ten shillings a day by his labour, and goes abroad, or sits idle, one half of that day, though he spends but sixpence during his diversion or idleness, ought not to reckon *that* the only expense; he has really spent, or rather thrown away, five shillings besides.
>
> Remember, that *credit* is money. If a man lets his money lie in my hands after it is due, he gives me the interest, or so much as I can make of it during that time. This amounts to a considerable sum where a man has good and large credit, and makes good use of it.
>
> Remember, that money is of the prolific, generating nature. Money can beget money, and its offspring can beget more, and so on. Five shillings turned is six, turned again it is seven and threepence, and so on, till it becomes a hundred pounds. The more there is of it, the more it produces every turning, so that the profits rise quicker and quicker. He that kills a breeding-sow, destroys all her offspring to the thousandth generation. He that murders a crown, destroys all that it might have produced, even scores of pounds.
>
> Remember this saying, *The good paymaster is lord of another man's purse*. He that is known to pay punctually and exactly to

the time he promises, may at any time, and on any occasion, raise all the money his friends can spare. This is sometimes of great use. After industry and frugality, nothing contributes more to the raising of a young man in the world than punctuality and justice in all his dealings; therefore never keep borrowed money an hour beyond the time you promised, lest a disappointment shut up your friend's purse for ever.

The most trifling actions that affect a man's credit are to be regarded. The sound of your hammer at five in the morning, or eight at night, heard by a creditor, makes him easy six months longer; but if he sees you at a billiard-table, or hears your voice at a tavern, when you should be at work, he sends for his money the next day; demands it, before he can receive it, in a lump.

It shows, besides, that you are mindful of what you owe; it makes you appear a careful as well as an honest man, and that still increases your credit.

Beware of thinking all your own that you possess, and of living accordingly. It is a mistake that many people who have credit fall into. To prevent this, keep an exact account for some time both of your expenses and your income. If you take the pains at first to mention particulars, it will have this good effect: you will discover how wonderfully small, trifling expenses mount up to large sums; and will discern what might have been, and may for the future be saved, without occasioning any great inconvenience.

For six pounds a year you may have the use of one hundred pounds, provided you are a man of known prudence and honesty.

He that spends a groat a day idly, spends idly above six pounds a year, which is the price for the use of one hundred pounds.

He that wastes idly a groat's worth of his time per day, one day with another, wastes the privilege of using one hundred pounds each day.

He that idly loses five shillings' worth of time, loses five shillings, and might as prudently throw five shillings into the sea.

He that loses five shillings, not only loses that sum, but all the advantage that might be made by turning it in dealing, which by the time that a young man becomes old, will amount to a considerable sum of money.[3]

It is Benjamin Franklin who preaches to us in these sentences, the same which Ferdinand Kürnberger satirizes in his clever and malicious *Picture of American Culture*[4] as the supposed confession of faith of the Yankee. That it is the spirit of capitalism which here speaks in characteristic fashion, no one will doubt, however little we may wish to claim that everything which could be understood as pertaining to that spirit is contained in it. Let us pause a moment to consider this passage, the philosophy of which Kürnberger sums up in the words, "They make tallow out of cattle and money out of men". The peculiarity of this philosophy of avarice appears to be the ideal of the honest man of recognized credit, and above all the idea of a duty of the individual toward the increase of his capital, which is assumed as an end in itself. Truly what is here preached is not simply a means of making one's way in the world, but a peculiar ethic. The infraction of its rules is treated not as foolishness but as forgetfulness of duty. That is the essence of the matter. It is not mere business astuteness, that sort of thing is common enough, it is an ethos. *This* is the quality which interests us.

When Jacob Fugger, in speaking to a business associate who had retired and who wanted to persuade him to do the same, since he had made enough money and should let others have a chance, rejected that as pusillanimity and answered that "he (Fugger) thought otherwise, he wanted to make money as long as he could",[5] the spirit of his statement is evidently quite different from that of Franklin. What in the former case was an expression of commercial daring and a personal inclination morally neutral,[6] in the latter takes on the character of an ethically coloured maxim for the conduct of life. The concept spirit of capitalism is here used in this specific sense,[7] it is the spirit of modern capitalism. For that we are here dealing only with Western European and American capitalism is obvious from the way in which the problem was stated. Capitalism existed in China, India, Babylon, in the classic world, and in the Middle Ages. But in all these cases, as we shall see, this particular ethos was lacking.

Now, all Franklin's moral attitudes are coloured with utilitarianism. Honesty is useful, because it assures credit; so are punctuality, industry, frugality, and that is the reason they are virtues. A logical deduction from this would be that where, for instance, the appearance of honesty serves the same purpose, that would suffice, and an unnecessary surplus of this virtue would evidently appear to Franklin's eyes as unproductive waste. And as a matter of fact, the story in his autobiography of his conversion to those virtues,[8] or the discussion of the value of a strict maintenance of the appearance of modesty, the assiduous belittlement of one's own deserts in order to gain general recognition later,[9] confirms this impression. According to Franklin, those virtues, like all others, are only in so far virtues as they are actually useful to the individual, and the surrogate of mere appearance is always sufficient when it accomplishes the end in view. It is a conclusion which is inevitable for strict utilitarianism. The impression of many Germans that the virtues professed by Americanism are pure hypocrisy seems to have been confirmed by this striking case. But in fact the matter is not by any means so simple. Benjamin Franklin's own character, as it appears in the really unusual candidness of his autobiography, belies that suspicion. The circumstance that he ascribes his recognition of the utility of virtue to a divine revelation which was intended to lead him in the path of righteousness, shows that something more than mere garnishing for purely egocentric motives is involved.

In fact, the *summum bonum*[10] of this ethic, the earning of more and more money, combined with the strict avoidance of all spontaneous enjoyment of life, is above all completely devoid of any eudæmonistic, not to say hedonistic, admixture. It is thought of so purely as an end in itself, that from the point of view of the happiness of, or utility to, the single individual, it appears entirely transcendental and absolutely irrational.[11] Man is dominated by the making of money, by acquisition as the ultimate purpose of his life. Economic acquisition is no longer subordinated to man as the means for the satisfaction of his material needs. This reversal of what we should call the natural relationship, so irrational from a naïve point of view, is evidently as definitely a leading principle of capitalism as it is foreign to all peoples not under capitalistic influence. At the same time it expresses a type of feeling which is closely connected with certain religious ideas. If we thus ask, *why* should "money be made out of men", Benjamin Franklin himself, although he was a colourless deist, answers in his autobiography with a quotation from the Bible, which his strict Calvinistic father drummed into him again and again in his youth: "Seest thou a man diligent in his business?[12] He shall stand before kings" (Prov. xxii. 29). The earning of money within the modern economic order is, so long as it is done legally, the result and the expression of virtue and proficiency in a calling; and this virtue and proficiency are, as it is now not difficult to see, the real Alpha and Omega of Franklin's ethic, as expressed in the passages we have quoted, as well as in all his works without exception.[13]

And in truth this peculiar idea, so familiar to us to-day, but in reality so little a matter of course, of one's duty in a calling, is what is most characteristic of the social ethic of capitalistic culture, and is in a sense the fundamental basis of it. It is an obligation which the individual is supposed to feel and does feel towards the content of his professional[14] activity, no matter in what it consists, in particular no matter whether it appears on the surface as a utilization of his personal powers, or only of his material possessions (as capital).

Of course, this conception has not appeared only under capitalistic conditions. On the contrary, we shall later trace its origins back to a time previous to the advent of capitalism. Still less, naturally, do we maintain that a conscious acceptance of these ethical maxims on the part of the individuals, entrepreneurs or labourers, in modern capitalistic enterprises, is a condition of the further existence of present-day capitalism. The capitalistic economy of the present day is an immense cosmos into which the individual is born, and which presents itself to him, at least as an individual, as an unalterable order of things in which he must live. It forces the individual, in so far as he is involved in the system of market relationships, to conform to capitalistic rules of action, The manufacturer who in the long run acts counter to these norms, will just as inevitably be eliminated from the economic scene as the worker who cannot or will not adapt himself to them will be thrown into the streets without a job.

Thus the capitalism of to-day, which has come to dominate economic life, educates and selects the economic subjects which it needs through a process of economic survival of the fittest. But here one can easily see the limits of the concept of selection as a means of historical explanation. In order that a manner of life so well adapted to the peculiarities of capitalism could be selected at all, i.e. should come to dominate others, it had to originate somewhere, and not in isolated individuals alone, but as a way of life common to whole groups of men. This origin is what really needs explanation. Concerning the doctrine of the more naïve historical materialism, that such ideas originate as a reflection or superstructure of economic situations, we shall speak more in detail below. At this point it will suffice for our purpose to call attention to the fact that without doubt, in the country of Benjamin Franklin's birth (Massachusetts), the spirit of capitalism (in the sense we have attached to it) was present before the capitalistic order. There were complaints of a peculiarly calculating sort of profit-seeking in New England, as distinguished from other parts of America, as early as 1632. It is further undoubted that capitalism remained far less developed in some of the neighbouring colonies, the later Southern States of the United States of America, in spite of the fact that these latter were founded by large capitalists for business motives, while the New England colonies were founded by preachers and seminary graduates with the help of small bourgeois, craftsmen and yoemen, for religious reasons. In this case the causal relation is certainly the reverse of that suggested by the materialistic standpoint.

But the origin and history of such ideas is much more complex than the theorists of the superstructure suppose. The spirit of capitalism, in the sense in which we are using the term, had to fight its way to supremacy against a whole world of hostile forces. A state of mind such as that expressed in the passages we have quoted from Franklin, and which called forth the applause of a whole people, would both in ancient times and in the Middle Ages[15] have been proscribed as the lowest sort of avarice and as an attitude entirely lacking in self-respect. It is, in fact, still regularly thus looked upon by all those social groups which are least involved in or adapted to modern capitalistic conditions. This is not wholly because the instinct of acquisition was in those times unknown or undeveloped, as has often been said. Nor because the *auri sacra fames*, the greed for gold, was then, or now, less powerful outside of bourgeois capitalism than within its peculiar sphere, as the illusions of modern romanticists are wont to believe. The difference between the capitalistic and pre-capitalistic spirits is not to be found at this point. The greed of the Chinese Mandarin, the old Roman aristocrat, or the modern peasant, can stand up to any comparison. And the *auri sacra fames*[16] of a Neapolitan cab-driver or *barcaiuolo*, and certainly of Asiatic representatives of similar trades, as well as of the craftsmen of southern European or Asiatic countries, is, as anyone can find out for himself, very much more intense, and especially more unscrupulous than that of, say, an Englishman in similar circumstances.[17]

The universal reign of absolute unscrupulousness in the pursuit of selfish interests by the making of money has been a specific characteristic of precisely those countries whose bourgeois-capitalistic development, measured according to Occidental standards, has remained backward. As every employer knows, the lack of *coscienziosità*[18] of the labourers[19] of such countries, for instance Italy as compared with Germany, has been, and to a certain extent still is, one of the principal obstacles to their capitalistic development. Capitalism cannot make use of the labour of those who practise the doctrine of undisciplined *liberum arbitrium*,[20] any more than it can make use of the business man who seems absolutely unscrupulous in his dealings with others, as we can learn from Franklin. Hence the difference does not lie in the degree of development of any impulse to make money. The *auri sacra fames* is as old as the history of man. But we shall see that those who submitted to it without reserve as an uncontrolled impulse, such as the Dutch sea-captain who "would go through hell for gain, even though he scorched his sails", were by no means the representatives of that attitude of mind from which the specifically modern capitalistic spirit as a mass phenomenon is derived, and that is what matters. At all periods of history, wherever it was possible, there has been ruthless acquisition, bound to no ethical norms whatever. Like war and piracy, trade has often been unrestrained in its relations with foreigners and those outside the group. The double ethic has permitted here what was forbidden in dealings among brothers.

Capitalistic acquisition as an adventure has been at home in all types of economic society which have known trade with the use of money and which have offered it opportunities, through *commenda*, farming of taxes, State loans, financing of wars, ducal courts and office-holders. Likewise the inner attitude of the adventurer, which laughs at all ethical limitations, has been universal. Absolute and conscious ruthlessness in acquisition has often stood in the closest connection with the strictest conformity to tradition. Moreover, with the breakdown of tradition and the more or less complete extension of free economic enterprise, even to within the social group, the new thing has not generally been ethically justified and encouraged, but only tolerated as a fact. And this fact has been treated either as ethically indifferent or as reprehensible, but unfortunately unavoidable. This has not only been the normal attitude of all ethical teachings, but, what is more important, also that expressed in the practical action of the average man of pre-capitalistic times, pre-capitalistic in the sense that the rational utilization of capital in a permanent enterprise and the rational capitalistic organization of labour had not yet become dominant forces in the determination of economic activity. Now just this attitude was one of the strongest inner obstacles which the adaptation of men to the conditions of an ordered bourgeois-capitalistic economy has encountered everywhere.

The most important opponent with which the spirit of capitalism, in the sense of a definite standard of life claiming ethical sanction, has had to struggle, was that type of attitude and reaction to new situations which we may designate as traditionalism. In this case also every attempt at a final definition must be held in abeyance. On the other hand, we must try to make the provisional meaning clear by citing a few cases. We will begin from below, with the labourers.

One of the technical means which the modern employer uses in order to secure the greatest possible amount of work from his men is the device of piece-rates. In agriculture, for instance, the gathering of the harvest is a case where the greatest possible intensity of labour is called for, since, the weather being uncertain, the difference between high profit and heavy loss may depend on the speed with which the harvesting can be done. Hence a system of piece-rates is almost universal in this case. And since the interest of the employer in a speeding-up of harvesting increases with the increase of the results and the intensity of the work, the attempt has again and again been made, by increasing the piece-rates of the workmen, thereby giving them an opportunity to earn what is for them a very high wage, to interest them in increasing their own efficiency. But a peculiar difficulty has been met with surprising frequency: raising the piece-rates has often had the result that not more but less has been accomplished in the same time, because the worker reacted to the increase not by increasing but by decreasing the amount of his work. A man, for instance, who at the rate of 1 mark per acre mowed 2½ acres per day and earned 2½ marks, when the rate was raised to 1.25 marks per acre mowed, not 3 acres, as he might easily have done, thus earning 3.75 marks, but only 2 acres, so that he could still earn

the 2½ marks to which he was accustomed. The opportunity of earning more was less attractive than that of working less. He did not ask:
how much can I earn in a day if I do as much work as possible? but:
how much must I work in order to earn the wage, 2½ marks, which
I earned before and which takes care of my traditional needs? This is
an example of what is here meant by traditionalism. A man does not
"by nature" wish to earn more and more money, but simply to live as
he is accustomed to live and to earn as much as is necessary for that
purpose. Wherever modern capitalism has begun its work of increasing the productivity of human labour by increasing its intensity, it has
encountered the immensely stubborn resistance of this leading trait
of pre-capitalistic labour. And to-day it encounters it the more, the
more backward (from a capitalistic point of view) the labouring
forces are with which it has to deal.

Another obvious possibility, to return to our example, since the
appeal to the acquisitive instinct through higher wage-rates failed,
would have been to try the opposite policy, to force the worker by
reduction of his wage-rates to work harder to earn the same amount
than he did before. Low wages and high profits seem even to-day to
a superficial observer to stand in correlation; everything which is paid
out in wages seems to involve a corresponding reduction of profits.
That road capitalism has taken again and again since its beginning.
For centuries it was an article of faith, that low wages were productive, i.e. that they increased the material results of labour so that, as
Pieter de la Cour, on this point, as we shall see, quite in the spirit of
the old Calvinism, said long ago, the people only work because and
so long as they are poor.

But the effectiveness of this apparently so efficient method has its
limits.[21] Of course the presence of a surplus population which it can
hire cheaply in the labour market is a necessity for the development
of capitalism. But though too large a reserve army may in certain
cases favour its quantitative expansion, it checks its qualitative development, especially the transition to types of enterprise which make
more intensive use of labour. Low wages are by no means identical
with cheap labour.[22] From a purely quantitative point of view the efficiency of labour decreases with a wage which is physiologically insufficient, which may in the long run even mean a survival of the unfit.
The present-day average Silesian mows, when he exerts himself to
the full, little more than two-thirds as much land as the better paid
and nourished Pomeranian or Mecklenburger, and the Pole, the further East he comes from, accomplishes progressively less than the
German. Low wages fail even from a purely business point of view
wherever it is a question of producing goods which require any sort
of skilled labour, or the use of expensive machinery which is easily
damaged, or in general wherever any great amount of sharp attention

or of initiative is required. Here low wages do not pay, and their effect is the opposite of what was intended. For not only is a developed sense of responsibility absolutely indispensable, but in general also an attitude which, at least during working hours, is freed from continual calculations of how the customary wage may be earned with a maximum of comfort and a minimum of exertion. Labour must, on the contrary, be performed as if it were an absolute end in itself, a calling. But such an attitude is by no means a product of nature. It cannot be evoked by low wages or high ones alone, but can only be the product of a long and arduous process of education. Today, capitalism, once in the saddle, can recruit its labouring force in all industrial countries with comparative ease. In the past this was in every case an extremely difficult problem.[23] And even today it could probably not get along without the support of a powerful ally along the way, which, as we shall see below, was at hand at the time of its development.

What is meant can again best be explained by means of an example. The type of backward traditional form of labour is today very often exemplified by women workers, especially unmarried ones. An almost universal complaint of employers of girls, for instance German girls, is that they are almost entirely unable and unwilling to give up methods of work inherited or once learned in favour of more efficient ones, to adapt themselves to new methods, to learn and to concentrate their intelligence, or even to use it at all. Explanations of the possibility of making work easier, above all more profitable to themselves, generally encounter a complete lack of understanding. Increases of piece-rates are without avail against the stone wall of habit. In general it is otherwise, and that is a point of no little importance from our view-point, only with girls having a specifically religious, especially a Pietistic, background. One often hears, and statistical investigation confirms it,[24] that by far the best chances of economic education are found among this group. The ability of mental concentration, as well as the absolutely essential feeling of obligation to one's job, are here most often combined with a strict economy which calculates the possibility of high earnings, and a cool self-control and frugality which enormously increase performance. This provides the most favourable foundation for the conception of labour as an end in itself, as a calling which is necessary to capitalism: the chances of overcoming traditionalism are greatest on account of the religious upbringing. This observation of present-day capitalism[25] in itself suggests that it is worth while to ask how this connection of adaptability to capitalism with religious factors may have come about in the days of the early development of capitalism. For that they were even then present in much the same form can be inferred from numerous facts. For instance, the dislike and the persecution which

Methodist workmen in the eighteenth century met at the hands of their comrades were not solely nor even principally the result of their religious eccentricities, England had seen many of those and more striking ones. It rested rather, as the destruction of their tools, repeatedly mentioned in the reports, suggests, upon their specific willingness to work as we should say to-day.

However, let us again return to the present, and this time to the entrepreneur, in order to clarify the meaning of traditionalism in his case.

Sombart, in his discussions of the genesis of capitalism,[26] has distinguished between the satisfaction of needs and acquisition as the two great leading principles in economic history. In the former case the attainment of the goods necessary to meet personal needs, in the latter a struggle for profit free from the limits set by needs, have been the ends controlling the form and direction of economic activity. What he calls the economy of needs seems at first glance to be identical with what is here described as economic traditionalism. That may be the case if the concept of needs is limited to traditional needs. But if that is not done, a number of economic types which must be considered capitalistic according to the definition of capital which Sombart gives in another part of his work,[27] would be excluded from the category of acquisitive economy and put into that of needs economy. Enterprises, namely, which are carried on by private entrepreneurs by utilizing capital (money or goods with a money value) to make a profit, purchasing the means of production and selling the product, i.e. undoubted capitalistic enterprises, may at the same time have a traditionalistic character. This has, in the course even of modern economic history, not been merely an occasional case, but rather the rule, with continual interruptions from repeated and increasingly powerful conquests of the capitalistic spirit. To be sure the capitalistic form of an enterprise and the spirit in which it is run generally stand in some sort of adequate relationship to each other, but not in one of necessary interdependence. Nevertheless, we provisionally use the expression spirit of (modern) capitalism[28] to describe that attitude which seeks profit rationally and systematically in the manner which we have illustrated by the example of Benjamin Franklin. This, however, is justified by the historical fact that that attitude of mind has on the one hand found its most suitable expression in capitalistic enterprise, while on the other the enterprise has derived its most suitable motive force from the spirit of capitalism.

But the two may very well occur separately. Benjamin Franklin was filled with the spirit of capitalism at a time when his printing business did not differ in form from any handicraft enterprise. And we shall see that at the beginning of modern times it was by no means the capitalistic entrepreneurs of the commercial aristocracy, who were either the sole or the predominant bearers of the attitude we have here called the spirit of capitalism.[29] It was much more the rising strata of the lower industrial middle classes. Even in the nineteenth century its classical representatives were not the elegant gentlemen of Liverpool and Hamburg, with their commercial fortunes handed down for generations, but the self-made parvenus of Manchester and Westphalia, who often rose from very modest circumstances. As early as the sixteenth century the situation was similar; the industries which arose at that time were mostly created by parvenus.[30]

The management, for instance, of a bank, a wholesale export business, a large retail establishment, or of a large putting-out enterprise dealing with goods produced in homes, is certainly only possible in the form of a capitalistic enterprise. Nevertheless, they may all be carried on in a traditionalistic spirit. In fact, the business of a large bank of issue cannot be carried on in any other way. The foreign trade of whole epochs has rested on the basis of monopolies and legal privileges of strictly traditional character. In retail trade—and we are not here talking of the small men without capital who are continually crying out for Government aid—the revolution which is making an end of the old traditionalism is still in full swing. It is the same development which broke up the old putting-out system, to which modern domestic labour is related only in form. How this revolution takes place and what is its significance may, in spite of the fact these things are so familiar, be again brought out by a concrete example.

Until about the middle of the past century the life of a putter-out was, at least in many of the branches of the Continental textile industry,[31] what we should to-day consider very comfortable. We may imagine its routine somewhat as follows: The peasants came with their cloth, often (in the case of linen) principally or entirely made from raw material which the peasant himself had produced, to the town in which the putter-out lived, and after a careful, often official, appraisal of the quality, received the customary price for it. The putter-out's customers, for markets any appreciable distance away, were middlemen, who also came to him, generally not yet following samples, but seeking traditional qualities, and bought from his warehouse, or, long before delivery, placed orders which were probably in turn passed on to the peasants. Personal canvassing of customers took place, if at all, only at long intervals. Otherwise correspondence sufficed, though the sending of samples slowly gained ground. The number of business hours was very moderate, perhaps five to six a day, sometimes considerably less; in the rush season, where there was one, more. Earnings were moderate; enough to lead a respectable life and in good times to put away a little. On the whole, relations among competitors were relatively good, with a large degree of agreement on the fundamentals of business. A long daily visit to the tavern, with often plenty to drink, and a congenial circle of friends, made life comfortable and leisurely.

The form of organization was in every respect capitalistic; the entrepreneur's activity was of a purely business character; the use of capital, turned over in the business, was indispensable; and finally, the objective aspect of the economic process, the book-keeping, was rational. But it was traditionalistic business, if one considers the spirit which animated the entrepreneur: the traditional manner of life, the traditional rate of profit, the traditional amount of work, the traditional manner of regulating the relationships with labour, and the essentially traditional circle of customers and the manner of attracting new ones. All these dominated the conduct of the business, were at the basis, one may say, of the *ethos* of this group of business men.

Now at some time this leisureliness was suddenly destroyed, and often entirely without any essential change in the form of organization, such as the transition to a unified factory, to mechanical weaving, etc. What happened was, on the contrary, often no more than this: some young man from one of the putting-out families went out into the country, carefully chose weavers for his employ, greatly increased the rigour of his supervision of their work, and thus turned them from peasants into labourers. On the other hand, he would begin to change his marketing methods by so far as possible going directly to the final consumer, would take the details into his own hands, would personally solicit customers, visiting them every year, and above all would adapt the quality of the product directly to their needs and wishes. At the same time he began to introduce the principle of low prices and large turnover. There was repeated what everywhere and always is the result of such a process of rationalization: those who would not follow suit had to go out of business. The idyllic state collapsed under the pressure of a bitter competitive struggle, respectable fortunes were made, and not lent out at interest, but always reinvested in the business. The old leisurely and comfortable attitude toward life gave way to a hard frugality in which some participated and came to the top, because they did not wish to consume but to earn, while others who wished to keep on with the old ways were forced to curtail their consumption.[32]

And, what is most important in this connection, it was not generally in such cases a stream of new money invested in the industry which brought about this revolution—in several cases known to me the whole revolutionary process was set in motion with a few thousands of capital borrowed from relations—but the new spirit, the spirit of modern capitalism, had set to work. The question of the motive forces in the expansion of modern capitalism is not in the first instance a question of the origin of the capital sums which were available for capitalistic uses, but, above all, of the development of the spirit of capitalism. Where it appears and is able to work itself out, it produces its own capital and monetary supplies as the means to its ends, but the reverse is not true.[33] Its entry on the scene was not generally peaceful. A flood of mistrust, sometimes of hatred, above all of moral indignation, regularly opposed itself to the first innovator. Often—I know of several cases of the sort—regular legends of mysterious shady spots in his previous life have been produced. It is very easy not to recognize that only an unusually strong character could save an entrepreneur of this new type from the loss of his temperate self-control and from both moral and economic shipwreck. Furthermore, along with clarity of vision and ability to act, it is only by virtue of very definite and highly developed ethical qualities that it has been possible for him to command the absolutely indispensable confidence of his customers and workmen. Nothing else could have given him the strength to overcome the innumerable obstacles, above all the infinitely more intensive work which is demanded of the modern entrepreneur. But these are ethical qualities of quite a different sort from those adapted to the traditionalism of the past.

And, as a rule, it has been neither dare-devil and unscrupulous speculators, economic adventurers such as we meet at all periods of economic history, nor simply great financiers who have earned through this change, outwardly so inconspicuous, but nevertheless so decisive for the penetration of economic life with the new spirit. On the contrary, they were men who had grown up in the hard school of life, calculating and daring at the same time, above all temperate and reliable, shrewd and completely devoted to their business, with strictly bourgeois opinions and principles.

One is tempted to think that these personal moral qualities have not the slightest relation to any ethical maxims, to say nothing of religious ideas, but that the essential relation between them is negative. The ability to free oneself from the common tradition, a sort of liberal enlightenment, seems likely to be the most suitable basis for such a business man's success. And to-day that is generally precisely the case. Any relationship between religious beliefs and conduct is generally absent, and where any exists, at least in Germany, it tends to be of the negative sort. The people filled with the spirit of capitalism to-day tend to be indifferent, if not hostile, to the Church. The thought of the pious boredom of paradise has little attraction for their active natures; religion appears to them as a means of drawing people away from labour in this world. If you ask them what is the meaning of their restless activity, why they are never satisfied with what they have, thus appearing so senseless to any purely worldly view of life, they would perhaps give the answer, if they know any at all: "to provide

*Business as the motivation itself*

for my children and grandchildren". But more often and, since that motive is not peculiar to them, but was just as effective for the traditionalist, more correctly, simply: that business with its continuous work has become a necessary part of their lives. That is in fact the only possible motivation, but it at the same time expresses what is, seen from the view-point of personal happiness, so irrational about this sort of life, where a man exists for the sake of his business, instead of the reverse.

Of course, the desire for the power and recognition which the mere fact of wealth brings plays its part. When the imagination of a whole people has once been turned toward purely quantitative bigness, as in the United States, this romanticism of numbers exercises an irresistible appeal to the poets among business men. Otherwise it is in general not the real leaders, and especially not the permanently successful entrepreneurs, who are taken in by it. In particular, the resort to entailed estates and the nobility, with sons whose conduct at the university and in the officers' corps tries to cover up their social origin, as has been the typical history of German capitalistic parvenu families, is a product of later decadence. The ideal type[34] of the capitalistic entrepreneur, as it has been represented even in Germany by occasional outstanding examples, has no relation to such more or less refined climbers. He avoids ostentation and unnecessary expenditure, as well as conscious enjoyment of his power, and is embarrassed by the outward signs of the social recognition which he receives. His manner of life is, in other words, often, and we shall have to investigate the historical significance of just this important fact, distinguished by a certain ascetic tendency, as appears clearly enough in the sermon of Franklin which we have quoted. It is, namely, by no means exceptional, but rather the rule, for him to have a sort of modesty which is essentially more honest than the reserve which Franklin so shrewdly recommends. He gets nothing out of his wealth for himself, except the irrational sense of having done his job well.

But it is just that which seems to the pre-capitalistic man so incomprehensible and mysterious, so unworthy and contemptible. That anyone should be able to make it the sole purpose of his life-work, to sink into the grave weighed down with a great material load of money and goods, seems to him explicable only as the product of a perverse instinct, the *auri sacra fames*.[35]

At present under our individualistic political, legal, and economic institutions, with the forms of organization and general structure which are peculiar to our economic order, this spirit of capitalism might be understandable, as has been said, purely as a result of adaptation. The capitalistic system so needs this devotion to the calling of making money, it is an attitude toward material goods which is so well suited to that system, so intimately bound up with the conditions of survival in the economic struggle for existence, that there can to-day no longer be any question of a necessary connection of that acquisitive manner of life with any single *Weltanschauung*.[36] In fact, it no longer needs the support of any religious forces, and feels the attempts of religion to influence economic life, in so far as they can still be felt at all, to be as much an unjustified interference as its regulation by the State. In such circumstances men's commercial and social interests do tend to determine their opinions and attitudes. Whoever does not adapt his manner of life to the conditions of capitalistic success must go under, or at least cannot rise. But these are phenomena of a time in which modern capitalism has become dominant and has become emancipated from its old supports. But as it could at one time destroy the old forms of mediæval regulation of economic life only in alliance with the growing power of the modern State, the same, we may say provisionally, may have been the case in its relations with religious forces. Whether and in what sense that was the case, it is our task to investigate. For that the conception of money-making as an end in itself to which people were bound, as a calling, was contrary to the ethical feelings of whole epochs, it is hardly necessary to prove. The dogma *Deo placere vix potest*[37] which was incorporated into the canon law and applied to the activities of the merchant, and which at the time (like the passage in the gospel about interest)[38] was considered genuine, as well as St. Thomas's characterization of the desire for gain as *turpitudo*[39] (which term even included unavoidable and hence ethically justified profit-making), already contained a high degree of concession on the part of the Catholic doctrine to the financial powers with which the Church had such intimate political relations in the Italian cities,[40] as compared with the much more radically anti-chrematistic views of comparatively wide circles. But even where the doctrine was still better accommodated to the facts, as for instance with Anthony of Florence, the feeling was never quite overcome, that activity directed to acquisition for its own sake was at bottom a *pudendum*[41] which was to be tolerated only because of the unalterable necessities of life in this world.

Some moralists of that time, especially of the nominalistic school, accepted developed capitalistic business forms as inevitable, and attempted to justify them, especially commerce, as necessary. The *industria*[42] developed in it they were able to regard, though not without contradictions, as a legitimate source of profit, and hence ethically unobjectionable. But the dominant doctrine rejected the spirit of capitalistic acquisition as *turpitudo*, or at least could not give it a positive ethical sanction. An ethical attitude like that of Benjamin Franklin would have been simply unthinkable. This was, above all, the attitude of capitalistic circles themselves. Their life-work was, so long as they clung to the tradition of the Church, at best something morally indifferent. It was tolerated, but was still, even if only on account of the continual danger of collision with the Church's doctrine on usury, somewhat dangerous to salvation. Quite considerable sums, as the sources show, went at the death of rich people to religious institutions as conscience money, at times even back to former debtors as *usura*[43] which had been unjustly taken from them. It was otherwise, along with heretical and other tendencies looked upon with disapproval, only in those parts of the commercial aristocracy which were already emancipated from the tradition. But even sceptics and people indifferent to the Church often reconciled themselves with it by gifts, because it was a sort of insurance against the uncertainties of what might come after death, or because (at least according to the very widely held latter view) an external obedience to the commands of the Church was sufficient to insure salvation.[44] Here the either non-moral or immoral character of their action in the opinion of the participants themselves comes clearly to light.

Now, how could activity, which was at best ethically tolerated, turn into a calling in the sense of Benjamin Franklin? The fact to be explained historically is that in the most highly capitalistic centre of that time, in Florence of the fourteenth and fifteenth centuries, the money and capital market of all the great political Powers, this attitude was considered ethically unjustifiable, or at best to be tolerated. But in the backwoods small bourgeois circumstances of Pennsylvania in the eighteenth century, where business threatened for simple lack of money to fall back into barter, where there was hardly a sign of large enterprise, where only the earliest beginnings of banking were to be found, the same thing was considered the essence of moral conduct, even commanded in the name of duty. To speak here of a reflection of material conditions in the ideal superstructure would be patent nonsense. What was the background of ideas which could account for the sort of activity apparently directed toward profit alone as a calling toward which the individual feels himself to have an ethical obligation? For it was this idea which gave the way of life of the new entrepreneur its ethical foundation and justification.

The attempt has been made, particularly by Sombart, in what are often judicious and effective observations, to depict economic rationalism as the salient feature of modern economic life as a whole. Undoubtedly with justification, if by that is meant the extension of the productivity of labour which has, through the subordination of the process of production to scientific points of view, relieved it from its dependence upon the natural organic limitations of the human individual. Now this process of rationalization in the field of technique and economic organization undoubtedly determines an important part of the ideals of life of modern bourgeois society. Labour in the service of a rational organization for the provision of humanity with material goods has without doubt always appeared to representatives of the capitalistic spirit as one of the most important purposes of their life-work. It is only necessary, for instance, to read Franklin's account of his efforts in the service of civic improvements in Philadelphia clearly to apprehend this obvious truth. And the joy and pride of having given employment to numerous people, of having had a part in the economic progress of his home town in the sense referring to figures of population and volume of trade which capitalism associated with the word, all these things obviously are part of the specific and undoubtedly idealistic satisfactions in life to modern men of business. Similarly it is one of the fundamental characteristics of an individualistic capitalistic economy that it is rationalized on the basis of rigorous calculation, directed with foresight and caution toward the economic success which is sought in sharp contrast to the hand-to-mouth existence of the peasant, and to the privileged traditionalism of the guild craftsman and of the adventurers' capitalism, oriented to the exploitation of political opportunities and irrational speculation.

It might thus seem that the development of the spirit of capitalism is best understood as part of the development of rationalism as a whole, and could be deduced from the fundamental position of rationalism on the basic problems of life. In the process Protestantism would only have to be considered in so far as it had formed a stage prior to the development of a purely rationalistic philosophy. But any serious attempt to carry this thesis through makes it evident that such a simple way of putting the question will not work, simply because of the fact that the history of rationalism shows a development which by no means follows parallel lines in the various departments of life. The rationalization of private law, for instance, if it is thought of as a logical simplification and rearrangement of the content of the law, was achieved in the highest hitherto known degree in the Roman law of late antiquity. But it remained most backward in some of the countries with the highest degree of economic rationalization, notably in England, where the Renaissance of Roman Law was overcome by the power of the great legal corporations, while it has always retained its supremacy in the Catholic countries of Southern Europe. The worldly rational philosophy of the eighteenth century did not find favour alone or even principally in the countries of highest capitalistic development. The doctrines of Voltaire are even to-day the common property of broad upper, and what is practically more important, middle-class groups in the Romance Catholic countries. Finally, if under practical rationalism is understood the type of attitude which sees and judges the world consciously in terms of the worldly interests of the individual ego, then this view of life was and is the special peculiarity of the peoples of the *liberum arbitrium*, such as the Italians and the French are in very flesh and blood. But we have already convinced ourselves that this is by no means the soil in which that relationship of a man to his calling as a task, which is necessary to capitalism, has pre-eminently grown. In fact, one may—this simple proposition, which is often forgotten should be placed at the beginning of every study which essays to deal with rationalism—rationalize life from fundamentally different basic points of view and in very different directions. Rationalism is an historical concept which covers a whole world of different things. It will be our task to find out whose intellectual child the particular concrete form of rational thought was, from which the idea of a calling and the devotion to labour in the calling has grown, which is, as we have seen, so irrational from the standpoint of purely eudæmonistic self-interest, but which has been and still is one of the most characteristic elements of our capitalistic culture. We are here particularly interested in the origin of precisely the irrational element which lies in this, as in every conception of a calling.

## Chapter 3. Luther's Conception of the Calling

### *Task of the investigation*

Now it is unmistakable that even in the German word *Beruf*, and perhaps still more clearly in the English *calling*, a religious conception, that of a task set by God, is at least suggested. The more emphasis is put upon the word in a concrete case, the more evident is the connotation. And if we trace the history of the word through the civilized languages, it appears that neither the predominantly Catholic peoples nor those of classical antiquity[1] have possessed any expression of similar connotation for what we know as a calling (in the sense of a life-task, a definite field in which to work), while one has existed for all predominantly Protestant peoples. It may be further shown that this is not due to any ethnical peculiarity of the languages concerned. It is not, for instance, the product of a Germanic spirit, but in its modern meaning the word comes from the Bible translations, through the spirit of the translator, not that of the original.[2] In Luther's translation of the Bible it appears to have first been used at a point in Jesus Sirach (xi. 20 and 21) precisely in our modern sense.[3] After that it speedily took on its present meaning in the everyday speech of all Protestant peoples, while earlier not even a suggestion of such a meaning could be found in the secular literature of any of them, and even, in religious writings, so far as I can ascertain, it is only found in one of the German mystics whose influence on Luther is well known.

Like the meaning of the word, the idea is new, a product of the Reformation. This may be assumed as generally known. It is true that certain suggestions of the positive valuation of routine activity in the world, which is contained in this conception of the calling, had already existed in the Middle Ages, and even in late Hellenistic antiquity. We shall speak of that later. But at least one thing was unquestionably new: the valuation of the fulfilment of duty in worldly affairs as the highest form which the moral activity of the individual could assume. This it was which inevitably gave every-day worldly activity a religious significance, and which first created the conception of a calling in this sense. The conception of the calling thus brings out that central dogma of all Protestant denominations which the Catholic division of ethical precepts into *præcepta*[4] and *consilia*[5] discards. The only way of living acceptably to God was not to surpass worldly morality in monastic asceticism, but solely through the fulfilment of the obligations imposed upon the individual by his position in the world. That was his calling.

Luther[6] developed the conception in the course of the first decade of his activity as a reformer. At first, quite in harmony with the prevailing tradition of the Middle Ages, as represented, for example, by Thomas Aquinas,[7] he thought of activity in the world as a thing of the flesh, even though willed by God. It is the indispensable natural condition of a life of faith, but in itself, like eating and drinking, morally neutral.[8] But with the development of the conception of *sola fide*[9] in all its consequences, and its logical result, the increasingly sharp emphasis against the Catholic *consilia evangelica*[10] of the monks as dictates of the devil, the calling grew in importance. The monastic life is not only quite devoid of value as a means of justification before God, but he also looks upon its renunciation of the duties of this world as the product of selfishness, withdrawing from temporal obligations. In contrast, labour in a calling appears to him as the outward expression of brotherly love. This he proves by the observation that the division of labour forces every individual to work for others, but his view-point is highly naïve, forming an almost grotesque contrast to Adam Smith's well-known statements on the same subject.[11] However, this justification, which is evidently essentially scholastic, soon disappears again, and there remains, more and more strongly emphasized, the statement that the fulfilment of worldly duties is under all circumstances the only way to live acceptably to God. It and it alone is the will of God, and hence every legitimate calling has exactly the same worth in the sight of God.[12]

That this moral justification of worldly activity was one of the most important results of the Reformation, especially of Luther's part in it, is beyond doubt, and may even be considered a platitude.[13] This attitude is worlds removed from the deep hatred of Pascal, in his contemplative moods, for all worldly activity, which he was deeply convinced could only be understood in terms of vanity or low cunning.[14] And it differs even more from the liberal utilitarian compromise with the world at which the Jesuits arrived. But just what the practical significance of this achievement of Protestantism was in detail is dimly felt rather than clearly perceived.

In the first place it is hardly necessary to point out that Luther cannot be claimed for the spirit of capitalism in the sense in which we have used that term above, or for that matter in any sense whatever. The religious circles which today most enthusiastically celebrate that great achievement of the Reformation are by no means friendly to capitalism in any sense. And Luther himself would, without doubt, have sharply repudiated any connection with a point of view like that of Franklin. Of course, one cannot consider his complaints against the great merchants of his time, such as the Fuggers,[15] as evidence in this case. For the struggle against the privileged position, legal or actual, of single great trading companies in the sixteenth and seventeenth centuries may best be compared with the modern campaign against the trusts, and can no more justly be considered in itself an expression of a traditionalistic point of view. Against these people, against the Lombards, the monopolists, speculators, and bankers patronized by the Anglican Church and the kings and parliaments of England and France, both the Puritans and the Huguenots carried on a bitter struggle.[16] Cromwell, after the battle of Dunbar (September 1650), wrote to the Long Parliament: "Be pleased to reform the abuses of all professions: and if there be any one that makes many poor to make a few rich, that suits not a Commonwealth." But, nevertheless, we will find Cromwell following a quite specifically capitalistic line of thought.[17] On the other hand, Luther's numerous statements against usury or interest in any form reveal a conception of the nature of capitalistic acquisition which, compared with that of late Scholasticism, is, from a capitalistic view-point, definitely backward.[18] Especially, of course, the doctrine of the sterility of money which Anthony of Florence had already refuted.

But it is unnecessary to go into detail. For, above all, the consequences of the conception of the calling in the religious sense for worldly conduct were susceptible to quite different interpretations. The effect of the Reformation as such was only that, as compared with the Catholic attitude, the moral emphasis on and the religious sanction of, organized worldly labour in a calling was mightily increased. The way in which the concept of the calling, which expressed this change, should develop further depended upon the religious evolution which now took place in the different Protestant

Churches. The authority of the Bible, from which Luther thought he had derived his idea of the calling, on the whole favoured a traditionalistic interpretation. The Old Testament, in particular, though in the genuine prophets it showed no sign of a tendency to excel worldly morality, and elsewhere only in quite isolated rudiments and suggestions, contained a similar religious idea entirely in this traditionalistic sense. Everyone should abide by his living and let the godless run after gain. That is the sense of all the statements which bear directly on worldly activities. Not until the Talmud is a partially, but not even then fundamentally, different attitude to be found. The personal attitude of Jesus is characterized in classical purity by the typical antique-Oriental plea: "Give us this day our daily bread." The element of radical repudiation of the world, as expressed in the $\mu\alpha\mu\omega\nu\tilde{\alpha}\varsigma\ \tau\tilde{\eta}\varsigma\ \dot{\alpha}\delta\iota\kappa\dot{\iota}\alpha\varsigma$[19] excluded the possibility that the modern idea of a calling should be based on his personal authority.[20] In the apostolic era as expressed in the New Testament, especially in St. Paul, the Christian looked upon worldly activity either with indifference, or at least essentially traditionalistically; for those first generations were filled with eschatological hopes. Since everyone was simply waiting for the coming of the Lord, there was nothing to do but remain in the station and in the worldly occupation in which the call of the Lord had found him, and labour as before. Thus he would not burden his brothers as an object of charity, and it would only be for a little while. Luther read the Bible through the spectacles of his whole attitude; at the time and in the course of his development from about 1518 to 1530 this not only remained traditionalistic but became ever more so.[21]

In the first years of his activity as a reformer he was, since he thought of the calling as primarily of the flesh, dominated by an attitude closely related, in so far as the form of world activity was concerned, to the Pauline eschatological indifference as expressed in 1 Cor. vii.[22] One may attain salvation in any walk of life; on the short pilgrimage of life there is no use in laying weight on the form of occupation. The pursuit of material gain beyond personal needs must thus appear as a symptom of lack of grace, and since it can apparently only be attained at the expense of others, directly reprehensible.[23] As he became increasingly involved in the affairs of the world, he came to value work in the world more highly. But in the concrete calling an individual pursued he saw more and more a special command of God to fulfil these particular duties which the Divine Will had imposed upon him. And after the conflict with the Fanatics and the peasant disturbances, the objective historical order of things in which the individual has been placed by God becomes for Luther more and more a direct manifestation of divine will.[24] The stronger and stronger emphasis on the providential element, even in particular events of life, led more and more to a traditionalistic interpretation based on the idea of Providence. The individual should remain once and for all in the station and calling in which God had placed him, and should restrain his worldly activity within the limits imposed by his established station in life. While his economic traditionalism was originally the result of Pauline indifference, it later became that of a more and more intense belief in divine providence,[25] which identified absolute obedience to God's will,[26] with absolute acceptance of things as they were. Starting from this background, it was impossible for Luther to establish a new or in any way fundamental connection between worldly activity and religious principles.[27] His acceptance of purity of doctrine as the one infallible criterion of the Church, which became more and more irrevocable after the struggles of the 'twenties, was in itself sufficient to check the development of new points of view in ethical matters.

Thus for Luther the concept of the calling remained traditionalistic.[28] His calling is something which man has to accept as a divine ordinance, to which he must adapt himself. This aspect outweighed the other idea which was also present, that work in the calling was a, or rather *the*, task set by God.[29] And in its further development, orthodox Lutheranism emphasized this aspect still more. Thus, for the time being, the only ethical result was negative; worldly duties were no longer subordinated to ascetic ones; obedience to authority and the acceptance of things as they were, were preached.[30] In this Lutheran form the idea of a calling had, as will be shown in our discussion of medieval religious ethics, to a considerable extent been anticipated by the German mystics. Especially in Tauler's equalization of the values of religious and worldly occupations, and the decline in valuation of the traditional forms of ascetic practices[31] on account of the decisive significance of the ecstatic-contemplative absorption of the divine spirit by the soul. To a certain extent Lutheranism means a step backward from the mystics, in so far as Luther, and still more his Church, had, as compared with the mystics, partly undermined the psychological foundations for a rational ethics. (The mystic attitude on this point is reminiscent partly of the Pietest and partly of the Quaker psychology of faith.[32]) That was precisely because he could not but suspect the tendency to ascetic self-discipline of leading to salvation by works, and hence he and his Church were forced to keep it more and more in the background.

Thus the mere idea of the calling in the Lutheran sense is at best of questionable importance for the problems in which we are interested. This was all that was meant to be determined here.[33] But this is not in the least to say that even the Lutheran form of the renewal of the religious life may not have had some practical significance for the objects of our investigation; quite the contrary. Only that significance evidently cannot be derived directly from the attitude of Luther and his Church to worldly activity, and is perhaps not altogether so easily grasped as the connection with other branches of Protestantism. It is thus well for us next to look into those forms in which a relation between practical life and a religious motivation can be more easily perceived than in Lutheranism. We have already called attention to the conspicuous part played by Calvinism and the Protestant sects in the history of capitalistic development. As Luther found a different spirit at work in Zwingli than in himself, so did his spiritual successors in Calvinism. And Catholicism has to the present day looked upon Calvinism as its real opponent.

Now that may be partly explained on purely political grounds. Although the Reformation is unthinkable without Luther's own personal religious development, and was spiritually long influenced by his personality, without Calvinism his work could not have had permanent concrete success. Nevertheless, the reason for this common repugnance of Catholics and Lutherans lies, at least partly, in the ethical peculiarities of Calvinism. A purely superficial glance shows that there is here quite a different relationship between the religious life and earthly activity than in either Catholicism or Lutheranism. Even in literature motivated purely by religious factors that is evident. Take for instance the end of the *Divine Comedy*, where the poet in Paradise stands speechless in his passive contemplation of the secrets of God, and compare it with the poem which has come to be called the *Divine Comedy of Puritanism*. Milton closes the last song of *Paradise Lost* after describing the *expulsion* from paradise as follows:—

> They, looking back, all the eastern side beheld
> Of paradise, so late their happy seat,
> Waved over by that flaming brand; the gate
> With dreadful faces thronged and fiery arms.
> Some natural tears they dropped, but wiped them soon:
> The world was all before them, there to choose
> Their place of rest, and Providence their guide.

And only a little before Michael had said to Adam:

> . . . "Only add
> Deeds to thy knowledge answerable; add faith;
> Add virtue, patience, temperance; add love,
> By name to come called Charity, the soul
> Of all the rest: then wilt thou not be loth
> To leave this Paradise, but shall possess
> A Paradise within thee, happier far."

One feels at once that this powerful expression of the Puritan's serious attention to this world, his acceptance of his life in the world as a task, could not possibly have come from the pen of a mediæval writer. But it is just as uncongenial to Lutheranism, as expressed for instance in Luther's and Paul Gerhard's chorales. It is now our task to replace this vague feeling by a somewhat more precise logical formulation, and to investigate the fundamental basis of these differences. The appeal to national character is generally a mere confession of ignorance, and in this case it is entirely untenable. To ascribe a unified national character to the Englishmen of the seventeenth century would be simply to falsify history. Cavaliers and Roundheads did not appeal to each other simply as two parties, but as radically distinct species of men, and whoever looks into the matter carefully must agree with them.[34] On the other hand, a difference of character between the English merchant adventurers and the old Hanseatic merchants is not to be found; nor can any other fundamental difference between the English and German characters at the end of the Middle Ages, which cannot easily be explained by the differences of their political history.[35] It was the power of religious influence, not alone, but more than anything else, which created the differences of which we are conscious to-day.[36]

We thus take as our starting-point in the investigation of the relationship between the old Protestant ethic and the spirit of capitalism the works of Calvin, of Calvinism, and the other Puritan sects. But it is not to be understood that we expect to find any of the founders or representatives of these religious movements considering the promotion of what we have called the spirit of capitalism as in any sense the end of his life-work. We cannot well maintain that the pursuit of worldly goods, conceived as an end in itself, was to any of them of positive ethical value. Once and for all it must be remembered that programmes of ethical reform never were at the centre of interest for any of the religious reformers (among whom, for our purposes, we must include men like Menno, George Fox, and Wesley). They were not the founders of societies for ethical culture nor the proponents of humanitarian projects for social reform or cultural ideals. The salvation of the soul and that alone was the centre of their life and work. Their ethical ideals and the practical results of their doctrines were all based on that alone, and were the consequences of purely religious motives. We shall thus have to admit that the cultural consequences of the Reformation were to a great extent, perhaps in the particular aspects with which we are dealing predominantly, unforeseen and even unwished-for results of the labours of the reformers. They were often far removed from or even in contradiction to all that they themselves thought to attain.

The following study may thus perhaps in a modest way form a contribution to the understanding of the manner in which ideas become effective forces in history. In order, however, to avoid any misunderstanding of the sense in which any such effectiveness of purely ideal motives is claimed at all, I may perhaps be permitted a few remarks in conclusion to this introductory discussion.

In such a study, it may at once be definitely stated, no attempt is made to evaluate the ideas of the Reformation in any sense, whether it concern their social or their religious worth. We have continually to deal with aspects of the Reformation which must appear to the truly religious consciousness as incidental and even superficial. For we are merely attempting to clarify the part which religious forces have played in forming the developing web of our specifically worldly modern culture, in the complex interaction of innumerable different historical factors. We are thus inquiring only to what extent certain characteristic features of this culture can be imputed to the influence of the Reformation. At the same time we must free ourselves from the idea that it is possible to deduce the Reformation, as a historically necessary result, from certain economic changes. Countless historical circumstances, which cannot be reduced to any economic law, and are not susceptible of economic explanation of any sort, especially purely political processes, had to concur in order that the newly created Churches should survive at all.

On the other hand, however, we have no intention whatever of maintaining such a foolish and doctrinaire thesis[37] as that the spirit of capitalism (in the provisional sense of the term explained above) could only have arisen as the result of certain effects of the Reformation, or even that capitalism as an economic system is a creation of the Reformation. In itself, the fact that certain important forms of capitalistic business organization are known to be considerably older than the Reformation is a sufficient refutation of such a claim. On the contrary, we only wish to ascertain whether and to what extent religious forces have taken part in the qualitative formation and the quantitative expansion of that spirit over the world. Furthermore, what concrete aspects of our capitalistic culture can be traced to them. In view of the tremendous confusion of interdependent influences between the material basis, the forms of social and political organization, and the ideas current in the time of the Reformation, we can only proceed by investigating whether and at what points certain correlations[38] between forms of religious belief and practical ethics can be worked out. At the same time we shall as far as possible clarify the manner and the general *direction* in which, by virtue of those relationships, the religious movements have influenced the development of material culture. Only when this has been determined with reasonable accuracy can the attempt be made to estimate to what extent the historical development of modern culture can be attributed to those religious forces and to what extent to others.

# Part II
# The Practical Ethics of the Ascetic Branches of Protestantism

## Chapter 4.
## The Religious Foundations of Worldly Asceticism

In history there have been four principal forms of ascetic Protestantism (in the sense of word here used): (1) Calvinism in the form which it assumed in the main area of its influence in Western Europe, especially in the seventeenth century; (2) Pietism; (3) Methodism; (4) the sects growing out of the Baptist movement.[1] None of these movements was completely separated from the others, and even the distinction from the nonascetic Churches of the Reformation is never perfectly clear. Methodism, which first arose in the middle of the eighteenth century within the Established Church of England, was not, in the minds of its founders, intended to form a new Church, but only a new awakening of the ascetic spirit within the old. Only in the course of its development, especially in its extension to America, did it become separate from the Anglican Church.           Escape from religion

Pietism first split off from the Calvinistic movement in England, and especially in Holland. It remained loosely connected with orthodoxy, shading off from it by imperceptible gradations, until at the end of the seventeenth century it was absorbed into Lutheranism under Spener's leadership. Though the dogmatic adjustment was not entirely satisfactory, it remained a movement within the Lutheran Church. Only the faction dominated by Zinzendorf, and affected by lingering Hussite and Calvinistic influences within the Moravian brotherhood, was forced, like Methodism against its will, to form a peculiar sort of sect. Calvinism and Baptism were at the beginning of their development sharply opposed to each other. But in the Baptism of the latter part of the seventeenth century they were in close contact. And even in the Independent sects of England and Holland at the beginning of the seventeenth century the transition was not abrupt. As Pietism shows, the transition to Lutheranism is also gradual, and the same is true of Calvinism and the Anglican Church, though both in external character and in the spirit of its most logical adherents the latter is more closely related to Catholicism. It is true that both the mass of the adherents and especially the staunchest champions of that ascetic movement which, in the broadest sense of a highly ambiguous word, has been called Puritanism,[2] did attack the foundations of Anglicanism; but even here the differences were only gradually worked out in the course of the struggle. Even if for the present we quite ignore the questions of government and organization which do not interest us here, the facts are just the same. The dogmatic differences, even the most important, such as those over the doctrines of predestination and justification, were combined in the most complex ways, and even at the beginning of the seventeenth century regularly, though not without exception, prevented the maintenance of unity in the Church. Above all, the types of moral conduct in which we are interested may be found in a similar manner among the adherents of the most various denominations, derived from any one of the four sources mentioned above, or a combination of several of them. We shall see that similar ethical maxims may be correlated with very different dogmatic foundations. Also the important literary tools for the saving of souls, above all the casuistic compendia of the various denominations, influenced each other in the course of time; one finds great similarities in them, in spite of very great differences in actual conduct.

It would almost seem as though we had best completely ignore both the dogmatic foundations and the ethical theory and confine our attention to the moral practice so far as it can be determined. That, however, is not true. The various different dogmatic roots of ascetic morality did no doubt die out after terrible struggles. But the original connection with those dogmas has left behind important traces in the later undogmatic ethics; moreover, only the knowledge of the original body of ideas can help us to understand the connection of that morality with the idea of the afterlife which absolutely dominated the most spiritual men of that time. Without its power, overshadowing everything else, no moral awakening which seriously influenced practical life came into being in that period.

We are naturally not concerned with the question of what was theoretically and officially taught in the ethical compendia of the time, however much practical significance this may have had through the influence of Church discipline, pastoral work, and preaching.[3] We are interested rather in something entirely different: the influence of those psychological sanctions which, originating in religious belief and the practice of religion, gave a direction to practical conduct and held the individual to it. Now these sanctions were to a large extent derived from the peculiarities of the religious ideas behind them. The men of that day were occupied with abstract dogmas to an extent which itself can only be understood when we perceive the connection of these dogmas with practical religious interests. A few observations on dogma,[4] which will seem to the nontheological reader as dull as they will hasty and superficial to the theologian, are indispensable. We can of course only proceed by presenting these religious ideas in the artificial simplicity of ideal types, as they could at best but seldom be found in history. For just because of the impossibility of drawing sharp boundaries in historical reality we can only hope to understand their specific importance from an investigation of them in their most consistent and logical forms.

## A. Calvinism

Now Calvinism[5] was the faith[6] over which the great political and cultural struggles of the sixteenth and seventeenth centuries were fought in the most highly developed countries, the Netherlands, England, and France. To it we shall hence turn first. At that time, and in general even to-day, the doctrine of predestination was considered its most characteristic dogma. It is true that there has been controversy as to whether it is the most essential dogma of the Reformed Church or only an appendage. Judgments of the importance of a historical phenomenon may be judgments of value or faith, namely, when they refer to what is alone interesting, or alone in the long run valuable in it. Or, on the other hand, they may refer to its influence on other historical processes as a causal factor. Then we are concerned with judgments of historical imputation. If now we start, as we must do here, from the latter standpoint and inquire into the significance which is to be attributed to that dogma by virtue of its cultural and historical consequences, it must certainly be rated very highly.[7] The movement which Oldenbarneveld led was shattered by it. The schism in the English Church became irrevocable under James I after the Crown and the Puritans came to differ dogmatically over just this doctrine. Again and again it was looked upon as the real element of political danger in Calvinism and attacked as such by those in authority.[8] The great synods of the seventeenth century, above all those of Dordrecht and Westminster, besides numerous smaller ones, made its elevation to canonical authority the central purpose of their work. It served as a rallying-point to countless heroes of the Church militant, and in both the eighteenth and the nineteenth centuries it caused schisms in the Church and formed the battle-cry of great new awakenings. We cannot pass it by, and since to-day it can no longer be assumed as known to all educated men, we can best learn its content from the authoritative words of the

Westminster Confession of 1647, which in this regard is simply repeated by both Independent and Baptist creeds.

> Chapter IX (of Free Will), No. 3. Man, by his fall into a state of sin, hath wholly lost all ability of will to any spiritual good accompanying salvation. So that a natural man, being altogether averse from that Good, and dead in sin, is not able, by his own strength, to convert himself, or to prepare himself thereunto.
>
> Chapter III (of God's Eternal Decree), No. 3. By the decree of God, for the manifestation of His glory, some men and angels are predestinated unto everlasting life, and others foreordained to everlasting death.
>
> No. 5. Those of mankind that are predestinated unto life, God before the foundation of the world was laid, according to His eternal and immutable purpose, and the secret counsel and good pleasure of His will, hath chosen in Christ unto everlasting glory, out of His mere free grace and love, without any foresight of faith or good works, or perseverance in either of them, or any other thing in the creature as conditions or causes moving Him thereunto, and all to the praise of His glorious grace.
>
> No. 7. The rest of mankind God was pleased, according to the unsearchable counsel of His own will, whereby He extendeth, or with-holdeth mercy, as He pleaseth, for the glory of His sovereign power over His creatures, to pass by, and to ordain them to dishonour and wrath for their sin, to the praise of His glorious justice.
>
> Chapter X (of Effectual Calling), No. 1. All those whom God hath predestinated unto life, and those only, He is pleased in His appointed and accepted time effectually to call by His word and spirit (out of that state of sin and death, in which they are by nature) . . . taking away their heart of stone, and giving unto them an heart of flesh; renewing their wills, and by His almighty power determining them to that which is good. . . .
>
> Chapter V (of Providence), No. 6. As for those wicked and ungodly men, whom God as a righteous judge, for former sins doth blind and harden, from them He not only with-holdeth His grace, whereby they might have been enlightened in their understandings and wrought upon in their hearts, but sometimes also withdraweth the gifts which they had and exposeth them to such objects as their corruption makes occasion of sin: and withal, gives them over to their own lusts, the temptations of the world, and the power of Satan: whereby it comes to pass that they harden themselves, even under those means, which God useth for the softening of others.[9]

"Though I may be sent to Hell for it, such a God will never command my respect", was Milton's well-known opinion of the doctrine.[10]

But we are here concerned not with the evaluation, but the historical significance of the dogma. We can only briefly sketch the question of how the doctrine originated and how it fitted into the framework of Calvinistic theology.

Two paths leading to it were possible. The phenomenon of the religious sense of grace is combined, in the most active and passionate of those great worshippers which Christianity has produced again and again since Augustine, with the feeling of certainty that that grace is the sole product of an objective power, and not in the least to be attributed to personal worth. The powerful feeling of lighthearted assurance, in which the tremendous pressure of their sense of sin is released, apparently breaks over them with elemental force and destroys every possibility of the belief that this overpowering gift of grace could owe anything to their own co-operation or could be connected with achievements or qualities of their own faith and will. At the time of Luther's greatest religious creativeness, when he was capable of writing his *Freiheit eines Christenmenschen*, God's secret decree was also to him most definitely the sole and ultimate source of his state of religious grace.[11] Even later he did not formally abandon it. But not only did the idea not assume a central position for him, but it receded more and more into the background, the more his position as responsible head of his Church forced him into practical politics. Melanchthon quite deliberately avoided adopting the dark and dangerous teaching in the Augsburg Confession, and for the Church fathers of Lutheranism it was an article of faith that grace was revocable (*amissibilis*), and could be won again by penitent humility and faithful trust in the word of God and in the sacraments.

With Calvin the process was just the opposite; the significance of the doctrine for him increased,[12] perceptibly in the course of his polemical controversies with theological opponents. It is not fully developed until the third edition of his *Institutes*, and only gained its position of central prominence after his death in the great struggles which the Synods of Dordrecht and Westminster sought to put an end to. With Calvin the *decretum horribile*[13] is derived not, as with Luther, from religious experience, but from the logical necessity of his thought; therefore its importance increases with every increase in the logical consistency of that religious thought. The interest of it is solely in God, not in man; God does not exist for men, but men for the sake of God.[14] All creation, including of course the fact, as it undoubtedly was for Calvin, that only a small proportion of men are chosen for eternal grace, can have any meaning only as means to the glory and majesty of God. To apply earthly standards of justice to His sovereign decrees is meaningless and an insult to His Majesty,[15] since He and He alone is free, i.e. is subject to no law. His decrees can only be understood by or even known to us in so far as it has been His pleasure to reveal them. We can only hold to these fragments of eternal truth. Everything else, including the meaning of our individual destiny, is hidden in dark mystery which it would be both impossible to pierce and presumptuous to question.

For the damned to complain of their lot would be much the same as for animals to bemoan the fact they were not born as men. For everything of the flesh is separated from God by an unbridgeable gulf and deserves of Him only eternal death, in so far as He has not decreed otherwise for the glorification of His Majesty. We know only that a part of humanity is saved, the rest damned. To assume that human merit or guilt plays a part in determining this destiny would be to think of God's absolutely free decrees, which have been settled from eternity, as subject to change by human influence, an impossible contradiction. The Father in heaven of the New Testament, so human and understanding, who rejoices over the repentance of a sinner as a woman over the lost piece of silver she has found, is gone. His place has been taken by a transcendental being, beyond the reach of human understanding, who with His quite incomprehensible decrees has decided the fate of every individual and regulated the tiniest details of the cosmos from eternity.[16] God's grace is, since His decrees cannot change, as impossible for those to whom He has granted it to lose as it is unattainable for those to whom He has denied it.

In its extreme inhumanity this doctrine must above all have had one consequence for the life of a generation which surrendered to its magnificent consistency. That was a feeling of unprecedented inner loneliness of the single individual.[17] In what was for the man of the age of the Reformation the most important thing in life, his eternal salvation, he was forced to follow his path alone to meet a destiny which had been decreed for him from eternity. No one could help him. No priest, for the chosen one can understand the word of God only in his own heart. No sacraments, for though the sacraments had been ordained by God for the increase of His glory, and must hence be scrupulously observed, they are not a means to the attainment of grace, but only the subjective *externa subsidia*[18] of faith. No Church, for though it was held that *extra ecclesiam nulla salus*[19] in the sense that whoever kept away from the true Church could never belong to God's chosen band,[20] nevertheless the membership of the external Church included the doomed. They should belong to it and be subjected to its discipline, not in order thus to attain salvation, that is impossible, but because, for the glory of God, they too must be forced to obey His commandments. Finally, even no God. For even Christ had died only for the elect,[21] for whose benefit God had decreed His martyrdom from eternity. This, the complete elimination of salvation through the Church and the sacraments (which was in Lutheranism by no means developed to its final conclusions), was what formed the absolutely decisive difference from Catholicism.

That great historic process in the development of religions, the elimination of magic from the world[22] which had begun with the old Hebrew prophets and, in conjunction with Hellenistic scientific thought, had repudiated all magical means to salvation as superstition and sin, came here to its logical conclusion. The genuine Puritan even rejected all signs of religious ceremony at the grave and buried his nearest and dearest without song or ritual in order that no superstition, no trust in the effects of magical and sacramental forces on salvation, should creep in.[23]

There was not only no magical means of attaining the grace of God for those to whom God had decided to deny it, but no means whatever. Combined with the harsh doctrines of the absolute transcendentality of God and the corruption of everything pertaining to the flesh, this inner isolation of the individual contains, on the one hand, the reason for the entirely negative attitude of Puritanism to all the sensuous and emotional elements in culture and in religion, because they are of no use toward salvation and promote sentimental illusions and idolatrous superstitions. Thus it provides a basis for a fundamental antagonism to sensuous culture of all kinds.[24] On the other hand, it forms one of the roots of that disillusioned and pessimistically inclined individualism[25] which can even to-day be identified in the national characters and the institutions of the peoples with a Puritan past, in such a striking contrast to the quite different spectacles through which the Enlightenment later looked upon men.[26] We can clearly identify the traces of the influence of the doctrine of predestination in the elementary forms of conduct and attitude toward life in the era with which we are concerned, even where its authority as a dogma was on the decline. It was in fact only the most extreme form of that exclusive trust in God in which we are here interested. It comes out for instance in the strikingly frequent repetition, especially in the English Puritan literature, of warnings against any trust in the aid of friendship of men.[27] Even the amiable Baxter counsels deep distrust of even one's closest friend, and Bailey directly exhorts to trust no one and to say nothing compromising to anyone. Only God should be your confidant.[28] In striking contrast to Lutheranism, this attitude toward life was also connected with the quiet disappearance of the private confession, of which Calvin was suspicious only on account of its possible sacramental misinterpretation, from all the regions of fully developed Calvinism. That was an occurrence of the greatest importance. In the first place it is a symptom of the type of influence this religion exercised. Further, however, it was a psychological stimulus to the development of their ethical attitude.

The means to a periodical discharge of the emotional sense of sin[29] was done away with.

Of the consequences for the ethical conduct of everyday life we speak later. But for the general religious situation of a man the consequences are evident. In spite of the necessity of membership in the true Church[30] for salvation, the Calvinist's intercourse with his God was carried on in deep spiritual isolation. To see the specific results[31] of this peculiar atmosphere, it is only necessary to read Bunyan's *Pilgrim's Progress*,[32] by far the most widely read book of the whole Puritan literature. In the description of Christian's attitude after he had realized that he was living in the City of Destruction and he had received the call to take up his pilgrimage to the celestial city, wife and children cling to him, but stopping his ears with his fingers and crying, "life, eternal life", he staggers forth across the fields. No refinement could surpass the naïve feeling of the tinker who, writing in his prison cell, earned the applause of a believing world, in expressing the emotions of the faithful Puritan, thinking only of his own salvation. It is expressed in the unctuous conversations which he holds with fellow-seekers on the way, in a manner somewhat reminiscent of Gottfried Keller's *Gerechte Kammacher*. Only when he himself is safe does it occur to him that it would be nice to have his family with him. It is the same anxious fear of death and the beyond which we feel so vividly in Alfonso of Liguori, as Döllinger has described him to us. It is worlds removed from that spirit of proud worldliness which Machiavelli expresses in relating the fame of those Florentine citizens who, in their struggle against the Pope and his excommunication, had held "Love of their native city higher than the fear for the salvation of their souls". And it is of course even farther from the feelings which Richard Wagner puts into the mouth of Siegmund before his fatal combat, "Grüsse mir Wotan, grüsse mir Wallhall—Doch von Wallhall's spröden Wonnen sprich du wahrlich mir nicht."[33] But the effects of this fear on Bunyan and Liguori are characteristically different. The same fear which drives the latter to every conceivable self-humiliation spurs the former on to a restless and systematic struggle with life. Whence comes this difference?

It seems at first a mystery how the undoubted superiority of Calvinism in social organization can be connected with this tendency to tear the individual away from the closed ties with which he is bound to this world.[34] But, however strange it may seem, it follows from the peculiar form which the Christian brotherly love was forced to take under the pressure of the inner isolation of the individual through the Calvinistic faith. In the first place it follows dogmatically.[35] The world exists to serve the glorification of God and for that purpose alone. The elected Christian is in the world only to increase this glory of God by fulfilling His commandments to the best of his ability. But

God requires social achievement of the Christian because He wills that social life shall be organized according to His commandments, in accordance with that purpose. The social[36] activity of the Christian in the world is solely activity *in majorem gloriam Dei*.[37] This character is hence shared by labour in a calling which serves the mundane life of the community. Even in Luther we found specialized labour in callings justified in terms of brotherly love. But what for him remained an uncertain, purely intellectual suggestion became for the Calvinists a characteristic element in their ethical system. Brotherly love, since it may only be practised for the glory of God[38] and not in the service of the flesh,[39] is expressed in the first place in the fulfil-ment of the daily tasks given by the *lex naturæ*[40] and in the process this fulfilment assumes a peculiarly objective and impersonal char-acter, that of service in the interest of the rational organization of our social environment. For the wonderfully purposeful organization and arrangement of this cosmos is, according both to the revelation of the Bible and to natural intuition, evidently designed by God to serve the utility of the human race. This makes labour in the service of imper-sonal social usefulness appear to promote the glory of God and hence to be willed by Him. The complete elimination of the theodicy prob-lem and of all those questions about the meaning of the world and of life, which have tortured others, was as self-evident to the Puritan as, for quite different reasons, to the Jew, and even in a certain sense to all the nonmystical types of Christian religion.

To this economy of forces Calvinism added another tendency which worked in the same direction. The conflict between the indi-vidual and the ethic (in Søren Kierkegaard's sense) did not exist for Calvinism, although it placed the individual entirely on his own responsibility in religious matters. This is not the place to analyse the reasons for this fact, or its significance for the political and economic rationalism of Calvinism. The source of the utilitarian character of Calvinistic ethics lies here, and important peculiarities of the Calvin-istic idea of the calling were derived from the same source as well.[41] But for the moment we must return to the special consideration of the doctrine of predestination.

For us the decisive problem is: How was this doctrine borne[42] in an age to which the after-life was not only more important, but in many ways also more certain, than all the interests of life in this world?[43] The question, Am I one of the elect? must sooner or later have arisen for every believer and have forced all other interests into the back-ground. And how can I be sure of this state of grace?[44] For Calvin himself this was not a problem. He felt himself to be a chosen agent of the Lord, and was certain of his own salvation. Accordingly, to the question of how the individual can be certain of his own election, he has at bottom only the answer that we should be content with the knowledge that God has chosen and depend further only on that implicit trust in Christ which is the result of true faith. He rejects in principle the assumption that one can learn from the conduct of others whether they are chosen or damned. It is an unjustifiable attempt to force God's secrets. The elect differ externally in this life in no way from the damned[45]; and even all the subjective experiences of the chosen are, as *ludibria spiritus sancti*,[46] possible for the damned with the single exception of that *finaliter*[47] expectant, trusting faith. The elect thus are and remain God's invisible Church.

Quite naturally this attitude was impossible for his followers as early as Beza, and, above all, for the broad mass of ordinary men. For them the *certitudo salutis*[48] in the sense of the recognizability of the state of grace necessarily became of absolutely dominant importance.[49] So, wherever the doctrine of predestination was held, the question could not be suppressed whether there were any infallible criteria by which membership in the *electi*[50] could be known. Not only has this question continually had a central importance in the development of the Pietism which first arose on the basis of the Reformed Church; it has in fact in a certain sense at times been fundamental to it. But when we consider the great political and social importance of the Reformed doctrine and practice of the Communion, we shall see how great a part was played during the whole seventeenth century outside of Pietism by the possibility of ascertaining the state of grace of the individual. On it depended, for instance, his admission to Communion, i.e. to the central religious ceremony which determined the social standing of the participants.

It was impossible, at least so far as the question of a man's own state of grace arose, to be satisfied[51] with Calvin's trust in the testimony of the expectant faith resulting from grace, even though the orthodox doctrine had never formally abandoned that criterion.[52] Above all, practical pastoral work, which had immediately to deal with all the suffering caused by the doctrine, could not be satisfied. It met these difficulties in various ways.[53] So far as predestination was not reinterpreted, toned down, or fundamentally abandoned,[54] two principal, mutually connected, types of pastoral advice appear. On the one hand it is held to be an absolute duty to consider oneself chosen, and to combat all doubts as temptations of the devil,[55] since lack of self-confidence is the result of insufficient faith, hence of imperfect grace. The exhortation of the apostle to make fast one's own call is here interpreted as a duty to attain certainty of one's own election and justification in the daily struggle of life. In the place of the humble sinners to whom Luther promises grace if they trust themselves to God in penitent faith are bred those self-confident saints[56] whom we can rediscover in the hard Puritan merchants of the heroic age of capitalism and in isolated instances down to the present. On

*[handwritten margin note: Destined to be saved or not, might as well succeed worldly]*

the other hand, in order to attain that self-confidence intense worldly activity is recommended as the most suitable means.[57] It and it alone disperses religious doubts and gives the certainty of grace.

That worldly activity should be considered capable of this achievement, that it could, so to speak, be considered the most suitable means of counteracting feelings of religious anxiety, finds its explanation in the fundamental peculiarities of religious feeling in the Reformed Church, which come most clearly to light in its differences from Lutheranism in the doctrine of justification by faith. These differences are analysed so subtly and with such objectivity and avoidance of value-judgments in Schneckenburger's excellent lectures,[58] that the following brief observations can for the most part simply rest upon his discussion.

The highest religious experience which the Lutheran faith strives to attain, especially as it developed in the course of the seventeenth century, is the *unio mystica*[59] with the deity.[60] As the name itself, which is unknown to the Reformed faith in this form, suggests, it is a feeling of actual absorption in the deity, that of a real entrance of the divine into the soul of the believer. It is qualitatively similar to the aim of the contemplation of the German mystics and is characterized by its passive search for the fulfilment of the yearning for rest in God.

Now the history of philosophy shows that religious belief which is primarily mystical may very well be compatible with a pronounced sense of reality in the field of empirical fact; it may even support it directly on account of the repudiation of dialectic doctrines. Furthermore, mysticism may indirectly even further the interests of rational conduct. Nevertheless, the positive valuation of external activity is lacking in its relation to the world. In addition to this, Lutheranism combines the *unio mystica* with that deep feeling of sin-stained unworthiness which is essential to preserve the *pœnitentia quotidiana*[61] of the faithful Lutheran, thereby maintaining the humility and simplicity indispensable for the forgiveness of sins. The typical religion of the Reformed Church, on the other hand, has from the beginning repudiated both this purely inward emotional piety of Lutheranism and the Quietist escape from everything of Pascal. A real penetration of the human soul by the divine was made impossible by the absolute transcendentality of God compared to the flesh: *finitum non est capax infiniti*.[62] The community of the elect with their God could only take place and be perceptible to them in that God worked (*operatur*) through them and that they were conscious of it. That is, their action originated from the faith caused by God's grace, and this faith in turn justified itself by the quality of that action. Deep-lying differences of the most important conditions of salvation[63] which apply to the classification of all practical religious activity appear here. The religious believer can make himself sure of his state

of grace either in that he feels himself to be the vessel of the Holy
Spirit or the tool of the divine will. In the former case his religious
life tends to mysticism and emotionalism, in the latter to ascetic
action; Luther stood close to the former type, Calvinism belonged
definitely to the latter. The Calvinist also wanted to be saved *sola
fide*.[64] But since Calvin viewed all pure feelings and emotions, no matter how exalted they might seem to be, with suspicion,[65] faith had to
be proved by its objective results in order to provide a firm foundation
for the *certitudo salutis*.[66] It must be a *fides efficax*,[67,68] the call to salvation an effectual calling (expression used in Savoy Declaration).

If we now ask further, by what fruits the Calvinist thought himself
able to identify true faith? the answer is: by a type of Christian conduct which served to increase the glory of God. Just what does so
serve is to be seen in his own will as revealed either directly through
the Bible or indirectly through the purposeful order of the world
which he has created (*lex naturæ*).[69,70] Especially by comparing the
condition of one's own soul with that of the elect, for instance the
patriarchs, according to the Bible, could the state of one's own grace
be known.[71] Only one of the elect really has the *fides efficax*,[72,73] only
he is able by virtue of his rebirth (*regeneratio*) and the resulting sanctification (*sanctificatio*) of his whole life, to augment the glory of God
by real, and not merely apparent, good works. It was through the consciousness that his conduct, at least in its fundamental character and
constant ideal (*propositum obœdientiæ*), rested on a power[74] within
himself working for the glory of God; that it is not only willed of God
but rather done by God[75] that he attained the highest good towards
which this religion strove, the certainty of salvation.[76] That it was
attainable was proved by 2 Cor. xiii. 5.[77,78] Thus, however useless
good works might be as a means of attaining salvation, for even the
elect remain beings of the flesh, and everything they do falls infinitely
short of divine standards, nevertheless, they are indispensable as a
sign of election.[79] They are the technical means, not of purchasing
salvation, but of getting rid of the fear of damnation. In this sense
they are occasionally referred to as directly necessary for salvation[80]
or the *possessio salutis*[81] is made conditional on them.[82]

In practice this means that God helps those who help themselves.[83]
Thus the Calvinist, as it is sometimes put, himself creates[84] his own
salvation, or, as would be more correct, the conviction of it. But this
creation cannot, as in Catholicism, consist in a gradual accumulation
of individual good works to one's credit, but rather in a systematic
self-control which at every moment stands before the inexorable
alternative, chosen or damned. This brings us to a very important
point in our investigation.

It is common knowledge that Lutherans have again and again
accused this line of thought, which was worked out in the Reformed

Churches and sects with increasing clarity,[85] of reversion to the doctrine of salvation by works.[86] And however justified the protest of the accused against identification of their dogmatic position with the Catholic doctrine, this accusation has surely been made with reason if by it is meant the practical consequences for the everyday life of the average Christian of the Reformed Church.[87] For a more intensive form of the religious valuation of moral action than that to which Calvinism led its adherents has perhaps never existed. But what is important for the practical significance of this sort of salvation by works must be sought in a knowledge of the particular qualities which characterized their type of ethical conduct and distinguished it from the everyday life of an average Christian of the Middle Ages. The difference may well be formulated as follows: the normal mediæval Catholic layman[88] lived ethically, so to speak, from hand to mouth. In the first place he conscientiously fulfilled his traditional duties. But beyond that minimum his good works did not necessarily form a connected, or at least not a rationalized, system of life, but rather remained a succession of individual acts. He could use them as occasion demanded, to atone for particular sins, to better his chances for salvation, or, toward the end of his life, as a sort of insurance premium. Of course the Catholic ethic was an ethic of intentions. But the concrete *intentio*[89] of the single act determined its value. And the single good or bad action was credited to the doer determining his temporal and eternal fate. Quite realistically the Church recognized that man was not an absolutely clearly defined unity to be judged one way or the other, but that his moral life was normally subject to conflicting motives and his action contradictory. Of course, it required as an ideal a change of life in principle. But it weakened just this requirement (for the average) by one of its most important means of power and education, the sacrament of absolution, the function of which was connected with the deepest roots of the peculiarly Catholic religion.

The rationalization of the world, the elimination of magic as a means to salvation,[90] the Catholics had not carried nearly so far as the Puritans (and before them the Jews) had done. To the Catholic[91] the absolution of his Church was a compensation for his own imperfection. The priest was a magician who performed the miracle of transubstantiation, and who held the key to eternal life in his hand. One could turn to him in grief and penitence. He dispensed atonement, hope of grace, certainty of forgiveness, and thereby granted release from that tremendous tension to which the Calvinist was doomed by an inexorable fate, admitting of no mitigation. For him such friendly and human comforts did not exist. He could not hope to atone for hours of weakness or of thoughtlessness by increased good will at other times, as the Catholic or even the Lutheran could. The God of

Calvinism demanded of his believers not single good works, but a life of good works combined into a unified system.[92] There was no place for the very human Catholic cycle of sin, repentance, atonement, release, followed by renewed sin. Nor was there any balance of merit for a life as a whole which could be adjusted by temporal punishments or the Churches' means of grace.

The moral conduct of the average man was thus deprived of its planless and unsystematic character and subjected to a consistent method for conduct as a whole. It is no accident that the name of Methodists stuck to the participants in the last great revival of Puritan ideas in the eighteenth century just as the term Precisians, which has the same meaning, was applied to their spiritual ancestors in the seventeenth century.[93] For only by a fundamental change in the whole meaning of life at every moment and in every action[94] could the effects of grace transforming a man from the *status naturæ*[95] to the *status gratiæ*[96] be proved.

The life of the saint was directed solely toward a transcendental end, salvation. But precisely for that reason it was thoroughly rationalized in this world and dominated entirely by the aim to add to the glory of God on earth. Never has the precept *omnia in majorem dei gloriam*[97] been taken with more bitter seriousness.[98] Only a life guided by constant thought could achieve conquest over the state of nature. Descartes's *cogito ergo sum*[99] was taken over by the contemporary Puritans with this ethical reinterpretation.[100] It was this rationalization which gave the Reformed faith its peculiar ascetic tendency, and is the basis both of its relationship[101] to and its conflict with Catholicism. For naturally similar things were not unknown to Catholicism.

Without doubt Christian asceticism, both outwardly and in its inner meaning, contains many different things. But it has had a definitely rational character in its highest Occidental forms as early as the Middle Ages, and in several forms even in antiquity. The great historical significance of Western monasticism, as contrasted with that of the Orient, is based on this fact, not in all cases, but in its general type. In the rules of St. Benedict, still more with the monks of Cluny, again with the Cistercians, and most strongly the Jesuits, it has become emancipated from planless otherworldliness and irrational self-torture. It had developed a systematic method of rational conduct with the purpose of overcoming the *status naturæ*, to free man from the power of irrational impulses and his dependence on the world and on nature. It attempted to subject man to the supremacy of a purposeful will,[102] to bring his actions under constant self-control with a careful consideration of their ethical consequences. Thus it trained the monk, objectively, as a worker in the service of the kingdom of God, and thereby further, subjectively, assured the salvation of his soul. This active self-control, which formed the end of the *exercitid*[103] of St. Ignatius and of the rational monastic virtues everywhere,[104] was also the most important practical ideal of Puritanism.[105] In the deep contempt with which the cool reserve of its adherents is contrasted, in the reports of the trials of its martyrs, with the undisciplined blustering of the noble prelates and officials[106] can be seen that respect for quiet self-control which still distinguishes the best type of English or American gentleman to-day.[107] To put it in our terms[108]: The Puritan, like every rational type of asceticism, tried to enable a man to maintain and act upon his constant motives, especially those which it taught him itself, against the emotions. In this formal psychological sense of the term it tried to make him into a personality. Contrary to many popular ideas, the end of this asceticism was to be able to lead an alert, intelligent life: the most urgent task the destruction of spontaneous, impulsive enjoyment, the most important means was to bring order into the conduct of its adherents. All these important points are emphasized in the rules of Catholic monasticism as strongly[109] as in the principles of conduct of the Calvinists.[110] On this methodical control over the whole man rests the enormous expansive power of both, especially the ability of Calvinism as against Lutheranism to defend the cause of Protestantism as the Church militant.

On the other hand, the difference of the Calvinistic from the mediæval asceticism is evident. It consisted in the disappearance of the *consilia evangelica*[111] and the accompanying transformation of asceticism to activity within the world. It is not as though Catholicism had restricted the methodical life to monastic cells. This was by no means the case either in theory or in practice. On the contrary, it has already been pointed out that, in spite of the greater ethical moderation of Catholicism, an ethically unsystematic life did not satisfy the highest ideals which it had set up even for the life of the layman.[112] The tertiary order of St. Francis was, for instance, a powerful attempt in the direction of an ascetic penetration of everyday life, and, as we know, by no means the only one. But, in fact, works like the *Nachfolge Christi* show, through the manner in which their strong influence was exerted, that the way of life preached in them was felt to be something higher than the everyday morality which sufficed as a minimum, and that this latter was not measured by such standards as Puritanism demanded. Moreover, the practical use made of certain institutions of the Church, above all of indulgences inevitably counteracted the tendencies toward systematic worldly asceticism. For that reason it was not felt at the time of the Reformation to be merely an unessential abuse, but one of the most fundamental evils of the Church.

But the most important thing was the fact that the man who, *par excellence*, lived a rational life in the religious sense was, and remained, alone the monk. Thus asceticism, the more strongly it gripped an individual, simply served to drive him farther away from everyday life, because the holiest task was definitely to surpass all worldly morality.[113] Luther, who was not in any sense fulfilling any law of development, but acting upon his quite personal experience, which was, though at first somewhat uncertain in its practical consequences, later pushed farther by the political situation, had repudiated that tendency, and Calvinism simply took this over from him.[114] Sebastian Franck struck the central characteristic of this type of religion when he saw the significance of the Reformation in the fact that now every Christian had to be a monk all his life. The drain of asceticism from everyday worldly life had been stopped by a dam, and those passionately spiritual natures which had formerly supplied the highest type of monk were now forced to pursue their ascetic ideals within mundane occupations.

But in the course of its development Calvinism added something positive to this, the idea of the necessity of proving one's faith in worldly activity.[115] Therein it gave the broader groups of religiously inclined people a positive incentive to asceticism. By founding its ethic in the doctrine of predestination, it substituted for the spiritual aristocracy of monks outside of and above the world the spiritual aristocracy of the predestined saints of God within the world.[116] It was an aristocracy which, with its *character indelebilis*,[117] was divided from the eternally damned remainder of humanity by a more impassable and in its invisibility more terrifying gulf,[118] than separated the monk of the Middle Ages from the rest of the world about him, a gulf which penetrated all social relations with its sharp brutality. This consciousness of divine grace of the elect and holy was accompanied by an attitude toward the sin of one's neighbour, not of sympathetic understanding based on consciousness of one's own weakness, but of hatred and contempt for him as an enemy of God bearing the signs of eternal damnation.[119] This sort of feeling was capable of such intensity that it sometimes resulted in the formation of sects. This was the case when, as in the Independent movement of the seventeenth century, the genuine Calvinist doctrine that the glory of God required the Church to bring the damned under the law, was outweighed by the conviction that it was an insult to God if an unregenerate soul should be admitted to His house and partake in the sacraments, or even, as a minister, administer them.[120] Thus, as a consequence of the doctrine of proof, the Donatist idea of the Church appeared, as in the case of the Calvinistic Baptists. The full logical consequence of the demand for a pure Church, a community of those proved to be in a state of grace, was not often drawn by forming sects. Modifications in the constitution of the Church resulted from the attempt to separate regenerate from unregenerate Christians, those who were from those who were not prepared for the sacrament, to keep the government of the Church or some other privilege in the hands of the former, and only to ordain ministers of whom there was no question.[121]

The norm by which it could always measure itself, of which it was evidently in need, this asceticism naturally found in the Bible. It is important to note that the well-known bibliocracy of the Calvinists held the moral precepts of the Old Testament, since it was fully as authentically revealed, on the same level of esteem as those of the New. It was only necessary that they should not obviously be applicable only to the historical circumstances of the Hebrews, or have been specifically denied by Christ. For the believer, the law was an ideal though never quite attainable norm[122] while Luther, on the other hand, originally had prized freedom from subjugation to the law as a divine privilege of the believer.[123] The influence of the God-fearing but perfectly unemotional wisdom of the Hebrews, which is expressed in the books most read by the Puritans, the Proverbs and the Psalms, can be felt in their whole attitude toward life. In particular, its rational suppression of the mystical, in fact the whole emotional side of religion, has rightly been attributed by Sanford[124] to the influence of the Old Testament. But this Old Testament rationalism was as such essentially of a small bourgeois, traditionalistic type, and was mixed not only with the powerful pathos of the prophets, but also with elements which encouraged the development of a peculiarly emotional type of religion even in the Middle Ages.[125] It was thus in the last analysis the peculiar, fundamentally ascetic, character of Calvinism itself which made it select and assimilate those elements of Old Testament religion which suited it best.

Now that systematization of ethical conduct which the asceticism of Calvinistic Protestantism had in common with the rational forms of life in the Catholic orders is expressed quite superficially in the way in which the conscientious Puritan continually supervised[126] his own state of grace. To be sure, the religious account-books in which sins, temptations, and progress made in grace were entered or tabulated were common to both the most enthusiastic Reformed circles[127] and some parts of modern Catholicism (especially in France), above all under the influence of the Jesuits. But in Catholicism it served the purpose of completeness of the confession, or gave the *directeur de l'âme*[128] a basis for his authoritarian guidance of the Christian (mostly female). The Reformed Christian, however, felt his own pulse with its aid. It is mentioned by all the moralists and theologians, while Benjamin Franklin's tabulated statistical book-keeping on his progress in the different virtues is a classic example.[129] On the other hand, the old mediæval (even ancient) idea of God's book-keeping is carried by Bunyan to the characteristically tasteless extreme of comparing the relation of a sinner to his God with that of customer and shopkeeper.

One who has once got into debt may well, by the product of all his virtuous acts, succeed in paying off the accumulated interest but never the principal.[130]

As he observed his own conduct, the later Puritan also observed that of God and saw His finger in all the details of life. And, contrary to the strict doctrine of Calvin, he always knew why God took this or that measure. The process of sanctifying life could thus almost take on the character of a business enterprise.[131] A thoroughgoing Christianization of the whole of life was the consequence of this methodical quality of ethical conduct into which Calvinism as distinct from Lutheranism forced men. That this rationality was decisive in its influence on practical life must always be borne in mind in order rightly to understand the influence of Calvinism. On the one hand we can see that it took this element to exercise such an influence at all. But other faiths as well necessarily had a similar influence when their ethical motives were the same in this decisive point, the doctrine of proof.

So far we have considered only Calvinism, and have thus assumed the doctrine of predestination as the dogmatic background of the Puritan morality in the sense of methodically rationalized ethical conduct. This could be done because the influence of that dogma in fact extended far beyond the single religious group which held in all respects strictly to Calvinistic principles, the Presbyterians. Not only the Independent Savoy Declaration of 1658, but also the Baptist Confession of Hanserd Knolly of 1689 contained it, and it had a place within Methodism. Although John Wesley, the great organizing genius of the movement, was a believer in the universality of Grace, one of the great agitators of the first generation of Methodists and their most consistent thinker, Whitefield, was an adherent of the doctrine. The same was true of the circle around Lady Huntingdon, which for a time had considerable influence. It was this doctrine in its magnificent consistency which, in the fateful epoch of the seventeenth century, upheld the belief of the militant defenders of the holy life that they were weapons in the hand of God, and executors of His providential will.[132] Moreover, it prevented a premature collapse into a purely utilitarian doctrine of good works in this world which would never have been capable of motivating such tremendous sacrifices for non-rational ideal ends.

The combination of faith in absolutely valid norms with absolute determinism and the complete transcendentality of God was in its way a product of great genius. At the same time it was, in principle, very much more modern than the milder doctrine, making greater concessions to the feelings which subjected God to the moral law. Above all, we shall see again and again how fundamental is the idea of proof for our problem. Since its practical significance as a psychological basis for rational morality could be studied in such purity in the doctrine of predestination, it was best to start there with the doctrine in its most consistent form. But it forms a recurring framework for the connection between faith and conduct in the denominations to be studied below. Within the Protestant movement the consequences which it inevitably had for the ascetic tendencies of the conduct of its first adherents form in principle the strongest antithesis to the relative moral helplessness of Lutheranism. The Lutheran *gratia amissibilis*,[133] which could always be regained through penitent contrition evidently, in itself, contained no sanction for what is for us the most important result of ascetic Protestantism, a systematic rational ordering of the moral life as a whole.[134] The Lutheran faith thus left the spontaneous vitality of impulsive action and naïve emotion more nearly unchanged. The motive to constant self-control and thus to a deliberate regulation of one's own life, which the gloomy doctrine of Calvinism gave, was lacking. A religious genius like Luther could live in this atmosphere of openness and freedom without difficulty and, so long as his enthusiasm was powerful enough, without danger of falling back into the *status naturalis*.[135] That simple, sensitive, and peculiarly emotional form of piety, which is the ornament of many of the highest types of Lutherans, like their free and spontaneous morality, finds few parallels in genuine Puritanism, but many more in the mild Anglicanism of such men as Hooker, Chillingsworth, etc. But for the everyday Lutheran, even the able one, nothing was more certain than that he was only temporarily, as long as the single confession or sermon affected him, raised above the *status naturalis*.

There was a great difference which was very striking to contemporaries between the moral standards of the courts of Reformed and of Lutheran princes, the latter often being degraded by drunkenness and vulgarity.[136] Moreover, the helplessness of the Lutheran clergy, with their emphasis on faith alone, against the ascetic Baptist movement, is well known. The typical German quality often called good nature (*Gemütlichkeit*) or naturalness contrasts strongly, even in the facial expressions of people, with the effects of that thorough destruction of the spontaneity of the *status naturalis* in the Anglo-American atmosphere, which Germans are accustomed to judge unfavourably as narrowness, unfreeness, and inner constraint. But the differences of conduct, which are very striking, have clearly originated in the lesser degree of ascetic penetration of life in Lutheranism as distinguished from Calvinism. The antipathy of every spontaneous child of nature to everything ascetic is expressed in those feelings. The fact is that Lutheranism, on account of its doctrine of grace, lacked a psychological sanction of systematic conduct to compel the methodical rationalization of life.

This sanction, which conditions the ascetic character of religion, could doubtless in itself have been furnished by various different religious motives, as we shall soon see. The Calvinistic doctrine of predestination was only one of several possibilities. But nevertheless we have become convinced that in its way it had not only a quite unique consistency, but that its psychological effect was extraordinarily powerful.[137] In comparison with it the non-Calvinistic ascetic movements, considered purely from the view-point of the religious motivation of asceticism, form an attenuation of the inner consistency and power of Calvinism.

But even in the actual historical development the situation was, for the most part, such that the Calvinistic form of asceticism was either imitated by the other ascetic movements or used as a source of inspiration or of comparison in the development of their divergent principles. Where, in spite of a different doctrinal basis, similar ascetic features have appeared, this has generally been the result of Church organization. Of this we shall come to speak in another connection.[138]

## B. Pietism

Historically the doctrine of predestination is also the starting-point of the ascetic movement usually known as Pietism. In so far as the movement remained within the Reformed Church, it is almost impossible to draw the line between Pietistic and non-Pietistic Calvinists.[139] Almost all the leading representatives of Puritanism are sometimes classed among the Pietists. It is even quite legitimate to look upon the whole connection between predestination and the doctrine of proof, with its fundamental interest in the attainment of the *certitudo salutis*[140] as discussed above, as in itself a Pietistic development of Calvin's original doctrines. The occurrence of ascetic revivals within the Reformed Church was, especially in Holland, regularly accompanied by a regeneration of the doctrine of predestination which had been temporarily forgotten or not strictly held to. Hence for England it is not customary to use the term Pietism at all.[141]

But even the Continental (Dutch and Lower Rhenish) Pietism in the Reformed Church was, at least fundamentally, just as much a simple intensification of the Reformed asceticism as, for instance, the doctrines of Bailey. The emphasis was placed so strongly on the *praxis pietatis*[142] that doctrinal orthodoxy was pushed into the background; at times, in fact, it seemed quite a matter of indifference. Those predestined for grace could occasionally be subject to dogmatic error as well as to other sins and experience showed that often those Christians who were quite uninstructed in the theology of the schools exhibited the fruits of faith most clearly, while on the other hand it became evident that mere knowledge of theology by no means guaranteed the proof of faith through conduct.[143]

Thus election could not be proved by theological learning at all.[144] Hence Pietism, with a deep distrust of the Church of the theologians,[145] to which—this is characteristic of it—it still belonged officially, began to gather the adherents of the *praxis pietatis* in conventicles removed from the world.[146] It wished to make the invisible Church of the elect visible on this earth. Without going so far as to form a separate sect, its members attempted to live, in this community, a life freed from all the temptations of the world and in all its details dictated by God's will, and thus to be made certain of their own rebirth by external signs manifested in their daily conduct. Thus the *ecclesiola*[147] of the true converts—this was common to all genuinely Pietistic groups—wished, by means of intensified asceticism, to enjoy the blissfulness of community with God in this life.

Now this latter tendency had something closely related to the Lutheran *unio mystica*,[148] and very often led to a greater emphasis on the emotional side of religion than was acceptable to orthodox Calvinism. In fact this may, from our view-point, be said to be the decisive characteristic of the Pietism which developed within the Reformed Church. For this element of emotion, which was originally quite foreign to Calvinism, but on the other hand related to certain mediæval forms of religion, led religion in practice to strive for the enjoyment of salvation in this world rather than to engage in the ascetic struggle for certainty about the future world. Moreover, the emotion was capable of such intensity, that religion took on a positively hysterical character, resulting in the alternation which is familiar from examples without number and neuropathologically understandable, of half-conscious states of religious ecstasy with periods of nervous exhaustion, which were felt as abandonment by God. The effect was the direct opposite of the strict and temperate discipline under which men were placed by the systematic life of holiness of the Puritan. It meant a weakening of the inhibitions which protected the rational personality of the Calvinist from his passions.[149] Similarly it was possible for the Calvinistic idea of the depravity of the flesh, taken emotionally, for instance in the form of the so-called worm-feeling, to lead to a deadening of enterprise in worldly activity.[150] Even the doctrine of predestination could lead to fatalism if, contrary to the predominant tendencies of rational Calvinism, it were made the object of emotional contemplation.[151] Finally, the desire to separate the elect from the world could, with a strong emotional intensity, lead to a sort of monastic community life of half-communistic character, as the history of Pietism, even within the Reformed Church, has shown again and again.[152]

But so long as this extreme effect, conditioned by this emphasis on emotion, did not appear, as long as Reformed Pietism strove to make

sure of salvation within the everyday routine of life in a worldly calling, the practical effect of Pietistic principles was an even stricter
ascetic control of conduct in the calling, which provided a still more
solid religious basis for the ethic of the calling, than the mere worldly
respectability of the normal Reformed Christian, which was felt by
the superior Pietist to be a second-rate Christianity. The religious
aristocracy of the elect, which developed in every form of Calvinistic
asceticism, the more seriously it was taken, the more surely, was then
organized, in Holland, on a voluntary basis in the form of conventicles within the Church. In English Puritanism, on the other hand, it
led partly to a virtual differentiation between active and passive
Christians within the Church organization, and partly, as has been
shown above, to the formation of sects.

On the other hand, the development of German Pietism from a
Lutheran basis, with which the names of Spener, Francke, and Zinzendorf are connected, led away from the doctrine of predestination. But
at the same time it was by no means outside the body of ideas of which
that dogma formed the logical climax, as is especially attested by
Spener's own account of the influence which English and Dutch
Pietism had upon him, and is shown by the fact that Bailey was read
in his first conventicles.[153]

From our special point of view, at any rate, Pietism meant simply
the penetration of methodically controlled and supervised, thus of
ascetic, conduct into the non-Calvinistic denominations.[154] But
Lutheranism necessarily felt this rational asceticism to be a foreign
element, and the lack of consistency in German Pietistic doctrines
was the result of the difficulties growing out of that fact. As a dogmatic basis of systematic religious conduct Spener combines
Lutheran ideas with the specifically Calvinistic doctrine of good
works as such which are undertaken with the "intention of doing
honour to God."[155] He also has a faith, suggestive of Calvinism, in the
possibility of the elect attaining a relative degree of Christian perfection.[156] But the theory lacked consistency. Spener, who was
strongly influenced by the mystics,[157] attempted, in a rather uncertain
but essentially Lutheran manner, rather to describe the systematic
type of Christian conduct which was essential to even his form of
Pietism than to justify it. He did not derive the *certitudo salutis*[158]
from sanctification; instead of the idea of proof, he adopted Luther's
somewhat loose connection between faith and works, which has been
discussed above.[159]

But again and again, in so far as the rational and ascetic element
of Pietism outweighed the emotional, the ideas essential to our thesis maintained their place. These were: (1) that the methodical development of one's own state of grace to a higher and higher degree of
certainty and perfection in terms of the law was a sign of grace;[160] and

(2) that "God's Providence works through those in such a state of perfection", i.e. in that He gives them His signs if they wait patiently and deliberate methodically.[161] Labour in a calling was also the ascetic activity *par excellence* for A. H. Francke;[162] that God Himself blessed His chosen ones through the success of their labours was as undeniable to him as we shall find it to have been to the Puritans.

And as a substitute for the double decree Pietism worked out ideas which, in a way essentially similar to Calvinism, though milder, established an aristocracy of the elect[163] resting on God's especial grace, with all the psychological results pointed out above. Among them belongs, for instance, the so-called doctrine of Terminism,[164] which was generally (though unjustly) attributed to Pietism by its opponents. It assumes that grace is offered to all men, but for everyone either once at a definite moment in his life or at some moment for the last time.[165] Anyone who let that moment pass was beyond the help of the universality of grace; he was in the same situation as those neglected by God in the Calvinistic doctrine. Quite close to this theory was the idea which Francke took from his personal experience, and which was very widespread in Pietism, one may even say predominant, that grace could only become effective under certain unique and peculiar circumstances, namely, after previous repentance.[166] Since, according to Pietist doctrine, not everyone was capable of such experiences, those who, in spite of the use of the ascetic methods recommended by the Pietists to bring it about, did not attain it, remained in the eyes of the regenerate a sort of passive Christian. On the other hand, by the creation of a method to induce repentance even the attainment of divine grace became in effect an object of rational human activity.

Moreover, the antagonism to the private confessional, which, though not shared by all—for instance, not by Francke—was characteristic of many Pietists, especially, as the repeated questions in Spener show, of Pietist pastors, resulted from this aristocracy of grace. This antagonism helped to weaken its ties with Lutheranism. The visible effects on conduct of grace gained through repentance formed a necessary criterion for admission to absolution; hence it was impossible to let *contritio*[167] alone suffice.[168]

Zinzendorf's conception of his own religious position, even though it vacillated in the face of attacks from orthodoxy, tended generally toward the instrumental idea. Beyond that, however, the doctrinal standpoint of this remarkable religious dilettante, as Ritschl calls him, is scarcely capable of clear formulation in the points of importance for us.[169] He repeatedly designated himself a representative of Pauline-Lutheran Christianity; hence he opposed the Pietistic type associated with Jansen with its adherence to the law. But the Brotherhood itself in practice upheld, as early as its Protocol of August 12, 1729, a standpoint which in many respects closely resembled that of the Calvinistic aristocracy of the elect.[170] And in spite of his repeated avowals of Lutheranism,[171] he permitted and encouraged it. The famous stand of attributing the Old Testament to Christ, taken on November 12, 1741, was the outward expression of somewhat the same attitude. However, of the three branches of the Brotherhood, both the Calvinistic and the Moravian accepted the Reformed ethics in essentials from the beginning. And even Zinzendorf followed the Puritans in expressing to John Wesley the opinion that even though a man himself could not, others could know his state of grace by his conduct.[172]

But on the other hand, in the peculiar piety of Herrnhut, the emotional element held a very prominent place. In particular Zinzendorf himself continually attempted to counteract the tendency to ascetic sanctification in the Puritan sense[173] and to turn the interpretation of good works in a Lutheran direction.[174] Also under the influence of the repudiation of conventicles and the retention of the confession, there developed an essentially Lutheran dependence on the sacraments. Moreover, Zinzendorf's peculiar principle that the childlikeness of religious feeling was a sign of its genuineness, as well as the use of the lot as a means of revealing God's will, strongly counteracted the influence of rationality in conduct. On the whole, within the sphere of influence of the Count,[175] the anti-rational, emotional elements predominated much more in the religion of the Herrnhuters than elsewhere in Pietism.[176] The connection between morality and the forgiveness of sins in Spangenberg's *Idea fides fratrum* is as loose[177] as in Lutheranism generally. Zinzendorf's repudiation of the Methodist pursuit of perfection is part, here as everywhere, of his fundamentally eudæmonistic ideal of having men experience eternal bliss (he calls it happiness) emotionally in the present,[178] instead of encouraging them by rational labour to make sure of it in the next world.[179]

Nevertheless, the idea that the most important value of the Brotherhood as contrasted with other Churches lay in an active Christian life, in missionary, and, which was brought into connection with it, in professional work in a calling,[180] remained a vital force with them. In addition, the practical rationalization of life from the standpoint of utility was very essential to Zinzendorf's philosophy.[181] It was derived for him, as for other Pietists, on the one hand from his decided dislike of philosophical speculation as dangerous to faith, and his corresponding preference for empirical knowledge;[182] on the other hand, from the shrewd common sense of the professional missionary. The Brotherhood was, as a great mission centre, at the same time a business enterprise. Thus it led its members into the paths of worldly asceticism, which everywhere first seeks for tasks and then carries them out carefully and systematically. However, the glorification of the apostolic poverty, of the disciples[183] chosen by God through pre-destination, which was derived from the example of the apostles as missionaries, formed another obstacle. It meant in effect a partial revival of the *consilia evangelica*.[184] The development of a rational eco-nomic ethic similar to the Calvinistic was certainly retarded by these factors, even though, as the development of the Baptist movement shows, it was not impossible, but on the contrary subjectively strongly encouraged by the idea of work solely for the sake of the calling.

All in all, when we consider German Pietism from the point of view important for us, we must admit a vacillation and uncertainty in the religious basis of its asceticism which makes it definitely weaker than the iron consistency of Calvinism, and which is partly the result of Lutheran influences and partly of its emotional character. To be sure, it is very one-sided to make this emotional element the distinguish-ing characteristic of Pietism as opposed to Lutheranism.[185] But com-pared to Calvinism, the rationalization of life was necessarily less intense because the pressure of occupation with a state of grace which had continually to be proved, and which was concerned for the future in eternity, was diverted to the present emotional state. The place of the self-confidence which the elect sought to attain, and continually to renew in restless and successful work at his calling, was taken by an attitude of humility and abnegation.[186] This in turn was partly the result of emotional stimulus directed solely toward spiritual experience; partly of the Lutheran institution of the confes-sion, which, though it was often looked upon with serious doubts by Pietism, was still generally tolerated.[187] All this shows the influence of the peculiarly Lutheran conception of salvation by the forgiveness of sins and not by practical sanctification. In place of the systematic rational struggle to attain and retain certain knowledge of future (otherworldly) salvation comes here the need to feel reconciliation and community with God now. Thus the tendency of the pursuit of present enjoyment to hinder the rational organization of economic life, depending as it does on provision for the future, has in a certain sense a parallel in the field of religious life.

Evidently, then, the orientation of religious needs to present emo-tional satisfaction could not develop so powerful a motive to ration-alize wordly activity, as the need of the Calvinistic elect for proof with their exclusive preoccupation with the beyond. On the other hand, it was considerably more favourable to the methodical pene-tration of conduct with religion than the traditionalistic faith of the orthodox Lutheran, bound as it was to the Word and the sacraments. On the whole Pietism from Francke and Spener to Zinzendorf tended toward increasing emphasis on the emotional side. But this was not in any sense the expression of an immanent law of development. The differences resulted from differences of the religious (and social) environments from which the leaders came. We cannot enter into that here, nor can we discuss how the peculiarities of German Pietism have affected its social and geographical extension.[188] We must again remind ourselves that this emotional Pietism of course shades off into the way of life of the Puritan elect by quite gradual stages. If we can, at least provisionally, point out any practical consequence of the difference, we may say that the virtues favoured by Pietism were more those on the one hand of the faithful official, clerk, labourer, or domestic worker,[189] and on the other of the predominantly patriarchal employer with a pious condescension (in Zinzendorf's manner). Calvinism, in comparison, appears to be more closely related to the hard legalism and the active enterprise of bourgeois-capitalistic entrepreneurs.[190] Finally, the purely emotional form of Pietism is, as Ritschl[191] has pointed out, a religious dilettantism for the leisure classes. However far this characterization falls short of being exhaustive, it helps to explain certain differences in the character (including the economic character) of peoples which have been under the influence of one or the other of these two ascetic movements.

## C. Methodism

The combination of an emotional but still ascetic type of religion with increasing indifference to or repudiation of the dogmatic basis of Calvinistic asceticism is characteristic also of the Anglo-American movement corresponding to Continental Pietism, namely Methodism.[192] The name in itself shows what impressed contemporaries as characteristic of its adherents: the methodical, systematic nature of conduct for the purpose of attaining the *certitudo salutis*.[193] This was from the beginning the centre of religious aspiration for this movement also, and remained so. In spite of all the differences, the undoubted relationship to certain branches of German Pietism[194] is shown above all by the fact that the method was used primarily to bring about the emotional act of conversion. And the emphasis on feeling, in John Wesley awakened by Moravian and Lutheran influences, led Methodism, which from the beginning saw its mission among the masses, to take on a strongly emotional character, especially in America. The attainment of repentance under certain circumstances involved an emotional struggle of such intensity as to lead to the most terrible ecstasies, which in America often took place in a public meeting. This formed the basis of a belief in the undeserved possession of divine grace and at the same time of an immediate consciousness of justification and forgiveness.

Now this emotional religion entered into a peculiar alliance, containing no small inherent difficulties, with the ascetic ethics which had for good and all been stamped with rationality by Puritanism. For one thing, unlike Calvinism, which held everything emotional to be illusory, the only sure basis for the *certitudo salutis* was in principle held to be a pure feeling of absolute certainty of forgiveness, derived immediately from the testimony of the spirit, the coming of which could be definitely placed to the hour. Added to this is Wesley's doctrine of sanctification which, though a decided departure from the orthodox doctrine, is a logical development of it. According to it, one reborn in this manner can, by virtue of the divine grace already working in him, even in this life attain sanctification, the consciousness of perfection in the sense of freedom from sin, by a second, generally separate and often sudden spiritual transformation. However difficult of attainment this end is, generally not till toward the end of one's life, it must inevitably be sought, because it finally guarantees the *certitudo salutis* and substitutes a serene confidence for the sullen worry of the Calvinist.[195] And it distinguishes the true convert in his own eyes and those of others by the fact that sin at least no longer has power over him.

In spite of the great significance of self-evident feeling, righteous conduct according to the law was thus naturally also adhered to. Whenever Wesley attacked the emphasis on works of his time, it was only to revive the old Puritan doctrine that works are not the cause, but only the means of knowing one's state of grace, and even this only when they are performed solely for the glory of God. Righteous conduct alone did not suffice, as he had found out for himself. The feeling of grace was necessary in addition. He himself sometimes described works as a condition of grace, and in the Declaration of August 9, 1771,[196] he emphasized that he who performed no good works was not a true believer. In fact, the Methodists have always maintained that they did not differ from the Established Church in doctrine, but only in religious practice. This emphasis on the fruits of belief was mostly justified by 1 John iii. 9; conduct is taken as a clear sign of rebirth.

But in spite of all that there were difficulties.[197] For those Methodists who were adherents of the doctrine of predestination, to think of the *certitudo salutis* as appearing in the immediate feeling[198] of grace and perfection instead of the consciousness of grace which grew out of ascetic conduct in continual proof of faith—since then the certainty of the *perservantia*[199] depended only on the single act of repentance—meant one of two things. For weak natures there was a fatalistic interpretation of Christian freedom, and with it the breakdown of methodical conduct; or, where this path was rejected, the self-confidence of the righteous man[200] reached untold heights, an emotional intensification of the Puritan type. In the face of the

attacks of opponents, the attempt was made to meet these consequences. On the one hand by increased emphasis on the normative
authority of the Bible and the indispensability of proof;[201] on the other
by, in effect, strengthening Wesley's anti-Calvinistic faction within the
movement with its doctrine that grace could be lost. The strong
Lutheran influences to which Wesley was exposed[202] through the
Moravians strengthened this tendency and increased the uncertainty
of the religious basis of the Methodist ethics.[203] In the end only the
concept of regeneration, an emotional certainty of salvation as the
immediate result of faith, was definitely maintained as the indispensable foundation of grace; and with it sanctification, resulting in (at
least virtual) freedom from the power of sin, as the consequent proof
of grace. The significance of external means of grace, especially the
sacraments, was correspondingly diminished. In any case, the general
awakening which followed Methodism everywhere, for example in
New England, meant a victory for the doctrine of grace and election.[204]

Thus from our view-point the Methodist ethic appears to rest on a
foundation of uncertainty similar to Pietism. But the aspiration to the
higher life, the second blessedness, served it as a sort of makeshift for
the doctrine of predestination. Moreover, being English in origin, its
ethical practice was closely related to that of English Puritanism, the
revival of which it aspired to be.

The emotional act of conversion was methodically induced. And
after it was attained there did not follow a pious enjoyment of community with God, after the manner of the emotional Pietism of
Zinzendorf, but the emotion, once awakened, was directed into a
rational struggle for perfection. Hence the emotional character of its
faith did not lead to a spiritualized religion of feeling like German
Pietism. It has already been shown by Schneckenburger that this fact
was connected with the less intensive development of the sense of sin
(partly directly on account of the emotional experience of conversion), and this has remained an accepted point in the discussion of
Methodism. The fundamentally Calvinistic character of its religious
feeling here remained decisive. The emotional excitement took the
form of enthusiasm which was only occasionally, but then powerfully
stirred, but which by no means destroyed the otherwise rational
character of conduct.[205] The regeneration of Methodism thus created
only a supplement to the pure doctrine of works, a religious basis for
ascetic conduct after the doctrine of predestination had been given
up. The signs given by conduct which formed an indispensable
means of ascertaining true conversion, even its condition as Wesley
occasionally says, were in fact just the same as those of Calvinism.
As a late product[206] we can, in the following discussion, generally
neglect Methodism, as it added nothing new to the development[207]
of the idea of calling.

## D. The Baptist Sects

The Pietism of the Continent of Europe and the Methodism of the Anglo-Saxon peoples are, considered both in their content of ideas and their historical significance, secondary movements.[208] On the other hand, we find a second independent source of Protestant asceticism besides Calvinism in the Baptist movement and the sects[209] which, in the course of the sixteenth and seventeenth centuries, came directly from it or adopted its forms of religious thought, the Baptists, Mennonites, and, above all, the Quakers.[210] With them we approach religious groups whose ethics rest upon a basis differing in principle from the Calvinistic doctrine. The following sketch, which only emphasizes what is important for us, can give no true impression of the diversity of this movement. Again we lay the principal emphasis on the development in the older capitalistic countries.

The feature of all these communities, which is both historically and in principle most important, but whose influence on the development of culture can only be made quite clear in a somewhat different connection, is something with which we are already familiar, the believer's Church.[211] This means that the religious community, the visible Church in the language of the Reformation Churches,[212] was no longer looked upon as a sort of trust foundation for supernatural ends, an institution, necessarily including both the just and the unjust, whether for increasing the glory of God (Calvinistic) or as a medium for bringing the means of salvation to men (Catholic and Lutheran), but solely as a community of personal believers of the reborn, and only these. In other words, not as a Church but as a sect.[213] This is all that the principle, in itself purely external, that only adults who have personally gained their own faith should be baptized, is meant to symbolize.[214] The justification through this faith was for the Baptists, as they have insistently repeated in all religious discussions, radically different from the idea of work in the world in the service of Christ, such as dominated the orthodox dogma of the older Protestantism.[215] It consisted rather in taking spiritual possession of His gift of salvation. But this occurred through individual revelation, by the working of the Divine Spirit in the individual, and only in that way. It was offered to everyone, and it sufficed to wait for the Spirit, and not to resist its coming by a sinful attachment to the world. The significance of faith in the sense of knowledge of the doctrines of the Church, but also in that of a repentant search for divine grace, was consequently quite minimized, and there took place, naturally with great modifications, a renaissance of Early Christian pneumatic doctrines. For instance, the sect to which Menno Simons in his *Fondamentboek* (1539) gave the first reasonably consistent doctrine, wished, like the other Baptist sects, to be the true blameless Church of Christ; like the apostolic community, consisting entirely of those personally awakened and called by God. Those who have been born again, and they alone, are brethren of Christ, because they, like Him, have been created in spirit directly by God.[216] A strict avoidance of the world, in the sense of all not strictly necessary intercourse with wordly people, together with the strictest bibliocracy in the sense of taking the life of the first generations of Christians as a model, were the results for the first Baptist communities, and this principle of avoidance of the world never quite disappeared so long as the old spirit remained alive.[217]

As a permanent possession, the Baptist sects retained from these dominating motives of their early period a principle with which, on a somewhat different foundation, we have already become acquainted in Calvinism, and the fundamental importance of which will again and again come out. They absolutely repudiated all idolatry of the flesh, as a detraction from the reverence due to God alone.[218] The Biblical way of life was conceived by the first Swiss and South German Baptists with a radicalism similar to that of the young St. Francis, as a sharp break with all the enjoyment of life, a life modelled directly on that of the Apostles. And, in truth, the life of many of the earlier Baptists is reminiscent of that of St. Giles. But this strict observation of Biblical precepts[219] was not on very secure foundations in its connection with the pneumatic character of the faith. What God had revealed to the prophets and apostles was not all that He could and would reveal. On the contrary, the continued life of the Word, not as a written document, but as the force of the Holy Spirit working in daily life, which speaks directly to any individual who is willing to hear, was the sole characteristic of the true Church. That, as Schwenkfeld taught as against Luther and later Fox against the Presbyterians, was the testimony of the early Christian communities. From this idea of the continuance of revelation developed the well-known doctrine, later consistently worked out by the Quakers, of the (in the last analysis decisive) significance of the inner testimony of the Spirit in reason and conscience. This did away, not with the authority, but with the sole authority, of the Bible, and started a development which in the end radically eliminated all that remained of the doctrine of salvation through the Church; for the Quakers even with Baptism and the Communion.[220]

The Baptist denominations along with the predestinationists, especially the strict Calvinists, carried out the most radical devaluation of all sacraments as means to salvation, and thus accomplished the religious rationalization of the world in its most extreme form. Only the inner light of continual revelation could enable one truly to understand even the Biblical revelations of God.[221] On the other hand, at least according to the Quaker doctrine which here drew the logical conclusion, its effects could be extended to people who had never known revelation in its Biblical form. The proposition *extra ecclesiam nulla salus*[222] held only for this invisible Church of those illuminated by the Spirit. Without the inner light, the natural man, even the man guided by natural reason,[223] remained purely a creature of the flesh, whose godlessness was condemned by the Baptists, including the Quakers, almost even more harshly than by the Calvinists. On the other hand, the new birth caused by the Spirit, if we wait for it and open our hearts to it, may, since it is divinely caused, lead to a state of such complete conquest of the power of sin,[224] that relapses, to say nothing of the loss of the state of grace, become practically impossible. However, as in Methodism at a later time, the attainment of that state was not thought of as the rule, but rather the degree of perfection of the individual was subject to development.

But all Baptist communities desired to be pure Churches in the sense of the blameless conduct of their members. A sincere repudiation of the world and its interests, and unconditional submission to God as speaking through the conscience, were the only unchallengeable signs of true rebirth, and a corresponding type of conduct was thus indispensable to salvation. And hence the gift of God's grace could not be earned, but only one who followed the dictates of his conscience could be justified in considering himself reborn. Good works in this sense were a *causa sine qua non*. As we see, this last reasoning of Barclay, to whose exposition we have adhered, was again the equivalent in practice of the Calvinistic doctrine, and was certainly developed under the influence of the Calvinistic asceticism, which surrounded the Baptist sects in England and the Netherlands. George Fox devoted the whole of his early missionary activity to the preaching of its earnest and sincere adoption.

But, since predestination was rejected, the peculiarly rational character of Baptist morality rested psychologically above all on the idea of expectant waiting for the Spirit to descend, which even to-day is characteristic of the Quaker meeting, and is well analysed by Barclay. The purpose of this silent waiting is to overcome everything impulsive and irrational, the passions and subjective interests of the natural man. He must be stilled in order to create that deep repose of the soul in which alone the word of God can be heard. Of course, this waiting might result in hysterical conditions, prophecy, and, as long as eschatological hopes survived, under certain circumstances even in an outbreak of chiliastic enthusiasm, as is possible in all similar types of religion. That actually happened in the movement which went to pieces in Münster.

But in so far as Baptism affected the normal workaday world, the idea that God only speaks when the flesh is silent evidently meant an incentive to the deliberate weighing of courses of action and their careful justification in terms of the individual conscience.[225] The later Baptist communities, most particularly the Quakers, adopted this quiet, moderate, eminently conscientious character of conduct. The radical elimination of magic from the world allowed no other psychological course than the practice of worldly asceticism. Since these communities would have nothing to do with the political powers and their doings, the external result also was the penetration of life in the calling with these ascetic virtues. The leaders of the earliest Baptist movement were ruthlessly radical in their rejection of worldliness. But naturally, even in the first generation, the strictly apostolic way of life was not maintained as absolutely essential to the proof of rebirth for everyone. Well-to-do bourgeois there were, even in this generation and even before Menno, who definitely defended the practical worldly virtues and the system of private property; the strict morality of the Baptists had turned in practice into the path prepared by the Calvinistic ethic.[226] This was simply because the road to the otherworldly monastic form of asceticism had been closed as unbiblical and savouring of salvation by works since Luther, whom the Baptists also followed in this respect.

Nevertheless, apart from the half-communistic communities of the early period, one Baptist sect, the so-called Dunckards (*Tunker, dompelaers*), has to this day maintained its condemnation of education and of every form of possession beyond that indispensable to life. And even Barclay looks upon the obligation to one's calling not in Calvinistic or even Lutheran terms, but rather Thomistically, as *naturali ratione*,[227] the necessary consequence of the believers having to live in the world.[228]

This attitude meant a weakening of the Calvinistic conception of the calling similar to those of Spener and the German Pietists. But, on the other hand, the intensity of interest in economic occupations was considerably increased by various factors at work in the Baptist sects. In the first place, by the refusal to accept office in the service of the State, which originated as a religious duty following from the repudiation of everything worldly. After its abandonment in principle it still remained, at least for the Mennonites and Quakers, effective in practice, because the strict refusal to bear arms or to take oaths formed a sufficient disqualification for office. Hand in hand with it in all Baptists' denominations went an invincible antagonism to any sort of aristocratic way of life. Partly, as with the Calvinists, it was a consequence of the prohibition of all idolatry of the flesh, partly a result of the aforementioned unpolitical or even anti-political principles. The whole shrewd and conscientious rationality of Baptist conduct was thus forced into non-political callings.

At the same time, the immense importance which was attributed by the Baptist doctrine of salvation to the rôle of the conscience as the revelation of God to the individual gave their conduct in worldly callings a character which was of the greatest significance for the development of the spirit of capitalism. We shall have to postpone its consideration until later, and it can then be studied only in so far as this is possible without entering into the whole political and social ethics of Protestant asceticism. But, to anticipate this much, we have already called attention to that most important principle of the capitalistic ethic which is generally formulated "honesty is the best policy".[229] Its classical document is the tract of Franklin quoted above. And even in the judgment of the seventeenth century the specific form of the worldly asceticism of the Baptists, especially the Quakers, lay in the practical adoption of this maxim.[230] On the other hand, we shall expect to find that the influence of Calvinism was exerted more in the direction of the liberation of energy for private acquisition. For in spite of all the formal legalism of the elect, Goethe's remark in fact applied often enough to the Calvinist: "The man of action is always ruthless; no one has a conscience but an observer."[231]

A further important element which promoted the intensity of the worldly asceticism of the Baptist denominations can in its full significance also be considered only in another connection. Nevertheless, we may anticipate a few remarks on it to justify the order of presentation we have chosen. We have quite deliberately not taken as a starting-point the objective social institutions of the older Protestant Churches, and their ethical influences, especially not the very important Church discipline. We have preferred rather to take the results which subjective adoption of an ascetic faith might have had in the conduct of the individual. This was not only because this side of the thing has previously received far less attention than the other, but also because the effect of Church discipline was by no means always a similar one. On the contrary, the ecclesiastical supervision of the life of the individual, which, as it was practised in the Calvinistic State Churches, almost amounted to an inquisition, might even retard that liberation of individual powers which was conditioned by the rational ascetic pursuit of salvation, and in some cases actually did so.

The mercantilistic regulations of the State might develop industries, but not, or certainly not alone, the spirit of capitalism; where they assumed a despotic, authoritarian character, they to a large extent directly hindered it. Thus a similar effect might well have resulted from ecclesiastical regimentation when it became excessively despotic. It enforced a particular type of external conformity, but in some cases weakened the subjective motives of rational conduct. Any discussion of this point[232] must take account of the great difference between the results of the authoritarian moral discipline of the Established Churches and the corresponding discipline in the sects which rested on voluntary submission. That the Baptist movement everywhere and in principle founded sects and not Churches was certainly as favourable to the intensity of their asceticism as was the case, to differing degrees, with those Calvinistic, Methodist, and Pietist communities which were driven by their situations into the formation of voluntary groups.[233]

It is our next task to follow out the results of the Puritan idea of the calling in the business world, now that the above sketch has attempted to show its religious foundations. With all the differences of detail and emphasis which these different ascetic movements show in the aspects with which we have been concerned, much the same characteristics are present and important in all of them.[234] But for our purposes the decisive point was, to recapitulate, the conception of the state of religious grace, common to all the denominations, as a status which marks off its possessor from the degradation of the flesh, from the world.[235]

On the other hand, though the means by which it was attained differed for different doctrines, it could not be guaranteed by any magical sacraments, by relief in the confession, nor by individual good works. That was only possible by proof in a specific type of conduct unmistakably different from the way of life of the natural man. From that followed for the individual an incentive methodically to supervise his own state of grace in his own conduct, and thus to penetrate it with asceticism. But, as we have seen, this ascetic conduct meant a rational planning of the whole of one's life in accordance with God's will. And this asceticism was no longer an *opus supererogationis*,[236] but something which could be required of everyone who would be certain of salvation. The religious life of the saints, as distinguished from the natural life, was—the most important point—no longer lived outside the world in monastic communities, but within the world and its institutions. This rationalization of conduct within this world, but for the sake of the world beyond, was the consequence of the concept of calling of ascetic Protestantism.

Christian asceticism, at first fleeing from the world into solitude, had already ruled the world which it had renounced from the monastery and through the Church. But it had, on the whole, left the naturally spontaneous character of daily life in the world untouched. Now it strode into the market-place of life, slammed the door of the monastery behind it, and undertook to penetrate just that daily routine of life with its methodicalness, to fashion it into a life in the world, but neither of nor for this world. With what result, we shall try to make clear in the following discussion.

# Chapter 5. Asceticism and the Spirit of Capitalism

In order to understand the connection between the fundamental religious ideas of ascetic Protestantism and its maxims for everyday economic conduct, it is necessary to examine with especial care such writings as have evidently been derived from ministerial practice. For in a time in which the beyond meant everything, when the social position of the Christian depended upon his admission to the Communion, the clergyman, through his ministry, Church discipline, and preaching, exercised an influence (as a glance at collections of *consilia, casus conscientiæ*,[1] etc., shows) which we modern men are entirely unable to picture. In such a time the religious forces which express themselves through such channels are the decisive influences in the formation of national character.

For the purposes of this chapter, though by no means for all purposes, we can treat ascetic Protestantism as a single whole. But since that side of English Puritanism which was derived from Calvinism gives the most consistent religious basis for the idea of the calling, we shall, following our previous method, place one of its representatives at the centre of the discussion. Richard Baxter stands out above many other writers on Puritan ethics, both because of his eminently practical and realistic attitude, and, at the same time, because of the universal recognition accorded to his works, which have gone through many new editions and translations. He was a Presbyterian and an apologist of the Westminster Synod, but at the same time, like so many of the best spirits of his time, gradually grew away from the dogmas of pure Calvinism. At heart he opposed Cromwell's usurpation as he would any revolution. He was unfavourable to the sects and the fanatical enthusiasm of the saints, but was very broadminded about external peculiarities and objective towards his opponents. He sought his field of labour most especially in the practical promotion of the moral life through the Church. In the pursuit of this end, as one of the most successful ministers known to history, he placed his services at the disposal of the Parliamentary Government, of Cromwell, and of the Restoration,[2] until he retired from office under the last, before St. Bartholomew's day. His *Christian Directory* is the most complete compendium of Puritan ethics, and is continually adjusted to the practical experiences of his own ministerial activity. In comparison we shall make use of Spener's *Theologische Bedenken*, as representative of German Pietism, Barclay's *Apology* for the Quakers, and some other representatives of ascetic ethics,[3] which, however, in the interest of space, will be limited as far as possible.[4]

Now, in glancing at Baxter's *Saints' Everlasting Rest*, or his *Christian Directory*, or similar works of others,[5] one is struck at first glance by the emphasis placed, in the discussion of wealth[6] and its acquisition, on the ebionitic elements of the New Testament.[7] Wealth as such is a great danger; its temptations never end, and its pursuit[8] is not only senseless as compared with the dominating importance of the Kingdom of God, but it is morally suspect. Here asceticism seems to have turned much more sharply against the acquisition of earthly goods than it did in Calvin, who saw no hindrance to the effectiveness of the clergy in their wealth, but rather a thoroughly desirable enhancement of their prestige. Hence he permitted them to employ their means profitably. Examples of the condemnation of the pursuit of money and goods may be gathered without end from Puritan writings, and may be contrasted with the late mediæval ethical literature, which was much more open-minded on this point.

Moreover, these doubts were meant with perfect seriousness; only it is necessary to examine them somewhat more closely in order to understand their true ethical significance and implications. The real moral objection is to relaxation in the security of possession,[9] the enjoyment of wealth with the consequence of idleness and the temptations of the flesh, above all of distraction from the pursuit of a righteous life. In fact, it is only because possession involves this danger of relaxation that it is objectionable at all. For the saints' everlasting rest is in the next world; on earth man must, to be certain of his state of grace, "do the works of him who sent him, as long as it is yet day." Not leisure and enjoyment, but only activity serves to increase the glory of God, according to the definite manifestations of His will.[10]

Waste of time is thus the first and in principle the deadliest of sins. The span of human life is infinitely short and precious to make sure of one's own election. Loss of time through sociability, idle talk,[11] luxury,[12] even more sleep than is necessary for health,[13] six to at most eight hours, is worthy of absolute moral condemnation.[14] It does not yet hold, with Franklin, that time is money, but the proposition is true in a certain spiritual sense. It is infinitely valuable because every hour lost is lost to labour for the glory of God.[15] Thus inactive contemplation is also valueless, or even directly reprehensible if it is at the expense of one's daily work.[16] For it is less pleasing to God than the active performance of His will in a calling.[17] Besides, Sunday is provided for that, and, according to Baxter, it is always those who are not diligent in their callings who have no time for God when the occasion demands it.[18]

Accordingly, Baxter's principal work is dominated by the continually repeated, often almost passionate preaching of hard, continuous bodily or mental labour.[19] It is due to a combination of two different motives.[20] Labour is, on the one hand, an approved ascetic technique,

as it always has been[21] in the Western Church, in sharp contrast not
only to the Orient but to almost all monastic rules the world over.[22]
It is in particular the specific defence against all those temptations
which Puritanism united under the name of the unclean life, whose
rôle for it was by no means small. The sexual asceticism of Puritanism differs only in degree, not in fundamental principle, from
that of monasticism; and on account of the Puritan conception of
marriage, its practical influence is more far-reaching than that of the
latter. For sexual intercourse is permitted, even within marriage,
only as the means willed by God for the increase of His glory according to the commandment, "Be fruitful and multiply."[23] Along with a
moderate vegetable diet and cold baths, the same prescription is
given for all sexual temptations as is used against religious doubts
and a sense of moral unworthiness: "Work hard in your calling."[24]
But the most important thing was that even beyond that labour came
to be considered in itself[25] the end of life, ordained as such by God.
St. Paul's "He who will not work shall not eat" holds unconditionally
for everyone.[26] Unwillingness to work is symptomatic of the lack of
grace.[27]

Here the difference from the mediæval view-point becomes quite
evident. Thomas Aquinas also gave an interpretation of that statement of St. Paul. But for him[28] labour is only necessary *naturali
ratione*[29] for the maintenance of individual and community. Where
this end is achieved, the precept ceases to have any meaning. Moreover, it holds only for the race, not for every individual. It does not
apply to anyone who can live without labour on his possessions, and
of course contemplation, as a spiritual form of action in the Kingdom
of God, takes precedence over the commandment in its literal sense.
Moreover, for the popular theology of the time, the highest form of
monastic productivity lay in the increase of the *Thesaurus ecclesiæ*[30]
through prayer and chant.

Now only do these exceptions to the duty to labour naturally no
longer hold for Baxter, but he holds most emphatically that wealth
does not exempt anyone from the unconditional command.[31] Even
the wealthy shall not eat without working, for even though they do
not need to labour to support their own needs, there is God's commandment which they, like the poor, must obey.[32] For everyone without exception God's Providence has prepared a calling, which he
should profess and in which he should labour. And this calling is not,
as it was for the Lutheran,[33] a fate to which he must submit and
which he must make the best of, but God's commandment to the
individual to work for the divine glory. This seemingly subtle difference had far-reaching psychological consequences, and became connected with a further development of the providential interpretation
of the economic order which had begun in scholasticism.

The phenomenon of the division of labour and occupations in society had, among others, been interpreted by Thomas Aquinas, to whom we may most conveniently refer, as a direct consequence of the divine scheme of things. But the places assigned to each man in this cosmos follow *ex causis naturalibus*[34] and are fortuitous (contingent in the Scholastic terminology). The differentiation of men into the classes and occupations established through historical development became for Luther, as we have seen, a direct result of the divine will. The perseverance of the individual in the place and within the limits which God had assigned to him was a religious duty.[35] This was the more certainly the consequence since the relations of Lutheranism to the world were in general uncertain from the beginning and remained so. Ethical principles for the reform of the world could not be found in Luther's realm of ideas; in fact it never quite freed itself from Pauline indifference. Hence the world had to be accepted as it was, and this alone could be made a religious duty.

But in the Puritan view, the providential character of the play of private economic interests takes on a somewhat different emphasis. True to the Puritan tendency to pragmatic interpretations, the providential purpose of the division of labour is to be known by its fruits. On this point Baxter expresses himself in terms which more than once directly recall Adam Smith's well-known apotheosis of the division of labour.[36] The specialization of occupations leads, since it makes the development of skill possible, to a quantitative and qualitative improvement in production, and thus serves the common good, which is identical with the good of the greatest possible number. So far, the motivation is purely utilitarian, and is closely related to the customary view-point of much of the secular literature of the time.[37]

But the characteristic Puritan element appears when Baxter sets at the head of his discussion the statement that "outside of a well-marked calling the accomplishments of a man are only casual and irregular, and he spends more time in idleness than at work", and when he concludes it as follows: "and he [the specialized worker] will carry out his work in order while another remains in constant confusion, and his business knows neither time nor place[38] . . . therefore is a certain calling the best for everyone". Irregular work, which the ordinary labourer is often forced to accept, is often unavoidable, but always an unwelcome state of transition. A man without a calling thus lacks the systematic, methodical character which is, as we have seen, demanded by worldly asceticism.

The Quaker ethic also holds that a man's life in his calling is an exercise in ascetic virtue, a proof of his state of grace through his conscientiousness, which is expressed in the care[39] and method with which he pursues his calling. What God demands is not labour in itself, but rational labour in a calling. In the Puritan concept of the calling the emphasis is always placed on this methodical character of worldly asceticism, not, as with Luther, on the acceptance of the lot which God has irretrievably assigned to man.[40]

Hence the question whether anyone may combine several callings is answered in the affirmative, if it is useful for the common good or one's own,[41] and not injurious to anyone, and if it does not lead to unfaithfulness in one of the callings. Even a change of calling is by no means regarded as objectionable, if it is not thoughtless and is made for the purpose of pursuing a calling more pleasing to God,[42] which means, on general principles, one more useful.

It is true that the usefulness of a calling, and thus its favour in the sight of God, is measured primarily in moral terms, and thus in terms of the importance of the goods produced in it for the community. But a further, and, above all, in practice the most important, criterion is found in private profitableness.[43] For if that God, whose hand the Puritan sees in all the occurrences of life, shows one of His elect a chance of profit, he must do it with a purpose. Hence the faithful Christian must follow the call by taking advantage of the opportunity.[44] "If God show you a way in which you may lawfully get more than in another way (without wrong to your soul or to any other), if you refuse this, and choose the less gainful way, you cross one of the ends of your calling, and you refuse to be God's steward, and to accept His gifts and use them for Him when He requireth it: you may labour to be rich for God, though not for the flesh and sin."[45]

Wealth is thus bad ethically only in so far as it is a temptation to idleness and sinful enjoyment of life, and its acquisition is bad only when it is with the purpose of later living merrily and without care. But as a performance of duty in a calling it is not only morally permissible, but actually enjoined.[46] The parable of the servant who was rejected because he did not increase the talent which was entrusted to him seemed to say so directly.[47] To wish to be poor was, it was often argued, the same as wishing to be unhealthy;[48] it is objectionable as a glorification of works and derogatory to the glory of God. Especially begging, on the part of one able to work, is not only the sin of slothfulness, but a violation of the duty of brotherly love according to the Apostle's own word.[49]

The emphasis on the ascetic importance of a fixed calling provided an ethical justification of the modern specialized division of labour. In a similar way the providential interpretation of profit-making justified the activities of the business man.[50] The superior indulgence of the *seigneur* and the parvenu ostentation of the *nouveau riche* are equally detestable to asceticism. But, on the other hand, it has the highest ethical appreciation of the sober, middle-class, self-made man.[51] "God blesseth His trade" is a stock remark about those good men[52] who had successfully followed the divine hints. The whole power of the God of the Old Testament, who rewards His people for their obedience in this life,[53] necessarily exercised a similar influence on the Puritan who, following Baxter's advice, compared his own state of grace with that of the heroes of the Bible,[54] and in the process interpreted the statements of the Scriptures as the articles of a book of statutes.

Of course, the words of the Old Testament were not entirely without ambiguity. We have seen that Luther first used the concept of the calling in the secular sense in translating a passage from Jesus Sirach. But the book of Jesus Sirach belongs, with the whole atmosphere expressed in it, to those parts of the broadened Old Testament with a distinctly traditionalistic tendency, in spite of Hellenistic influences. It is characteristic that down to the present day this book seems to enjoy a special favour among Lutheran German peasants,[55] just as the Lutheran influence in large sections of German Pietism has been expressed by a preference for Jesus Sirach.[56]

The Puritans repudiated the Apocrypha as not inspired, consistently with their sharp distinction between things divine and things of the flesh.[57] But among the canonical books that of Job had all the more influence. On the one hand it contained a grand conception of the absolute sovereign majesty of God, beyond all human comprehension, which was closely related to that of Calvinism. With that, on the other hand, it combined the certainty which, though incidental for Calvin, came to be of great importance for Puritanism, that God would bless His own in this life—in the book of Job only—and also in the material sense.[58] The Oriental quietism, which appears in several of the finest verses of the Psalms and in the Proverbs, was interpreted away, just as Baxter did with the traditionalistic tinge of the passage in the 1st Epistle to the Corinthians, so important for the idea of the calling.

But all the more emphasis was placed on those parts of the Old Testament which praise formal legality as a sign of conduct pleasing to God. They held the theory that the Mosaic Law had only lost its validity through Christ in so far as it contained ceremonial or purely historical precepts applying only to the Jewish people, but that otherwise it had always been valid as an expression of the natural law, and must hence be retained.[59] This made it possible, on the one hand, to eliminate elements which could not be reconciled with modern life. But still, through its numerous related features, Old Testament morality was able to give a powerful impetus to that spirit of self-righteous and sober legality which was so characteristic of the worldly asceticism of this form of Protestantism.[60]

Thus when authors, as was the case with several contemporaries as well as later writers, characterize the basic ethical tendency of Puritanism, especially in England, as English Hebraism[61] they are, correctly understood, not wrong. It is necessary, however, not to think of Palestinian Judaism at the time of the writing of the Scriptures, but of Judaism as it became under the influence of many centuries of formalistic, legalistic, and Talmudic education. Even then one must be very careful in drawing parallels. The general tendency of the older Judaism toward a naïve acceptance of life as such was far removed from the special characteristics of Puritanism. It was, however, just as far—and this ought not to be overlooked—from the economic ethics of mediæval and modern Judaism, in the traits which determined the positions of both in the development of the capitalistic ethos. The Jews stood on the side of the politically and speculatively oriented adventurous capitalism; their ethos was, in a word, that of pariah-capitalism. But Puritanism carried the ethos of the rational organization of capital and labour. It took over from the Jewish ethic only what was adapted to this purpose.

To analyse the effects on the character of peoples of the penetration of life with Old Testament norms—a tempting task which, however, has not yet satisfactorily been done even for Judaism[62]—would be impossible within the limits of this sketch. In addition to the relationships already pointed out, it is important for the general inner attitude of the Puritans, above all, that the belief that they were God's chosen people saw in them a great renaissance.[63] Even the kindly Baxter thanked God that he was born in England, and thus in the true Church, and nowhere else. This thankfulness for one's own perfection by the grace of God penetrated the attitude toward life[64] of the Puritan middle class, and played its part in developing that formalistic, hard, correct character which was peculiar to the men of that heroic age of capitalism.

Let us now try to clarify the points in which the Puritan idea of the calling and the premium it placed upon ascetic conduct was bound directly to influence the development of a capitalistic way of life. As we have seen, this asceticism turned with all its force against one thing: the spontaneous enjoyment of life and all it had to offer. This is perhaps most characteristically brought out in the struggle over the *Book of Sports*[65] which James I and Charles I made into law expressly as a means of counteracting Puritanism, and which the latter ordered to be read from all the pulpits. The fanatical opposition of the Puritans to the ordinances of the King, permitting certain popular amusements on Sunday outside of Church hours by law, was not only explained by the disturbance of the Sabbath rest, but also by resentment against the intentional diversion from the ordered life of the saint, which it caused. And, on his side, the King's threats of severe punishment for every attack on the legality of those sports were motivated by his purpose of breaking the anti-authoritarian ascetic tendency of Puritanism, which was so dangerous to the State. The feudal and monarchical forces protected the pleasure seekers against the rising middle-class morality and the anti-authoritarian ascetic conventicles, just as to-day capitalistic society tends to protect those willing to work against the class morality of the proletariat and the anti-authoritarian trade union.

As against this the Puritans upheld their decisive characteristic, the principle of ascetic conduct. For otherwise the Puritan aversion to sport, even for the Quakers, was by no means simply one of principle. Sport was accepted if it served a rational purpose, that of recreation necessary for physical efficiency. But as a means for the spontaneous expression of undisciplined impulses, it was under suspicion; and in so far as it became purely a means of enjoyment, or awakened pride, raw instincts or the irrational gambling instinct, it was of course strictly condemned. Impulsive enjoyment of life, which leads away both from work in a calling and from religion, was as such the enemy of rational asceticism, whether in the form of seigneurial sports, or the enjoyment of the dance-hall or the public-house of the common man.[66]

Its attitude was thus suspicious and often hostile to the aspects of culture without any immediate religious value. It is not, however, true that the ideals of Puritanism implied a solemn, narrow-minded contempt of culture. Quite the contrary is the case at least for science, with the exception of the hatred of Scholasticism. Moreover, the great men of the Puritan movement were thoroughly steeped in the culture of the Renaissance. The sermons of the Presbyterian divines abound with classical allusions,[67] and even the Radicals, although they objected to it, were not ashamed to display that kind of learning in theological polemics. Perhaps no country was ever so full of graduates as New England in the first generation of its existence. The satire of their opponents, such as, for instance, Butler's *Hudibras*, also attacks primarily the pedantry and highly trained dialectics of the Puritans. This is partially due to the religious valuation of knowledge which followed from their attitude to the Catholic *fides implicita*.[68]

But the situation is quite different when one looks at nonscientific literature,[69] and especially the fine arts. Here asceticism descended like a frost on the life of "merrie old England". And not only worldly merriment felt its effect. The Puritan's ferocious hatred of everything which smacked of superstition, of all survivals of magical or sacramental salvation, applied to the Christmas festivities and the May Pole[70] and all spontaneous religious art. That there was room in Holland for a great, often uncouthly realistic art[71] proves only how far from completely the authoritarian moral discipline of that country was able to counteract the influence of the court and the regents (a class of *rentiers*), and also the joy in life of the parvenu bourgeoisie, after the short supremacy of the Calvinistic theocracy had been transformed into a moderate national Church, and with it Calvinism had perceptibly lost in its power of ascetic influence.[72]

The theatre was obnoxious to the Puritans,[73] and with the strict exclusion of the erotic and of nudity from the realm of toleration, a radical view of either literature or art could not exist. The conceptions of idle talk, of superfluities,[74] and of vain ostentation, all designations of an irrational attitude without objective purpose, thus not ascetic, and especially not serving the glory of God, but of man, were always at hand to serve in deciding in favour of sober utility as against any artistic tendencies. This was especially true in the case of decoration of the person, for instance clothing.[75] That powerful tendency toward uniformity of life, which to-day so immensely aids the capitalistic interest in the standardization of production,[76] had its ideal foundations in the repudiation of all idolatry of the flesh.[77]

Of course we must not forget that Puritanism included a world of contradictions, and that the instinctive sense of eternal greatness in art was certainly stronger among its leaders than in the atmosphere of the Cavaliers.[78] Moreover, a unique genius like Rembrandt, however little his conduct may have been acceptable to God in the eyes of the Puritans, was very strongly influenced in the character of his work by his religious environment.[79] But that does not alter the picture as a whole. In so far as the development of the Puritan tradition could, and in part did, lead to a powerful spiritualization of personality, it was a decided benefit to literature. But for the most part that benefit only accrued to later generations.

Although we cannot here enter upon a discussion of the influence of Puritanism in all these directions, we should call attention to the fact that the toleration of pleasure in cultural goods, which contributed to purely æsthetic or athletic enjoyment, certainly always ran up against one characteristic limitation: they must not cost anything. Man is only a trustee of the goods which have come to him through God's grace. He must, like the servant in the parable, give an account of every penny entrusted to him,[80] and it is at least hazardous to spend any of it for a purpose which does not serve the glory of God but only one's own enjoyment.[81] What person, who keeps his eyes open, has not met representatives of this view-point even in the present?[82] The idea of a man's duty to his possessions, to which he subordinates himself as an obedient steward, or even as an acquisitive machine, bears with chilling weight on his life. The greater the possessions the heavier, if the ascetic attitude toward life stands the test, the feeling of responsibility for them, for holding them undiminished for the glory of God and increasing them by restless effort. The origin of this type of life also extends in certain roots, like so many aspects of the spirit of capitalism, back into the Middle Ages.[83] But it was in the ethic of ascetic Protestantism that it first found a consistent ethical foundation. Its significance for the development of capitalism is obvious.[84]

This worldly Protestant asceticism, as we may recapitulate up to this point, acted powerfully against the spontaneous enjoyment of possessions; it restricted consumption, especially of luxuries. On the other hand, it had the psychological effect of freeing the acquisition of goods from the inhibitions of traditionalistic ethics. It broke the bonds of the impulse of acquisition in that it not only legalized it, but (in the sense discussed) looked upon it as directly willed by God. The campaign against the temptations of the flesh, and the dependence on external things, was, as besides the Puritans the great Quaker apologist Barclay expressly says, not a struggle against the rational acquisition, but against the irrational use of wealth.

But this irrational use was exemplified in the outward forms of luxury which their code condemned as idolatry of the flesh,[85] however natural they had appeared to the feudal mind. On the other hand, they approved the rational and utilitarian uses of wealth which were willed by God for the needs of the individual and the community. They did not wish to impose mortification[86] on the man of wealth, but the use of his means for necessary and practical things. The idea of comfort characteristically limits the extent of ethically permissible expenditures. It is naturally no accident that the development of a manner of living consistent with that idea may be observed earliest and most clearly among the most consistent representatives of this whole attitude toward life. Over against the glitter and ostentation of feudal magnificence which, resting on an unsound economic basis, prefers a sordid elegance to a sober simplicity, they set the clean and solid comfort of the middle-class home as an ideal.[87]

On the side of the production of private wealth, asceticism condemned both dishonesty and impulsive avarice. What was condemned as covetousness, Mammonism, etc., was the pursuit of riches for their own sake. For wealth in itself was a temptation. But here asceticism was the power "which ever seeks the good but ever creates evil";[88] what was evil in its sense was possession and its temptations. For, in conformity with the Old Testament and in analogy to the ethical valuation of good works, asceticism looked upon the pursuit of wealth as an end in itself as highly reprehensible; but the attainment of it as a fruit of labour in a calling was a sign of God's blessing. And even more important: the religious valuation of restless, continuous, systematic work in a worldly calling, as the highest means to asceticism, and at the same time the surest and most evident proof of rebirth and genuine faith, must have been the most powerful conceivable lever for the expansion of that attitude toward life which we have here called the spirit of capitalism.[89]

When the limitation of consumption is combined with this release of acquisitive activity, the inevitable practical result is obvious: accumulation of capital through ascetic compulsion to save.[90] The restraints which were imposed upon the consumption of wealth naturally served to increase it by making possible the productive investment of capital. How strong this influence was is not, unfortunately, susceptible of exact statistical demonstration. In New England the connection is so evident that it did not escape the eye of so discerning a historian as Doyle.[91] But also in Holland, which was really only dominated by strict Calvinism for seven years, the greater simplicity of life in the more seriously religious circles, in combination with great wealth, led to an excessive propensity to accumulation.[92]

That, furthermore, the tendency which has existed everywhere and at all times, being quite strong in Germany to-day, for middle-class fortunes to be absorbed into the nobility, was necessarily checked by the Puritan antipathy to the feudal way of life, is evident. English Mercantilist writers of the seventeenth century attributed the superiority of Dutch capital to English to the circumstance that newly acquired wealth there did not regularly seek investment in land. Also, since it is not simply a question of the purchase of land, it did not there seek to transfer itself to feudal habits of life, and thereby to remove itself from the possibility of capitalistic investment.[93] The high esteem for agriculture as a peculiarly important branch of activity, also especially consistent with piety, which the Puritans shared, applied (for instance in Baxter) not to the landlord, but to the yeoman and farmer, in the eighteenth century not to the squire, but the rational cultivator.[94] Through the whole of English society in the time since the seventeenth century goes the conflict between the squirearchy, the representatives of "merrie old England", and the Puritan circles of widely varying social influence.[95] Both elements, that of an unspoiled naïve joy of life, and of a strictly regulated, reserved self-control, and conventional ethical conduct are even to-day combined to form the English national character.[96] Similarly, the early history of the North American Colonies is dominated by the sharp contrast of the adventurers, who wanted to set up plantations with the labour of indentured servants, and live as feudal lords, and the specifically middle-class outlook of the Puritans.[97]

As far as the influence of the Puritan outlook extended, under all circumstances—and this is, of course, much more important than the mere encouragement of capital accumulation—it favoured the development of a rational bourgeois economic life; it was the most important, and above all the only consistent influence in the development of that life. It stood at the cradle of the modern economic man.

To be sure, these Puritanical ideals tended to give way under excessive pressure from the temptations of wealth, as the Puritans themselves knew very well. With great regularity we find the most genuine adherents of Puritanism among the classes which were rising from a lowly status,[98] the small bourgeois and farmers, while the *beati possidentes*,[99] even among Quakers, are often found tending to repudiate the old ideals.[100] It was the same fate which again and again befell the predecessor of this worldly asceticism, the monastic asceticism of the Middle Ages. In the latter case, when rational economic activity had worked out its full effects by strict regulation of conduct and limitation of consumption, the wealth accumulated either succumbed directly to the nobility, as in the time before the Reformation, or monastic discipline threatened to break down, and one of the numerous reformations became necessary.

In fact the whole history of monasticism is in a certain sense the history of a continual struggle with the problem of the secularizing influence of wealth. The same is true on a grand scale of the worldly asceticism of Puritanism. The great revival of Methodism, which preceded the expansion of English industry toward the end of the eighteenth century, may well be compared with such a monastic reform. We may hence quote here a passage[101] from John Wesley himself which might well serve as a motto for everything which has been said above. For it shows that the leaders of these ascetic movements understood the seemingly paradoxical relationships which we have here analysed perfectly well, and in the same sense that we have given them.[102] He wrote:

> I fear, wherever riches have increased, the essence of religion has decreased in the same proportion. Therefore I do not see how it is possible, in the nature of things, for any revival of true religion to continue long. For religion must necessarily produce both industry and frugality, and these cannot but produce riches. But as riches increase, so will pride, anger, and love of the world in all its branches. How then is it possible that Methodism, that is, a religion of the heart, though it flourishes now as a green bay tree, should continue in this state? For the Methodists in every place grow diligent and frugal; consequently they increase in goods. Hence they proportionately increase in pride, in anger, in the desire of the flesh, the desire of the eyes, and the pride of life. So, although the form of religion remains, the spirit is swiftly vanishing away. Is there no way to prevent this—this continual decay of pure religion? We ought not to prevent people from being diligent and frugal; *we must exhort all Christians to gain all they can, and to save all they can; that is, in effect, to grow rich.*[103]

There follows the advice that those who gain all they can and save all they can should also give all they can, so that they will grow in grace and lay up a treasure in heaven. It is clear that Wesley here expresses, even in detail, just what we have been trying to point out.[104]

As Wesley here says, the full economic effect of those great religious movements, whose significance for economic development lay above all in their ascetic educative influence, generally came only after the peak of the purely religious enthusiasm was past. Then the intensity of the search for the Kingdom of God commenced gradually to pass over into sober economic virtue; the religious roots died out slowly, giving way to utilitarian worldliness. Then, as Dowden puts it, as in *Robinson Crusoe*, the isolated economic man who carries on missionary activities on the side[105] takes the place of the lonely spiritual search for the Kingdom of Heaven of Bunyan's pilgrim, hurrying through the market-place of Vanity.

When later the principle "to make the most of both worlds" became dominant in the end, as Dowden has remarked, a good conscience simply became one of the means of enjoying a comfortable bourgeois life, as is well expressed in the German proverb about the soft pillow. What the great religious epoch of the seventeenth century bequeathed to its utilitarian successor was, however, above all an amazingly good, we may even say a pharisaically good, conscience in the acquisition of money, so long as it took place legally. Every trace of the *deplacere vix potest*[106] has disappeared.[107]

A specifically bourgeois economic ethic had grown up. With the consciousness of standing in the fullness of God's grace and being visibly blessed by Him, the bourgeois business man, as long as he remained within the bounds of formal correctness, as long as his moral conduct was spotless and the use to which he put his wealth was not objectionable, could follow his pecuniary interests as he would and feel that he was fulfilling a duty in doing so. The power of religious asceticism provided him in addition with sober, conscientious, and unusually industrious workmen, who clung to their work as to a life purpose willed by God.[108]

Finally, it gave him the comforting assurance that the unequal distribution of the goods of this world was a special dispensation of Divine Providence, which in these differences, as in particular grace, pursued secret ends unknown to men.[109] Calvin himself had made the much-quoted statement that only when the people, i.e. the mass of labourers and craftsmen, were poor did they remain obedient to God.[110] In the Netherlands (Pieter de la Court and others), that had been secularized to the effect that the mass of men only labour when necessity forces them to do so. This formulation of a leading idea of capitalistic economy later entered into the current theories of the productivity of low wages. Here also, with the dying out of the religious root, the utilitarian interpretation crept in unnoticed, in the line of development which we have again and again observed.

Mediæval ethics not only tolerated begging but actually glorified it in the mendicant orders. Even secular beggars, since they gave the person of means opportunity for good works through giving alms, were sometimes considered an estate and treated as such. Even the Anglican social ethic of the Stuarts was very close to this attitude. It remained for Puritan Asceticism to take part in the severe English Poor Relief Legislation which fundamentally changed the situation. And it could do that, because the Protestant sects and the strict Puritan communities actually did not know any begging in their own midst.[111]

On the other hand, seen from the side of the workers, the Zinzendorf branch of Pietism, for instance, glorified the loyal worker who did not seek acquisition, but lived according to the apostolic model, and was thus endowed with the *charisma*[112] of the disciples.[113] Similar ideas had originally been prevalent among the Baptists in an even more radical form.

Now naturally the whole ascetic literature of almost all denominations is saturated with the idea that faithful labour, even at low wages, on the part of those whom life offers no other opportunities, is highly pleasing to God. In this respect Protestant Asceticism added in itself nothing new. But it not only deepened this idea most powerfully, it also created the force which was alone decisive for its effectiveness: the psychological sanction of it through the conception of this labour as a calling, as the best, often in the last analysis the only means of attaining certainty of grace.[114] And on the other hand it legalized the exploitation of this specific willingness to work, in that it also interpreted the employer's business activity as a calling.[115] It is obvious how powerfully the exclusive search for the Kingdom of God only through the fulfilment of duty in the calling, and the strict asceticism which Church discipline naturally imposed, especially on the propertyless classes, was bound to affect the productivity of labour in the capitalistic sense of the word. The treatment of labour as a calling became as characteristic of the modern worker as the corresponding attitude toward acquisition of the business man. It was a perception of this situation, new at his time, which caused so able an observer as Sir William Petty to attribute the economic power of Holland in the seventeenth century to the fact that the very numerous dissenters in that country (Calvinists and Baptists) "are for the most part thinking, sober men, and such as believe that Labour and Industry is their duty towards God".[116]

Calvinism opposed organic social organization in the fiscal-monopolistic form which it assumed in Anglicanism under the Stuarts, especially in the conceptions of Laud, this alliance of Church and State with the monopolists on the basis of a Christian-social ethical foundation. Its leaders were universally among the most passionate opponents of this type of politically privileged commercial, putting-out, and colonial capitalism. Over against it they placed the individualistic motives of rational legal acquisition by virtue of one's own ability and initiative. And, while the politically privileged monopoly industries in England all disappeared in short order, this attitude played a large and decisive part in the development of the industries which grew up in spite of and against the authority of the State.[117] The Puritans (Prynne, Parker) repudiated all connection with the large-scale capitalistic courtiers and projectors as an ethically suspicious class. On the other hand, they took pride in their own superior middle-class business morality, which formed the true reason for the persecutions to which they were subjected on the part of those circles. Defoe proposed to win the battle against dissent by boycotting bank credit and withdrawing deposits. The difference of the two types of capitalistic attitude went to a very large extent hand in hand with religious differences. The opponents of the Nonconformists, even in the eighteenth century, again and again ridiculed them for personifying the spirit of shopkeepers, and for having ruined the ideals of old England. Here also lay the difference of the Puritan economic ethic from the Jewish; and contemporaries (Prynne) knew well that the former and not the latter was the bourgeois capitalistic ethic.[118]

One of the fundamental elements of the spirit of modern capitalism, and not only of that but of all modern culture: rational conduct on the basis of the idea of the calling, was born—that is what this discussion has sought to demonstrate—from the spirit of Christian asceticism. One has only to re-read the passage from Franklin, quoted at the beginning of this essay, in order to see that the essential elements of the attitude which was there called the spirit of capitalism are the same as what we have just shown to be the content of the Puritan worldly asceticism,[119] only without the religious basis, which by Franklin's time had died away. The idea that modern labour has an ascetic character is of course not new. Limitation to specialized work, with a renunciation of the Faustian universality of man which it involves, is a condition of any valuable work in the modern world; hence deeds and renunciation inevitably condition each other to-day. This fundamentally ascetic trait of middle-class life, if it attempts to be a way of life at all, and not simply the absence of any, was what Goethe wanted to teach, at the height of his wisdom, in the *Wanderjahren*,[120] and in the end which he gave to the life of his *Faust*.[121] For him the realization meant a renunciation, a departure from an age of full and beautiful humanity, which can no more be repeated in the course of our cultural development than can the flower of the Athenian culture of antiquity.

The Puritan wanted to work in a calling; we are forced to do so. For when asceticism was carried out of monastic cells into everyday life, and began to dominate worldly morality, it did its part in building the tremendous cosmos of the modern economic order. This order is now bound to the technical and economic conditions of machine production which to-day determine the lives of all the individuals who are born into this mechanism, not only those directly concerned with economic acquisition, with irresistible force. Perhaps it will so determine them until the last ton of fossilized coal is burnt. In Baxter's view the care for external goods should only lie on the shoulders of the "saint like a light cloak, which can be thrown aside at any moment."[122] But fate decreed that the cloak should become an iron cage.[123]

Since asceticism undertook to remodel the world and to work out its ideals in the world, material goods have gained an increasing and finally an inexorable power over the lives of men as at no previous period in history. To-day the spirit of religious asceticism—whether finally, who knows?—has escaped from the cage. But victorious capitalism, since it rests on mechanical foundations, needs its support no longer. The rosy blush of its laughing heir, the Enlightenment, seems also to be irretrievably fading, and the idea of duty in one's calling prowls about in our lives like the ghost of dead religious beliefs. Where the fulfilment of the calling cannot directly be related to the highest spiritual and cultural values, or when, on the other hand, it need not be felt simply as economic compulsion, the individual generally abandons the attempt to justify it at all. In the field of its highest development, in the United States, the pursuit of wealth, stripped of its religious and ethical meaning, tends to become associated with purely mundane passions, which often actually give it the character of sport.[124]

No one knows who will live in this cage in the future, or whether at the end of this tremendous development entirely new prophets will arise, or there will be a great rebirth of old ideas and ideals, or, if neither, mechanized petrification, embellished with a sort of convulsive self-importance. For of the last stage of this cultural development, it might well be truly said: "Specialists without spirit, sensualists without heart; this nullity imagines that it has attained a level of civilization never before achieved."

But this brings us to the world of judgments of value and of faith, with which this purely historical discussion need not be burdened. The next task would be rather to show the significance of ascetic rationalism, which has only been touched in the foregoing sketch, for the content of practical social ethics, thus for the types of organization and the functions of social groups from the conventicle to the State. Then its relations to humanistic rationalism,[125] its ideals of life and cultural influence; further to the development of philosophical and scientific empiricism, to technical development and to spiritual ideals would have to be analysed. Then its historical development from the mediæval beginnings of worldly asceticism to its dissolution into pure utilitarianism would have to be traced out through all the areas of ascetic religion. Only then could the quantitative cultural significance of ascetic Protestantism in its relation to the other plastic elements of modern culture be estimated.

Here we have only attempted to trace the fact and the direction of its influence to their motives in one, though a very important point. But it would also further be necessary to investigate how Protestant Asceticism was in turn influenced in its development and its character by the totality of social conditions, especially economic.[126] The modern man is in general, even with the best will, unable to give religious ideas a significance for culture and national character which they deserve. But it is, of course, not my aim to substitute for a one-sided materialistic an equally one-sided spiritualistic causal interpretation of culture and of history. Each is equally possible,[127] but each, if it does not serve as the preparation, but as the conclusion of an investigation, accomplishes equally little in the interest of historical truth.[128]

# Notes

## AUTHOR'S INTRODUCTION

1. *Ständestaat*. The term refers to the late form taken by feudalism in Europe in its transition to absolute monarchy.—TRANSLATOR'S NOTE.
2. Here, as on some other points, I differ from our honoured master, Lujo Brentano (in his work to be cited later). Chiefly in regard to terminology, but also on questions of fact. It does not seem to me expedient to bring such different things as acquisition of booty and acquisition by management of a factory together under the same category; still less to designate every tendency to the acquisition of money as the spirit of capitalism as against other types of acquisition. The second sacrifices all precision of concepts, and the first the possibility of clarifying the specific difference between Occidental capitalism and other forms. Also in Simmel's *Philosophie des Geldes* money economy and capitalism are too closely identified, to the detriment of his concrete analysis. In the writings of Werner Sombart, above all in the second edition of his most important work, *Der moderne Kapitalismus*, the *differentia specifica* [what is specific to] of Occidental capitalism—at least from the view-point of my problem—the rational organization of labour, is strongly overshadowed by genetic factors which have been operative everywhere in the world.
3. *Commenda* was a form of mediæval trading association, entered into *ad hoc* for carrying out one sea voyage. A producer or exporter of goods turned them over to another who took them abroad (on a ship provided sometimes by one party, sometimes by the other) and sold them, receiving a share in the profits. The expenses of the voyage were divided between the two in agreed proportion, while the original shipper bore the risk. See Weber, "Handelsgesellschaften im Mittelalter" [*The History of Commercial Partnerships in the Middle Ages*], *Gesammelte Aufsätze zur Sozial- und Wirtschaftsgeschichte*, pp. 323–8.—TRANSLATOR'S NOTE.
4. The sea loan, used in maritime commerce in the Middle Ages, was "a method of insuring against the risks of the sea without violating the prohibitions against usury. . . . When certain risky maritime ventures were to be undertaken, a certain sum . . . was obtained for the cargo belonging to such and such a person or capitalist. If the ship was lost, no repayment was exacted by the lender; if it reached port safely, the borrower paid a considerable premium, sometimes 50 per cent." Henri Sée, *Modern Capitalism*, p. 189.—TRANSLATOR'S NOTE.
5. A form of company between the partnership and the limited liability corporation. At least one of the participants is made liable without limit, while the others enjoy limitation of liability to the amount of their investment.—TRANSLATOR'S NOTE.
6. Mercenary leaders (Italian) [*Editor*].
7. Workshops [*Editor*].
8. Naturally the difference cannot be conceived in absolute terms. The politically oriented capitalism (above all tax-farming) of Mediterranean and Oriental antiquity, and even of China and India, gave rise to rational, continuous enterprises whose book-keeping—though known to us only in pitiful fragments—probably had a rational character. Furthermore, the politically oriented adventurers' capitalism has been closely associated

with rational bourgeois capitalism in the development of modern banks, which, including the Bank of England, have for the most part originated in transactions of a political nature, often connected with war. The difference between the characters of Paterson, for instance—a typical promoter—and of the members of the directorate of the Bank who gave the keynote to its permanent policy, and very soon came to be known as the "Puritan usurers of Grocers' Hall", is characteristic of it. Similarly, we have the aberration of the policy of this most solid bank at the time of the South Sea Bubble. Thus the two naturally shade off into each other. But the difference is there. The great promoters and financiers have no more created the rational organization of labour than—again in general and with individual exceptions—those other typical representatives of financial and political capitalism, the Jews. That was done, typically, by quite a different set of people.

9.  Household [Editor].

10. For Weber's discussion of the ineffectiveness of slave labour, especially so far as calculation is concerned, see his essay, "Agrarverhältnisse im Altertum" [The Agrarian Sociology of Ancient Civilizations], in the volume Gesammelte Aufsätze zur Sozial- und Wirtschaftsgeschichte.—TRANSLATOR'S NOTE.

11. That is, in the whole series of Aufsätze zur Religionssoziologie, not only in the essay here translated. See translator's preface.—TRANSLATOR'S NOTE.

12. The Protestant Ethic and the Spirit of Capitalism was originally published in 1904–1905 as two articles [Editor].

13. A project that Weber worked on in the 1910s and which represented a continuation of The Protestant Ethic [Editor].

14. The remains of my knowledge of Hebrew are also quite inadequate.

15. Scholars and writers [Editor].

16. I need hardly point out that this does not apply to attempts like that of Karl Jasper's (in his book Psychologie der Weltanschauungen, 1919), nor to Klages's Charakterologie, and similar studies which differ from our own in their point of departure. There is no space here for a criticism of them.

17. The only thing of this kind which Weber ever wrote is the section on "Religionssoziologie" in his large work Wirtschaft und Gesellschaft. It was left unfinished by him and does not really close the gap satisfactorily.—TRANSLATOR'S NOTE.

18. Some years ago an eminent psychiatrist expressed the same opinion to me.

## I THE PROBLEM

1.  From the voluminous literature which has grown up around this essay I cite only the most comprehensive criticisms. (1) F. Rachfahl, "Kalvinismus und Kapitalismus", Internationale Wochenschrift für Wissenschaft, Kunst und Technik (1909), Nos. 39–43. In reply, my article: "Antikritisches zum Geist des Kapitalismus," Archiv für Sozialwissenschaft und Sozialpolitik (Tübingen), XX, 1910 [The Protestant Ethic Debate, eds. David Chalcraft and Austin Harrington]. Then Rachfahl's reply to that: "Nochmals Kalvinismus und Kapitalismus", 1910, Nos. 22–25, of the Internationale Wochenschrift. Finally my "Antikritisches Schlusswort", Archiv, XXXI [The Protestant Ethic Debate, eds. David Chalcraft and Austin Harrington]. (Brentano, in the criticism presently to be referred to, evidently did not know of this last phase of the discussion, as he does not refer to it.) I have not incorporated anything in this edition from the somewhat unfruitful polemics against Rachfahl. He is an author whom I otherwise admire, but who has in this instance ventured into a field which he has not thoroughly mastered. I have only added a few supplementary references from my anti-critique, and have attempted, in new passages and footnotes, to make impossible any future misunderstanding. (2) W. Sombart, in his book Der Bourgeois (Munich and Leipzig, 1913, also translated into English under the title The Quintessence of Capitalism, London, 1915), to which I shall return in footnotes below, Finally (3) Lujo Brentano in Part II of the Appendix to his Munich address (in the Academy of Sciences, 1913) on Die Anfänge des modernen Kapitalismus, which was published in 1916. (Since Weber's death Brentano has somewhat expanded these essays and incorporated them into his recent book Der wirtschaftende Mensch in der Geschichte.—TRANSLATOR'S NOTE.) I shall also refer to this criticism in special footnotes in the proper places. I invite anyone who may be interested to convince himself by comparison that I have not in revision left out, changed the meaning of, weakened, or added materially different statements to, a single sentence of my essay which contained any essential point. There was no occasion to do so, and the development of my exposition will convince anyone who still doubts. The two latter writers engaged in a more bitter quarrel with each other than with me. Brentano's criticism of Sombart's book, Die Juden und das Wirtschaftsleben, I consider in many points well founded, but often very unjust, even

apart from the fact that Brentano does not himself seem to understand the real essence of the problem of the Jews (which is entirely omitted from this essay, but will be dealt with later [in a later section of the *Religionssoziologie* (*Economy and Society*, pp. 611–23—*Editor*)—TRANSLATOR'S NOTE]).

From theologians I have received numerous valuable suggestions in connection with this study. Its reception on their part has been in general friendly and impersonal, in spite of wide differences of opinion on particular points. This is the more welcome to me since I should not have wondered at a certain antipathy to the manner in which these matters must necessarily be treated here. What to a theologian is valuable in his religion cannot play a very large part in this study. We are concerned with what, from a religious point of view, are often quite superficial and unrefined aspects of religious life, but which, and precisely because they were superficial and unrefined, have often influenced outward behaviour most profoundly.

Another book which, besides containing many other things, is a very welcome confirmation of and supplement to this essay in so far as it deals with our problem, is the important work of E. Troeltsch, *Die Soziallehren der christlichen Kirchen und Gruppen* (Tübingen, 1912). It deals with the history of the ethics of Western Christianity from a very comprehensive point of view of its own. I here refer the reader to it for general comparison instead of making repeated references to special points. The author is principally concerned with the doctrines of religion, while I am interested rather in their practical results.

2. The exceptions are explained, not always, but frequently, by the fact that the religious leanings of the labouring force of an industry are naturally, in the first instance, determined by those of the locality in which the industry is situated, or from which its labour is drawn. This circumstance often alters the impression given at first glance by some statistics of religious adherence, for instance in the Rhine provinces. Furthermore, figures can naturally only be conclusive if individual specialized occupations are carefully distinguished in them. Otherwise very large employers may sometimes be grouped together with master craftsmen who work alone, under the category of "proprietors of enterprises." Above all, the fully developed capitalism of the present day, especially so far as the great unskilled lower strata of labour are concerned, has become independent of any influence which religion may have had in the past. I shall return to this point.

3. Compare, for instance, Schell, *Der Katholizismus als Prinzip des Fortschrittes* (Würzburg, 1897), p. 31, and v. Hertling, *Das Prinzip des Katholizismus und die Wissenschaft* (Freiburg, 1899), p. 58.

4. One of my pupils has gone through what is at this time the most complete statistical material we possess on this subject: the religious statistics of Baden. See Martin Offenbacher, "Konfession und soziale Schichtung", *Eine Studie über die wirtschaftliche Lage der Katholiken und Protestanten in Baden* (Tübingen und Leipzig, 1901), Vol. IV, part v, of the *Volkswirtschaftliche Abhandlungen der badischen Hochschulen*. The facts and figures which are used for illustration below are all drawn from this study.

5. For instance, in 1895 in Baden there was taxable capital available for the tax on returns from capital:

> Per 1,000 Protestants . . . . . . 954,000 marks
> Per 1,000 Catholics . . . . . . . 589,000 marks

It is true that the Jews, with over four millions per 1,000, were far ahead of the rest. (For details see Offenbacher, *op. cit.*, p. 21.)

6. On this point compare the whole discussion in Offenbacher's study.

7. On this point also Offenbacher brings forward more detailed evidence for Baden in his first two chapters.

8. The population of Baden was composed in 1895 as follows: Protestants, 37.0 per cent.; Catholics, 61.3 per cent.; Jewish, 1.5 per cent. The students of schools beyond the compulsory public school stage were, however, divided as follows (Offenbacher, p. 16):

| | Protestant. | Catholic. | Jews. |
|---|---|---|---|
| | Per Cent. | Per Cent. | Per Cent. |
| *Gymnasien* | 43 | 46 | 9.5 |
| *Realgymnasien* | 69[a] | 31 | 9 |
| *Oberrealschulen* | 52 | 41 | 7 |
| *Realschulen* | 49 | 40 | 11 |
| *Höhere Bürgerschulen* | 51 | 37 | 12 |
| Average | 48 | 42 | 10 |

[a] [Error by Weber; should be 60, not 69—*Editor*]

(In the *Gymnasium* the main emphasis is on the classics. In the *Realgymnasium* Greek is dropped and Latin reduced in favour of modern languages, mathematics and science. The *Realschule* and *Oberrealschule* are similar to the latter except that Latin is dropped entirely in favour of modern languages. See G. E. Bolton, *The Secondary School System in Germany*, New York, 1900.—TRANSLATOR'S NOTE.)

The same thing may be observed in Prussia, Bavaria, Würtemberg, Alsace-Lorraine, and Hungary (see figures in Offenbacher, pp. 16 ff.).

9.  See the figures in the preceding note, which show that the Catholic attendance at secondary schools, which is regularly less than the Catholic share of the total population by a third, only exceeds this by a few per cent. in the case of the grammar schools (mainly in preparation for theological studies). With reference to the subsequent discussion it may further be noted as characteristic that in Hungary those affiliated with the Reformed Church exceed even the average Protestant record of attendance at secondary schools. (See Offenbacher, p. 19, note.)

10. For the proofs see Offenbacher, p. 54, and the tables at the end of his study.

11. Especially well illustrated by passages in the works of Sir William Petty, to be referred to later.

12. Petty's reference to the case of Ireland is very simply explained by the fact that the Protestants were only involved in the capacity of absentee landlords. If he had meant to maintain more he would have been wrong, as the situation of the Scotch-Irish shows. The typical relationship between Protestantism and capitalism existed in Ireland as well as elsewhere. (On the Scotch-Irish see C. A. Hanna, *The Scotch-Irish*, two vols., Putnam, New York.)

13. This is not, of course, to deny that the latter facts have had exceedingly important consequences. As I shall show later, the fact that many Protestant sects were small and hence homogeneous minorities, as were all the strict Calvinists outside of Geneva and New England, even where they were in possession of political power, was of fundamental significance for the development of their whole character, including their manner of participation in economic life. The migration of exiles of all the religions of the earth, Indian, Arabian, Chinese, Syrian, Phœnician, Greek, Lombard, to other countries as bearers of the commercial lore of highly developed areas, has been of universal occurrence and has nothing to do with our problem. Brentano, in the essay to which I shall often refer, *Die Anfänge des modern Kapitalismus*, calls to witness his own family. But bankers of foreign extraction have existed at all times and in all countries as the representatives of commercial experience and connections. They are not peculiar to modern capitalism, and were looked upon with ethical mistrust by the Protestants (see below). The case of the Protestant families, such as the Muralts, Pestalozzi, etc., who migrated to Zurich from Locarno, was different. They very soon became identified with a specifically modern (industrial) type of capitalistic development.

14. Offenbacher, *op. cit.*, p. 58.

15. Unusually good observations on the characteristic peculiarities of the different religions in Germany and France, and the relation of these differences to other cultural elements in the conflict of nationalities in Alsace are to be found in the fine study of W. Wittich, "Deutsche und französische Kultur im Elsass", *Illustrierte Elsässische Rundschau* (1900, also published separately).

16. This, of course, was true only when some possibility of capitalistic development in the area in question was present.

17. On this point see, for instance, Dupin de St. André "L'ancienne église réformée de Tours. Les membres de l'église", *Bull. de la soc. de l'hist. du Protest.*, 4, p. 10. Here again one might, especially from the Catholic point of view, look upon the desire for emancipation from monastic or ecclesiastical control as the dominant motive. But against that view stands not only the judgment of contemporaries (including Rabelais), but also, for instance, the qualms of conscience of the first national synods of the Huguenots (for instance 1st Synod, C. partic. qu. 10 in Aymon, *Synod. Nat.*, p. 10), as to whether a banker might become an elder of the Church; and in spite of Calvin's own definite stand, the repeated discussions in the same bodies of the permissibility of taking interest occasioned by the questions of ultra-scrupulous members. It is partly explained by the number of persons having a direct interest in the question, but at the same time the wish to practise *usuraria pravitas* [depraved usury] without the necessity of confession could not have been alone decisive. The same, see below, is true of Holland. Let it be said explicitly that the prohibition of interest in the canon law will play no part in this investigation.

18. Gothein, *Wirtschaftsgeschichte des Schwarzwaldes*, I, p. 67.

19. In connection with this see Sombart's brief comments (*Der moderne Kapitalismus*, first edition, p. 380). Later, under the influence of a study of F. Keller (*Unternehmung und Mehrwert*, Publications of the Goerres-Gesellschaft, XII), which, in spite of many good observations (which in this connection, however, are not new), falls below the standard

of other recent works of Catholic apologetics, Sombart, in what is in these parts in my opinion by far the weakest of his larger works (*Der Bourgeois*), has unfortunately maintained a completely untenable thesis, to which I shall refer in the proper place.

20. That the simple fact of a change of residence is among the most effective means of intensifying labour is thoroughly established (compare note 13 above). The same Polish girl who at home was not to be shaken loose from her traditional laziness by any chance of earning money, however tempting, seems to change her entire nature and become capable of unlimited accomplishment when she is a migratory worker in a foreign country. The same is true of migratory Italian labourers. That this is by no means entirely explicable in terms of the educative influence of the entrance into a higher cultural environment, although this naturally plays a part, is shown by the fact that the same thing happens where the type of occupation, as in agricultural labour, is exactly the same as at home. Furthermore, accommodation in labour barracks, etc., may involve a degradation to a standard of living which would never be tolerated at home. The simple fact of working in quite different surroundings from those to which one is accustomed breaks through the tradition and is the educative force. It is hardly necessary to remark how much of American economic development is the result of such factors. In ancient times the similar significance of the Babylonian exile for the Jews is very striking, and the same is true of the Parsees. But for the Protestants, as is indicated by the undeniable difference in the economic characteristics of the Puritan New England colonies from Catholic Maryland, the Episcopal South, and mixed Rhode island, the influence of their religious belief quite evidently plays a part as an independent factor. Similarly in India, for instance, with the Jains.

21. It is well known in most of its forms to be a more or less moderated Calvinism or Zwinglianism.

22. In Hamburg, which is almost entirely Lutheran, the only fortune going back to the seventeenth century is that of a well-known Reformed family (kindly called to my attention by Professor A. Wahl).

23. It is thus not new that the existence of this relationship is maintained here. Lavelye, Matthew Arnold, and others already perceived it. What is new, on the contrary, is the quite unfounded denial of it. Our task here is to explain the relation.

24. Naturally this does not mean that official Pietism, like other religious tendencies, did not at a later date, from a patriarchal point of view, oppose certain progressive features of capitalistic development, for instance, the transition from domestic industry to the factory system. What a religion has sought after as an ideal, and what the actual result of its influence on the lives of its adherents has been, must be sharply distinguished, as we shall often see in the course of our discussion. On the specific adaptation of Pietists to industrial labour, I have given examples from a Westphalian factory in my article, "Zur Psychophysik der gewerblichen Arbeit", *Archiv für Sozialwissenschaft und Sozielpolitik*, XXVIII, and at various other times.

## 2 THE SPIRIT OF CAPITALISM

1. Belonging to a type, but with its own specific features [*Editor*].

2. These passages represent a very brief summary of some aspects of Weber's methodological views. At about the same time that he wrote this essay he was engaged in a thorough criticism and revaluation of the methods of the Social Sciences, the result of which was a point of view in many ways different from the prevailing one, especially outside of Germany. In order thoroughly to understand the significance of this essay in its wider bearings on Weber's sociological work as a whole it is necessary to know what his methodological aims were. Most of his writings on this subject have been assembled since his death (in 1920) in the volume *Gesammelte Aufsätze zur Wissenschaftslehre*. A shorter exposition of the main position is contained in the opening chapters of *Wirtschaft und Gesellschaft* [*Economy and Society*], *Grundriss der Sozialökonomik*, III.—TRANSLATOR'S NOTE.

3. The final passage is from *Necessary Hints to Those That would Be Rich* (written 1736, Works, Sparks edition, II, p. 80), the rest from *Advice to a Young Tradesman* (written 1748, Sparks edition, II, pp. 87 ff.). The italics in the text are Franklin's.

4. *Der Amerikamüde* (Frankfurt, 1835), well known to be an imaginative paraphrase of Lenau's impressions of America. As a work of art the book would to-day be somewhat difficult to enjoy, but it is incomparable as a document of the (now long since blurred-over) differences between the German and the American outlook, one may even say of the type of spiritual life which, in spite of everything, has remained common to all Germans, Catholic and Protestant alike, since the German mysticism of the Middle Ages, as against the Puritan capitalistic valuation of action.

5. Sombart has used this quotation as a motto for his section dealing with the genesis of capitalism (*Der moderne Kapitalismus*, first edition, I, p. 193. See also p. 390).

6. Which quite obviously does not mean either that Jacob Fugger was a morally indifferent or an irreligious man, or that Benjamin Franklin's ethic is completely covered by the above quotations. It scarcely required Brentano's quotations (*Die Anfänge des modernen Kapitalismus*, pp. 150 ff.) to protect this well-known philanthropist from the misunderstanding which Brentano seems to attribute to me. The problem is just the reverse: how could such a philanthropist come to write these particular sentences (the especially characteristic form of which Brentano has neglected to reproduce) in the manner of a moralist?

7. This is the basis of our difference from Sombart in stating the problem. Its very considerable practical significance will become clear later. In anticipation, however, let it be remarked that Sombart has by no means neglected this ethical aspect of the capitalistic entrepreneur. But in his view of the problem it appears as a result of capitalism, whereas for our purposes we must assume the opposite as an hypothesis. A final position can only be taken up at the end of the investigation. For Sombart's view see *op. cit.*, pp. 357, 380, etc. His reasoning here connects with the brilliant analysis given in Simmel's *Philosophie des Geldes* (final chapter). Of the polemics which he has brought forward against me in his *Bourgeois* I shall come to speak later. At this point any thorough discussion must be postponed.

8. "I grew convinced that truth, sincerity, and integrity in dealings between man and man were of the utmost importance to the felicity of life; and I formed written resolutions, which still remain in my journal book to practise them ever while I lived. Revelation had indeed no weight with me as such; but I entertained an opinion that, though certain actions might not be bad because they were forbidden by it, or good because it commanded them, yet probably these actions might be forbidden because they were bad for us, or commanded because they were beneficial to us in their own nature, all the circumstances of things considered." *Autobiography* (ed. F. W. Pine, Henry Holt, New York, 1916), p. 112.

9. "I therefore put myself as much as I could out of sight and started it"—that is the project of a library which he had initiated—"as a scheme of a *number of friends*, who had requested me to go about and propose it to such as they thought lovers of reading. In this way my affair went on smoothly, and I ever after practised it on such occasions; and from my frequent successes, can heartily recommend it. The present little sacrifice of your vanity will afterwards be amply repaid. If it remains awhile uncertain to whom the merit belongs, someone more vain than yourself will be encouraged to claim it, and then even envy will be disposed to do you justice by plucking those assumed feathers and restoring them to their right owner." *Autobiography*, p. 140.

10. Supreme good [*Editor*].

11. Brentano (*op. cit.*, pp. 125, 127, note 1) takes this remark as an occasion to criticize the later discussion of "that rationalization and discipline" to which worldly asceticism* has subjected men. That, he says, is a rationalization toward an irrational mode of life. He is, in fact, quite correct. A thing is never irrational in itself, but only from a particular rational point of view. For the unbeliever every religious way of life is irrational, for the hedonist every ascetic standard, no matter whether, measured with respect to its particular basic values, that opposing asceticism is a rationalization. If this essay makes any contribution at all, may it be to bring out the complexity of the only superficially simple concept of the rational.

12. Should be "Calling" [*Editor*]. This seemingly paradoxical term has been the best translation I could find for Weber's *innerweltliche Askese*, which means asceticism practised within the world as contrasted with *ausserweltliche Askese*, which withdraws from the world (for instance into a monastery). Their precise meaning will appear in the course of Weber's discussion. It is one of the prime points of his essay that asceticism does not need to flee from the world to be ascetic. I shall consistently employ the terms worldly and otherworldly to denote the contrast between the two kinds of asceticism.—TRANSLATOR'S NOTE.

13. In reply to Brentano's (*Die Anfänge des modernen Kapitalismus*, pp. 150 ff.) long and somewhat inaccurate apologia for Franklin, whose ethical qualities I am supposed to have misunderstood, I refer only to this statement, which should, in my opinion, have been sufficient to make that apologia superfluous.

14. The two terms profession and calling I have used in translation of the German *Beruf*, whichever seemed best to fit the particular context. Vocation does not carry the ethical connotation in which Weber is interested. It is especially to be remembered that profession in this sense is not contrasted with business, but it refers to a particular attitude toward one's occupation, no matter what that occupation may be. This should become abundantly clear from the whole of Weber's argument.—TRANSLATOR'S NOTE.

15. I make use of this opportunity to insert a few anti-critical remarks in advance of the main argument. Sombart (*Bourgeois*) makes the untenable statement that this ethic of Franklin is a word-for-word repetition of some writings of that great and versatile genius of the

Renaissance, Leon Battista Alberti, who besides theoretical treatises on Mathematics, Sculpture, Painting, Architecture, and Love (he was personally a woman-hater), wrote a work in four books on household management (*Della Famiglia*). (Unfortunately, I have not at the time of writing been able to procure the edition of Mancini, but only the older one of Bonucci.) The passage from Franklin is printed above word for word. Where then are corresponding passages to be found in Alberti's work, especially the maxim "time is money", which stands at the head, and the exhortations which follow it? The only passage which, so far as I know, bears the slightest resemblance to it is found towards the end of the first book of *Della Famiglia* (ed. Bonucci, II, p. 353), where Alberti speaks in very general terms of money as the *nervus rerum* [major driving force] of the household, which must hence be handled with special care, just as Cato spoke in *De Re Rustica*. To treat Alberti, who was very proud of his descent from one of the most distinguished cavalier families of Florence (*Nobilissimi Cavalieri, op. cit.*, pp. 213, 228, 247, etc.), as a man of mongrel blood who was filled with envy for the noble families because his illegitimate birth, which was not in the least socially disqualifying, excluded him as a bourgeois from association with the nobility, is quite incorrect. It is true that the recommendation of large enterprises as alone worthy of a *nobile è onesta famiglia* [noble and honest family] and a *libero è nobile animo* [free and noble spirit], and as costing less labour is characteristic of Alberti (p. 209; compare *Del governo della Famiglia*, IV, p. 55, as well as p. 116 in the edition for the Pandolfini). Hence the best thing is a putting-out business for wool and silk. Also an ordered and painstaking regulation of his household, i.e. the limiting of expenditure to income. This is the *santa masserizia* [prudent management], which is thus primarily a principle of maintenance, a given standard of life, and not of acquisition (as no one should have understood better than Sombart). Similarly, in the discussion of the nature of money, his concern is with the management of consumption funds (money or *possessioni*), not with that of capital; all that is clear from the expression of it which is put into the mouth of Gianozzo. He recommends, as protection against the uncertainty of *fortuna*, early habituation to continuous activity, which is also (pp. 73–4) alone healthy in the long run, *in cose magnifiche è ample* [magnificent and grand things], and avoidance of laziness, which always endangers the maintenance of one's position in the world. Hence a careful study of a suitable trade in case of a change of fortune, but every *opera mercenaria* [venal activity] is unsuitable (*op. cit.*, I, p. 209). His idea of *tranquillita dell' animo* [peace of mind] and his strong tendency toward the Epicurean λάθε βιῶγας (*vivere a sè stesso* [live off one's own means], p. 262); especially his dislike of any office (p. 258) as a source of unrest, of making enemies, and of becoming involved in dishonourable dealings; the ideal of life in a country villa; his nourishment of vanity through the thought of his ancestors; and his treatment of the honour of the family (which on that account should keep its fortune together in the Florentine manner and not divide it up) as a decisive standard and ideal—all these things would in the eyes of every Puritan have been sinful idolatry of the flesh, and in those of Benjamin Franklin the expression of incomprehensible aristocratic nonsense. Note, further, the very high opinion of literary things (for the *industria* [hard work] is applied principally to literary and scientific work), which is really most worthy of a man's efforts. And the expression of the *masserizia*, in the sense of "rational conduct of the household" as the means of living independently of others and avoiding destitution, is in general put only in the mouth of the illiterate Gianozzo as of equal value. Thus the origin of this concept, which comes (see below) from monastic ethics, is traced back to an old priest (p. 249).

Now compare all this with the ethic and manner of life of Benjamin Franklin, and especially of his Puritan ancestors; the works of the Renaissance *littérateur* addressing himself to the humanistic aristocracy, with Franklin's works addressed to the masses of the lower middle class (he especially mentions clerks) and with the tracts and sermons of the Puritans, in order to comprehend the depth of the difference. The economic rationalism of Alberti, everywhere supported by references to ancient authors, is most clearly related to the treatment of economic problems in the works of Xenophon (whom he did not know), of Cato, Varro, and Columella (all of whom he quotes), except that especially in Cato and Varro, *acquisition* as such stands in the foreground in a different way from that to be found in Alberti. Furthermore, the very occasional comments of Alberti on the use of the *fattori* [factors], their division of labour and discipline, on the unreliability of the peasants, etc., really sound as if Cato's homely wisdom were taken from the field of the ancient slave-using household and applied to that of free labour in domestic industry and the metayer system. When Sombart (whose reference to the Stoic ethic is quite misleading) sees economic rationalism as "developed to its farthest conclusions" as early as Cato, he is, with a correct interpretation, not entirely wrong. It is possible to unite the *diligens pater familias* [conscientiousness] of the Romans with the ideal of the *massajo* [management] of Alberti under the same category. It is above all characteristic for Cato that a landed estate is valued and judged as an object for the investment of consumption funds. The concept of *industria*, on the other hand, is differently coloured on account of Christian influence. And there is just the difference. In the conception of *industria*, which comes from monastic asceticism and which was developed by monastic writers, lies the seed of an *ethos* which was fully developed later in the Protestant worldly asceticism. Hence, as we shall often point out, the relationship of the two, which, however, is less close to the official Church doctrine of St. Thomas than to the Florentine and Siennese mendicant-moralists. In Cato and also in Alberti's own writings this *ethos* is lacking; for both it is a matter of worldly wisdom, not of ethic. In Franklin there is also a utilitarian strain. But the ethical quality of the sermon to young business men is impossible to mistake, and that is the characteristic thing. A lack of care in the handling of money means to him that one so to speak murders capital embryos, and hence it is an ethical defect.

An inner relationship of the two (Alberti and Franklin) exists in fact only in so far as Alberti, whom Sombart calls pious, but who actually, although he took the sacraments and held a Roman benefice, like so many humanists, did not himself (except for two quite colourless passages) in any way make use of religious motives as a justification of the manner of life he recommended, had not yet, Franklin on the other hand no longer, related his recommendation of economy to religious conceptions. Utilitarianism, in Alberti's preference for wool and silk manufacture, also the mercantilist social utilitarianism "that many people should be given employment" (see Alberti, *op. cit.*, p. 292), is in this field at least formally the sole justification for the one as for the other. Alberti's discussions of this subject form an excellent example of the sort of economic rationalism which really existed as a reflection of economic conditions, in the work of authors interested purely in "the thing for its own sake" everywhere and at all times; in the Chinese classicism and in Greece and Rome no less than in the Renaissance and the age of the Enlightenment. There is no doubt that just as in ancient times with Cato, Varro, and Columella, also here with Alberti and others of the same type, especially in the doctrine of *industria*, a sort of economic rationality is highly developed. But how can anyone believe that such a literary *theory* could develop into a revolutionary force at all comparable to the way in which a religious belief was able to set the sanctions of salvation and damnation on the fulfillment of a particular (in this case methodically rationalized) manner of life? What, as compared with it, a really religiously oriented rationalization of conduct looks like, may be seen, outside of the Puritans of all denominations, in the cases of the Jains, the Jews, certain ascetic sects of the Middle Ages, the Bohemian Brothers (an offshoot of the Hussite movement), the Skoptsi and Stundists in Russia, and numerous monastic orders, however much all these may differ from each other.

The essential point of the difference is (to anticipate) that an ethic based on religion places certain psychological sanctions (not of an economic character) on the maintenance of the attitude prescribed by it, sanctions which, so long as the religious belief remains alive, are highly effective, and which mere worldly wisdom like that of Alberti does not have at its disposal. Only in so far as these sanctions work, and, above all, in the direction in which they work, which is often very different from the doctrine of the theologians, does such an ethic gain an independent influence on the conduct of life and thus on the economic order. This is, to speak frankly, the point of this whole essay, which I had not expected to find so completely overlooked.

Later on I shall come to speak of the theological moralists of the late Middle Ages, who were relatively friendly to capital (especially Anthony of Florence and Bernhard of Siena), and whom Sombart has also seriously misinterpreted. In any case Alberti did not belong to that group. Only the concept of *industria* did he take from monastic lines of thought, no matter through what intermediate links. Alberti, Pandolfini, and their kind are representatives of that attitude which, in spite of all its outward obedience, was inwardly already emancipated from the tradition of the Church. With all its resemblance to the current Christian ethic, it was to a large extent of the antique pagan character, which Brentano thinks I have ignored in its significance for the development of modern economic thought (and also modern economic policy). That I do not deal with its influence here is quite true. It would be out of place in a study of the Protestant ethic and the spirit of capitalism. But, as will appear in a different connection, far from denying its significance, I have been and am for good reasons of the opinion that its sphere and direction of influence were entirely different from those of the Protestant ethic (of which the spiritual ancestry, of no small practical importance, lies in the sects and in the ethics of Wyclif and Hus). It was not the mode of life of the rising bourgeoisie which was influenced by this other attitude, but the policy of statesmen and princes; and these two partly, but by no means always, convergent lines of development should for purposes of analysis be kept perfectly distinct. So far as Franklin is concerned, his tracts of advice to business men, at present used for school reading in America, belong in fact to a category of works which have influenced practical life, far more than Alberti's large book, which hardly became known outside of learned circles. But I have expressly denoted him as a man who stood beyond the direct influence of the Puritan view of life, which had paled considerably in the meantime, just as the whole English enlightenment, the relations of which to Puritanism have often been set forth.

16. The holy or accursed lust for gold [*Editor*].
17. Unfortunately Brentano (*op. cit.*) has thrown every kind of struggle for gain, whether peaceful or warlike, into one pot, and has then set up as the specific criterion of capitalistic (as contrasted, for instance, with feudal) profit-seeking, its acquisitiveness of *money* (instead of land). Any further differentiation, which alone could lead to a clear conception, he has not only refused to make, but has made against the concept of the spirit of (modern) capitalism which we have formed for our purposes, the (to me) incomprehensible objection that it already includes in its assumptions what is supposed to be proved.
18 Conscientiousness [*Editor*].
19. Compare the, in every respect, excellent observations of Sombart, *Die deutsche Volkswirtschaft im 19ten Jahrhundert*, p. 123. In general I do not need specially to point out, although the following studies go back in their most important points of view to much older work, how much they owe in their development to the mere existence of Sombart's important works, with their pointed formulations and this even, perhaps especially, where they take a different road. Even those who feel themselves continually and decisively disagreeing with Sombart's views, and who reject many of his theses, have the duty to do so only after a thorough study of his work.
20. Free will [*Editor*].
21. Of course we cannot here enter into the question of where these limits lie, nor can we evaluate the familiar theory of the relation between high wages and the high productivity of labour which was first suggested by Brassey, formulated and maintained theoretically by Brentano, and both historically and theoretically by Schulze-Gaevernitz. The discussion was again opened by Hasbach's penetrating studies (*Schmollers Jahrbuch*, 1903, pp. 385–91 and 417 ff.), and is not yet finally settled. For us it is here sufficient to assent to the fact which is not, and cannot be, doubted by anyone, that low wages and high profits, low wages and favourable opportunities for industrial development, are at least not simply identical, that generally speaking training for capitalistic culture, and with it the possibility of capitalism as an economic system, are not brought about simply through mechanical financial operations. All examples are purely illustrative.
22. It must be remembered that this was written twenty-five years ago, when the above statement was by no means the commonplace that it is now, even among economists, to say nothing of business men.—TRANSLATOR'S NOTE.
23. The establishment even of capitalistic industries has hence often not been possible without large migratory movements from areas of older culture. However correct Sombart's remarks on the difference between the personal skill and trade secrets of the handicraftsman and the scientific, objective modern technique may be, at the time of the rise of capitalism the difference hardly existed. In fact the, so to speak, ethical qualities of the capitalistic workman (and to a certain extent also of the entrepreneur) often had a higher scarcity value than the skill of the craftsman, crystallized in traditions hundreds of years old. And even present-day industry is not yet by any means entirely independent in its choice of location of such qualities of the population, acquired by long-standing tradition and education in intensive labour. It is congenial to the scientific prejudices of to-day, when such a dependence is observed to ascribe it to congenital racial qualities rather than to tradition and education, in my opinion with very doubtful validity.
24. See my "Zur Psychophysik der gewerblichen Arbeit", *Archiv für Sozialwissenschaft und Sozialpolitik*, XXVIII.
25. The foregoing observations might be misunderstood. The tendency of a well-known type of business man to use the belief that "religion must be maintained for the people" for his own purpose, and the earlier not uncommon willingness of large numbers, especially of the Lutheran clergy, from a general sympathy with authority, to offer themselves as black police when they wished to brand the strike as sin and trade unions as furtherers of cupidity, all these are things with which our present problem has nothing to do. The factors discussed in the text do not concern occasional but very common facts, which, as we shall see, continually recur in a typical manner.
26. *Der moderne Kapitalismus*, first edition, 1, p. 62.
27. *Ibid.*, p. 195.
28. Naturally that of the modern rational enterprise peculiar to the Occident, not of the sort of capitalism spread over the world for three thousand years, from China, India, Babylon, Greece, Rome, Florence, to the present, carried on by usurers, military contractors, traders in offices, tax-farmers, large merchants, and financial magnates. See the Introduction.
29. The assumption is thus by no means justified *a priori*, that is all I wish to bring out here, that on the one hand the technique of the capitalistic enterprise, and on the other the spirit of professional work which gives to capitalism its expansive energy, must have had their original roots in the same social classes. Similarly with the social relationships of religious beliefs. Calvinism was historically one of the agents of education in the spirit of capitalism. But in the Netherlands, the large moneyed interests were, for reasons which

will be discussed later, not predominately adherents of strict Calvinism, but Arminians. The rising middle and small bourgeoisie, from which entrepreneurs were principally recruited, were for the most part here and elsewhere typical representatives both of capitalistic ethics and of Calvinistic religion. But that fits in very well with our present thesis: there were at all times large bankers and merchants. But a rational capitalistic organization of industrial labour was never known until the transition from the Middle Ages to modern times took place.

30. On this point see the good Zurich dissertation of J. Maliniak (1913).

31. The following picture has been put together as an ideal type from conditions found in different industrial branches and at different places. For the purposes of illustration which it here serves, it is of course of no consequence that the process has not in any one of the examples we have in mind taken place in precisely the manner we have described.

32. For this reason, among others, it is not by chance that this first period of incipient (economic) rationalism in German industry was accompanied by certain other phenomena, for instance the catastrophic degradation of taste in the style of articles of everyday use.

33. This is not to be understood as a claim that changes in the supply of the precious metals are of no economic importance.

34. This is meant to refer to the type of entrepreneur (business man) whom we are making the object of our study, not any empirical average type. On the concept of the ideal type see my discussion in the *Archiv für Sozialwissenschaft und Sozialpolitik*, XIX, No. 1 [*The Methodology of the Social Sciences*, pp. 89–105]. (Republished since Weber's death in the *Gesammelte Aufsätze zur Wissenschaftslehre*. The concept was first thoroughly developed by Weber himself in these essays, and is likely to be unfamiliar to non-German readers. It is one of the most important aspects of Weber's methodological work, referred to in a note above—TRANSLATOR'S NOTE.)

35. Holy or accursed lust for gold [*Editor*].

36. Worldview [*Editor*].

37. A merchant can hardly ever please God [*Editor*].

38. This is perhaps the most appropriate place to make a few remarks concerning the essay of F. Keller, already referred to (volume 12 of the publications of the Görres-Gesellschaft), and Sombart's observations (*Der Bourgeois*) in following it up, so far as they are relevant in the present context. That an author should criticize a study in which the canonical prohibition of interest (except in one incidental remark which has no connection with the general argument) is not even mentioned, on the assumption that this prohibition of interest, which has a parallel in almost every religious ethic in the world, is taken to be the decisive criterion of the difference between the Catholic and Protestant ethics, is almost inconceivable. One should really only criticize things which one has read, or the argument of which, if read, one has not already forgotten. The campaign against *usuraria pravitas* [depraved usury] runs through both the Huguenot and the Dutch Church history of the sixteenth century; Lombards, i.e. bankers, were by virtue of that fact alone often excluded from communion (see Chap. 1, note 17). The more liberal attitude of Calvin (which did not, however, prevent the inclusion of regulations against usury in the first plan of the ordinances) did not gain a definite victory until Salmasius. Hence the difference did not lie at this point; quite the contrary. But still worse are the author's own arguments on this point. Compared to the works of Funck and other Catholic scholars (which he has not, in my opinion, taken as fully into consideration as they deserve), and the investigations of Endemann, which, however obsolete in certain points to-day, are still fundamental, they make a painful impression of superficiality. To be sure, Keller has abstained from such excesses as the remarks of Sombart (*Der Bourgeois*, p. 321) that one noticed how the "pious gentlemen" (Bernard of Siena and Anthony of Florence) "wished to excite the spirit of enterprise by every possible means", that is, since they, just like nearly everyone else concerned with the prohibition of interest, interpreted it in such a way as to exempt what we should call the productive investment of capital. That Sombart, on the one hand, places the Romans among the heroic peoples, and on the other, what is for his work as a whole an impossible contradiction, considers economic rationalism to have been developed to its final consequences in Cato (p. 267), may be mentioned by the way as a symptom that this is a book with a thesis in the worst sense.

He has also completely misrepresented the significance of the prohibition of interest. This cannot be set forth here in detail. At one time it was often exaggerated, then strongly underestimated, and now, in an era which produces Catholic millionaires as well as Protestant, has been turned upside down for apologetic purposes. As is well known, it was not, in spite of Biblical authority, abolished until the last century by order of the *Congregatio S. Officii*, and then only *temporum ratione habita* and indirectly, namely, by forbidding confessors to worry their charges by questions about *usuraria pravitas*, even though no claim to obedience was given up in case it should be restored. Anyone who has made a thorough study of the extremely complicated history of the doctrine cannot claim, considering the endless controversies over, for instance, the justification of the purchase of bonds, the discounting of notes and various other contracts (and above all considering the order of the *Congregatio S. Officii* [organ of the Catholic Church], mentioned above, concerning a municipal loan), that the prohibition of interest was only intended to apply to emergency loans, nor that it had the intention of preserving capital, or that it was even an aid to capitalistic enterprise (p. 25). The truth is that the Church came to reconsider the prohibition of interest comparatively late. At the time when this happened the forms of purely business investment were not loans at fixed interest rate, but the *fœnus nauticum, commenda, societas maris*, and the *dare ad proficuum de mari* (a loan in which the shares of gain and loss were adjusted according to degrees of risk), and were, considering the character of the return on loans to productive enterprise, necessarily of that sort. These were not (or only according to a few rigorous canonists) held to fall under the ban, but when investment at a definite rate of interest and discounting became possible and customary, the first sort of loans also encountered very troublesome difficulties from the prohibition, which led to various drastic measures of the merchant guilds (black lists). But the treatment of usury on the part of the canonists was generally purely legal and formal, and was certainly free from any such tendency to protect capital as Keller ascribes to it. Finally, in so far as any attitude towards capitalism as such can be ascertained, the decisive factors were: on the one hand, a traditional, mostly inarticulate hostility towards the growing power of capital which was impersonal, and hence not readily amenable to ethical control (as it is still reflected in Luther's pronouncements about the Fuggers and about the banking business); on the other hand, the necessity of accommodation to practical needs. But we cannot discuss this, for, as has been said, the prohibition of usury and its fate can have at most a symptomatic significance for us, and that only to a limited degree.

The economic ethic of the Scotists, and especially of certain mendicant theologians of the fourteenth century, above all Bernhard of Siena and Anthony of Florence, that is monks with a specifically rational type of asceticism, undoubtedly deserves a separate treatment, and cannot be disposed of incidentally in our discussion. Otherwise I should be forced here, in reply to criticism, to anticipate what I have to say in my discussion of the economic ethics of Catholicism in its positive relations to capitalism. These authors attempt, and in that anticipate some of the Jesuits, to present the profit of the merchant as a reward for his *industria*, and thus ethically to justify it. (Of course, even Keller cannot claim more.)

The concept and the approval of *industria* come, of course, in the last analysis from monastic asceticism, probably also from the idea of *masserizia* [management], which Alberti, as he himself says through the mouth of Gianozzo, takes over from clerical sources. We shall later speak more fully of the sense in which the monastic ethics is a forerunner of the worldly ascetic denominations of Protestantism. In Greece, among the Cynics, as shown by late-Hellenic tombstone inscriptions, and, with an entirely different background, in Egypt, there were suggestions of similar ideas. But what is for us the most important thing is entirely lacking both here and in the case of Alberti. As we shall see later, the characteristic Protestant conception of the proof of one's own salvation, the *certitudo salutis* in a calling, provided the psychological sanctions which this religious belief put behind the *industria*. But that Catholicism could not supply, because its means to salvation were different. In effect these authors are concerned with an ethical doctrine, not with motives to practical action, dependent on the desire for salvation. Furthermore, they are, as is very easy to see, concerned with concessions to practical necessity, not, as was worldly asceticism, with deductions from fundamental religious postulates. (Incidentally, Anthony and Bernhard have long ago been better dealt with than by Keller.) And even these concessions have remained an object of controversy down to the present. Nevertheless the significance of these monastic ethical conceptions as symptoms is by no means small.

But the real roots of the religious ethics which led the way to the modern conception of a calling lay in the sects and the heterodox movements, above all in Wyclif; although Brodnitz (*Englische Wirtschaftsgeschichte*), who thinks his influence was so great that Puritanism found nothing left for it to do, greatly overestimates his significance. All that cannot be gone into here. For here we can only discuss incidentally whether and to what extent the Christian ethic of the Middle Ages had in fact already prepared the way for the spirit of capitalism.

39. Turpitude [*Editor*].
40. The words μηδὲν ἀπελπίζοντες [with no hope for anything in return] (Luke vi. 35) and the translation of the Vulgate, *nihil inde sperantes* [hoping for nothing from it], are thought (according to A. Merx) to be a corruption of μηδένα ἀπελπίζοντες (or *meminem desperantes*) [do not despair of anyone], and thus to command the granting of loans to all brothers, including the poor, without saying anything at all about interest. The passage *Deo placere vix potest* [a merchant can hardly ever please God] is now thought to be of Arian origin (which, if true, makes no difference to our contentions).

41. Something to be ashamed of [*Editor's*].
42. Hard work [*Editor's*].
43. Excessive and immoral rate of interest [*Editor's*].
44. How a compromise with the prohibition of usury was achieved is shown, for example, in Book 1, chapter 65, of the statutes of the *Arte di Calimala* (at present I have only the Italian edition in Emiliani-Guidici, *Stor. dei Com. Ital.*, III, p. 246), "Procurino i consoli con quelli frate, che parrà loro, che perdono si faccia e come fare si possa il meglio per l'amore di ciascuno, del dono, merito o guiderdono, ovvero interesse per l'anno presente e secondo che altra volta fatto fue" [The consuls must make sure that they confess to the brothers they judge most likely to pardon them, and that they do it in a way most appropriate to the gift, service, or award received, in terms of the interest exacted for the past year, according to custom]. It is thus a way for the guild to secure exemption for its members on account of their official positions, without defiance of authority. The suggestions immediately following, as well as the immediately preceding idea to book all interest and profits as gifts, are very characteristic of the amoral attitude towards profits on capital. To the present stock exchange black list against brokers who hold back the difference between top price and actual selling price, often corresponded the outcry against those who pleaded before the ecclesiastical court with the *exceptio usurariæ pravitatis* [exemption from depraved usury].

## 3 LUTHER'S CONCEPTION OF THE CALLING

1. Of the ancient languages only Hebrew has any similar concept. Most of all in the word מְלָאכָה. It is used for sacerdotal functions (Exod. xxxv. 21; Neh. xi. 22; 1 Chron. ix. 13; xiii. 4; xxvi. 30), for business in the service of the king (especially 1 Sam. viii. 16; 1 Chron. iv. 23; xxix. 26), for the service of a royal official (Esther iii. 9; ix. 3), of a superintendant of labour (2 Kings xii, 12), of a slave (Gen. xxxix, 11), of labour in the fields (1 Chron. xxvii. 26), of craftsmen (Exod. xxxi. 5; xxxv. 21; 1 Kings vii. 14), for traders (Psa. cvii. 23), and for worldly activity of any kind in the passage, Sirach xi. 20, to be discussed later. The word is derived from the root לאַר, to send, thus meaning originally a task. That it originated in the ideas current in Solomon's bureaucratic kingdom of serfs (*Fronstaat*), built up as it was according to the Egyptian model, seems evident from the above references. In meaning, however, as I learn from A. Merx, this root concept had become lost even in antiquity. The word came to be used for any sort of labour, and in fact became fully as colourless as the German *Beruf*, with which it shared the fate of being used primarily for mental and not manual functions. The expression (חק), assignment, task, lesson, which also occurs in Sirach xi. 20, and is translated in the Septuagint with διαθήκη, is also derived from the terminology of the servile bureaucratic regime of the time, as is דכיוס (Exod. v. 13, cf. Exod. v. 14), where the Septuagint also uses διαθήκη for task. In Sirach xliii. 10 it is rendered in the Septuagint with κρίμα. In Sirach xi. 20 it is evidently used to signify the fulfillment of God's commandments, being thus related to our calling. On this passage in Jesus Sirach reference may here be made to Smend's well-known book on Jesus Sirach, and for the words διαθήκη, ἔργον, πόνος, to his *Index zur Weisheit des Jesus Sirach* (Berlin, 1907). As is well known, the Hebrew text of the Book of Sirach was lost, but has been rediscovered by Schechter, and in part supplemented by quotations from the Talmud. Luther did not possess it, and these two Hebrew concepts could not have had any influence on his use of language. (See below on Prov. xxii. 29.)

In Greek there is no term corresponding in ethical connotation to the German or English words at all. Where Luther, quite in the spirit of the modern usage (see below), translates Jesus Sirach xi. 20 and 21, *bleibe in deinem Beruf* [remain in your calling], the Septuagint has at one point ἔργον, at the other, which however seems to be an entirely corrupt passage, πόνος (the Hebrew original speaks of the shining of divine help!). Otherwise in antiquity τὰ προσήκοντο is used in the general sense of duties. In the works of the Stoics κάματος occasionally carries similar connotations, though its linguistic source is indifferent (called to my attention by A. Dieterich). All other expressions (such as τάξις etc.) have no ethical implications.

In Latin what we translate as calling, a man's sustained activity under the division of labour, which is thus (normally) his source of income and in the long run the economic basis of his existence, is, aside from the colourless *opus*, expressed with an ethical content, at least similar to that of the German word, either by *officium* (from *opificium*, which was originally ethically colourless, but later, as especially in Seneca *de benef*, IV, p. 18, came to mean *Beruf*); or by *munus*, derived from the compulsory obligations of the old civic community; or finally by *professio*. This last word was also characteristically used in this sense for public obligations, probably being derived from the old tax declarations of the citizens. But later it came to be applied in the special modern sense of the liberal professions (as in *professio bene dicendi*), and in this narrower meaning had a significance in every way similar to the German *Beruf*, even in the more spiritual sense of the word, as when Cicero says of someone "non intelligit quid profiteatur", in the sense of "he does not know his real profession". The only difference is that it is, of course, definitely secular without any religious connotation. That is even more true of *ars*, which in Imperial times was used for handicraft. The Vulgate translates the above passages from Jesus Sirach, at one point with *opus*, the other (verse 21) with *locus*, which in this case means something like social station. The addition of *mandaturam tuorum* comes from the ascetic Jerome, as Brentano quite rightly remarks, without, however, here or elsewhere, calling attention to the fact that this was characteristic of precisely the ascetic use of the term, before the Reformation in an otherworldly, afterwards in a worldly, sense. It is furthermore uncertain from what text Jerome's translation was made. An influence of the old liturgical meaning of מְלָאכָה does not seem to be impossible.

In the Romance languages only the Spanish *vocacion* in the sense of an inner call to something, from the analogy of a clerical office, has a connotation partly corresponding to that of the German word, but it is never used to mean calling in the external sense. In the Romance Bible translations the Spanish *vocacion*, the Italian *vocazione* and *chiamamento*, which otherwise have a meaning partly corresponding to the Lutheran and Calvinistic usage to be discussed presently, are used only to translate the κλῆσις; of the New Testament, the call of the Gospel to eternal salvation, which in the Vulgate is *vocatio*. Strange to say, Brentano, *op. cit.*, maintains that this fact, which I have myself adduced to defend my view, is evidenced for the existence of the concept of the calling in the sense which it had later, before the Reformation. But it is nothing of the kind. κλῆσις had to be translated by *vocatio*. But where and when in the Middle Ages was it used in our sense? The fact of this translation, and in spite of it, the lack of any application of the word to worldly callings is what is decisive. *Chiamamento* is used in this manner along with *vocazione* in the Italian Bible translation of the fifteenth century, which is printed in the *Collezione di opere inedite e rare* (Bologna, 1887), while the modern Italian translations use the latter alone. On the other hand, the words used in the Romance languages for calling in the external worldly sense of regular acquisitive activity carry, as appears from all the dictionaries and from a report of my friend Professor Baist (of Freiburg), no religious connotation whatever. This is so no matter whether they are derived from *ministerium* or *officium*, which originally had a certain religious colouring, or from *ars*, *professio*, and *implicare (impeigo)*, from which it has been entirely absent from the beginning. The passages in Jesus Sirach mentioned above, where Luther used *Beruf*, are translated: in French, v. 20, *office*; v. 21, *labeur* (Calvinistic translation); Spanish, v. 20, *obra*; v. 21, *lugar* (following the Vulgate); recent translations, *posto* (Protestant). The Protestants of the Latin countries, since they were minorities, did not exercise, possibly without even making the attempt, such a creative influence over their respective languages as Luther did over the still less highly rationalized (in an academic sense) German official language.

2. On the other hand, the *Augsburg Confession* only contains the idea implicitly and but partially developed. Article XVI (ed. by Kolde, p. 43) teaches: "Meanwhile it (the Gospel) does not dissolve the ties of civil or domestic economy, but strongly enjoins us to maintain them as ordinances of God and in such ordinances (*ein jeder nach seinem Beruf*) to exercise charity." (Translated by Rev. W. H. Teale, Leeds, 1842.)

(In Latin it is only "et in talibus ordinationibus exercere caritatem". The English is evidently translated directly from the Latin, and does not contain the idea which came into the German version.—Translator's Note.)

The conclusion drawn, that one must obey authority, shows that here *Beruf* is thought of, at least primarily, as an objective order in the sense of the passage in 1 Cor. vii. 20.

And Article XXVII (Kolde, p. 83) speaks of *Beruf* (Latin in *vocatione sua*) only in connection with estates ordained by God: clergy, magistrates, princes, lords, etc. But even this is true only of the German version of the *Konkordienbuch*, while in the German *Ed. princeps* the sentence is left out.

Only in Article XXVI (Kolde, p. 81) is the word used in a sense which at least includes our present meaning: "that he did chastise his body, not to deserve by that discipline remission of sin, but to have his body in bondage and apt to spiritual things, and to do his calling". Translated by Richard Taverner, Philadelphia Publications Society, 1888. (Latin *juxta vocationem suam*.)

3. According to the lexicons, kindly confirmed by my colleagues Professors Braune and Hoops, the word *Beruf* (Dutch *beroep*, English *calling*, Danish *kald*, Swedish *kallelse*) does not occur in any of the languages which now contain it in its present worldly (secular) sense before Luther's translation of the Bible. The Middle High German, Middle Low German, and Middle Dutch words, which sound like it, all mean the same as *Ruf* in modern German, especially inclusive, in late mediæval times, of the calling (vocation) of a candidate to a clerical benefice by those with the power of appointment. It is a special case

which is also often mentioned in the dictionaries of the Scandinavian languages. The word is also occasionally used by Luther in the same sense. However, even though this special use of the word may have promoted its change of meaning, the modern conception of *Beruf* undoubtedly goes linguistically back to the Bible translations by Protestants, and any anticipation of it is only to be found, as we shall see later, in Tauler (died 1361). All the languages which were fundamentally influenced by the Protestant Bible translations have the word, all of which this was not true (like the Romance languages) do not, or at least not in its modern meaning.

Luther renders two quite different concepts with *Beruf*. First the Pauline κλῆσις in the sense of the call to eternal salvation through God. Thus: 1 Cor. i. 26; Eph. i. 18; iv. 1, 4; 2 Thess. i. 11; Heb. iii. 1; 2 Peter i. 10. All these cases concern the purely religious idea of the call through the Gospel taught by the apostle; the word κλῆσις has nothing to do with worldly callings in the modern sense. The German Bibles before Luther use in this case *ruffunge* (so in all those in the Heidelberg Library), and sometimes instead of "von Gott geruffet" say "von Gott gefordert". Secondly; however, he, as we have already seen, translates the words in Jesus Sirach discussed in the previous note (in the Septuagint ἔν τῷ ἔργῳ σου παλαιώθητι and καὶ ἔμμενε τῷ πόνῳ σου), with "beharre in deinem Beruf" and "bliebe in deinem Beruf" [remain in your calling], instead of "bliebe bei deiner Arbeit" [remain in your work]. The later (authorized) Catholic translations (for instance that of Fleischütz, Fulda, 1781) have (as in the New Testament passages) simply followed him. Luther's translation of the passage in the Book of Sirach is, so far as I know, the first case in which the German word *Beruf* appears in its present purely secular sense. The preceding exhortation, verse 20, στῆθι εν διαθήκῃ σου he translates "bliebe in Gottes Wort" [remain in God's word], although Sirach xiv. 1 and xliii. 10 show that, corresponding to the Hebrew רח, which (according to quotations in the Talmud) Sirach used, διαθήκη really did mean something similar to our calling, namely one's fate or assigned task. In its later and present sense the word *Beruf* did not exist in the German language, nor, so far as I can learn, in the works of the older Bible translators or preachers. The German Bibles before Luther rendered the passage from Sirach with *Werk*. Berthold of Regensburg, at the points in his sermons where the modern would say *Benif*, uses the word *Arbeit*. The usage was thus the same as in antiquity. The first passage I know, in which not *Beruf* but *Ruf* (as a translation of κλῆσις) is applied to purely worldly labour, is in the fine sermon of Tauler on Ephesians iv (Works, Basle edition, f. 117. v), of peasants who *misten* [cause trouble] go: they often fare better "so sie folgen einfeltiglich irem Ruff denn die geistlichen Menschen, die auf ihren Ruf nicht Acht haben." [if they followed their own call instead of the clergy who do not represent their own call]. The word in this sense did not find its way into everyday speech. Although Luther's usage at first vacillates between *Ruf* and *Beruf* (see *Werke*, Erlangen edition, p. 51.), that he was directly influenced by Tauler is by no means certain, although the *Freiheit eines Christenmenschen* is in many respects similar to this sermon of Tauler. But in the purely worldly sense of Tauler, Luther did not use the word *Ruf*. (This against Denifle, *Luther*, p. 163.)

Now evidently Sirach's advice in the version of the Septuagint contains, apart from the general exhortation to trust in God, no suggestion of a specifically religious valuation of secular labour in a calling. The term πόνος, toil, in the corrupt second passage would be rather the opposite, if it were not corrupted. What Jesus Sirach says simply corresponds to the exhortation of the psalmist (Psa. xxxvii. 3), "Dwell in the land, and feed on his faithfulness", as also comes out clearly in the connection with the warning not to let oneself be blinded with the works of the godless, since it is easy for God to make a poor man rich. Only the opening exhortation to remain in the רח (verse 20) has a certain resemblance to the κλῆσις of the Gospel, but here Luther did not use the word *Beruf* for the Greek διαθήκη. The connection between Luther's two seemingly quite unrelated uses of the word *Beruf* is found in the first letter to the Corinthians and its translation.

In the usual modern editions, the whole context in which the passage stands is as follows, 1 Cor. vii. 17 (English, King James version [American revision, 1901]): "(17) Only as the Lord hath distributed to each man, as God hath called each, so let him walk. And so ordain I in all churches. (18) Was any man called being circumcised? let him not become uncircumcised. Hath any man been called in uncircumcision? let him not be circumcised. (19) Circumcision is nothing and uncircumcision is nothing; but the keeping of the commandments of God. (20) Let each man abide in that calling wherein he was called (ἐν τῇ κλήσει ἦ ἐκλήθη; an undoubted Herbraism, as Professor Merx tells me). (21) Wast thou called being a bondservant? care not for it; nay even if thou canst become free use it rather. (22) For he that was called in the Lord being a bondservant is the Lord's freedman; likewise he that was called being free is Christ's bondservant. (23) Ye were bought with a price; become not bondservants of men. (24) Brethren, let each man, wherein he was called, therein abide with God."

In verse 29 follows the remark that time is shortened, followed by the well-known commandments motivated by eschatological expectations: (31) to possess women as though one did not have them, to buy as though one did not have what one had bought, etc. In verse 20 Luther, following the older German translations, even in 1523 in his exigesis of this chapter, renders κλῆσις with *Beruf* [call], and interprets it with *Stand* [social status]. (Erlangen ed., LI, p. 51.)

In fact it is evident that the word κλῆσις at this point, and only at this, corresponds approximately to the Latin *status* and the German *Stand* (status of marriage, status of a servant, etc.). But of course not as Brentano, *op. cit.*, p. 137, assumes, in the modern sense of *Beruf*. Brentano can hardly have read this passage, or what I have said about it, very carefully. In a sense at least suggesting it this word, which is etymologically related to ἐκκλησία an assembly which has been called, occurs in Greek literature, so far as the lexicons tell, only once in a passage from Dionysius of Halicarnassus, where it corresponds to the Latin *classis*, a word borrowed from the Greek, meaning that part of the citizenry which has been called to the colours. Theophylaktos (eleventh-twelfth century) interprets 1 Cor. vii. 20: ἐνοίῳ βιῳ καὶ ἐν οἴῳ τάλματι καὶ πολιτεύματι ὄν ἐττίστευσεν [one should stay in the position of one's calling in life, classes, and one's activities as a citizen]. (My colleague Professor Deissmann called my attention to this passage.) Now, even in our passage, κλῆσις does not correspond to the modern *Beruf*. But having translated κλῆσις with *Beruf* in the eschatologically motivated exhortation, that everyone should remain in his present status, Luther, when he later came to translate the Apocrypha, would naturally, on account of the similar content of the exhortations alone, also use *Beruf* for πόνος in the traditionalistic and anti-chrematistic commandment of Jesus Sirach, that everyone should remain in the same business. This is what is important and characteristic. The passage in 1 Cor. vii. 17 does not, as has been pointed out, use κλῆσις at all in the sense of *Beruf*, a definite field of activity.

In the meantime (or about the same time), in the *Augsburg Confession*, the Protestant dogma of the uselessness of the Catholic attempt to excel worldly morality was established, and in it the expression "einem jeglichen nach seinem Beruf" [every person according to his calling] was used (see previous note). In Luther's translation, both this and the positive valuation of the order in which the individual was placed, as holy, which was gaining ground just about the beginning of the 1530s, stand out. It was a result of his more and more sharply defined belief in special Divine Providence, even in the details of life, and at the same time of his increasing inclination to accept the existing order of things in the world as immutably willed by God. *Vocatio*, in the traditional Latin, meant the divine call to a life of holiness, especially in a monastery or as a priest. But now, under the influence of this dogma, life in a worldly calling came for Luther to have the same connotation. For he now translated πόνος and ἔργον in Jesus Sirach with *Beruf*, for which, up to that time, there had been only the (Latin) analogy, coming from the monastic translation. But a few years earlier, in Prov. xxii. 29, he had still translated the Hebrew מְלָאכָה, which was the original of ἔργον in the Greek text of Jesus Sirach, and which, like the German *Beruf* and the Scandinavian *kald, kallelse*, originally related to a *spiritual* call (*Beruf*), as in other passages (Gen. xxxix. 11), with *Geschäft* (Septuagint ἔργον, Vulgate *opus*, English Bibles *business*, and correspondingly in the Scandinavian and all the other translations before me).

The word *Beruf*, in the modern sense which he had finally created, remained for the time being entirely Lutheran. To the Calvinists the Apocrypha are entirely uncanonical. It was only as a result of the development which brought the interest in proof of salvation to the fore that Luther's concept was taken over, and then strongly emphasized by them. But in their first (Romance) translations they had no such word available, and no power to create one in the usage of a language already so stereotyped.

As early as the sixteenth century the concept of *Beruf* in its present sense became established in secular literature. The Bible translators before Luther had used the word *Berufung* [appointment to a position] for κλῆσις (as for instance in the Heidelberg versions of 1462–66 and 1485), and the Eck translation of 1537 says "in dem Ruf, worin er beruft ist" [in the call to which one is called]. Most of the later Catholic translators directly follow Luther. In England, the first of all, Wyclif's translation (1382), used *cleping* (the Old English word which was later replaced by the borrowed *calling*). It is quite characteristic of the Lollard ethics to use a word which already corresponded to the later usage of the Reformation. Tyndale's translation of 1534, on the other hand, interprets the idea in terms of *status*: "in the same state wherein he was called", as also does the Geneva Bible of 1557. Cranmer's official translation of 1539 substituted *calling* for *state*, while the (Catholic) Bible of Rheims (1582), as well as the Anglican Court Bibles of the Elizabethan era, characteristically return to vocation, following the Vulgate.

That for England, Cranmer's Bible translation is the source of the Puritan conception of calling in the sense of *Beruf*, trade, has already, quite correctly, been pointed out by

Murray. As early as the middle of the sixteenth century calling is used in that sense. In 1588 unlawful callings are referred to, and in 1603 greater callings in the sense of higher occupations, etc. (see Murray). Quite remarkable is Brentano's idea (*op. cit.*, p. 139), that in the Middle Ages *vocatio* was not translated with *Beruf*, and that this concept was not known, because only a free man could engage in a *Beruf*, and freemen, in the middle-class professions, did not exist at that time. Since the whole social structure of the mediæval crafts, as opposed to those of antiquity, rested upon free labour, and, above all, almost all the merchants were freemen, I do not clearly understand this thesis.

4. What is commanded [*Editor*].

5. What is advised [*Editor*].

6. Compare with the following the instructive discussion in K. Eger, *Die Anschauung Luthers vom Beruf* (Giessen, 1900). Perhaps its only serious fault, which is shared by almost all other theological writers, is his insufficiently clear analysis of the concept of *lex naturæ*. On this see E. Troeltsch in his review of Seeberg's *Dogmengeschichte*, and now above all in the relevant parts of his *Soziallehren der christlichen Kirchen*.

7. For when Thomas Aquinas represents the division of men into estates and occupational groups as the work of divine providence, by that he means the objective cosmos of society. But that the individual should take up a particular calling (as we should say; Thomas, however, says *ministerium* or *officium*) is due to *causæ naturales* [natural causes]. *Quæst. quodlibetal*, VII, Art. 17c. "Hæc autem diversificatio hominum in diversis officiis contingit primo ex divina providentia, quæ ita hominum status distribuit . . . secundo etiam ex causis naturalibus, ex quibus contingit, quod in diversis hominibus sunt diversæ inclinationes ad diversa officia . . ." [This division of people in different occupations comes firstly from God's providence, according to which these are allotted. This apportioning is due, secondly, to natural causes for different inclinations toward the different occupations that exist in different people.]

   Quite similar to Pascal's view-point when he says that it is chance which determines the choice of a calling. See on Pascal, A. Koester, *Die Ethik Pascals* (1907). Of the organic systems of religious ethics, only the most complete of them, the Indian, is different in this respect. The difference between the Thomistic and the Protestant ideas of the calling is so evident that we may dismiss it for the present with the above quotation. This is true even as between the Thomistic and the later Lutheran ethics, which are very similar in many other respects, especially in their emphasis on Providence. We shall return later to a discussion of the Catholic view-point. On Thomas Aquinas, see Mauren brecher, *Thomas von Aquino's Stellung zum Wirtschaftsleben seiner Zeit*, 1888. Otherwise, where Luther agrees with Thomas in details, he has probably been influenced rather by the general doctrines of Scholasticism than by Thomas in particular. For, according to Denifle's investigations, he seems really not to have known Thomas very well. See Denifle, *Luther und Luthertum* (1903), p. 501, and on it, Koehler, *Ein Wort zu Denifles Luther* (1904), p. 25.

8. In *Von der Freiheit eines Cristenmenschen*, (1) the double nature of man is used for the justification of worldly duties in the sense of the *lex naturæ* [here the natural order of the world). From that it follows (Erlangen edition, 27, p. 188) that man is inevitably bound to his body and to the social community. (2) In this situation he will (p. 196: this is a second justification), if he is a believing Christian, decide to repay God's act of grace, which was done for pure love, by love of his neighbour. With this very loose connection between faith and love is combined (3) (p. 190) the old ascetic justification of labour as a means of securing to the inner man mastery over the body. (4) Labour is hence, as the reasoning is continued with another appearance of the idea of *lex naturæ* in another sense (here, natural morality), an original instinct given by God to Adam (before the fall), which he has obeyed "solely to please God". Finally (5) (pp. 161 and 199), there appears, in connection with Matt. vii. 18 f., the idea that good work in one's ordinary calling is and must be the result of the renewal of life, caused by faith, without, however, developing the most important Calvinistic idea of proof. The powerful emotion which dominates the work explains the presence of such contradictory ideas.

9. By faith alone [*Editor*].

10. Evangelical councils [*Editor*].

11. "It is not from the benevolence of the butcher, the brewer, or the baker, that we expect our dinner, but from their regard to their own interest. We address ourselves, not to their humanity, but to their self-love; and never talk to them of our own necessities, but of their advantages" (*Wealth of Nations*, Book I, chap. ii).

12. "Omnia enim per te operabitur (Deus), mulgebit per te vaccam et servilissima quæque opera faciet, ac maxima pariter et minima ipsi grata erunt" [in effect, it is through you that He (God) will operate everything, milk the cow and perform the most servile tasks; the great as well as the low tasks please him equally] (*Exigesis of Genesis, Opera lat. exeget.*, ed., Elsperger, VII, p. 213). The idea is found before Luther in Tauler, who holds the spiritual and the worldly *Ruf* to be in principle of equal value. The difference from

the Thomistic view is common to the German mystics and Luther. It may be said that Thomas, principally to retain the moral value of contemplation, but also from the viewpoint of the mendicant friar, is forced to interpret Paul's doctrine that "if a man will not work he shall not eat" in the sense that labour, which is of course necessary *lege naturæ* [through the law], is imposed upon the human race as a whole, but not on all individuals. The gradation in the value of forms of labour, from the *opera servilia* [servile work] of the peasants upwards, is connected with the specific character of the mendicant friars, who were for material reasons bound to the town as a place of domicile. It was equally foreign to the German mystics and to Luther, the peasant's son; both of them, while valuing all occupations equally, looked upon their order of rank as willed by God. For the relevant passages in Thomas see Maurenbrecher, *op. cit.*, pp. 65 ff.

13. It is astonishing that some investigators can maintain that such a change could have been without effect upon the actions of men. I confess my inability to understand such a view.

14. "Vanity is so firmly imbedded in the human heart that a camp-follower, a kitchen-helper, or a porter, boast and seek admirers. . . ." (Faugeres edition, I, p. 208. Compare Koester, *op. cit.*, pp. 17, 136 ff.). On the attitude of Port Royal and the Jansenists to the calling, to which we shall return, see now the excellent study of Dr. Paul Honigsheim, *Die Staats- und Soziallehren der französischen Jansenisten im 17ten Jahrhundert* (Heidelberg Historical Dissertation, 1914. It is a separately printed part of a more comprehensive work on the *Vorgeschichte der französischen Aufklärung*. Compare especially pp. 138 ff.).

15. Apropos of the Fuggers, he thinks that it "cannot be right and godly for such a great and regal fortune to be piled up in the lifetime of one man". That is evidently the peasant's mistrust of capital. Similarly (*Grosser Sermon vom Wucher*, Erlangen edition, XX, p. 109) investment in securities he considers ethically undesirable, because it is "ein neues behendes erfunden Ding" [a newly discovered clever thing] i.e. because it is to him economically incomprehensible; somewhat like margin trading to the modern clergyman.

16. The difference is well worked out by H. Levy (in his study, *Die Grundlagen des ökonomischen Liberalismus in der Geschichte der englischen Volkswirtschaft*, Jena, 1912). Compare also, for instance, the petition of the Levellers in Cromwell's army of 1653 against monopolies and companies, given in Gardiner, *Commonwealth*, II, p. 179. Laud's regime, on the other hand, worked for a Christian, social, economic organization under the joint leadership of Crown and Church, from which the King hoped for political and fiscal-monopolistic advantages. It was against just this that the Puritans were struggling.

17. What I understand by this may be shown by the example of the proclamation addressed by Cromwell to the Irish in 1650, with which he opened his war against them and which formed his reply to the manifestos of the Irish (Catholic) clergy of Clonmacnoise of December 4 and 13, 1649. The most important sentences follow: "Englishmen had good inheritances (namely in Ireland) which many of them purchased with their money . . . they had good leases from Irishmen for long time to come, great stocks thereupon, houses and plantations erected at their cost and charge. . . . You broke the union . . . at a time when Ireland was in perfect peace and when, through the example of English industry, through commerce and traffic, that which was in the nation's hands was better to them than if all Ireland had been in their possession. . . . Is God, will God be with you? I am confident He will not."

This proclamation, which is suggestive of articles in the English Press at the time of the Boer War, is not characteristic, because the capitalistic interests of Englishmen are held to be the justification of the war. That argument could, of course, have just as well been made use of, for instance, in a quarrel between Venice and Genoa over their respective spheres of influence in the Orient (which, in spite of my pointing it out here, Brentano, *op. cit.*, p. 142, strangely enough holds against me). On the contrary, what is interesting in the document is that Cromwell, with the deepest personal conviction, as everyone who knows his character will agree, bases the moral justification of the subjection of the Irish, in calling God to witness, on the fact that English capital has taught the Irish to work. (The proclamation is in Carlyle, and is also reprinted and analysed in Gardiner, *History of the Commonwealth*, I, pp. 163 f.)

18. This is not the place to follow the subject farther. Compare the authors cited in note 21 below.

19. Mammon of unrighteousness [*Editor*].

20. Compare the remarks in Jülicher's fine book, *Die Gleichnisreden Jesu*, II, pp. 108, 636 f.

21. With what follows, compare above all the discussion in Eger, *op. cit.* Also Schneckenburger's fine work, which is even to-day not yet out of date (*Vergleichende Darstellung der lutherischen und reformierten Lehrbegriffe*, Grüder, Stuttgart, 1855). Luthardt's *Ethik Luthers*, p. 84 of the first edition, the only one to which I have had access, gives no real picture of the development. Further compare Seeberg, *Dogmengeschichte*, II, pp. 262 ff. The article on *Beruf* in the *Realenzyklopädie für protestantische Theologie und Kirche* is valueless. Instead of a scientific analysis of the conception and its origin, it contains all sorts of rather sentimental observations on all possible subjects, such as the position of

women, etc. Of the economic literature on Luther, I refer here only to Schmoller's studies ("Geschichte der Nationalökonomischen Ansichten in Deutschland während der
Reformationszeit", *Zeitschrift f. Staatswiss.*, XVI, 1860); Wiskemann's prize essay (1861);
and the study of Frank G. Ward ("Darstellung und Würdigung von Luthers Ansichten
vom Staat und seinen wirtschaftlichen Aufgaben", *Conrads Abhandlungen*, XXI, Jena,
1898). The literature on Luther in commemoration of the anniversary of the Reformation, part of which is excellent, has, so far as I can see, made no definite contribution to
this particular problem. On the social ethics of Luther (and the Lutherans) compare, of
course, the relevant parts of Troeltsch's *Soziallehren.*

22. *Analysis of the Seventh Chapter of the First Epistle to the Corinthians*, 1523, Erlangen edi-
    tion, LI, p. 1. Here Luther still interprets the idea of the freedom of every calling before
    God in the sense of this passage, so as to emphasize (1) that certain human institutions
    should be repudiated (monastic vows, the prohibition of mixed marriages, etc.), (2) that
    the fulfillment of traditional worldly duties to one's neighbour (in itself indifferent before
    God) is turned into a commandment of brotherly love. In fact this characteristic reason-
    ing (for instance pp. 55, 56) fundamentally concerns the question of the dualism of the
    *lex naturæ* in its relations with divine justice.

23. Compare the passage from *Von Kaufhandlung und Wucher*, which Sombart rightly uses
    as a motto for his treatment of the handicraft spirit (= traditionalism): "Darum musst du
    dir fürsetzen, nichts denn deine ziemliche Nahrung zu suchen in solchem Handel,
    danach Kost, Mühe, Arbeit und Gefahr rechnen und überschlagen und also dann die
    Ware selbst setzen, steigern oder niedern, dass du solcher Arbeit und Mühe Lohn davon
    hasst." The principle is formulated in a thoroughly Thomistic spirit.

24. As early as the letter to H. von Sternberg of 1530, in which he dedicates the Exigesis of
    the 117th Psalm to him, the estate of the lower nobility appears to him, in spite of its
    moral degradation, as ordained of God (Erlangen edition, XL, pp. 282 ff.). The decisive
    influence of the Münzer disturbances in developing this view-point can clearly be seen
    in the letter (p. 282). Compare also Eger, *op. cit.,* p. 150.

25. Also in the analysis of the 111th Psalm, verses 5 and 6 (Erlangen edition, XL, pp.
    215–16), written in 1530, the starting-point is the polemics against withdrawal from the
    world into monasteries. But in this case the *lex naturæ* [natural law] (as distinct from pos-
    itive law made by the Emperor and the Jurists) is directly identical with divine justice. It
    is God's ordinance, and includes especially the division of the people into classes (p. 215).
    The equal value of the classes is emphasized, but only in the sight of God.

26. As taught especially in the works *Von Konzilien und Kirchen* (1539) and *Kurzer Beken-
    ntnis vom heiligen Sakrament* (1545).

27. How far in the background of Luther's thought was the most important idea of proof of
    the Christian in his calling and his worldly conduct, which dominated Calvinism, is
    shown by this passage from *Von Konzilien und Kirchen* (1539, Erlangen edition, XXV, p.
    376): "Besides these seven principal signs there are more superficial ones by which the
    holy Christian Church can be known. If we are not unchaste nor drunkards, proud, inso-
    lent, nor extravagant, but chaste, modest, and temperate." According to Luther these
    signs are not so infallible as the others (purity of doctrine, prayer, etc.). "Because certain
    of the heathen have borne themselves so and sometimes even appeared holier than Chris-
    tians." Calvin's personal position was, as we shall see, not very different, but that was not
    true of Puritanism. In any case, for Luther the Christian serves God only *in vocatione*
    [when in a vocation], not *per vocationem* [for a vocation] (Eger, pp. 117 ff.). Of the idea
    of proof, on the other hand (more, however, in its Pietistic than its Calvinistic form), there
    are at least isolated suggestions in the German mystics (see for instance in Seeberg, *Dog-
    mengeschichte*, p. 195, the passage from Suso, as well as those from Tauler quoted above),
    even though it was understood only in a psychological sense.

28. His final position is well expressed in some parts of the exegesis of Genesis (in the *op. lat.
    exeget.* edited by Elsperger).

    Vol. IV, p. 109: "Neque hæc fuit levis tentatio, intentum esse suæ vocationi et de aliis
    non esse curiosum. . . . Paucissimi sunt, qui sua sorte vivant contenti . . . (p. 111). Nos-
    trum autem est, ut vocanti Deo pareamus . . . (p. 112). Regula igitur hæc servanda est, ut
    unusquisque maneat in sua vocatione et suo dono contentus vivat, de aliis autem non sit
    curiosus" [It is not easy to apply oneself to one's own calling, without caring about those
    of others. . . . Those who are only concerned with their own fate are rare indeed. . . . (p.
    111). It behooves us to obey God when he calls us. . . . (p. 112) That is why one must
    observe this rule: that everyone stays in their own calling, and is content with his lot, with-
    out being concerned with others . . . ]. In effect that is thoroughly in accordance with
    Thomas Aquinas's formulation of traditionalism (*Secunda secundæ*, Quest. 118, Art. 1):
    "Unde necese eat, quod bonum hominis circa ea consistat in quadam mensura, dum scil-
    icet homo . . . quærit habere exteriores divitas, prout sunt necessariæ ad vitam ejus secun-
    dum suam conditionem. Et ideo in excessu hujus mensuræ consistit peccatum, dum

scilicet aliquis supra debitum modum vult eas vel acquirere vel retinere, quod pertinet ad avaritiam" [It follows necessarily that from this viewpoint the good of man consists of being measured in his pursuit of outer riches and only wanting what is necessary for one's existence and conforms to one's station in life. This is why it is a sin to go beyond this, for example when one wants to acquire or keep riches beyond this measure, which is a sign of cupidity]. The sinfulness of the pursuit of acquisition beyond the point set by the needs of one's station in life is based by Thomas on the *lex naturæ* as revealed by the purpose (ratio) of external goods; by Luther, on the other hand, on God's will. On the relation of faith and the calling in Luther see also Vol. VII, p. 225: ". . . quando es fidelis, tum placent Deo etiam physica, carnalia, animalia, officia, sive edas, sive bibas, sive vigiles, sive dormias, quæ mere corporalia et animalia sunt. Tanta res est fides. . . . Verum est quidem, placere Deo etiam in impiis sedulitatem et industriam in officio [ . . . from the moment that you believe, even physical, bodily and animalistic functions please God; that you eat, that you drink, that you are awake or sleep, all purely bodily or animalistic functions. Faith is so great. . . . But the truth is that even for the nonbelievers, energy and application to one's task please God]. [This activity in practical life is a virtue *lege naturæ*] [through the law] sed obstat incredulitas et vana gloria, ne possint opera sua referre ad gloriam Dei [But their lack of faith and their vain glory prevents them from carrying out their task for the glory of God . . . ] [reminiscent of Calvinistic ways of speaking). . . . Merentur igitur etiam impiorum bona opera in hac quidem vita præmia sua [That is why the good work of non-believers merit reward, at least in this life] [as distinct from Augustine's 'vitia specie virtutum palliata'] ["vices disguised as virtues"] sed non numerantur, non colliguntur in altero" [but they are not counted or considered in the world beyond].

29. In the *Kirchenpostille* it runs (Erlangen edition, X, pp. 233, 235–6): "Everyone is called to some calling." He should wait for this call (on p. 236 it even becomes command) and serve God in it. God takes pleasure not in man's achievements but in his obedience in this respect.

30. This explains why, in contrast to what has been said above about the effects of Pietism on women workers, modern business men sometimes maintain that strict Lutheran domestic workers to-day often, for instance in Westphalia, think very largely in traditional terms. Even without going over to the factory system, and in spite of the temptation of higher earnings, they resist changes in methods of work, and in explanation maintain that in the next world such trifles won't matter anyway. It is evident that the mere fact of Church membership and belief is not in itself of essential significance for conduct as a whole. It has been much more concrete religious values and ideals which have influenced the development of capitalism in its early stages and, to a lesser extent, still do.

31. Compare Tauler, Basle edition, *Bl.*, pp. 161 ff.

32. Compare the peculiarly emotional sermon of Tauler referred to above, and the following one, 17, 18, verse 20.

33. Since this is the sole purpose of these present remarks on Luther, I have limited them to a brief preliminary sketch, which would, of course, be wholly inadequate as an appraisal of Luther's influence as a whole.

34. One who shared the philosophy of history of the Levellers would be in the fortunate position of being able to attribute this in turn to racial differences. They believed themselves to be the defenders of the Anglo-Saxon birthright, against the descendants of William the Conqueror and the Normans. It is astonishing enough that it has not yet occurred to anyone to maintain that the plebeian Roundheads were round-headed in the anthropometric sense!

35. Especially the English national pride, a result of Magna Charta and the great wars. The saying, so typical to-day, "She looks like an English girl" on seeing any pretty foreign girl, is reported as early as the fifteenth century.

36. These differences have, of course, persisted in England as well. Especially the Squirearchy has remained the centre of "merrie old England" down to the present day, and the whole period since the Reformation may be looked upon as a struggle of the two elements in English society. In this point I agree with M. J. Bonn's remarks (in the *Frankfurter Zeitung*) on the excellent study of v. Schulze-Gaevernitz on British Imperialism. Compare H. Levy in the *Archiv für Sozialwissenschaft und Sozialpolitik*, 46, 3.

37. In spite of this and the following remarks, which in my opinion are clear enough, and have never been changed, I have again and again been accused of this.

38. "Elective affinities" is generally considered a more appropriate translation of *Wahlverwandtschaften* than Parsons' "correlations." [*Editor*]

## 4 THE RELIGIOUS FOUNDATIONS OF WORLDLY ASCETICISIM

1. Zwinglianism we do not discuss separately, since after a short lease of power it rapidly lost in importance. Arminianism, the dogmatic peculiarity of which consisted in the repudiation of the doctrine of predestination in its strict form, and which also repudiated worldly

asceticism, was organized as a sect only in Holland (and the United States). In this chapter it is without interest to us, or has only the negative interest of having been the religion of the merchant patricians in Holland (see below). In dogma it resembled the Anglican Church and most of the Methodist denominations. Its Erastian position (i.e. upholding the sovereignty of the State even in Church matters) was, however, common to all the authorities with purely political interests: the Long Parliament in England, Elizabeth, the Dutch States-General, and, above all, Oldenbarnereldt.

2. On the development of the concept of Puritanism see, above all, Sanford, *Studies and Reflections of the Great Rebellion*, p. 65 f. When we use the expression it is always in the sense which it took on in the popular speech of the seventeenth century, to mean the ascetically inclined religious movements in Holland and England without distinction of Church organization or dogma, thus including Independents, Congregationalists, Baptists, Mennonites, and Quakers.

3. This has been badly misunderstood in the discussion of these questions. Especially Sombart, but also Brentano, continually cite the ethical writers (mostly those of whom they have heard through me) as codifications of rules of conduct without ever asking which of them were supported by psychologically effective religious sanctions.

4. I hardly need to emphasize that this sketch, so far as it is concerned solely with the field of dogma, falls back everywhere on the formulations of the literature of the history of the Church and of doctrine. It makes no claim whatever to originality. Naturally I have attempted, so far as possible, to acquaint myself with the sources for the history of the Reformation. But to ignore in the process the intensive and acute theological research of many decades, instead of, as is quite indispensable, allowing oneself to be led from it to the sources, would have been presumption indeed. I must hope that the necessary brevity of the sketch has not led to incorrect formulations, and that I have at least avoided important misunderstandings of fact. The discussion contributes something new for those familiar with theological literature only in the sense that the whole is, of course, considered from the point of view of our problem. For that reason many of the most important points, for instance the rational character of this asceticism and its significance for modern life, have naturally not been emphasized by theological writers.

This aspect, and in general the sociological side, has, since the appearance of this study, been systematically studied in the work of E. Troeltsch, mentioned above, whose *Gerhard und Melancthon*, as well as numerous reviews in the *Gött. Gel. Anz.*, contained several preliminary studies to his great work. For reasons of space the references have not included everything which has been used, but for the most part only those works which that part of the text follows, or which are directly relevant to it. These are often older authors, where our problems have seemed closer to them. The insufficient pecuniary resources of German libraries have meant that in the provinces the most important source materials or studies could only be had from Berlin or other large libraries on loan for very short periods. This is the case with Voët, Baxter, Tyermans, Wesley, all the Methodist, Baptist, and Quaker authors, and many others of the earlier writers not contained in the *Corpus Reformatorum*. For any thorough study the use of English and American libraries is almost indispensable. But for the following sketch it was necessary (and possible) to be content with material available in Germany. In America recently the characteristic tendency to deny their own sectarian origins has led many university libraries to provide little or nothing new of that sort of literature. It is an aspect of the general tendency to the secularization of American life which will in a short time have dissolved the traditional national character and changed the significance of many of the fundamental institutions of the country completely and finally. It is now necessary to fall back on the small orthodox sectarian colleges.

5. On Calvin and Calvinism, besides the fundamental work of Kampschulte, the best source of information is the discussion of Erick Marcks (in his *Coligny*). Campbell, *The Puritans in Holland, England, and America* (2 vols.), is not always critical and unprejudiced. A strongly partisan anti-Calvinistic study is Pierson, *Studien over Johan Calvijn*. For the development in Holland compare, besides Motley, the Dutch classics, especially Groen van Prinsterer, *Geschiedenis v.h. Vaderland; La Hollande et l'influence de Calvin* (1864); *Le parti anti-révolutionnaire et confessionnel dans l'église des P.B.* (1860) (for modern Holland); further, above all, Fruin's *Tien jaren mit den tachtigjarigen oorlog*, and especially Naber, *Calvinist of Libertijnsch*. Also W. J. F. Nuyens, *Gesch. der kerkel. an pol. geschillen in de Rep. d. Ver. Prov.* (Amsterdam, 1886); A. Köhler, *Die Niederl. ref. Kirche* (Erlangen, 1856), for the nineteenth century. For France, besides Polenz, now Baird, *Rise of the Huguenots*. For England, besides Carlyle, Macaulay, Masson, and, last but not least, Ranke, above all, now the various works of Gardiner and Firth. Further, Taylor, *A Retrospect of the Religious Life in England* (1854), and the excellent book of Weingarten, *Die englischen Revolutionskirchen*. Then the article on the English Moralists by E. Troeltsch in the *Realenzyklopädie für protestantische Theologie und Kirche*, third edition, and of course his *Soziallehren*. Also E. Bernstein's excellent essay in the *Geschichte des Sozialismus*

(Stuttgart, 1895, I, p. 50 ff.). The best bibliography (over seven thousand titles) is in Dexter, *Congregationalism of the Last Three Hundred Years* (principally, though not exclusively, questions of Church organization). The book is very much better than Price (*History of Nonconformism*), Skeats, and others. For Scotland see, among others, Sack, *Die Kirche von Schottland* (1844), and the literature on John Knox. For the American colonies the outstanding work is Doyle, *The English in America*. Further, Daniel Wait Howe, *The Puritan Republic*; J. Brown, *The Pilgrim Fathers of New England and their Puritan Successors* (third edition, Revell). Further references will be given later.

For the differences of doctrine the following presentation is especially indebted to Schneckenburger's lectures cited above. Ritschl's fundamental work, *Die christliche Lehre von der Rechtfertigung und Versöhnung* (references to Vol. III of third edition), in its mixture of historical method with judgments of value, shows the marked peculiarities of the author, who with all his fine acuteness of logic does not always give the reader the certainty of objectivity. Where, for instance, he differs from Schneckenburger's interpretation I am often doubtful of his correctness, however little I presume to have an opinion of my own. Further, what he selects out of the great variety of religious ideas and feelings as the Lutheran doctrine often seems to be determined by his own preconceptions. It is what Ritschl himself conceives to be of permanent value in Lutheranism. It is Lutheranism as Ritschl would have had it, not always as it was. That the works of Karl Müller, Seeberg, and others have everywhere been made use of it is unnecessary to mention particularly. If in the following I have condemned the reader as well as myself to the penitence of a malignant growth of footnotes, it has been done in order to give especially the non-theological reader an opportunity to check up the validity of this sketch by the suggestion of related lines of thought.

6. In the following discussion we are not primarily interested in the origin, antecedents, or history of these ascetic movements, but take their doctrines as given in a state of full development.

7. For the following discussion I may here say definitely that we are not studying the personal views of Calvin, but Calvinism, and that in the form to which it had evolved by the end of the sixteenth and in the seventeenth centuries in the great areas where it had a decisive influence and which were at the same time the home of capitalistic culture. For the present, Germany is neglected entirely, since pure Calvinism never dominated large areas here. Reformed is, of course, by no means identical with Calvinistic.

8. Even the Declaration agreed upon between the University of Cambridge and the Archbishop of Canterbury on the 17th Article of the Anglican Confession, the so-called Lambeth Article of 1595, which (contrary to the official version) expressly held that there was also predestination to eternal death, was not ratified by the Queen. The Radicals (as in *Hanserd Knolly's Confession*) laid special emphasis on the express predestination to death (not only the admission of damnation, as the milder doctrine would have it).

9. *Westminster Confession*, fifth official edition, London, 1717. Compare the Savoy and the (American) *Hanserd Knolly's Declarations*. On predestination and the Huguenots see, among others, Polenz, I, pp. 545 ff.

10. On Milton's theology see the essay of Eibach in the *Theol. Studien und Kritiken*, 1879. Macaulay's essay on it, on the occasion of Sumner's translation of the *Doctrina Christiana*, rediscovered in 1823 (Tauchnitz edition, 185, pp. 1 ff.), is superficial. For more detail see the somewhat too schematic six-volume English work of Masson, and the German biography of Milton by Stern which rests upon it. Milton early began to grow away from the doctrine of predestination in the form of the double decree, and reached a wholly free Christianity in his old age. In his freedom from the tendencies of his own time he may in a certain sense be compared to Sebastian Franck. Only Milton was a practical and positive person, Franck predominantly critical. Milton is a Puritan only in the broader sense of the rational organization of his life in the world in accordance with the divine will, which formed the permanent inheritance of later times from Calvinism. Franck could be called a Puritan in much the same sense. Both, as isolated figures, must remain outside our investigation.

11. "Hic est fides summus gradus; credere Deum esse clementem, qui tam paucos salvat, justum, qui sua voluntate nos damnabiles facit" [Such is the supreme degree of faith: that we believe in the clemency of God, he who saves so few; that we believe in his justice, he who has made us into condemned beings], is the text of the famous passage in *De servo arbitrio*.

12. The truth is that both Luther and Calvin believed fundamentally in a double God (see Ritschl's remarks in *Geschichte des Pietismus* and Köstlin, *Gott in Realenzyklopädie für protestantische Theologie und Kirche*, third edition), the gracious and kindly Father of the New Testament, who dominates the first books of the *Institutio Christiana*, and behind him the *Deus absconditus* [hidden God] as an arbitrary despot. For Luther, the God of the New Testament kept the upper hand, because he avoided reflection on metaphysical questions as useless and dangerous, while for Calvin the idea of a transcendental God won out. In the

popular development of Calvinism, it is true, this idea could not be maintained, but what took his place was not the Heavenly Father of the New Testament but the Jehovah of the Old.

13. Horrible decree [on predestination] [*Editor*].

14. Compare on the following: Scheibe, *Calvins Prädestinationslehre* (Halle, 1897). On Calvinistic theology in general, Heppe, *Dogmatik des evangelisch-reformierten Kirche* (Elberfeld, 1861).

15. *Corpus Reformatorum*, LXXVII, pp. 186 ff.

16. The preceding exposition of the Calvinistic doctrine can be found in much the same form as here given, for instance in Hoornbeek's *Theologia practica* (Utrecht, 1663), L. II, c. 1; *de predestinatione*, the section stands characteristically directly under the heading *De Deo*. The Biblical foundation for it is principally the first chapter of the Epistle to the Ephesians. It is unnecessary for us here to analyse the various inconsistent attempts to combine with the predestination and providence of God the responsibility and free will of the individual. They began as early as in Augustine's first attempt to develop the doctrine.

17. "The deepest community (with God) is found not in institutions or corporations or churches, but in the secrets of a solitary heart", as Dowden puts the essential point in his fine book *Puritan and Anglican* (p. 234). This deep spiritual loneliness of the individual applied as well to the Jansenists of Port Royal, who were also predestinationists.

18. External helps [*Editor*].

19. Outside the Church, there is no salvation [*Editor*].

20. "Contra qui huiusmodi cœtum [namely a Church which maintains a pure doctrine, sacraments, and Church discipline] contemnunt . . . salutis suæ certi esse non possunt; et qui in illo contemtu perseverat electus non est" [On the contrary, those who have contempt for an assembly of this type . . . cannot be assured of their salvation; and he who persists in such contempt is not among the chosen]. Olevian, *De subst. Fœd.*, p. 222.

21. "It is said that God sent His Son to save the human race, but that was not His purpose, He only wished to help a few out of their degradation—and I say unto you that God died only for the elect" (sermon held in 1609 at Broek, near Rogge, Wtenbogaert, II, p. 9. Compare Nuyens, *op. cit.*, II, p. 232). The explanation of the role of Christ is also confused in *Hanserd Knolly's Confession*. It is everywhere assumed that God did not need His instrumentality.

22. *Entzauberung der Welt* [disenchantment of the world]. On this process see the other essays in my *Wirtschaftsethik der Weltreligionen* [*The Economic Ethics of the World Religions*]. The peculiar position of the old Hebrew ethic, as compared with the closely related ethics of Egypt and Babylon, and its development after the time of the prophets, rested, as is shown there, entirely on this fundamental fact, the rejection of sacramental magic as a road to salvation. (This process is for Weber one of the most important aspects of the broader process of rationalization, in which he sums up his philosophy of history. See various parts of *Wirtschaft und Gesellschaft* [*Economy and Society*] and H. Grab, *Der Begriff des Rationalen bei Max Weber*.—TRANSLATOR'S NOTE.)

23. Similarly the most consistent doctrine held that baptism was required by positive ordinance, but was not necessary to salvation. For that reason the strictly Puritan Scotch and English Independents were able to maintain the principle that children of obvious reprobates should not be baptized (for instance, children of drunkards). An adult who desired to be baptized, but was not yet ripe for the communion, the Synod of Edam of 1586 (Art. 32, 1) recommended should be baptized only if his conduct were blameless, and he should have placed his desires *sonder superstitie* [beyond being influenced by superstitions].

24. This negative attitude toward all sensuous culture is, as Dowden, *op. cit.*, shows, a very fundamental element of Puritanism.

25. The expression individualism includes the most heterogeneous things imaginable. What is here understood by it will, I hope, be clear from the following discussion. In another sense of the word, Lutheranism has been called individualistic, because it does not attempt any ascetic regulation of life. In yet another quite different sense the word is used, for example, by Dietrich Schäfer when in his study, "Zur Beurteilung des Wormser Konkordats", *Abh. d. Berl. Akad.* (1905), he calls the Middle Ages the era of pronounced individuality because, for the events relevant for the historian, irrational factors then had a significance which they do not possess to-day. He is right, but so perhaps are also those whom he attacks in his remarks, for they mean something quite different, when they speak of individuality and individualism. Jacob Burckhardt's brilliant ideas are to-day at least partly out of date, and a thorough analysis of these concepts in historical terms would at the present time be highly valuable to science. Quite the opposite is, of course, true when the play impulse causes certain historians to define the concept in such a way as to enable them to use it as a label for any epoch of history they please.

26. And in a similar, though naturally less sharp, contrast to the later Catholic doctrine. The deep pessimism of Pascal, which also rests on the doctrine of predestination, is, on the

other hand, of Jansenist origin, and the resulting individualism of renunciation by no means agrees with the official Catholic position. See the study by Honigsheim on the French Jansenists, referred to in Chap. 3, note 14.

27. The same holds for the Jansenists.

28. Bailey, *Praxis pietatis* (German edition, Leipzig, 1724); p. 187. Also P. J. Spener in his *Theologische Bedenken* (according to third edition, Halle, 1712) adopts a similar standpoint. A friend seldom gives advice for the glory of God, but generally for mundane (though not necessarily egotistical) reasons. "He [the knowing man] is blind in no man's cause, but best sighted in his own. He confines himself to the circle of his own affairs and thrusts not his fingers into needless fires. He sees the falseness of it [the world] and therefore learns to trust himself ever, others so far as not to be damaged by their disappointment", is the philosophy of Thomas Adams (*Works of the Puritan Divines*, p. 11). Bailey (*Praxis pietatis*, p. 176) further recommends every morning before going out among people to imagine oneself going into a wild forest full of dangers, and to pray God for the "cloak of foresight and righteousness". This feeling is characteristic of all the ascetic denominations without exception, and in the case of many Pietists led directly to a sort of hermit's life within the world. Even Spangenberg in the (Moravian) *Idea fides fratum*, p. 382, calls attention with emphasis to Jer. xvii. 5: "Cursed is the man who trusteth in man." To grasp the peculiar misanthropy of this attitude, note also Hoornbeek's remarks (*Theologia practica*, I, p. 882) on the duty to love one's enemy: "Denique hoc magis nos ulcisimur, quo proximum, inultum nobis, tradimus ultori Deo—Quo quis plus se ulscitur, eo minus id pro ipso agit Deus" [We invite revenge on ourselves more likely as a result of what we see in a vindictive God and what we attribute to him. But when a person takes revenge it is he and not God who is acting]. It is the same transfer of vengeance that is found in the parts of the Old Testament written after the exile; a subtle intensification and refinement of the spirit of revenge compared to the older "eye for an eye". On brotherly love, see below, note 39.

29. Of course the confessional did not have only that effect. The explanations, for instance, of Muthmann, *Z. f. Rel. Psych.*, I, Heft 2, p. 65, are too simple for such a highly complex psychological problem as the confessional.

30. This is a fact which is of especial importance for the interpretation of the psychological basis of Calvinistic social organizations. They all rest on spiritually individualistic, rational motives. The individual never enters emotionally into them. The glory of God and one's own salvation always remain above the threshold of consciousness. This accounts for certain characteristic features of the social organization of peoples with a Puritan past even to-day.

31. The fundamentally anti-authoritarian tendency of the doctrine, which at bottom undermined every responsibility for ethical conduct or spiritual salvation on the part of Church or State as useless, led again and again to its proscription, as, for instance, by the States-General of the Netherlands. The result was always the formation of conventicles (as after 1614).

32. On Bunyan compare the biography of Froude in the *English Men of Letters* series, also Macaulay's superficial sketch (*Miscel. Works*, II, p. 227). Bunyan was indifferent to the denominational distinctions within Calvinism, but was himself a strict Calvinistic Baptist.

33. "Greet for me Wotan, greet for me Valhalla—But truly do not speak of Valhalla's cold delights to me" [*Editor*].

34. It is tempting to refer to the undoubted importance for the social character of Reformed Christianity of the necessity for salvation, following from the Calvinistic idea of "incorporation into the body of Christ" (Calvin, *Instit. Christ*, III, 11, 10), of reception into a community conforming to the divine prescriptions. From our point of view, however, the centre of the problem is somewhat different. That doctrinal tenet could have been developed in a Church of purely institutional character (*anstaltsmässig*), and, as is well known, this did happen. But in itself it did not possess the psychological force to awaken the initiative to form such communities nor to imbue them with the power which Calvinism possessed. Its tendency to form a community worked itself out very largely in the world outside the Church organizations ordained by God. Here the belief that the Christian proved (see below) his state of grace by action *in majorem Dei gloriam* [to the greater glory of God] was decisive, and the sharp condemnation of idolatry of the flesh and of all dependence on personal relations to other men was bound unperceived to direct this energy into the field of objective (impersonal) activity. The Christian who took the proof of his state of grace seriously acted in the service of God's ends, and these could only be impersonal. Every purely emotional, that is not rationally motivated, personal relation of man to man easily fell in the Puritan, as in every ascetic ethic, under the suspicion of idolatry of the flesh. In addition to what has already been said, this is clearly shown for the case of friendship by the following warning: "It is an irrational act and not fit for a rational creature to love any one farther than reason will allow us. . . . It very often taketh up men's minds so as to hinder their love of God" (Baxter, *Christian Directory*, IV, p. 253). We shall meet such arguments again and again.

The Calvinist was fascinated by the idea that God in creating the world, including the order of society, must have willed things to be objectively purposeful as a means of adding to His glory; not the flesh for its own sake, but the organization of the things of the flesh under His will. The active energies of the elect, liberated by the doctrine of predestination, thus flowed into the struggle to rationalize the world. Especially the idea that the public welfare, or as Baxter (*Christian Directory*, IV, p. 262) puts it, quite in the sense of later liberal rationalism, "The good of the many" (with a somewhat forced reference to Rom. ix. 3), was to be preferred to any personal or private good of the individual, followed, although not in itself new, for Puritanism from the repudiation of idolatry of the flesh. The traditional American objection to performing personal service is probably connected, besides the other important causes resulting from democratic feelings, at least indirectly with that tradition. Similarly, the relative immunity of formerly Puritan peoples to Cæsarism, and, in general, the subjectively free attitude of the English to their great statesmen as compared with many things which we have experienced since 1878 in Germany positively and negatively. On the one hand, there is a greater willingness to give the great man his due, but, on the other, a repudiation of all hysterical idolization of him and of the naïve idea that political obedience could be due anyone from thankfulness. On the sinfulness of the belief in authority, which is only permissible in the form of an impersonal authority, the Scriptures, as well as of an excessive devotion to even the most holy and virtuous of men, since that might interfere with obedience to God, see Baxter, *Christian Directory* (second edition, 1678), I, p. 56. The political consequences of the renunciation of idolatry of the flesh and the principle which was first applied only to the Church but later to life in general, that God alone should rule, do not belong in this investigation.

35. Of the relation between dogmatic and practical psychological consequence we shall often have to speak. That the two are not identical it is hardly necessary to remark.

36. Social, used of course without any of the implications attached to the modern sense of the word, meaning simply activity within the Church, politics, or any other social organization.

37. For the greater glory of God [*Editor*].

38. "Good works performed for any other purpose than the glory of God are sinful" (*Hanserd Knolly's Confession*, chap. xvi).

39. What such an impersonality of brotherly love, resulting from the orientation of life solely to God's will, means in the field of religious group life itself may be well illustrated by the attitude of the China Inland Mission and the International Missionaries Alliance (see Warneck, *Gesch. d. prot. Missionären*, pp. 99, 111). At tremendous expense an army of missionaries was fitted out, for instance one thousand for China alone, in order by itinerant preaching to offer the Gospel to all the heathen in a strictly literal sense, since Christ had commanded it and made His second coming dependent on it. Whether these heathen should be converted to Christianity and thus attain salvation, even whether they could understand the language in which the missionary preached, was a matter of small importance and could be left to God, Who alone could control such things. According to Hudson Taylor (see Warneck, *op. cit.*), China has about fifty million families; one thousand missionaries could each reach fifty families per day (!) or the Gospel could be presented to all the Chinese in less than three years. It is precisely the same manner in which, for instance, Calvinism carried out its Church discipline. The end was not the salvation of those subject to it, which was the affair of God alone (in practice their own) and could not be in any way influenced by the means at the disposal of the Church, but simply the increase of God's glory. Calvinism as such is not responsible for those feats of missionary zeal, since they rest on an interdenominational basis. Calvin himself denied the duty of sending missions to the heathen since a further expansion of the Church is *unius Dei opus* [the work of the single God]. Nevertheless, they obviously originate in the ideas, running through the whole Puritan ethic, according to which the duty to love one's neighbour is satisfied by fulfilling God's commandments to increase His glory. The neighbour thereby receives all that is due him, and anything further is God's affair. Humanity in relation to one's neighbour has, so to speak, died out. That is indicated by the most various circumstances.

Thus, to mention a remnant of that atmosphere, in the field of charity of the Reformed Church, which in certain respects is justly famous, the Amsterdam orphans, with (in the twentieth century!) their coats and trousers divided vertically into a black and a red, or a red and a green half, a sort of fool's costume, and brought in parade formation to church, formed, for the feelings of the past, a highly uplifting spectacle. It served the glory of God precisely to the extent that all personal and human feelings were necessarily insulted by it. And so, as we shall see later, even in all the details of private life. Naturally all that signified only a tendency and we shall later ourselves have to make certain qualifications. But as one very important tendency of this ascetic faith, it was necessary to point it out here.

40. Natural law [*Editor*].

41. In all these respects the ethic of Port Royal, although predestinationist, takes quite a different standpoint on account of its mystical and otherworldly orientation, which is in so far Catholic (see Honigsheim, *op. cit.*).

42. Hundeshagen (*Beitr. z. Kirchenverfassungsgesch. u. Kirchenpolitik*, 1864, 1, p. 37) takes the view, since often repeated, that predestination was a dogma of the theologians, not a popular doctrine. But that is only true if the people is identified with the mass of the uneducated lower classes. Even then it has only limited validity. Köhler (*op. cit.*) found that in the forties of the nineteenth century just those masses (meaning the *petite bourgeoisie* of Holland) were thoroughly imbued with predestination. Anyone who denied the double decree was to them a heretic and a condemned soul. He himself was asked about the time of his rebirth (in the sense of predestination). Da Costa and the separation of de Kock were greatly influenced by it. Not only Cromwell, in whose case Zeller (*Das Theologische System Zwinglis*, p. 17) has already shown the effects of the dogma most effectively, but also his army knew very well what it was about. Moreover, the canons of the synods of Dordrecht and Westminster were national questions of the first importance. Cromwell's tryers and ejectors admitted only believers in predestination, and Baxter (*Life*, I, p. 72), although he was otherwise its opponent, considers its effect on the quality of the clergy to be important. That the Reformed Pietists, the members of the English and Dutch conventicles, should not have understood the doctrine is quite impossible. It was precisely what drove them together to seek the *certitudo salutis*.

   What significance the doctrine of predestination does or does not have when it remains a dogma of the theologians is shown by perfectly orthodox Catholicism, to which it was by no means strange as an esoteric doctrine under various forms. What is important is that the idea of the individual's obligation to consider himself of the elect and prove it to himself was always denied. Compare for the Catholic doctrine, for instance, A. Van Wyck, *Tract. de prædestinatione* (Cologne, 1708). To what extent Pascal's doctrine of predestination was correct, we cannot inquire here.

   Hundeshagen, who dislikes the doctrine, evidently gets his impressions primarily from German sources. His antipathy is based on the purely deductive opinion that it necessarily leads to moral fatalism and antinomianism. This opinion has already been refuted by Zeller, *op. cit.* That such a result was possible cannot, of course, be denied. Both Melanchthon and Wesley speak of it. But it is characteristic that in both cases it is combined with an emotional religion of faith. For them, lacking the rational idea of proof, this consequence was in fact not unnatural.

   The same consequences appeared in Islam. But why? Because the Mohammedan idea was that of predetermination, not predestination, and was applied to fate in this world, not in the next. In consequence the most important thing, the proof of the believer in predestination, played no part in Islam. Thus only the fearlessness of the warrior (as in the case of *moira*) [death in battle is in God's hands] could result, but there were no consequences for rationalization of life; there was no religious sanction for them. See the (Heidelberg) theological dissertation of F. Ullrich, *Die Vorherbestimmungslehre im Islam u. Christenheit*, 1900. The modifications of the doctrine which came in practice, for instance Baxter, did not disturb it in essence so long as the idea that the election of God, and its proof, fell upon the concrete individual, was not shaken. Finally, and above all, all the great men of Puritanism (in the broadest sense) took their departure from this doctrine, whose terrible seriousness deeply influenced their youthful development. Milton like, in declining order it is true, Baxter, and, still later, the free-thinker Franklin. Their later emancipation from its strict interpretation is directly parallel to the development which the religious movement as a whole underwent in the same direction. And all the great religious revivals, at least in Holland, and most of those in England, took it up again.

43. As is true in such a striking way of the basic atmosphere of Bunyan's *Pilgrim's Progress*.

44. This question meant less to the later Lutheran, even apart from the doctrine of predestination, than to the Calvinist. Not because he was less interested in the salvation of his soul, but because, in the form which the Lutheran Church had taken, its character as an institution for salvation (*Heilsanstalt*) came to the fore. The individual thus felt himself to be an object of its care and dependent on it. The problem was first raised within Lutheranism characteristically enough through the Pietist movement. The question of *certitudo salutis* itself has, however, for every non-sacramental religion of salvation, whether Buddhism, Jainism, or anything else, been absolutely fundamental; that must not be forgotten. It has been the origin of all psychological drives of a purely religious character.

45. Thus expressly in the letter to Bucer, *Corp. Ref.* 29, pp. 883 f. Compare with that again Scheibe, *op. cit.*, p. 30.

46. Playthings of the Holy Spirit [*Editor*].

47. Ultimate [*Editor*].

48. Certainty of Salvation [*Editor*].

49. The *Westminster Confession* (XVIII, p. 2) also assures the elect of indubitable certainty of grace, although with all our activity we remain useless servants and the struggle against evil lasts one's whole life long. But even the chosen one often has to struggle long and hard to attain the *certitudo* which the consciousness of having done his duty gives him and of which a true believer will never entirely be deprived.

50. Chosen [*Editor*].

51. The orthodox Calvinistic doctrine referred to faith and the consciousness of community with God in the sacraments, and mentioned the "other fruits of the Spirit" only incidentally. See the passages in Heppe, *op. cit.*, p. 425. Calvin himself most emphatically denied that works were indications of favour before God, although he, like the Lutherans, considered them the fruits of belief (*Instit. Christ*, III, 2, 37, 38). The actual evolution to the proof of faith through works, which is characteristic of asceticism, is parallel to a gradual modification of the doctrines of Calvin. As with Luther, the true Church was first marked off primarily by purity of doctrine and sacraments, but later the *disciplina* came to be placed on an equal footing with the other two. This evolution may be followed in the passages given by Heppe, *op. cit.*, pp. 194–5, as well as in the manner in which Church members were acquired in the Netherlands by the end of the sixteenth century (express subjection by agreement to Church discipline as the principal prerequisite).

52. For example, Olevian, *De substantia fœderis gratuiti inter Deum et electos* (1585), p. 257; Heidegger, *Corpus Theologiæ*, XXIV, p. 87; and other passages in Heppe, *Dogmatik der ev. ref. Kirche* (1861), p. 425.

53. On this point see the remarks of Schneckenburger, *op. cit.*, p. 48.

54. Thus, for example, in Baxter the distinction between mortal and venial sin reappears in a truly Catholic sense. The former is a sign of the lack of grace which can only be attained by the conversion of one's whole life. The latter is not incompatible with grace.

55. As held in many different shades by Baxter, Bailey, Sedgwick, Hoornbeek. Further see examples given by Schneckenburger, *op. cit.*, p. 262.

56. The conception of the state of grace as a sort of social estate (somewhat like that of the ascetics of the early Church) is very common. See for instance Schortinghuis, *Het innige Christendom* (1740 proscribed by the States-General)!

57. Thus, as we shall see later, in countless passages, especially the conclusion, of Baxter's *Christian Directory*. This recommendation of worldly activity as a means of overcoming one's own feeling of moral inferiority is reminiscent of Pascal's psychological interpretation of the impulse of acquisition and ascetic activity as means to deceive oneself about one's own moral worthlessness. For him the belief in predestination and the conviction of the original sinfulness of everything pertaining to the flesh resulted only in renunciation of the world and the recommendation of contemplation as the sole means of lightening the burden of sin and attaining certainty of salvation. Of the orthodox Catholic and the Jansenist versions of the idea of calling an acute analysis has been made by Dr. Paul Honigsheim in the dissertation cited above (part of a larger study, which it is hoped will be continued). The Jansenists lacked every trace of a connection between certainty of salvation and worldly activity. Their concept of calling has, even more strongly than the Lutheran or even the orthodox Catholic, the sense of acceptance of the situation in life in which one finds oneself, sanctioned not only, as in Catholicism by the social order, but also by the voice of one's own conscience (Honigsheim, *op. cit.*, pp. 139 ff.).

58. The very lucidly written sketch of Lobstein in the *Festgabe für H. Holtzmann*, which starts from his view-point, may also be compared with the following. It has been criticized for too sharp an emphasis on the *certitudo salutis*. But just at this point Calvin's theology must be distinguished from Calvinism, the theological system from the needs of religious practice. All the religious movements which have affected large masses have started from the question, "How can I become certain of my salvation?" As we have said, it not only plays a central part in this case but in the history of all religions, even in India. And could it well be otherwise?

59. Mystical union [*Editor*].

60. Of course it cannot be denied that the full development of this conception did not take place until late Lutheran times (Prætorius, Nicolai, Meisner). It is present, however, even in Johannes Gerhard, quite in the sense meant here. Hence Ritschl in Book IV of his *Geschichte des Pietismus* (II, pp. 3 ff.) interprets the introduction of this concept into Lutheranism as a Renaissance or an adoption of Catholic elements. He does not deny (p. 10) that the problem of individual salvation was the same for Luther as for the Catholic Mystics, but he believes that the solution was precisely opposite in the two cases. I can, of course, have no competent opinion of my own. That the atmosphere of *Die Freiheit eines Christenmenschen* is different, on the one hand, from the sweet flirtation with the *liebem Jesulein* [dear child-like Jesus] of the later writers, and on the other from Tauler's religious feeling, is naturally obvious to anyone. Similarly the retention of the mystic-magical element in Luther's doctrines of the Communion certainly has different religious motives from

the Bernhardine piety, the "Song of Songs feeling" to which Ritschl again and again returns as the source of the bridal relations with Christ. But might not, among other things, that doctrine of the Communion have favoured the revival of mystical religious emotions? Further, it is by no means accurate to say that (p. 11, *op. cit.*) the freedom of the mystic consisted entirely in isolation from the world. Especially Tauler has, in passages which from the point of view of the psychology of religion are very interesting, maintained that the order which is thereby brought into thoughts concerning worldly activities is one practical result of the nocturnal contemplation which he recommends, for instance, in case of insomnia. "Only thereby [the mystical union with God at night before going to sleep] is reason clarified and the brain strengthened, and man is the whole day the more peacefully and divinely guided by virtue of the inner discipline of having truly united himself with God: then all his works shall be set in order. And thus when a man has forewarned (= prepared) himself of his work, and has placed his trust in virtue; then if he comes into the world, his works shall be virtuous and divine" (*Predigten*, fol. 318). Thus we see, and we shall return to the point, that mystic contemplation and a rational attitude toward the calling are not in themselves mutually contradictory. The opposite is only true when the religion takes on a directly hysterical character, which has not been the case with all mystics nor even all Pietists.

61. Daily penitence [*Editor*].
62. The finite cannot understand the infinite [*Editor*].
63. On this see the introduction to the following essays on the *Wirtschaftsethik der Weltreligionen* ["The Social Psychology of the World Religions" in *From Max Weber*] (not included in this translation: German in *Gesammelte Aufsätze zur Religionssoziologie.*— TRANSLATOR'S NOTE).
64. By faith alone [*Editor*].
65. In this assumption Calvinism has a point of contact with official Catholicism. But for the Catholics there resulted the necessity of the sacrament of repentance; for the Reformed Church that of practical proof through activity in the world.
66. Certainty of salvation [*Editor*].
67. See, for instance, Beza (*De prædestinat doct ex prælect.* in Rom 9a, Raph. Eglino exc. 1584), p. 133: "Sicut ex operibus vere bonis ad sanctificationis donum, a sanctificatione ad fidem—ascendimus: ita ex certis illis effectis non quamvis vocationem, sed efficacem illam et ex hac vocatione electionem et ex electione donum prædestinationis in Christo tam firmam quam immotus est Dei thronus certissima connexione effectorum et acausarum colligimus. . . ." [Just as we are given the gift of salvation by doing good works, and from these ascend to salvation, so do we acquire from continuous actions an effective and not just a random calling. Through Christ we then attain through this calling the gift of predestination. It has come to us from an effective connection between activity and principles, as immovable as God's throne.] Only with regard to the signs of damnation is it necessary to be careful, since it is a matter of final judgment. On this point the Puritans first differed. See further the thorough discussion of Schneckenburger, *op. cit.*, who to be sure only cites a limited category of literature. In the whole Puritan literature this aspect comes out. "It will not be said, did you believe?—but: were you Doers or Talkers only?" says Bunyan. According to Baxter (*The Saints' Everlasting Rest*, chap. xii), who teaches the mildest form of predestination, faith means subjection to Christ in heart and in deed. "Do what you are able first, and then complain of God for denying you grace if you have cause", was his answer to the objection that the will was not free and God alone was able to insure salvation (*Works of the Puritan Divines*, IV, p. 155). The investigation of Fuller (the Church historian) was limited to the one question of practical proof and the indications of his state of grace in his conduct, The same with Howe in the passage referred to elsewhere. Any examination of the *Works of the Puritan Divines* gives ample proofs.

Not seldom the conversion to Puritanism was due to Catholic ascetic writings, thus, with Baxter, a Jesuit tract. These conceptions were not wholly new compared with Calvin's own doctrine (*Instit. Christ*, chap. i, original edition of 1536, pp. 97, 113). Only for Calvin himself the certainty of salvation could not be attained in this manner (p. 147). Generally one referred to 1 John iii. 5 and similar passages. The demand for *fides efficax* is not—to anticipate—limited to the Calvinists. Baptist confessions of faith deal, in the article on predestination, similarly with the fruits of faith ("and that its—regeneration—proper evidence appears in the holy fruits of repentance and faith and newness of life"—Article 7 of the Confession printed in the *Baptist Church Manual* by J. N. Brown, D.D., Philadelphia, *Am. Bapt. Pub. Soc.*). In the same way the tract (under Mennonite influence), *Oliif—Tacxken*, which the Harlem Synod adopted in 1649, begins on page 1 with the question of how the children of God are to be known, and answers (p. 10): "Nu al is't dat dasdanigh vruchtbare ghelove alleene zii het seker fondamentale kennteeken—om de conscientien der gelovigen in het nieuwe verbondt der genade Gods te versekeren" [but only this fertile faith is the very sure sign . . . that can assure the believers that they are in God's new grace].

68. Effective faith

69. Law of nature [*Editor*].
70. Of the significance of this for the material content of social ethics some hint has been given above. Here we are interested not in the content, but in the motives of moral action.
71. How this idea must have promoted the penetration of Puritanism with the Old Testament Hebrew spirit is evident.
72. By faith alone [*Editor*].
73. Thus the Savoy Declaration says of the members of the *ecclesia pura* that they are "saints by effectual calling, visibly manifested by their profession and walking".
74. "A Principle of Goodness", Charnock in the *Works of the Puritan Divines*, p. 175.
75. Conversion is, as Sedgwick puts it, an "exact copy of the decree of predestination". And whoever is chosen is also called to obedience and made capable of it, teaches Bailey. Only those whom God calls to His faith (which is expressed in their conduct) are true believers, not merely temporary believers, according to the (Baptist) Confession of Hanserd Knolly.
76. Compare, for instance, the conclusion to Baxter's *Christian Directory*.
77. "Examine yourselves, to see whether you are in the faith"—2 Cor, xiii.5 [*Editor*].
78. Thus, for instance, Charnock, *Self-Examination*, p. 183, in refutation of the Catholic doctrine of *dubitatio*.
79. This argument recurs again and again in Hoornbeek, *Theologia practica*. For instance, I, p. 160; II, pp. 70, 72, 182.
80. For instance, the *Conf. Helvet*, 16, says "et improprie his [the works] *salus adtribuitur*" [salvation is improperly imputed to them (the works)].
81. Possession of salvation [*Editor*].
82. With all the above compare Schneckenburger, pp. 80 ff.
83. Augustine is supposed to have said "si non es prædestinatus, fac ut prædestineris" [act as if you were predestined, even if you are not].
84. One is reminded of a saying of Goethe with essentially the same meaning: "How can a man know himself? Never by observation, but through action. Try to do your duty and you will know what is in you. And what is your duty? Your daily task."
85. For though Calvin himself held that saintliness must appear on the surface (*Instit. Christ*, IV, pp. 1, 2, 7, 9), the dividing-line between saints and sinners must ever remain hidden from human knowledge. We must believe that where God's pure word is alive in a Church, organized and administered according to his law, some of the elect, even though we do not know them, are present.
86. The Calvinistic faith is one of the many examples in the history of religions of the relation between the logical and the psychological consequences for the practical religious attitude to be derived from certain religious ideas. Fatalism is, of course, the only logical consequence of predestination. But on account of the idea of proof the psychological result was precisely the opposite. For essentially similar reasons the followers of Nietzsche claim a positive ethical significance for the idea of eternal recurrence. This case, however, is concerned with responsibility for a future life which is connected with the active individual by no conscious thread of continuity, while for the Puritan it was *tua res agitur* [your own affairs are in question]. Even Hoornbeek (*Theologia practica*, I, p. 159) analyses the relation between predestination and action well in the language of the times. The *electi* [the chosen] are, on account of their election, proof against fatalism because in their rejection of it they prove themselves "quos ipsa electio sollicitos reddit et diligentes officiorum" [those whose election makes them anxious and careful about their tasks]. The practical interests cut off the fatalistic consequences of logic (which, however, in spite of everything occasionally did break through).

But, on the other hand, the content of ideas of a religion is, as Calvinism shows, far more important than William James (*Varieties of Religious Experience*, 1902, pp. 444 f.) is inclined to admit. The significance of the rational element in religious metaphysics is shown in classical form by the tremendous influence which especially the logical structure of the Calvinistic concept of God exercised on life. If the God of the Puritans has influenced history as hardly another before or since, it is principally due to the attributes which the power of thought had given him. James's pragmatic valuation of the significance of religious ideas according to their influence on life is incidentally a true child of the world of ideas of the Puritan home of that eminent scholar. The religious experience as such is of course irrational, like every experience. In its highest, mystical form it is even the experience. In its highest, mystical form it is even the experience κατ᾽ ἐξοχὴν [par excellence], and, as James has well shown, is distinguished by its absolute incommunicability. It has a specific character and appears as knowledge, but cannot be adequately reproduced by means of our lingual and conceptual apparatus. It is further true that every religious experience loses some of its content in the attempt of rational formulation, the further the conceptual formulation goes, the more so. That is the reason for many of the tragic conflicts of all rational theology, as the Baptist sects of the seventeenth century already knew. But that irrational element, which is by no means peculiar to religious experience, but applies (in different senses and to different degrees) to every experience, does not prevent its being of the greatest practical importance, of what particular type the system of ideas is, that captures and moulds the immediate experience of religion in its own way. For from this source develop, in times of great influence of the Church on life and of strong interest in dogmatic considerations within it, most of those differences between the various religions in their ethical consequences which are of such great practical importance. How unbelievably intense, measured by present standards, the dogmatic interests even of the layman were, everyone knows who is familiar with the historical sources. We can find a parallel to-day only in the at bottom equally superstitious belief of the modern proletariat in what can be accomplished and proved by science.

87. Baxter, *The Saints' Everlasting Rest*, I, p. 6, answers to the question: "Whether to make salvation our end be not mercenary or legal? It is property mercenary when we expect it as wages for work done. . . . Otherwise it is only such a mercenarism as Christ commandeth . . . and if seeking Christ be mercenary, I desire to be so mercenary." Nevertheless, many Calvinists who are considered orthodox do not escape falling into a very crass sort of mercenariness. According to Bailey, *Praxis pietatis*, p. 262, alms are a means of escaping temporal punishment. Other theologians urged the damned to perform good works, since their damnation might thereby become somewhat more bearable, but the elect because God will then not only love them without cause but *ob causam* [for a cause], which shall certainly sometime have its reward. The apologists have also made certain small concessions concerning the significance of good works for the degree of salvation (Schneckenburger, *op. cit.*, p. 101).

88. Here also it is absolutely necessary, in order to bring out the characteristic differences, to speak in terms of ideal types, thus in a certain sense doing violence to historical reality. But without this a clear formulation would be quite impossible considering the complexity of the material. In how far the differences which we here draw as sharply as possible were merely relative, would have to be discussed separately. It is, of course, true that the official Catholic doctrine, even in the Middle Ages, itself set up the ideal of a systematic sanctification of life as a whole. But it is just as certain (1) that the normal practice of the Church, directly on account of its most effective means of discipline, the confession, promoted the unsystematic way of life discussed in the text, and further (2) that the fundamentally rigorous and cold atmosphere in which he lived and the absolute isolation of the Calvinst were utterly foreign to mediæval lay-Catholicism.

89. Intention [*Editor*].

90. The absolutely fundamental importance of this factor will, as has already once been pointed out, gradually become clear in the essays on the *Wirtschaftsethik der Weltreligionen* [*The Economic Ethics of the World Religions*].

91. And to a certain extent also to the Lutheran. Luther did not wish to eliminate this last vestige of sacramental magic.

92. Compare, for instance, Sedgwick, *Buss- und Gnadenlehre* (German by Roscher, 1689). The repentant man has a fast rule to which he holds himself exactly, ordering thereby his whole life and conduct (p. 591). He lives according to the law, shrewdly, wakefully, and carefully (p. 596). Only a permanent change in the whole man can, since it is a result of predestination, cause this (p. 852). True repentance is always expressed in conduct (p. 361). The difference between only morally good work and *opera spiritualia* [spiritual task] lies, as Hoornbeek (*op. cit.*, I, IX, chap. ii) explains, in the fact that the latter are the results of a regenerate life (*op. cit.*, 1, p. 160). A continuous progress in them is discernible which can only be achieved by the supernatural influence of God's grace (p. 150). Salvation results from the transformation of the whole man through the grace of God (pp. 190 f.). These ideas are common to all Protestantism, and are of course found in the highest ideals of Catholicism as well. But their consequences could only appear in the Puritan movements of worldly asceticism, and above all only in those cases did they have adequate psychological sanctions.

93. The latter name is, especially in Holland, derived from those who modelled their lives precisely on the example of the Bible (thus with Voet). Moreover, the name Methodists occurs occasionally among the Puritans in the seventeenth century.

94. For, as the Puritan preachers emphasize (for instance Bunyan in the *Pharisee and the Publican, Works of the Puritan Divines*, p. 126), every single sin would destroy everything which might have been accumulated in the way of merit by good works in a lifetime, if, which is unthinkable, man were alone able to accomplish anything which God should necessarily recognize as meritorious, or even could live in perfection for any length of time. Thus Puritanism did not think as did Catholicism in terms of a sort of account with calculation of the balance, a simile which was common even in antiquity, but of the definite alternative of grace or damnation held for a life as a whole. For suggestions of the bank account idea see note 131.

95. State of nature [*Editor*].

96. State of grace [*Editor*].

97. For the greater glory of God [*Editor*].
98. Therein lies the distinction from the mere Legality and Civility which Bunyan has living as associates of Mr. Worldly-Wiseman in the City called Morality.
99. I think, therefore I am [*Editor*].
100. Charnock, *Self-Examination* (*Works of the Puritan Divines*, p. 172): "Reflection and knowledge of self is a prerogative of a rational nature." Also the footnote: "Cogito, ergo sum is the first principle of the new philosophy."
101. This is not yet the place to discuss the relationship of the theology of Duns Scotus to certain ideas of ascetic Protestantism. It never gained official recognition, but was at best tolerated and at times proscribed. The later specific repugnance of the Pietists to Aristotelean philosophy was shared by Luther, in a somewhat different sense, and also by Calvin in conscious antagonism to Catholicism (cf. *Instit. Christ*, II, chap. xii, p. 4; IV, chap. xvii, p. 24). The "primacy of the will", as Kahl has put it, is common to all these movements.
102. Thus, for instance, the article on "Asceticism" in the Catholic *Church Lexicon* defines its meaning entirely in harmony with its highest historical manifestations. Similarly Seeberg in the *Realenzyklopädie für protestantische Theologie und Kirche*. For the purpose of this study we must be allowed to use the concept as we have done. That it can be defined in other ways, more broadly as well as more narrowly, and is generally so defined, I am well aware.
103. Religious exercises [*Editor*].
104. In Hudibras (*1st Song*, 18, 19) the Puritans are compared with the bare-foot Franciscans. A report of the Genoese Ambassador, Ficeschi, calls Cromwell's army an assembly of monks.
105. In view of the close relationship between otherworldly monastic asceticism and active worldly asceticism, which I here expressly maintain, I am surprised to find Brentano (*op. cit.*, p. 134 and elsewhere) citing the ascetic labour of the monks and its recommendation against me. His whole "Exkurs" against me culminates in that. But that continuity is, as anyone can see, a fundamental postulate of my whole thesis: the Reformation took rational Christian asceticism and its methodical habits out of the monasteries and placed them in the service of active life in the world. Compare the following discussion, which has not been altered.
106. So in the many reports of the trials of Puritan heretics cited in Neal's *History of the Puritans* and Crosby's *English Baptists*.
107. Sanford, *op. cit.* (and both before and after him many others), has found the origin of the ideal of reserve in Puritanism. Compare on that ideal also the remarks of James Bryce on the American college in Vol. II of his *American Commonwealth*. The ascetic principle of self-control also made Puritanism one of the fathers of modern military discipline. (On Maurice of Orange as a founder of modern army organization, see Roloff, *Preuss. Jahrb.*, 1903, III, p. 255.) Cromwell's Ironsides, with cocked pistols in their hands, and approaching the enemy at a brisk trot without shooting, were not the superiors of the Cavaliers by virtue of their fierce passion, but, on the contrary, through their cool self-control, which enabled their leaders always to keep them well in hand. The knightly storm-attack of the Cavaliers, on the other hand, always resulted in dissolving their troops into atoms. See Firth, *Cromwell's Army*.
108. See especially Windelband, *Ueber Willensfreiheit*, pp. 77 ff.
109. Only not so unmixed. Contemplation, sometimes combined with emotionalism, is often combined with these rational elements. But again contemplation itself is methodically regulated.
110. According to Richard Baxter everything is sinful which is contrary to the reason given by God as a norm of action. Not only passions which have a sinful content, but all feelings which are senseless and intemperate as such. They destroy the countenance and, as things of the flesh, prevent us from rationally directing all action and feeling to God, and thus insult Him. Compare what is said of the sinfulness of anger (*Christian Directory*, second edition, 1698, p. 285. Tauler is cited on p. 287). On the sinfulness of anxiety, *Ebenda*, I, p. 287. That it is idolatry if our appetite is made the "rule or measure of eating" is maintained very emphatically (*op. cit.*, I, pp. 310, 316, and elsewhere). In such discussions reference is made everywhere to the Proverbs and also to Plutarch's *De tranquilitate Animi*, and not seldom to ascetic writings of the Middle Ages: St. Bernard, Bonaventura, and others. The contrast to "who does not love wine, women, and song . . ." could hardly be more sharply drawn than by the extension of the idea of idolatry to all sensuous pleasures, so far as they are not justified by hygienic considerations, in which case they (like sport within these limits, but also other recreations) are permissible. See below (Chapter 5) for further discussion. Please note that the sources referred to here and elsewhere are neither dogmatic nor edifying works, but grew out of practical ministry, and thus give a good picture of the direction which its influence took.
111. Evangelical counsels [*Editor*].

112. I should regret it if any evaluation of one or the other form of religion should be read into this discussion. We are not concerned with that here. It is only a question of the influence of certain things which, from a purely religious point of view, are perhaps incidental, but important for practical conduct.

113. On this, see especially the article "Moralisten, englische", by E. Troeltsch, in the *Realenzyklopädie für protestantische Theologie und Kirche*, third edition.

114. How much influence quite definite religious ideas and situations, which seem to be historical accidents, have had is shown unusually clearly by the fact that in the circles of Pietism of a Reformed origin the lack of monasteries was occasionally directly regretted, and that the communistic experiments of Labadie and others were simply a substitute for monastic life.

115. As early even as several confessions of the time of the Reformation. Even Ritschl (*Pietismus*, I, p. 258 f.) does not deny, although he looks upon the later development as a deterioration of the ideas of the Reformation, that, for instance, in *Conf. Gall.* 25, 26, *Conf. Belg.* 29, *Conf. Helv.* post, 17, the true Reformed Church was defined by definitely empirical attributes, and that to this true Church believers were not accounted without the attribute of moral activity. (See above, note 52).

116. "Bless God that we are not of the many" (Thomas Adams, *Works of the Puritan Divines*, p. 138).

117. Indelible mark [*Editor*].

118. The idea of the birthright, so important in history, thus received an important confirmation in England. "The firstborn which are written in heaven. . . . As the firstborn is not to be defeated in his inheritance, and the enrolled names are never to be obliterated, so certainly they shall inherit eternal life" (Thomas Adams, *Works of the Puritan Divines*, p. xiv).

119. The Lutheran emphasis on penitent grief is foreign to the spirit of ascetic Calvinism, not in theory, but definitely in practice. For it is of no ethical value to the Calvinist; it does not help the damned, while for those certain of their election, their own sin, so far as they admit it to themselves, is a symptom of backwardness in development. Instead of repenting of it they hate it and attempt to overcome it by activity for the glory of God. Compare the explanation of Howe (Cromwell's chaplain 1656–58) in *Of Men's Enmity against God and of Reconciliation between God and Man* (*Works of English Puritan Divines*, p. 237): "The carnal mind is enmity against God. It is the mind, therefore, not as speculative merely, but as practical and active that must be renewed", and, p. 246: "Reconciliation . . . must begin in (1) a deep conviction . . . of your former enmity . . . I have been alienated from God. . . . (2) (p. 251) a clear and lively apprehension of the monstrous iniquity and wickedness thereof." The hatred here is that of sin, not of the sinner. But as early as the famous letter of the Duchess Renata d'Este (Leonore's mother) to Calvin, in which she speaks of the hatred which she would feel toward her father and husband if she became convinced they belonged to the damned, is shown the transfer to the person. At the same time it is an example of what was said above [pp. 104–6] of how the individual became loosed from the ties resting on his natural feelings, for which the doctrine of predestination was responsible.

120. "None but those who give evidence of being regenerate or holy persons ought to be received or counted fit members of visible Churches. Where this is wanting, the very essence of a Church is lost", as the principle is put by Owen, the Independent-Calvinistic Vice-Chancellor of Oxford under Cromwell (*Inv. into the Origin of Ev. Ch.*). Further, see the following essay (not translated here.—TRANSLATOR).

121. See following essay (not translated here [*Editor*]).

122. *Cat. Genev.*, p. 149. Bailey, *Praxis pietatis*, p. 125: "In life we should act as though no one but Moses had authority over us."

123. "The law appears to the Calvinist as an ideal norm of action. It oppresses the Lutheran because it is for him unattainable." In the Lutheran catechism it stands at the beginning in order to arouse the necessary humility, in the Reformed catechism it generally stands after the Gospel. The Calvinists accused the Lutherans of having a "virtual reluctance to becoming holy" (Möhler), while the Lutherans accused the Calvinists of an "unfree servitude to the law", and of arrogance.

124. *Studies and Reflections of the Great Rebellion*, pp. 79 f.

125. Among these the Song of Songs is especially noteworthy. It was for the most part simply ignored by the Puritans. Its Oriental eroticism has influenced the development of certain types of religion, such as that of St. Bernard.

126. On the necessity of this self-observation, see the sermon of Charnock, already referred to, on 2 Cor. xiii, 5, *Works of the Puritan Divines*, pp. 161 ff.

127. Most of the theological moralists recommended it. Thus Baxter, *Christian Directory*, II, pp. 77 ff., who, however, does not gloss over its dangers.

128. Spiritual guide [*Editor*].

129. Moral book-keeping has, of course, been widespread elsewhere. But the emphasis which was placed upon it as the sole means of knowledge of the eternal decree of salvation or

damnation was lacking, and with it the most important psychological sanction for care and exactitude in this calculation.

130. This was the significant difference from other attitudes which were superficially similar.

131. Baxter (*Saints' Everlasting Rest*, chap. xii) explains God's invisibility with the remark that just as one can carry on profitable trade with an invisible foreigner through correspondence, so is it possible by means of holy commerce with an invisible God to get possession of the one priceless pearl. These commercial similes rather than the forensic ones customary with the older moralists and the Lutherans are thoroughly characteristic of Puritanism, which in effect makes man buy his own salvation. Compare further the following passage from a sermon: "We reckon the value of a thing by that which a wise man will give for it, who is not ignorant of it nor under necessity. Christ, the Wisdom of God, gave Himself, His own precious blood, to redeem souls, and He knew what they were and had no need of them" (Matthew Henry, *The Worth of the Soul, Works of the Puritan Divines*, p. 313).

132. In contrast to that, Luther himself said: "Weeping goes before action and suffering excells all accomplishment" (*Weinen geht vor Wirken und Leiden übertrifft alles tun*).

133. Loss of grace [*Editor*].

134. This is also shown most clearly in the development of the ethical theory of Lutheranism. On this see Hoennicke, *Studien zur altprotestantischen Ethik* (Berlin, 1902), and the instructive review of it by E. Troeltsch, *Gött. Gel. Anz.*, 1902, No. 8. The approach of the Lutheran doctrine, especially to the older orthodox Calvinistic, was in form often very close. But the difference of religious background was always apparent. In order to establish a connection between morality and faith, Melanchthon had placed the idea of repentance in the foreground. Repentance through the law must precede faith, but good works must follow it, otherwise it cannot be the truly justifying faith—almost a Puritan formula. Melanchthon admitted a certain degree of perfection to be attainable on earth. He had, in fact, originally taught that justification was given in order to make men capable of good works, and in increasing perfection lay at least the relative degree of blessedness which faith could give in this world. Also later Lutheran theologians held that good works are the necessary fruits of faith, that faith results in a new external life, just as the Reformed preachers did. The question in what good works consist Melanchthon, and especially the later Lutherans, answered more and more by reference to the law. There remained of Luther's original doctrines only the lesser degree of seriousness with which the Bible, especially the particular norms of the Old Testament, was taken. The decalogue remained, as a codification of the most important ideas of the natural moral law, the essential norm of human action. But there was no firm limit connecting its legal validity with the more and more strongly emphasized importance of faith for justification, because this faith (see above) had a fundamentally different psychological character from the Calvinistic.

The true Lutheran standpoint of the early period had to be abandoned by a Church which looked upon itself as an institution for salvation. But another had not been found. Especially was it impossible, for fear of losing their dogmatic foundation (*sola fide!*) [by faith alone], to accept the ascetic rationalization of conduct as the moral task of the individual. For there was no motive to give the idea of proof such a significance as it attained in Calvinism through the doctrine of predestination. Moreover, the magical interpretation of the sacraments, combined with the lack of this doctrine, especially the association of the *regeneratio* [regeneration of hope for salvation], or at least its beginning with baptism, necessarily, assuming as it did the universality of grace, hindered the development of methodical morality. For it weakened the contrast between the state of nature and the state of grace, especially when combined with the strong Lutheran emphasis on original sin. No less important was the entirely forensic interpretation of the act of justification which assumed that God's decrees might be changed through the influence of particular acts of repentance of the converted sinner. And that was just the element to which Melanchthon gave increasing emphasis. The whole development of his doctrine, which gave increasing weight to repentance, was intimately connected with his profession of the freedom of the will. That was what primarily determined the *un*methodical character of Lutheran conduct.

Particular acts of grace for particular sins, not the development of an aristocracy of saints creating the certainty of their own salvation, was the necessary form salvation took for the average Lutheran, as the retention of the confession proves. Thus it could develop neither a morality free from the law nor a rational asceticism in terms of the law. Rather the law remained in an unorganic proximity to faith as an ideal, and, moreover, since the strict dependence on the Bible was avoided as suggesting salvation by works, it remained uncertain, vague, and, above all, unsystematic in its content. Their conduct remained, as Troeltsch has said of their ethical theory, a "sum of mere beginnings which never quite materialized"; which, "taught in particular, uncertain, and unrelated maxims", did not succeed in "working out an articulate system of conduct", but formed essentially, following the development through which Luther himself (see above) had gone, a resignation to things as they were in matters both small and great. The resignation of the

Germans to foreign cultures, their rapid change of nationality, of which there is so much complaint, is clearly to be attributed, along with certain political circumstances in the history of the nation, in part to the results of this influence, which still affects all aspects of our life. The subjective assimilation of culture remained weak because it took place primarily by means of a passive absorption of what was authoritatively presented.

135. State of nature [*Editor*].

136. On these points, see the gossipy book of Tholuck, *Vorgeschichte des Rationalismus*.

137. On the quite different results of the Mohammedan doctrine of predestination (or rather predetermination) and the reasons for it, see the theological dissertation (Heidelberg) of F. Ullrich, *Die Vorherbestimmungslehre im Islam u. Ch.*, 1912. On that of the Jansenists, see P. Honigsheim, *op. cit.*

138. See the following essay in this collection (not translated here).

139. Ritschl, *Geschichte des Pietismus*, I, p. 152, attempts to distinguish them for the time before Labadie (only on the basis of examples from the Netherlands) (1) in that the Pietists formed conventicles; (2) they held the doctrine of the "worthlessness of existence in the flesh" in a "manner contrary to the Protestant interests in salvation"; (3) "the assurance of grace in the tender relationship with the Lord Jesus" was sought in an un-Calvinistic manner. The last criterion applies for this early period only to one of the cases with which he deals. The idea of worthlessness of the flesh was in itself a true child of the Calvinistic spirit, and only where it led to practical renunciation of the world was it antagonistic to normal Protestantism. The conventicles, finally, had been established to a certain extent (especially for catechistic purposes) by the Synod of Dordrecht itself. Of the criteria of Pietism analysed in Ritschl's previous discussion, those worth considering are (1) the greater precision with which the letter of the Bible was followed in all external affairs of life, as Gisbert Voet for a time urged; (2) the treatment of justification and reconciliation with God, not as ends in themselves, but simply as means toward a holy ascetic life as can be seen perhaps in Lodensteyn, but as is also suggested by Melanchthon [see above, note 104] (n. 134, p. 128); (3) the high value placed on repentance as a sign of true regeneration, as was first taught by W. Teellinck; (4) abstention from communion when unregenerate persons partake of it (of which we shall speak in another connection). Connected with that was the formation of conventicles with a revival of prophecy, i.e. interpretation of the Scriptures by laymen, even women. That went beyond the limits set by the canons of Dordrecht.

Those are all things forming departures, sometimes considerable, from both the doctrine and practice of the Reformers. But compared with the movements which Ritschl does not include in his treatment, especially the English Puritans, they form, except for No. 3, only a continuation of tendencies which lay in the whole line of development of this religion. The objectivity of Ritschl's treatment suffers from the fact that the great scholar allows his personal attitude towards the Church or, perhaps better, religious policy, to enter in, and, in his antipathy to all peculiarly ascetic forms of religion, interprets any development in that direction as a step back into Catholicism. But, like Catholicism, the older Protestantism included all sorts and conditions of men. But that did not prevent the Catholic Church from repudiating rigorous worldly asceticism in the form of Jansenism; just as Pietism repudiated the peculiar Catholic Quietism of the seventeenth century. From our special view-point Pietism differs not in degree, but in kind from Calvinism only when the increasing fear of the world leads to flight from ordinary economic life and the formation of monastic-communistic conventicles (Labadie). Or, which has been attributed to certain extreme Pietists by their contemporaries, they were led deliberately to neglect worldly duties in favour of contemplation. This naturally happened with particular frequency when contemplation began to assume the character which Ritschl calls Bernardism, because it suggests St. Bernard's interpretation of the Song of Songs; a mystical, emotional form of religion seeking the *unio mystica* [mystical union] with an esoteric sexual tinge. Even from the view-point of religious psychology alone this is undoubtedly something quite different from Calvinism, including its ascetic form exemplified by men like Voet. Ritschl, however, everywhere attempts to connect this quietism with the Pietist asceticism and thus to bring the latter under the same indictment; in doing so he puts his finger on every quotation from Catholic mysticism or asceticism which he can find in Pietist literature. But English and Dutch moralists and theologians who are quite beyond suspicion cite Bernard, Bonaventura, and Thomas à Kempis. The relationship of all the Reformation Churches to the Catholic past was very complex and, according to the point of view which is emphasized, one or another appears most closely related to Catholicism or certain sides of it.

140. Certainty of salvation [*Editor*].

141. The illuminating article on "Pietism" by Mirbt in the third edition of the *Realenzyklopädie für protestantische Theologie und Kirche*, treats the origin of Pietism, leaving its Protestant antecedents entirely on one side, as a purely personal religious experience of Spener, which is somewhat improbable. As an introduction to Pietism, Gustav Freytag's description in *Bilder der deutschen Vergangenheit* is still worth reading. For the beginnings of

English Pietism in the contemporary literature, compare W. Whitaker, *Prima Instituto disciplinaque pietatis* (1570).

142. Practice of piety [*Editor*].

143. It is well known that this attitude made it possible for Pietism to be one of the main forces behind the idea of toleration. At this point we may insert a few remarks on that subject. In the West its historical origin, if we omit the humanistic indifference of the Enlightenment, which in itself has never had great practical influence, is to be found in the following principal sources: (1) Purely political expediency (type: William of Orange). (2) Mercantilism (especially clear for the City of Amsterdam, but also typical of numerous cities, landlords, and rulers who received the members of sects as valuable for economic progress). (3) The radical wing of Calvinism. Predestination made it fundamentally impossible for the State really to promote religion by intolerance. It could not thereby save a single soul. Only the idea of the glory of God gave the Church occasion to claim its help in the suppression of heresy. Now the greater the emphasis on the membership of the preacher, and all those that partook of the communion, in the elect, the more intolerable became the interference of the State in the appointment of the clergy. For clerical positions were often granted as beneficies to men from the universities only because of their theological training, though they might be personally unregenerate. In general, any interference in the affairs of the religious community by those in political power, whose conduct might often be unsatisfactory, was resented. Reformed Pietism strengthened this tendency by weakening the emphasis on doctrinal orthodoxy and by gradually undermining the principle of *extra ecclesiam nulla salus* [there is no salvation outside the Church].

Calvin had regarded the subjection of the damned to the divine supervision of the Church as alone consistent with the glory of God; in New England the attempt was made to constitute the Church as an aristocracy of proved saints. Even the radical Independents, however, repudiated every interference of temporal or any sort of hierarchical powers with the proof of salvation which was only possible within the individual community. The idea that the glory of God requires the subjection of the damned to the discipline of the Church was gradually superseded by the other idea, which was present from the beginning and became gradually more prominent, that it was an insult to His glory to partake of the Communion with one rejected by God. That necessarily led to voluntarism, for it led to the believers' Church the religious community which included only the twice-born. Calvinistic Baptism, to which, for instance, the leader of the Parliament of Saints Praisegod Barebones belonged, drew the consequences of this line of thought with great emphasis. Cromwell's army upheld the liberty of conscience and the parliament of saints even advocated the separation of Church and State, because its members were good Pietists, thus on positive religious grounds. (4) The Baptist sects, which we shall discuss later, have from the beginning of their history most strongly and consistently maintained the principle that only those personally regenerated could be admitted to the Church. Hence they repudiated every conception of the Church as an institution (*Anstalt*) and every interference of the temporal power. Here also it was for positive religious reasons that unconditional toleration was advocated.

The first man who stood out for absolute toleration and the separation of Church and State, almost a generation before the Baptists and two before Roger Williams, was probably John Browne. The first declaration of a Church group in this sense appears to be the resolution of the English Baptists in Amsterdam of 1612 or 1613: "The magistrate is not to middle with religion or matters of conscience . . . because Christ is the King and Law-giver of the Church and conscience." The first official document of a Church which claimed the positive protection of liberty of conscience by the State as a right was probably Article 44 of the Confession of the Particular Baptists of 1644.

Let it be emphatically stated again that the idea sometimes brought forward, that toleration as such was favourable to capitalism, is naturally quite wrong. Religious toleration is neither peculiar to modern times nor to the West. It has ruled in China, in India, in the great empires of the Near East in Hellenistic times, in the Roman Empire and the Mohammedan Empires for long periods to a degree only limited by reasons of political expediency (which form its limits to-day also!) which was attained nowhere in the world in the sixteenth and seventeenth centuries. Moreover, it was least strong in those areas which were dominated by Puritanism, as, for instance, Holland and Zeeland in their period of political and economic expansion or in Puritan old or New England. Both before and after the Reformation, religious intolerance was peculiarly characteristic of the Occident as of the Sassanian Empire. Similarly, it has prevailed in China, Japan, and India at certain particular times, though mostly for political reasons. Thus toleration as such certainly has nothing whatever to do with capitalism. The real question, Who benefited by it? Of the consequences of the believers' Church we shall speak further in the following article.

144. This idea is illustrated in its practical application by Cromwell's tryers, the examiners of candidates for the position of preacher. They attempted to ascertain not only the knowl-

edge of theology, but also the subjective state of grace of the candidate. See also the following article.

145. The characteristic Pietistic distrust of Aristotle and classical philosophy in general is suggested in Calvin himself (compare *Instit. Christ*, II, chap. ii, p. 4; III, chap. xxiii, p. 5; IV, chap. xvii, p. 24). Luther in his early days distrusted it no less, but that was later changed by the humanistic influence (especially of Melanchthon) and the urgent need of ammunition for apologetic purposes. That everything necessary for salvation was contained in the Scriptures plainly enough for even the untutored was, of course, taught by the Westminster Confession (chap. i, No. 7.), in conformity with the whole Protestant tradition.

146. The official Churches protested against this, as, for example, in the shorter catechism of the Scotch Presbyterian Church of 1648, sec. vii. Participation of those not members of the same family in family devotions was forbidden as interference with the prerogatives of the office. Pietism, like every ascetic community-forming movement, tended to loosen the ties of the individual with domestic patriarchalism, with its interest in the prestige of office.

147. Little church [*Editor*].

148. Mystical union [*Editor*].

149. We are here for good reasons intentionally neglecting discussion of the psychological, in the technical sense of the word, aspect of these religious phenomena, and even its terminology has been as far as possible avoided. The firmly established results of psychology, including psychiatry, do not as present go far enough to make them of use for the purposes of the historical investigation of our problems without prejudicing historical judgments. The use of its terminology would only form a temptation to hide phenomena which were immediately understandable, or even sometimes trivial, behind a veil of foreign words, and thus give a false impression of scientific exactitude, such as is unfortunately typical of Lamprecht. For a more serious attempt to make use of psychological concepts in the interpretation of certain historical mass phenomena, see W. Hellpach, *Grundlinien zu einer Psychologie der Hysterie*, chap. xii, as well as his *Nervosität und Kultur*. I cannot here attempt to explain that in my opinion even this many-sided writer has been harmfully influenced by certain of Lamprecht's theories. How completely worthless, as compared with the older literature, Lamprecht's schematic treatment of Pietism is (in Vol. VII of the *Deutsche Geschichte*) everyone knows who has the slightest acquaintance with the literature.

150. Thus with the adherents of Schortinghuis's *Innige Christendom*. In the history of religion it goes back to the verse about the servant of God in Isaiah and the 22nd Psalm.

151. This appeared occasionally in Dutch Pietism and then under the influence of Spinoza.

152. Labadie, Teersteegen, etc.

153. Perhaps this appears most clearly when he (Spener !) disputes the authority of the Government to control the conventicles except in cases of disorder and abuses, because it concerns a fundamental right of Christians guaranteed by apostolic authority (*Theologische Bedenken*, II, pp. 81 f.). That is, in principle, exactly the Puritan standpoint regarding the relations of the individual to authority and the extent to which individual rights, which follow *ex jure divino* [from divine law] and are therefore inalienable, are valid. Neither this heresy, nor the one mentioned farther on in the text, has escaped Ritschl (*Pietismus*, II, pp. 115, 157). However unhistorical the positivistic (not to say philistine) criticism to which he has subjected the idea of natural rights to which we are nevertheless indebted for not much less than everything which even the most extreme reactionary prizes as his sphere of individual freedom, we naturally agree entirely with him that in both cases an organic relationship to Spener's Lutheran standpoint is lacking.

The conventicles (*collegia pietatis*) themselves, to which Spener's famous *Pia Desideria* gave the theoretical basis, and which he founded in practice, corresponded closely in essentials to the English prophesyings which were first practised in John of Lasco's London Bible Classes (1547), and after that were a regular feature of all forms of Puritanism which revolted against the authority of the Church. Finally, he bases his well-known repudiation of the Church discipline of Geneva on the fact that its natural executors, the third estate (*status œconomicus*: the Christian laity), were not even a part of the organization of the Lutheran Church. On the other hand, in the discussion of excommunication the lay members' recognition of the Consistorium appointed by the prince as representatives of the third estate is weakly Lutheran.

154. The name Pietism in itself, which first occurs in Lutheran territory, indicates that in the opinion of contemporaries it was characteristic of it that a methodical business was made out of *pietas* [piety].

155. It is, of course, granted that though this type of motivation was primarily Calvinistic it is not exclusively such. It is also found with special frequency in some of the oldest Lutheran Church constitutions.

156. In the sense of Heb. v. 13, 14. Compare Spener, *Theologische Bedenken*, I, p. 306.

157. Besides Bailey and Baxter (see *Consilia theologica*, III, 6, 1; 1, 47; 3, 6), Spener was especially fond of Thomas à Kempis, and even more of Tauler—whom he did not

entirely understand (*op. cit.*, III, 61, 1, No. 1). For detailed discussion of the latter, see *op. cit.*, I, 1, 1, No. 7. For him Luther is derived directly from Tauler.

158. Certainty of salvation [*Editor*].

159. See in Ritschl, *op. cit.*, II, p. 113. He did not accept the repentance of the later Pietists (and of Luther) as the sole trustworthy indication of true conversion (*Theologische Bedenken*, III, p. 476). On sanctification as the fruit of thankfulness in the belief of forgiveness, a typically Lutheran idea, see passages cited by Ritschl, *op. cit.*, p. 115, note 2. On the *certitudo salutis* see, on the one hand, *Theologische Bedenken*, I, p. 324: "true belief is not so much felt emotionally as known by its fruits" (love and obedience to God); on the other, *Theologische Bedenken*, I, p. 335 f.: "As far as anxiety that they should be assured of salvation and grace is concerned, it is better to trust to our books, the Lutheran, than to the English writings." But on the nature of sanctification he was at one with the English view-point.

160. Of this the religious account books which A. H. Francke recommended were external symptoms. The methodical practice and habit of virtue was supposed to cause its growth and the separation of good from evil. This is the principal theme of Francke's book, *Von des Christen Vollkommenheit*.

161. The difference between this rational Pietist belief in Providence and its orthodox interpretation is shown characteristically in the famous controversy between the Pietists of Halle and the orthodox Lutheran Löscher. Löscher in his *Timotheus Verinus* goes so far as to contrast everything that is attained by human action with the decrees of Providence. On the other hand, Francke's consistent view was that the sudden flash of clarity over what is to happen, which comes as a result of quiet waiting for decision, is to be considered as "God's hint", quite analogous to the Quaker psychology, and corresponding to the general ascetic idea that rational methods are the way to approach nearer to God. It is true that Zinzendorf, who in one most vital decision entrusted the fate of his community to lot, was far from Francke's form of the belief in Providence. Spener, *Theologische Bedenken*, I, p. 314, referred to Tauler for a description of the Christian resignation in which one should bow to the divine will, and not cross it by hasty action on one's own responsibility, essentially the position of Francke. Its effectiveness as compared to Puritanism is essentially weakened by the tendency of Pietism to seek peace in this world, as can everywhere be clearly seen. "First righteousness, then peace", as was said in opposition to it in 1904 by a leading Baptist (G. White in an address to be referred to later) in formulating the ethical programme of his denomination (*Baptist Handbook*, 1904, p. 107).

162. *Lect. paraenet.*, IV, p. 271.

163. Ritschl's criticism is directed especially against this continually recurrent idea. See the work of Francke containing the doctrine which has already been referred to. (See note 124 above) (n. 60).

164. It occurs also among English Pietists who were not adherents of predestination, for instance Goodwin. On him and others compare Heppe, *Geschichte des Pietismus in der reformierten Kirche* (Leiden, 1879), a book which even with Ritschl's standard work cannot yet be dispensed with for England, and here and there also for the Netherlands. Even in the nineteenth century in the Netherlands Köhler, *Die Niederl. ref. Kirche*, was asked about the exact time of his rebirth.

165. They attempted thus to counteract the lax results of the Lutheran doctrine of the recoverability of grace (especially the very frequent conversion *in extremis*) [under extreme circumstances].

166. Against the corresponding necessity of knowing the day and hour of conversion as an indispensable sign of its genuineness. See Spener, *Theologische Bedenken*, II, 6, 1, p. 197. Repentance was as little known to him as Luther's *terrores conscientiæ* to Melanchthon.

167. Sorrow for sin [*Editor*].

168. At the same time, of course, the anti-authoritarian interpretation of the universal priesthood, typical of all asceticism, played a part. Occasionally the minister was advised to delay absolution until proof was given of genuine repentance which, as Ritschl rightly says, was in principle Calvinistic.

169. The essential points for our purposes are most easily found in Putt, *Zinzendorf's Theologie* (3 vols., Gotha, 1869), I, pp. 325, 345, 381, 412, 429, 433 f., 444, 448; II, pp. 372, 381, 385, 409 f.; III, pp. 131, 167, 176. Compare also Bernh. Becker, *Zinzendorf und sein Christentum* (Leipzig, 1900), Book III, chap. iii.

170. "In no religion do we recognize as brothers those who have not been washed in the blood of Christ and continue thoroughly changed in the sanctity of the Spirit. We recognize no evident (= visible) Church of Christ except where the Word of Cod is taught in purity and where the members live in holiness as children of God following its precepts." The last sentence, it is true, is taken from Luther's smaller catechism but, as Ritschl points out, there it serves to answer the question how the Name of God shall be made holy, while here it serves to delimit the Church of the saints.

171. It is true that he only considered the Augsburg Confession to be a suitable document of

the Lutheran Christian faith if, as he expressed it in his disgusting terminology, a *Wund-brühe* [healing liquid] had been poured upon it. To read him is an act of penitence because his language, in its insipid melting quality, is even worse than the frightful Christo-turpentine of F. T. Vischer (in his polemics with the Munich *christoterpe*).

172. See Plitt, *op. cit.*, I, p. 346. Even more decisive is the answer, quoted in Plitt, *op. cit.*, I, p. 381, to the question whether good works are necessary to salvation. "Unnecessary and harmful to the attainment of salvation, but after salvation is attained so necessary that he who does not perform them is not really saved." Thus here also they are not the cause of salvation, but the sole means of recognizing it.

173. For instance, through those caricatures of Christian freedom which Ritschl, *op cit.*, III, p. 381, so severely criticizes.

174. Above all in the greater emphasis on the idea of retributive punishment in the doctrine of salvation, which, after the repudiation of his missionary attempts by the American sects, he made the basis of his method of sanctification. After that he places the retention of childlikeness and the virtues of humble resignation in the foreground as the end of Herrnhut asceticism, in sharp contrast to the inclination of his own community to an asceticism closely analogous to the Puritan.

175. Which, however, had its limits. For this reason alone it is wrong to attempt to place Zinzendorf's religion in a scheme of social psychological evolutionary stages, as Lamprecht does. Furthermore, however, his whole religious attitude is influenced by nothing more strongly than the fact that he was a Count with an outlook fundamentally feudal. Further, the emotional side of it would, from the point of view of social psychology, fit just as well into the period of the sentimental decadence of chivalry as in that of sensitiveness. If social psychology gives any clue to its difference from West European rationalism, it is most likely to be found in the patriarchal traditionalism of Eastern Germany.

176. This is evident from Zinzendorf's controversy with Dippel just as, after his death, the doctrines of the Synod of 1764 bring out the character of the Herrnhut community as an institution for salvation. See Ritschl's criticism, *op. cit.*, III, pp. 443 f.

177. Compare, for instance, §§ 151, 153, 160. That sanctification may not take place in spite of true penitence and the forgiveness of sins is evident, especially from the remarks on p. 311, and agrees with the Lutheran doctrine of salvation just as it is in disagreement with that of Calvinism (and Methodism).

178. Compare Zinzendorf's opinion, cited in Plitt, *op. cit.*, ll, p. 345. Similarly Spangenberg, *Idea Fidei*, p. 325.

179. Compare, for instance, Zinzendorf's remark on Matt. xx. 28, cited by Plitt, *op. cit.*, III, p. 131: "When I see a man to whom God has given a great gift, I rejoice and gladly avail myself of the gift. But when I note that he is not content with his own, but wishes to increase it further, I consider it the beginning of that person's ruin." In other words, Zinzendorf denied, especially in his conversation with John Wesley in 1743, that there could be progress in holiness, because he identified it with justification and found it only in the emotional relationship to Christ (Plitt, I, p. 413). In place of the sense of being the instrument of God comes the possession of the divine; mysticism, not asceticism (in the sense to be discussed in the introduction to the following essays) (not here translated.—TRANSLATOR'S NOTE). As is pointed out there, a present, worldly state of mind is naturally what the Puritan really seeks for also. But for him the state which he interprets as the *certitudo salutis* is the feeling of being an active instrument.

180. But which, precisely on account of this mystical tendency, did not receive a consistent ethical justification. Zinzendorf rejects Luther's idea of divine worship in the calling as the decisive reason for performing one's duty in it. It is rather a return for the "Saviour's loyal services" (Plitt, II, p. 411).

181. His saying that "a reasonable man should not be without faith and a believer should not be unreasonable" is well known. See his *Sokrates, d. i. Aufrichtige Anzeige verschiedener nicht sowohl unbekannter als vielmehr in Abfall geratener Hauptwahrheiten* (1725). Further, his fondness for such authors as Bayle.

182. The decided propensity of Protestant asceticism for empiricism, rationalized on a mathematical basis, is well known, but cannot be further analysed here. On the development of the sciences in the direction of mathematically rationalized exact investigation, the philosophical motives of it and their contrast to Bacon's view-point, see Windelband, *Geschichte der Philosophie*, pp. 305–7, especially the remark on p. 305, which rightly denies that modern natural science can be understood as the product of material and technical interests. Highly important relationships exist, of course, but they are much more complex. See further Windelband, *Neuere Phil.*, I, pp. 40 ff. For the attitude of Protestant asceticism the decisive point was, as may perhaps be most clearly seen in Spener's *Theologische Bedenken*, I, p. 232; III, p. 260, that just as the Christian is known by the fruits of his belief, the knowledge of God and His designs can only be attained through a knowledge of His works. The favourite science of all Puritan, Baptist, or Pietist Christianity was thus physics, and next

to it all those other natural sciences which used a similar method, especially mathematics. It was hoped from the empirical knowledge of the divine laws of nature to ascend to a grasp of the essence of the world, which on account of the fragmentary nature of the divine revelation, a Calvinistic idea, could never be attained by the method of metaphysical speculation. The empiricism of the seventeenth century was the means for asceticism to seek God in nature. It seemed to lead to God, philosophical speculation away from Him. In particular Spener considers the Aristotelean philosophy to have been the most harmful element in Christian tradition. Every other is better, especially the Platonic: *Cons. Theol.*, III; 6, 1, Dist. 2, No. 13. Compare further the following characteristic passage: "Unde pro Cartesio quid dicam non habeo [he had not read him], semper tamen optavi et opto, ut Deus viros excitet, qui veram philosophiam vel tandem oculis sisterent in qua nullius hominis attenderetur auctoritas, sed sana tantum magistri nescia ratio", Spener, *Cons. Theol.*, II, 5, No. 2. The significance of this attitude of ascetic Protestantism for the development of education, especially technical education is well known. Combined with the attitude to *fides implicita* [implicit faith] they furnished a pedagogical programme.

183. "That is a type of men who seek their happiness in four main ways: (1) to be insignificant, despised, and abased; (2) to neglect all things they do not need for the service of their Lord; (3) either to possess nothing or to give away again what they receive; (4) to work as wage labourers, not for the sake of the wage, but of the calling in the service of the Lord and their neighbour" (*Rel. Reden*, II, p. 180; Plitt, *op. cit.*, I, p. 445). Not everyone can or may become a disciple, but only those who receive the call of the Lord. But according to Zinzendorf's own confession (Plitt, op. cit., I, p. 449) there still remain difficulties, for the Sermon on the Mount applies formally to all. The resemblance of this free universality of love to the old Baptist ideals is evident.

184. Evangelical counsels [*Editor*].

185. An emotional intensification of religion was by no means entirely unknown to Lutheranism even in its later period. Rather the ascetic element, the way of life which the Lutheran suspected of being salvation by works, was the fundamental difference in this case.

186. A healthy fear is a better sign of grace than certainty, says Spener, *Theologische Bedenken*, I, p. 324. In the Puritan writers we, of course, also find emphatic warnings against false certainty; but at least the doctrine of predestination, so far as its influence determined religious practice, always worked in the opposite direction.

187. The psychological effect of the confessional was everywhere to relieve the individual of responsibility for his own conduct, that is why it was sought, and that weakened the rigorous consistency of the demands of asceticism.

188. How important at the same time, even for the form of the Pietist faith, was the part played by purely political factors, has been indicated by Ritschl in his study of Württemberg Pietism.

189. See Zinzendorf's statement [quoted above, note 183].

190. Of course Calvinism, in so far as it is genuine, is also patriarchal. The connection, for instance, of the success of Baxter's activities with the domestic character of industry in Kidderminster is evident from his autobiography. See the passage quoted in the *Works of the Puritan Divines*, p. 38: "The town itself upon the weaving of Kidderminster stuffs, and as they stand in their loom, they can set a book before them, or edify each other. . . ." Nevertheless, there is a difference between patriarchalism based on Pietism and on the Calvinistic and especially the Baptist ethics. This problem can only be discussed in another connection.

191. *Lehre von der Rechtfertigung und Versöhnung*, third edition, I, p. 598. That Frederick William I called Pietism a religion for the leisure class is more indicative of his own Pietism than that of Spener and Francke. Even this king knew very well why he had opened his realm to the Pietists by his declaration of toleration.

192. As an introduction to Methodism the excellent article *Methodismus* by Loofs in the *Realenzyklopädie für protestantische Theologie und Kirche* is particularly good. Also the works of Jacoby (especially the *Handbuch des Methodismus*), Kolde, Jüngst, and Southey are useful. On Wesley: Tyerman, *Life and Times of John Wesley* is popular. One of the best libraries on the history of Methodism is that of Northwestern University, Evanston, Ill. A sort of link between classical Puritanism and Methodism was formed by the religious poet Isaac Watts, a friend of the chaplain of Oliver Cromwell (Howe) and then of Richard Cromwell. Whitefield is said to have sought his advice (cf. Skeats, *op. cit.*, pp. 254 f.).

193. Certainty of salvation [*Editor*].

194. Apart from the personal influence of the Wesleys the similarity is historically determined, on the one hand, by the decline of the dogma of predestination, on the other by the powerful revival of the *sola fide* [by faith alone] in the founders of Methodism, especially motivated by its specific missionary character. This brought forth a modified rejuvenation of certain mediæval methods of revival preaching and combined them with Pietistic forms. It certainly does not belong in a general line of development toward subjectivism, since in

this respect it stood behind not only Pietism, but also the Bernardine religion of the Middle Ages.

195. In this manner Wesley himself occasionally characterized the effect of the Methodist faith. The relationship to Zinzendorf's *Glückseligkeit* is evident.

196. Given in Watson's *Life of Wesley,* p. 331 (German edition).

197. J. Schneckenburger, *Vorlesungen über die Lehrbegriffe der kleinen protestantischen Kirchenparteien,* edited by Hundeshagen (Frankfurt, 1863), p. 147.

198. Whitefield, the leader of the predestinationist group which after his death dissolved for lack of organization, rejected Wesley's doctrine of perfection in its essentials. In fact, it is only a makeshift for the real Calvinistic idea of proof.

199. Resoluteness [*Editor*].

200. Schneckenburger, *op. cit.,* p. 145. Somewhat different in Loofs, *op. cit.* Both results are typical of all similar religious phenomena.

201. Thus in the conference of 1770. The first conference of 1744 had already recognized that the Biblical words came "within a hair" of Calvinism on the one hand and Antinomianism on the other. But since they were so obscure it was not well to be separated by doctrinal differences so long as the validity of the Bible as a practical norm was upheld.

202. The Methodists were separated from the Herrnhuters by their doctrine of the possibility of sinless perfection, which Zinzendorf, in particular, rejected. On the other hand, Wesley felt the emotional element in the Herrnhut religion to be mysticism and branded Luther's interpretation of the law as blasphemous. This shows the barrier which existed between Lutheranism and every kind of rational religious conduct.

203. John Wesley emphasizes the fact that everywhere, among Quakers, Presbyterians, and High Churchmen, one must believe in dogmas, except in Methodism. With the above, compare the rather summary discussion in Skeats, *History of the Free Churches of - England, 1688–1851.*

204. Compare Dexter, *Congregationalism,* pp. 455 ff.

205. Though naturally it might interfere with it, as is to-day the case among the American negroes. Furthermore, the often definitely pathological character of Methodist emotionalism as compared to the relatively mild type of Pietism may possibly, along with purely historical reasons and the publicity of the process, be connected with the greater ascetic penetration of life in the areas where Methodism is widespread. Only a neurologist could decide that.

206. Loofs, *op. cit.,* p. 750, strongly emphasizes the fact that Methodism is distinguished from other ascetic movements in that it came after the English Enlightenment, and compares it with the (surely much less pronounced) German Renaissance of Pietism in the first third of the nineteenth century. Nevertheless, it is permissible, following Ritschl, *Lehre von der Rechtfertigung und Versöhnung,* I, pp. 568 f., to retain the parallel with the Zinzendorf form of Pietism, which, unlike that of Spener and Francke, was already itself a reaction against the Enlightenment. However, this reaction takes a very different course in Methodism from that of the Herrnhuters, at least so far as they were influenced by Zinzendorf.

207. But which, as is shown by the passage from John Wesley (p. 92), it developed in the same way and with the same effect as the other ascetic denominations.

208. And, as we have seen, milder forms of the consistent ascetic ethics of Puritanism; while if, in the popular manner, one wished to interpret these religious conceptions as only exponents or reflections of capitalistic institutions, just the opposite would have to be the case.

209. Of the Baptists only the so-called General Baptists go back to the older movement. The Particular Baptists were, as we have pointed out already, Calvinists, who in principle limited Church membership to the regenerate, or at least personal believers, and hence remained in principle voluntarists and opponents of any State Church. Under Cromwell, no doubt, they were not always consistent in practice. Neither they nor the General Baptists, however important they are as the bearers of the Baptist tradition, give us any occasion for an especial dogmatic analysis here. That the Quakers, though formally a new foundation of George Fox and his associates, were fundamentally a continuation of the Baptist tradition, is beyond question. The best introduction to their history, including their relations to Baptists and Mennonites, is Robert Barclay, *The Inner Life of the Religious Societies of the Commonwealth,* 1876. On the history of the Baptists, compare, among others, H. M. Dexter, *The True Story of John Smyth, the Se-Baptist,* as told by himself and his contemporaries, Boston, 1881 (also J. C. Lang in *The Baptist Quarterly Review,* 1883, p. 1); J. Murch, *A History of the Presb. and Gen. Bapt. Church in the West of England,* London, 1835; A. H. Newman, *History of the Baptist Church in the U.S.,* New York, 1894 (*Am. Church Hist. Series,* vol. 2); Vedder, *A Short History of the Baptists,* London, 1897; E. B. Bax, *Rise and Fall of the Anabaptists,* New York, 1902; G. Lorimer, *The Baptists in History,* 1902; J. A. Seiss, *The Baptist System Examined,* Lutheran Publication Society, 1902; further material in the *Baptist Handbook,* London, 1896 ff.; *Baptist Manuals,* Paris, 1891–93; *The Baptist Quarterly Review;* and the *Bibliotheca Sacra,* Oberlin, 1900.

The best Baptist library seems to be that of Colgate College in the State of New York. For the history of the Quakers the collection in Devonshire House in London is considered the best (not available to me). The official modern organ of orthodoxy is the *American Friend*, edited by Professor Jones; the best Quaker history that of Rowntree. In addition Rufus B. Jones, *George Fox, an Autobiography*, Phila., 1903; Alton C. Thomas, *A History of the Society of Friends in America*, Phila., 1895; Edward Grubbe, *Social Aspects of the Quaker Faith*, London, 1899. Also the copious and excellent biographical literature.

210. It is one of the many merits of Karl Müller's *Kirchengeschichte* to have given the Baptist movement, great in its way, even though outwardly unassuming, the place it deserved in his work. It has suffered more than any other from the pitiless persecution of all the Churches, because it wished to be a sect in the specific sense of that word. Even after five generations it was discredited before the eyes of all the world by the debacle of the related eschatological experiment in Münster. And, continually oppressed and driven underground, it was long after its origin before it attained a consistent formulation of its religious doctrines. Thus it produced even less theology than would have been consistent with its principles, which were themselves hostile to a specialized development of its faith in God as a science. That was not very pleasing to the older professional theologians, even in its own time, and it made little impression on them. But many more recent ones have taken the same attitude. In Ritschl, *Pietismus*, I, pp. 22 f., the rebaptizers are not very adequately, in fact, rather contemptuously, treated. One is tempted to speak of a theological bourgeois standpoint. That, in spite of the fact that Cornelius's fine work (*Geschichte des Münsterschen Aufruhrs*) had been available for decades.

Here also Ritschl everywhere sees a retrogression from his standpoint toward Catholicism, and suspects direct influences of the radical wing of the Franciscan tradition. Even if such could be proved in a few cases, these threads would be very thin. Above all, the historical fact was probably that the official Catholic Church, wherever the worldly asceticism of the laity went as far as the formation of conventicles, regarded it with the utmost suspicion and attempted to encourage the formation of orders, thus outside the world, or to attach it as asceticism of the second grade to the existing orders and bring it under control. Where this did not succeed, it felt the danger that the practice of subjectivist ascetic morality might lead to the denial of authority and to heresy, just as, and with the same justification, the Elizabethan Church felt toward the half-Pietistic prophesying Bible conventicles, even when their conformism was undoubted; a feeling which was expressed by the Stuarts in their *Book of Sports*, of which later. The history of numerous heretical movements, including, for instance, the Humiliati and the Beguins, as well as the fate of St. Francis, are the proofs of it. The preaching of the mendicant friars, especially the Franciscans, probably did much to prepare the way for the ascetic lay morality of Calvinist-Baptist Protestantism. But the numerous close relationships between the asceticism of Western monasticism and the ascetic conduct of Protestantism, the importance of which must continually be stressed for our particular problems, are based in the last analysis on the fact that important factors are necessarily common to every asceticism on the basis of Biblical Christianity. Furthermore, every asceticism, no matter what its faith, has need of certain tried methods of subduing the flesh.

Of the following sketch it may further be remarked that its brevity is due to the fact that the Baptist ethic is of only very limited importance for the problem considered primarily in this study, the development of the religious background of the bourgeois idea of the calling. It contributed nothing new whatever to it. The much more important social aspect of the movement must for the present remain untouched. Of the history of the older Baptist movement, we can, from the view-point of our problem, present here only what was later important for the development of the sects in which we are interested: Baptists, Quakers, and, more incidentally, Mennonites.

211. See above note 120.

212. On their origin and changes, see A. Ritschl in his *Gesammelte Aufsätze*, pp. 69 f.

213. Naturally the Baptists have always repudiated the designation of a sect. They form *the* Church in the sense of the Epistle to the Ephesians v. 27. But in our terminology they form a sect not only because they lack all relation to the State. The relation between Church and State of early Christianity was even for the Quakers (Barclay) their ideal; for to them, as to many Pietists, only a Church under the Cross was beyond suspicion of its purity. But the Calvinists as well, *faute de mieux* [for want of better], similarly even the Catholic Church in the same circumstances, were forced to favour the separation of Church and State under an unbelieving State or under the Cross. Neither were they a sect, because induction to membership in the Church took place *de facto* through a contract between the congregation and the candidates. For that was formally the case in the Dutch Reformed communities (as a result of the original political situation) in accordance with the old Church constitution (see v. Hoffmann, *Kirchenverfassungsrecht der niederl. Reformierten*, Leipzig, 1902).

On the contrary, it was because such a religious community could only be voluntarily organized as a sect, not compulsorily as a Church, if it did not wish to include the unregenerate and thus depart from the Early Christian ideal. For the Baptist communities it was an essential of the very idea of their Church, while for the Calvinists it was an historical accident. To be sure, that the latter were also urged by very definite religious motives in the direction of the believers' Church has already been indicated. On the distinction between Church and sect, see the following essay. The concept of sect which I have adopted here has been used at about the same time and, I assume, independently from me, by Kattenbusch in the *Realenzyklopädie für protestantische Theologie und Kirche* (Article *Sekte*). Troeltsch in his *Die Soziallehren der christlichen Kirchen und Gruppen* accepts it and discusses it more in detail. See also below, the introduction to the essays on the *Wirtschaftsethik der Weltreligionen* (not in this volume [*Editor*]).

214. How important this symbol was, historically, for the conservation of the Church community, since it was an unambiguous and unmistakable sign, has been very clearly shown by Cornelius, *op. cit.*

215. Certain approaches to it in the Mennonites' doctrine of justification need not concern us here.

216. This idea is perhaps the basis of the religious interest in the discussion of questions like the incarnation of Christ and his relationship to the Virgin Mary, which, often as the sole purely dogmatic part, stands out so strangely in the oldest documents of Baptism (for instance the confessions printed in Cornelius, *op. cit.*, Appendix to Vol. II. On this question, see K. Müller, *Kirchengeschichte*, II, i, p. 330). The difference between the christology of the Reformed Church and the Lutheran (in the doctrine of the so-called *communicatio idiomatum*) [communication of idioms] seems to have been based on similar religious interests.

217. It was expressed especially in the original strict avoidance even of everyday intercourse with the excommunicated, a point at which even the Calvinists, who in principle held the opinion that worldly affairs were not affected by spiritual censure, made large concessions. See the following essay (not in this volume [*Editor*]).

218. How this principle was applied by the Quakers to seemingly trivial externals (refusal to remove the hat, to kneel, bow, or use formal address) is well known. The basic idea is to a certain extent characteristic of all asceticism. Hence the fact that true asceticism is always hostile to authority. In Calvinism the principle appeared in that only Christ should rule in the Church. In the case of Pietism one may think of Spener's attempts to find a Biblical justification of titles. Catholic asceticism, so far as ecclesiastical authority was concerned, broke through this tendency in its oath of obedience, by interpreting obedience itself in ascetic terms. The overturning of this principle in Protestant asceticism is the historical basis of the peculiarities of even the contemporary democracy of the peoples influenced by Puritanism as distinct from that of the Latin spirit. It is also part of the historical background of that lack of respect of the American which is, as the case may be, so irritating or so refreshing.

219. No doubt this was true from the beginning for the Baptists essentially only of the New Testament, not to the same extent of the Old. Especially the Sermon on the Mount enjoyed a peculiar prestige as a programme of social ethic in all denominations.

220. Even Schwenkfeld had considered the outward performance of the sacraments an *adiaphoron* [a matter of indifference from a religious viewpoint], while the General Baptists and the Mennonites held strictly to Baptism and the Communion, the Mennonites to the washing of feet in addition. On the other hand, for the predestinationists the depreciation, in fact for all except the communion—one may even say the suspicion—in which the sacraments were held, went very far. See the following essay (not in this volume [*Editor*]).

221. On this point the Baptist denominations, especially the Quakers (Barclay, *Apology for the True Christian Divinity*, fourth edition, London, 1701, kindly placed at my disposal by Eduard Bernstein), referred to Calvin's statements in the *Instit. Christ*, III, p. 2, where in fact quite unmistakable suggestions of Baptist doctrine are to be found. Also the older distinction between the Word of God as that which God had revealed to the patriarchs, the prophets, and the apostles, and the Holy Scriptures as that part of it which they had written down, was, even though there was no historical connection, intimately related to the Baptist conception of revelation. The mechanical idea of inspiration, and with it the strict bibliocracy of the Calvinists, was just as much the product of their development in one direction in the course of the sixteenth century as the doctrine of the inner light of the Quakers, derived from Baptist sources, was the result of a directly opposite development. The sharp differentiation was also in this case partly a result of continual disputes.

222. There is no salvation outsidde the church [*Editor*].

223. That was emphasized strongly against certain tendencies of the Socinians. The natural reason knows nothing whatever of God (Barclay, *op. cit.*, p. 102). That meant that the part played by the *lex naturæ* [natural law] elsewhere in Protestantism was altered. In principle

there could be no general rules, no moral code, for the calling which everyone had, and which is different for every individual, is revealed to him by God through his conscience. We should do, not the good in the general sense of natural reason, but God's will as it is written in our hearts and known through the conscience (Barclay, pp. 73, 76). This irrationality of morality, derived from the exaggerated contrast between the divine and the flesh, is expressed in these fundamental tenets of Quaker ethics: "What a man does contrary to his faith, though his faith may be wrong, is in no way acceptable to God—though the thing might have been lawful to another" (Barclay, p. 487). Of course that could not be upheld in practice. The "moral and perpetual statutes acknowledged by all Christians" are, for instance, for Barclay the limit of toleration. In practice the contemporaries felt their ethic, with certain peculiarities of its own, to be similar to that of the Reformed Pietists. "Everything good in the Church is suspected of being Quakerism", as Spener repeatedly points out. It thus seems that Spener envied the Quakers this reputation. *Cons. Theol.*, III, 6, 1, Dist. 2, No. 64. The repudiation of oaths on the basis of a passage in the Bible shows that the real emancipation from the Scriptures had not gone far. The significance for social ethics of the principle, "Do unto others as you would that they should do unto you", which many Quakers regarded as the essence of the whole Christian ethics, need not concern us here.

224. The necessity of assuming this possibility Barclay justifies because without it "there should never be a place known by the Saints wherein they might be free of doubting and despair, which—is most absurd". It is evident that the *certitudo salutis* [certainty of salvation] depends upon it. Thus Barclay, *op. cit.*, p. 20.

225. There thus remains a difference in type between the Calvinistic and the Quaker rationalization of life. But when Baxter formulates it by saying that the spirit is supposed by the Quakers to act upon the soul as on a corpse, while the characteristically formulated Calvinistic principle is "reason and spirit are conjunct principles" (*Christian Directory*, II, p. 76), the distinction was no longer valid for his time in this form.

226. Thus in the very careful articles "Menno" and "Mennoniten" by Cramer in the *Realenzyklopädie für protestantische Theologie und Kirche*, especially p. 604. However excellent these articles are, the article "Baptisten" in the same encyclopedia is not very penetrating and in part simply incorrect. Its author does not know, for instance, the *Publications of the Hanserd Knolly's Society*, which are indispensable for the history of Baptism.

227. Naturally rational [*Editor*].

228. Thus Barclay, *op. cit.*, p. 404, explains that eating, drinking, and acquisition are natural, not spiritual acts, which may be performed without the special sanction of God. The explanation is in reply to the characteristic objection that if, as the Quakers teach, one cannot pray without a special motion of the Spirit, the same should apply to ploughing. It is, of course, significant that even in the modern resolutions of Quaker Synods the advice is sometimes given to retire from business after acquiring a sufficient fortune, in order, withdrawn from the bustle of the world, to be able to live in devotion to the Kingdom of God alone. But the same idea certainly occurs occasionally in other denominations, including Calvinism. That betrays the fact that the acceptance of the bourgeois practical ethics by these movements was the worldly application of an asceticism which had originally fled from the world.

229. Veblen in his suggestive book *The Theory of Business Enterprise* is of the opinion that this motto belongs only to early capitalism. But economic supermen, who, like the present captains of industry, have stood beyond good and evil, have always existed, and the statement is still true of the broad strata underlying strata of business men.

230. We may here again expressly call attention to the excellent remarks of Eduard Bernstein, *op. cit.* To Kautsky's highly schematic treatment of the Baptist movement and his theory of heretical communism in general (in the first volume of the same work) we shall return on another occasion.

231. "In civil actions it is good to be as the many, in religious to be as the best", says, for example, Thomas Adams (*Works of the Puritan Divines*, p. 138). That sounds somewhat more drastic than it is meant to be. It means that the Puritan honesty is formalistic legality, just as the uprightness which the sometime Puritan people like to claim as a national virtue is something specifically different from the German *Ehrlichkeit* [honesty]. Some good remarks on the subject from the educational standpoint may be found in the *Preuss. Jahrb.*, CXII (1903), p. 226. The formalism of the Puritan ethic is in turn the natural consequence of its relation to the law.

232. Something is said on this in the following essay (not in this volume [*Editor*]).

233. This is the reason for the economic importance of the ascetic Protestant, but not Catholic, minorities.

234. That the difference of dogmatic basis was not inconsistent with the adoption of the most important interest in proof is to be explained in the last analysis by the historical peculiarities of Christianity in general which cannot be discussed here.

235. "Since God hath gathered us to be a people", says Barclay, *op. cit.*, p. 357. I myself heard

a Quaker sermon at Haverford College which laid great emphasis on the interpretation of saints as meaning separate.

236. An achievement of the few [*Editor*].

## 5 ASCETICISM AND THE SPIRIT OF CAPITALISM

1. Various Church documents [*Editor*].

2. See the excellent sketch of his character in Dowden, *op. cit.* A passable introduction to Baxter's theology, after he had abandoned a strict belief in the double decree, is given in the introduction to the various extracts from his works printed in the *Works of the Puritan Divines* (by Jenkyn). His attempt to combine universal redemption and personal election satisfied no one. For us it is important only that he even then held to personal election, i.e. to the most important point for ethics in the doctrine of predestination. On the other hand, his weakening of the forensic view of redemption is important as being suggestive of baptism.

3. Tracts and sermons by Thomas Adams, John Howe, Matthew Henry, J. Janeway, Stuart Charnock, Baxter, Bunyan, have been collected in the ten volumes of the *Works of the Puritan Divines* (London, 1845–8), though the choice is often somewhat arbitrary. Editions of the works of Bailey, Sedgwick, and Hoornbeek have already been referred to.

4. We could just as well have included Voet and other continental representatives of worldly asceticism. Brentano's view that the whole development was purely Anglo-Saxon is quite wrong. My choice is motivated mainly (though not exclusively) by the wish to present the ascetic movement as much as possible in the second half of the seventeenth century, immediately before the change to utilitarianism. It has unfortunately been impossible, within the limits of this sketch, to enter upon the fascinating task of presenting the characteristics of ascetic Protestantism through the medium of the biographical literature; the Quakers would in this connection be particularly important, since they are relatively little known in Germany.

5. For one might just as well take the writings of Gisbert Voet, the proceedings of the Huguenot Synods, or the Dutch Baptist literature. Sombart and Brentano have unfortunately taken just the ebionitic parts of Baxter, which I myself have strongly emphasized, to confront me with the undoubted capitalistic backwardness of his doctrines. But (1) one must know this whole literature thoroughly in order to use it correctly, and (2) not overlook the fact that I have attempted to show how, in spite of its anti-mammonistic doctrines, the spirit of this ascetic religion nevertheless, just as in the monastic communities, gave birth to economic rationalism because it placed a premium on what was most important for it: the fundamentally ascetic rational motives. That fact alone is under discussion and is the point of this whole essay.

6. Similarly in Calvin, who was certainly no champion of bourgeois wealth (see the sharp attacks on Venice and Antwerp in *Jes. Opp.*, III, 140a, 308a).

7. *Saints' Everlasting Rest*, chaps. x, xii. Compare Bailey (*Praxis Pietatis*, p. 182) or Matthew Henry (*The Worth of the Soul, Works of the Puritan Divines*, p. 319). "Those that are eager in pursuit of worldly wealth despise their Soul, not only because the Soul is neglected and the body preferred before it, but because it is employed in these pursuits" (Psa. cxxvii. 2). On the same page, however, is the remark to be cited below about the sinfulness of all waste of time, especially in recreations. Similarly in almost the whole religious literature of English-Dutch Puritanism. See for instance, Hoornbeek's (*op cit.*, L, X, ch. 18, 18) Phillipics against *avaritia*. This writer is also affected by sentimental pietistic influences. See the praise of *tranquillitas animi* [silent soul] which is much more pleasing to God than the *sollicitudo* [activities] of this world. Also Bailey, referring to the well-known passage in Scripture, is of the opinion that "A rich man is not easily saved" (*op. cit.*, p. 182). The Methodist catechisms also warn against "gathering treasure on this earth". For Pietism this is quite obvious, as also for the Quakers. Compare Barday (*op. cit.*, p. 517), ". . . and therefore beware of such temptations as to use their callings as an engine to be richer".

8. For not wealth alone, but also the impulsive pursuit of it (or what passed as such) was condemned with similar severity. In the Netherlands the South Holland Synod of 1574 declared, in reply to a question, that money-lenders should not be admitted to communion even though the business was permitted by law; and the Deventer Provincial Synod of 1598 (Art. 24) extended this to the employees of money-lenders. The Synod of Gorichem in 1606 prescribed severe and humiliating conditions under which the wives of usurers might be admitted, and the question was discussed as late as 1644 and 1657 whether Lombards should be admitted to communion (this against Brentano, who cites his own Catholic ancestors, although foreign traders and bankers have existed in the whole European and Asiatic world for thousands of years). Gisbert Voet (*Disp. Theol.*, IV, 1667, *de usuris*, p. 665) still wanted to exclude the Trapezites (Lombards, Piedmontese).

The same was true of the Huguenot Synods. This type of capitalistic classes were not the typical representatives of the philosophy or the type of conduct with which we are concerned. They were also not new as compared with antiquity or the Middle Ages.

9. Developed in detail in the tenth chapter of the *Saints' Everlasting Rest*. He who should seek to rest in the shelter of possessions which God gives, God strikes even in this life. A self-satisfied enjoyment of wealth already gained is almost always a symptom of moral degradation, If we had everything which we could have in this world, would that be all we hoped for? Complete satisfaction of desires is not attainable on earth because God's will has decreed it should not be so.

10. *Christian Directory*, I, pp. 375–6. "It is for action that God maintaineth us and our activities; work is the moral as well as the natural end of power. . . . It is action that God is most served and honoured by. . . . The public welfare or the good of the many is to be valued above our own." Here is the connecting-point for the transition from the will of God to the purely utilitarian view-point of the later liberal theory. On the religious sources of Utilitarianism, see below in the text and above, chap. 4, note 182.

11. The commandment of silence has been, starting from the Biblical threat of punishment for every useless word, especially since the Cluny monks, a favourite ascetic means of education in self-control. Baxter also speaks in detail of the sinfulness of unnecessary words. Its place in his character has been pointed out by Sanford, *op. cit.*, pp. 90 ff.

What contemporaries felt as the deep melancholy and moroseness of the Puritans was the result of breaking down the spontaneity of the *status naturalis* [state of nature], and the condemnation of thoughtless speech was in the service of this end. When Washington Irving (*Bracebridge Hall*, chap. xxx) seeks the reason for it partly in the calculating spirit of capitalism and partly in the effect of political freedom, which promotes a sense of responsibility, it may be remarked that it does not apply to the Latin peoples. For England the situation was probably that: (1) Puritanism enabled its adherents to create free institutions and still become a world power; and (2) it transformed that calculating spirit (what Sombart calls *Rechenhaftigkeit*), which is in truth essential to capitalism, from a mere means to economy into a principle of general conduct.

12. *Op. cit.*, I, p. 111.

13. *Op. cit.*, I, pp. 383 f.

14. Similarly on the preciousness of time, see Barclay, *op. cit.*, p. 14.

15. Baxter, *op. cit.*, I, p. 79. "Keep up a high esteem of time and be every day more careful that you lose none of your time, than you are that you lose none of your gold and silver. And if vain recreation, dressings, feastings, idle talk, unprofitable company, or sleep be any of them temptations to rob you of any of your time, accordingly heighten your watchfulness." "Those that are prodigal of their time despise their own souls", says Matthew Henry (*Worth of the Soul, Works of the Puritan Divines*, p. 315). Here also Protestant asceticism follows a well-beaten track. We are accustomed to think it characteristic of the modern man that he has no time, and for instance, like Goethe in the *Wanderjahren* to measure the degree of capitalistic development by the fact that the clocks strike every quarter-hour. So also Sombart in his *Kapitalismus*. We ought not, however, to forget that the first people to live (in the Middle Ages) with careful measurement of time were the monks, and that the church bells were meant above all to meet their needs.

16. Compare Baxter's discussion of the calling, *op. cit.*, I, pp. 108 ff. Especially the following passage : "Question : But may I not cast off the world that I may only think of my salvation? Answer: You may cast off all such excess of worldly cares or business as unnecessarily hinder you in spiritual things. But you may not cast off all bodily employment and mental labour in which you may serve the common good. Everyone as a member of Church or Commonwealth must employ their parts to the utmost for the good of the Church and the Commonwealth. To neglect this and say: I will pray and meditate, is as if your servant should refuse his greatest work and tie himself to some lesser, easier part. And God hath commanded you some way or other to labour for your daily bread and not to live as drones of the sweat of others only." God's commandment to Adam, "In the sweat of thy brow", and Paul's declaration, "He who will not work shall not eat", are also quoted. It has always been known of the Quakers that even the most well-to-do of them have had their sons learn a calling, for ethical and not, as Alberti recommends, for utilitarian reasons.

17. Here are points where Pietism, on account of its emotional character, takes a different view. Spener, although he emphasizes in characteristic Lutheran fashion that labour in a calling is worship of God (*Theologische Bedenken*, III, p. 445), nevertheless holds that the restlessness of business affairs distracts one from God, a most characteristic difference from Puritanism.

18. I, *op. cit.*, p. 242. "It's they that are lazy in their callings that can find no time for holy duties." Hence the idea that the cities, the seat of the middle class with its rational business activities, are the seats of ascetic virtue. Thus Baxter says of his hand-loom weavers in Kidderminster: "And their constant converse and traffic with London doth much to

promote civility and piety among tradesmen . . ." in his autobiography (*Works of the Puritan Divines*, p. 38). That the proximity of the capital should promote virtue would astonish modern clergymen, at least in Germany. But Pietism also inclined to similar views. Thus Spener, speaking of a young colleague, writes: "At least it appears that among the great multitudes in the cities, though the majority is quite depraved, there are nevertheless a number of good people who can accomplish much, while in villages often hardly anything good can be found in a whole community" (*Theologische Bedenken*, I, 66, p. 303). In other words, the peasant is little suited to rational ascetic conduct. Its ethical glorification is very modern. We cannot here enter into the significance of this and similar statements for the question of the relation of asceticism to social classes.

19. Take, for instance, the following passages (*op. cit.*, pp. 336 f.): "Be wholly taken up in diligent business of your lawful callings when you are not exercised in the more immediate service of God." "Labour hard in your callings." "See that you have a calling which will find you employment for all the time which God's immediate service spareth."

20. That the peculiar ethical valuation of labour and its dignity was not originally a Christian idea nor even peculiar to Christianity has recently again been strongly emphasized by Harnack (*Mitt. des Ev.-Soz Kongr.*, 14. Folge, 1905, Nos. 3, 4, p. 48).

21. Similarly in Pietism (Spener, *op. cit.*, III, pp. 429–30). The characteristic Pietist version is that loyalty to a calling which is imposed upon us by the fall serves to annihilate one's own selfish will. Labour in the calling is, as a service of love to one's neighbour, a duty of gratitude for God's grace (a Lutheran idea), and hence it is not pleasing to God that it should be performed reluctantly (*op. cit.*, III, p. 272). The Christian should thus "prove himself as industrious in his labour as a worldly man" (III, p. 278). That is obviously less drastic than the Puritan version.

22. The significance of this important difference, which has been evident ever since the Benedictine rules, can only be shown by a much wider investigation.

23. "A sober procreation of children" is its purpose according to Baxter. Similarly Spener, at the same time with concessions to the coarse Lutheran attitude, which makes the avoidance of immorality, which is otherwise unavoidable, an accessory aim. Concupiscence as an accompaniment of sexual intercourse is sinful even in marriage. For instance, in Spener's view it is a result of the fall which transformed such a natural, divinely ordained process into something inevitably accompanied by sinful sensations, which is hence shameful. Also in the opinion of various Pietistic groups the highest form of Christian marriage is that with the preservation of virginity, the next highest that in which sexual intercourse is only indulged in for the procreation of children, and so on down to those which are contracted for purely erotic or external reasons and which are, from an ethical standpoint, concubinage. On these lower levels a marriage entered into for purely economic reasons is preferred (because after all it is inspired by rational motives) to one with erotic foundations. We may here neglect the Herrnhut theory and practice of marriage. Rationalistic philosophy (Christian Wolff) adopted the ascetic theory in the form that what was designed as a means to an end, concupiscence and its satisfaction, should not be made an end in itself.

The transition to a pure, hygienically oriented utilitarianism had already taken place in Franklin, who took approximately the ethical standpoint of modern physicians, who understand by chastity the restriction of sexual intercourse to the amount desirable for health, and who have, as is well known, even given theoretical advice as to how that should be accomplished. As soon as these matters have become the object of purely rational consideration the same development has everywhere taken place. The Puritan and the hygienic sex-rationalist generally tread very different paths, but here they understand each other perfectly. In a lecture, a zealous adherent of hygienic prostitution—it was a question of the regulation of brothels and prostitutes—defended the moral legitimacy of extramarital intercourse (which was looked upon as hygienically useful) by referring to its poetic justification in the case of Faust and Margaret. To treat Margaret as a prostitute and to fail to distinguish the powerful sway of human passions from sexual intercourse for hygienic reasons, both are thoroughly congenial to the Puritan standpoint. Similar, for instance, is the typical specialist's view, occasionally put forward by very distinguished physicians, that a question which extends so far into the subtlest problems of personality and of culture as that of sexual abstinence should be dealt with exclusively in the forum of the physician (as an expert). For the Puritan the expert was the moral theorist, now he is the medical man; but the claim of competence to dispose of the questions which seem to us somewhat narrow-minded is, with opposite signs of course, the same in both cases.

But with all its prudery, the powerful idealism of the Puritan attitude can show positive accomplishments, even from the point of view of race conservation in a purely hygienic sense, while modern sex hygiene, on account of the appeal to unprejudicedness which it is forced to make, is in danger of destroying the basis of all its success. How, with the rationalistic interpretation of sexual relations among peoples influenced by Puritanism, a certain refinement and spiritual and ethical penetration of marital relationships, with a blossoming of matrimonial chivalry, has grown up, in contrast to the patriarchal sentimentality (*Brodem*), which is typical of Germany even in the circles of the intellectual aristocracy, must necessarily remain outside this discussion. Baptist influences have played a part in the emancipation of woman; the protection of her freedom of conscience, and the extension of the idea of the universal priesthood to her were here also the first breaches in patriarchal ideas.

24. This recurs again and again in Baxter. The Biblical basis is regularly either the passages in Proverbs, which we already know from Franklin (xxii. 29), or those in praise of labour (xxxi. 16). Cf. *op. cit.*, I, pp. 377, 382, etc.

25. Even Zinzendorf says at one point : "One does not only work in order to live, but one lives for the sake of one's work, and if there is no more work to do one suffers or goes to sleep" (Plitt, *op. cit.*, I, p. 428).

26. Also a symbol of the Mormons closes (after quotations) with the words : "But a lazy or indolent man cannot be a Christian and be saved. He is destined to be struck down and cast from the hive." But in this case it was primarily the grandiose discipline, half-way between monastery and factory, which placed the individual before the dilemma of labour or annihilation and, of course in connection with religious enthusiasm and only possible through it, brought forth the astonishing economic achievements of this sect.

27. Hence (*op. cit.*, I, p. 380) its symptoms are carefully analysed. Sloth and idleness are such deadly sins because they have a cumulative character. They are even regarded by Baxter as "destroyers of grace" (*op. cit.*, I, pp. 279–80). That is, they are the antitheses of the methodical life.

28. See above, chap. 3, note 7.

29. And naturally rational [*Editor*].

30. Treasure of the Church [*Editor*].

31. Baxter, *op. cit.*, I, pp. 108 ff. Especially striking are the following passages : "Question: But will not wealth excuse us? Answer: It may excuse you from some sordid sort of work by making you more serviceable to another, but you are no more excused from service of work . . . than the poorest man." Also, p. 376: "Though they [the rich] have no outward want to urge them, they have as great a necessity to obey God . . . God hath strictly commanded it [labour] to all." Chap. 4, note 57.

32. Similarly Spener (*op. cit.*, III, pp. 338, 425), who for this reason opposes the tendency to early retirement as morally objectionable, and, in refuting an objection to the taking of interest, that the enjoyment of interest leads to laziness, emphasizes that anyone who was in a position to live upon interest would still be obligated to work by God's commandment.

33. Including Pietism. Whenever a question of change of calling arises, Spener takes the attitude that after a certain calling has once been entered upon, it is a duty of obedience to Providence to remain and acquiesce in it.

34. From natural causes [*Editor*].

35. The tremendous force, dominating the whole of conduct, with which the Indian religious teaching sanctions economic traditionalism in terms of chances of favourable rebirth, I have shown in the essays on the *Wirtschaftsethik der Weltreligionen* [*The Economic Ethics of the World Religions*]. It is an excellent example by which to show the difference between mere ethical theories and the creation of psychological sanctions with a religious background for certain types of conduct. The pious Hindu could advance in the scale of transmigration only by the strictly traditional fulfilment of the duties of the caste of his birth. It was the strongest conceivable religious basis for traditionalism. In fact, the Indian ethic is in this respect the most completely consistent antithesis of the Puritan, as in another respect (traditionalism of the caste structure) it is opposed to the Hebrew.

36. Baxter, *op. cit.*, I, p. 377.

37. But this does not mean that the Puritan view-point was historically derived from the latter. On the contrary, it is an expression of the genuinely Calvinistic idea that the cosmos of the world serves the glory of God. The utilitarian turn, that the economic cosmos should serve the good of the many, the common good, etc., was a consequence of the idea that any other interpretation of it would lead to aristocratic idolatry of the flesh, or at least did not serve the glory of God, but only fleshly cultural ends. But God's will, as it is expressed (chap. 4, note 39) in the purposeful arrangements of the economic cosmos, can, so far as secular ends are in question at all, only be embodied in the good of the community, in impersonal usefulness. Utilitarianism is thus, as has already been pointed out, the result of the impersonal character of brotherly love and the repudiation of all glorification of this world by the exclusiveness of the Puritan *in majorem Dei gloriam* [for the greater glory of God].

How completely this idea, that all idolatry of the flesh is inconsistent with the glory of God and hence unconditionally bad, dominated ascetic Protestantism is clearly shown by the doubts and hesitation which it cost even Spener, who certainly was not infected with democracy, to maintain the use of titles as ἀδιάφορον [indifferent from the view of religion] against numerous objections. He finally comforted himself with the reflection that even in the Bible the Prætor Festus was given the title of κράτιστος [the All Powerful] by the Apostles. The political side of the question does not arise in this connection.

38. "The inconstant man is a stranger in his own house", says Thomas Adams (*Works of the Puritan Divines*, p. 77).

39. On this, see especially George Fox's remarks in the *Friends' Library* (ed. W. & T. Evans, Philadelphia, 1837), I, p. 130.

40. Above all, this sort of religious ethic cannot be regarded as a reflex of economic conditions. The specialization of occupations had, if anything, gone further in mediæval Italy than in the England of that period.

41. For, as is often pointed out in the Puritan literature, God never commanded "love thy neighbour more than thyself", but only as thyself. Hence self-regard is also a duty. For instance, a man who can make better use of his possessions, to the greater glory of God, than his neighbour, is not obliged by the duty of brotherly love to part with them.

42. Spener is also close to this view-point. But even in the case of transfer from commercial occupations (regarded as especially dangerous to virtue) to theology, he remains hesitant and on the whole opposed to it (*op. cit.*, III, pp. 435, 443; I, p. 524). The frequent occurrence of the reply to just this question (of the permissibility of changing a calling) in Spener's naturally biassed opinion shows, incidentally, how eminently practical the different ways of interpreting 1 Corinthians vii were.

43. Such ideas are not to be found, at least in the writings, of the leading Continental Pietists. Spener's attitude vacillates between the Lutheran (that of satisfaction of needs) and Mercantilist arguments for the usefulness of the prosperity of commerce, etc. (*op. cit.*, III, pp. 330, 332; I, p. 418: "the cultivation of tobacco brings money into the country and is thus useful, hence not sinful". Compare also III, pp. 426–7, 429, 434). But he does not neglect to point out that, as the example of the Quakers and the Mennonites shows, one can make profit and yet remain pious; in fact, that even especially high profits, as we shall point out later, may be the direct result of pious uprightness (*op. cit.*, p. 435).

44. These views of Baxter are not a reflection of the economic environment in which he lived. On the contrary, his autobiography shows that the success of his home missionary work was partly due to the fact that the Kidderminster tradesmen were not rich, but earned food and raiment, and that the master craftsmen had to live from hand to mouth just as their employees did. "It is the pool who receive the glad tidings of the Gospel." Thomas Adams remarks on the pursuit of gain : "He [the knowing man] knows . . . that money may make a man richer, not better, and thereupon chooseth rather to sleep with a good conscience than a full purse . . . therefore desires no more wealth than an honest man may bear away" (*Works of the Puritan Divines*, LI). But he does want that much, and that means that every formally honest gain is legitimate.

45. Thus Baxter, *op. cit.*, I, chap. x, 1, 9 (par. 24); I, p. 378, 2. In Prov. xxiii. 4: "Weary thyself not to be rich" means only "riches for our fleshly ends must not ultimately be intended". Possession in the feudal-seigneurial form of its use is what is odious (cf. the remark, *op. cit.*, I, p. 380, on the "debauched part of the gentry"), not possession in itself. Milton, in the first *Defensio pro populo Anglicano*, held the well-known theory that only the middle class can maintain virtue. That middle class here means bourgeoisie as against the aristocracy is shown by the statement that both luxury and necessity are unfavourable to virtue.

46. This is most important. We may again add the general remark: we are here naturally not so much concerned with what concepts the theological moralists developed in their ethical theories, but, rather, what was the effective morality in the life of believers—that is, how the religious background of economic ethics affected practice. In the casuistic literature of Catholicism, especially the Jesuit, one can occasionally read discussions which—for instance on the question of the justification of interest, into which we do not enter here—sound like those of many Protestant casuists, or even seem to go farther in permitting or tolerating things. The Puritans have since often enough been reproached that their ethic is at bottom the same as that of the Jesuits. Just as the Calvinists often cite Catholic moralists, not only Thomas Aquinas, Bernhard of Clairvaux, Bonaventura, etc., but also contemporaries, the Catholic casuists also took notice of heretical ethics. We cannot discuss all that here.

But quite apart from the decisive fact of the religious sanction of the ascetic life for the layman, there is the fundamental difference, even in theory, that these latitudinarian ideas within Catholicism were the products of peculiarly lax ethical theories, not sanctioned by the authority of the Church, but opposed by the most serious and strictest disciples of it. On the other hand, the Protestant idea of the calling in effect placed the most serious enthusiasts for asceticism in the service of capitalistic acquisition. What in the one case might under certain conditions be allowed, appeared in the other as a positive moral good. The fundamental differences of the two ethics, very important in practice, have been finally crystallized, even for modern times, by the Jansenist controversy and the Bull *Unigenitus*.

47. "You may labour in that manner as tendeth most to your success and lawful gain. You are bound to improve all your talents." There follows the passage cited above in the text. A

direct parallel between the pursuit of wealth in the Kingdom of Heaven and the pursuit of success in an earthly calling is found in Janeway, *Heaven upon Earth* (*Works of the Puritan Divines*, p. 275).

48. Even in the Lutheran Confession of Duke Christopher of Württemberg, which was submitted to the Council of Trent, objection is made to the oath of poverty. He who is poor in his station should bear it, but if he swore to remain so it would be the same as if he swore to remain sick or to maintain a bad reputation.

49. Thus in Baxter and also in Duke Christopher's confession. Compare further passages like: ". . . the vagrant rogues whose lives are nothing but an exorbitant course; the main begging", etc. (Thomas Adams, *Works of the Puritan Divines*, p. 259). Even Calvin had strictly forbidden begging, and the Dutch Synods campaigned against licences to beg. During the epoch of the Stuarts, especially Laud's regime under Charles I, which had systematically developed the principle of public poor relief and provision of work for the unemployed, the Puritan battle-cry was: "Giving alms is no charity" (title of Defoe's later well-known work). Towards the end of the seventeenth century they began the deterrent system of workhouses for the unemployed (compare Leonard, *Early History of English Poor Relief*, Cambridge, 1900, and H. Levy, *Die Grundlagen des ökonomischen Liberalismus in der Geschichte der englischen Volkswirtschaft*, Jena, 1912, pp. 69 ff.).

50. The President of the Baptist Union of Great Britain and Ireland, G. White, said emphatically in his inaugural address before the assembly in London in 1903 (*Baptist Handbook*, 1904, p. 104): "The best men on the roll of our Puritan Churches were men of affairs, who believed that religion should permeate the whole of life."

51. Here also lies the characteristic difference from all feudal view-points. For the latter only the descendants of the parvenu (political or social) can reap the benefit of his success in a recognized station (characteristically expressed in the Spanish *Hidalgo* [parvenu] = *hijo d'algo* = *filius de aliquo* where the *aliquid* means an inherited property). However rapidly these differences are to-day fading out in the rapid change and Europeanization of the American national character, nevertheless the precisely opposite bourgeois attitude which glorifies business success and earnings as a symptom of mental achievement, but has no respect for mere inherited wealth, is still sometimes represented there. On the other hand, in Europe (as James Bryce once remarked) in effect almost every social honour is now purchasable for money, so long as the buyer has not himself stood behind the counter, and carries out the necessary metamorphosis of his property (formation of trusts, etc.). Against the aristocracy of blood, see for instance Thomas Adams, *Works of the Puritan Divines*, p. 216.

52. That was, for instance, already true of the founder of the Familist sect, Hendrik Nicklaes, who was a merchant (Barclay, *Inner Life of the Religious Societies of the Commonwealth*, p. 34).

53. This is, for instance, definitely true for Hoornbeek, since Matt. v. 5 and 1 Tim. iv. 8 also made purely worldly promises to the saints (*op. cit.*, I, p. 193). Everything is the work of God's Providence, but in particular He takes care of His own. *Op. cit.*, p. 192: "Super alios autem summa cura et modis singularissimis versatur Dei providentia circa fideles." [more than to others, Providence extends with an enormous solicitude to the faithful and in appropriate ways]. There follows a discussion of how one can know that a stroke of luck comes not from the *communis providentia* [common ordering of the world], but from that special care. Bailey also (*op. cit.*, p. 191) explains success in worldly labours by reference to Providence. That prosperity is often the reward of a godly life is a common expression in Quaker writings (for example see such an expression as late as 1848 in *Selection from the Christian Advices*, issued by the General Meeting of the Society of Friends, London, sixth edition, 1851, p. 209). We shall return to the connection with the Quaker ethics.

54. Thomas Adams's analysis of the quarrel of Jacob and Esau may serve as an example of this attention to the patriarchs, which is equally characteristic of the Puritan view of life (*Works of the Puritan Divines*, p. 235): "His [Esau's] folly may be argued from the base estimation of the birthright" [the passage is also important for the development of the idea of the birthright, of which more later] "that he would so lightly pass from it and on so easy condition as a pottage." But then it was perfidious that he would not recognize the sale, charging he had been cheated. He is, in other words, "a cunning hunter, a man of the fields"; a man of irrational, barbarous life; while Jacob, "a plain man, dwelling in tents", represents the "man of grace".

The sense of an inner relationship to Judaism, which is expressed even in the well-known work of Roosevelt, Köhler (*op. cit.*) found widespread among the peasants in Holland. But, on the other hand, Puritanism was fully conscious of its differences from Hebrew ethics in practical affairs, as Prynne's attack on the Jews (apropos of Cromwell's proposals for toleration) plainly shows. See below, note 62).

55. *Zur bäuerlichen Glaubens- und Sittenlehre*. Von einem thüring schen Landpfarrer, second edition, Gotha, 1890, p. 16. The peasants who are here described are characteristic

products of the Lutheran Church. Again and again I wrote Lutheran in the margin when the excellent author spoke of peasant religion in general.

56. Compare for instance the passage cited in Ritschl, *Pietismus* II, p. 158. Spener also bases his objections to change of calling and pursuit of gain partly on passages in Jesus Sirach. *Theologische Bedenken*, III, p. 426.

57. It is true that Bailey, nevertheless, recommends reading them, and references to the Apocrypha occur now and then, though naturally not often. I can remember none to Jesus Sirach just now (though perhaps by chance).

58. Where outward success comes to persons evidently damned, the Calvinist (as for instance Hoornbeek) comforts himself with the reflection, following the theory of stubbornness, that God allows it to them in order to harden them and make their doom the more certain.

59. We cannot go farther into this point in this connection. We are here interested only in the formalistic character of Puritan righteousness. On the significance of Old Testament ethics for the *lex naturæ* there is much in Troeltsch's *Soziallehren*.

60. The binding character of the ethical norms of the Scriptures goes for Baxter (*Christian Directory*, III, p. 173 f.) so far that they are (1) only a transcript of the law of nature, or (2) hear the "express character of universality and perpetuity".

61. For instance Dowden (with reference to Bunyan), *op. cit.*, p. 39.

62. More on this point in the essays on the *Wirtschaftsethik der Weltreligionen* [*The Economic Ethics of the World Religions*]. The enormous influence which, for instance, the second commandment ("thou shalt not make unto thee a graven image") has had on the development of the Jewish character, its rationality and abhorrence of sensuous culture, cannot be analysed here. However, it may perhaps be noted as characteristic that one of the leaders of the Educational Alliance in the United States, an organization which carries on the Americanization of Jewish immigrants on a grand scale and with astonishing success, told me that one of the first purposes aimed at in all forms of artistic and social educational work was emancipation from the second commandment. To the Israelite's prohibition of any anthropomorphic representation of God corresponds in Puritanism the somewhat different but in effect similar prohibition of idolatry of the flesh.

As far as Talmudic Judaism is concerned, some fundamental traits of Puritan morality are certainly related to it. For instance, it is stated in the Talmud (in Wünsche, *Babyl. Talmud*, II, p. 34) that it is better and will be more richly rewarded by God if one does a good deed for duty's sake than one which is not commanded by the law. In other words, loveless fulfillment of duty stands higher ethically than sentimental philanthropy. The Puritan ethics would accept that in essentials. Kant in effect also comes close to it, being partly of Scotch ancestry and strongly influenced by Pietism in his bringing up. Though we cannot discuss the subject here, many of his formulations are closely related to ideas of ascetic Protestantism. But nevertheless the Talmudic ethic is deeply saturated with Oriental traditionalism. "R. Tanchum said to Ben Chanilai, 'Never alter a custom'" (Gemara to Mischna. VII, i, 86b, No. 93, in Wünsche. It is a question of the standard of living of day labourers. The only exception to the conformity is relation to strangers.

Moreover, the Puritan conception of lawfulness as proof evidently provided a much stronger motive to positive action than the Jewish unquestioned fulfillment of all commandments. The idea that success reveals the blessing of God is of course not unknown to Judaism. But the fundamental difference in religious and ethical significance which it took on for Judaism on account of the double ethic prevented the appearance of similar results at just the most important point. Acts toward a stranger were allowed which were forbidden toward a brother. For that reason alone it was impossible for success in this field of what was not commanded but only allowed to be a sign of religious worth and a motive to methodical conduct in the way in which it was for the Puritan. On this whole problem, which Sombart, in his book *Die Juden und das Wirtschaftsleben*, has often dealt with incorrectly, see the essays referred to above. The details have no place here.

The Jewish ethics, however strange that may at first sound, remained very strongly traditionalistic. We can likewise not enter into the tremendous change which the inner attitude toward the world underwent with the Christian form of the ideas of grace and salvation which contained in a peculiar way the seeds of new possibilities of development. On Old Testament lawfulness compare for example Ritschl, *Die christliche Lehre von der Rechtfertigung und Versöhnung*, II, p. 265.

To the English Puritans, the Jews of their time were representatives of that type of capitalism which was involved in war, Government contracts, State monopolies, speculative promotions, and the construction and financial projects of princes, which they themselves condemned. In fact the difference may, in general, with the necessary qualifications, be formulated: that Jewish capitalism was speculative pariah-capitalism, while the Puritan was bourgeois organization of labour.

63. The truth of the Holy Scriptures follows for Baxter in the last analysis from the "wonderful difference of the godly and ungodly", the absolute difference of the renewed man

from others, and God's evident quite special care for His chosen people (which *may* of course be expressed in temptations), *Christian Directory*, I, p. 165.

64. As a characterization of this, it is only necessary to read how tortuously even Bunyan, who still occasionally approaches the atmosphere of Luther's *Freiheit eines Christenmenschen* (for example in *Of the Law and a Christian, Works of the Puritan Divines*, p. 254), reconciles himself with the parable of the Pharisee and the Publican (see the sermon *The Pharisee and the Publican, op. cit.*, p. 100) Why is the Pharisee condemned? He does not truly keep God's commandments, for he is evidently a sectarian who is only concerned with external details and ceremonies (p. 107), but above all because he ascribes merit to himself, and at the same time, like the Quakers, thanks God for virtue by misuse of His name. In a sinful manner he exalts this virtue (p. 126), and thus implicitly contests God's predestination (p. 139). His prayer is thus idolatry of the flesh, and that is the reason it is sinful. On the other hand, the publican is, as the honesty of his confession shows, spiritually reborn, for, as it is put with a characteristic Puritan mitigation of the Lutheran sense of sin, "to a right and sincere conviction of sin there must be a conviction of the probability of mercy" (p. 209).

65. Printed in Gardiner's *Constitutional Documents*. One may compare this struggle against anti-authoritarian asceticism with Louis XIV's persecution of Port Royal and the Jansenists.

66. Calvin's own standpoint was in this respect distinctly less drastic, at least in so far as the finer aristocratic forms of the enjoyment of life were concerned. The only limitation is the Bible. Whoever adheres to it and has a good conscience, need not observe his every impulse to enjoy life with anxiety. The discussion in Chapter X of the *Instit. Christ* (for instance, "nec fugere ea quoque possumus quæ videntur oblectatione magis quam necessitate inservire") [we cannot escape what serves pleasure more than necessity] might in itself have opened the way to a very lax practice. Along with increasing anxiety over the *certitudo salutis* the most important circumstance for the later disciples was, however, as we shall point out in another place, that in the era of the *ecclesia militans* it was the small bourgeoisie who were the principal representatives of Calvinistic ethics.

67. Thomas Adams (*Works of the Puritan Divines*, p. 3) begins a sermon on the "three divine sisters" ("but love is the greatest of these") with the remark that even Paris gave the golden apple to Aphrodite!

68. Confusing faith, as the Puritans conceived it [*Editor*].

69. Novels and the like should not be read; they are "wastetimes" (Baxter, *Christian Directory*, I, p. 51). The decline of lyric poetry and folk-music, as well as the drama, after the Elizabethan age in England is well known. In the pictorial arts Puritanism perhaps did not find very much to suppress. But very striking is the decline from what seemed to be a promising musical beginning (England's part in the history of music was by no means unimportant) to that absolute musical vacuum which we find typical of the Anglo-Saxon peoples later, and even to-day. Except for the negro churches, and the professional singers whom the Churches now engage as attractions (Trinity Church in Boston in 1904 for $8,000 annually), in America one also hears as community singing in general only a noise which is intolerable to German ears (partly analogous things in Holland also).

70. Just the same in Holland, as the reports of the Synods show. (See the resolutions on the Maypole in the Reitmaas Collection, VI, 78, 139.)

71. That the "Renaissance of the Old Testament" and the Pietistic orientation to certain Christian attitudes hostile to beauty in art, which in the last analysis go back to Isaiah and the 22nd Psalm, must have contributed to making ugliness more of a possible object for art, and that the Puritan repudiation of idolatry of the flesh played a part, seems likely. But in detail everything seems uncertain. In the Roman Church quite different demagogic motives led to outwardly similar effects, but, however, with quite different artistic results. Standing before Rembrandt's *Saul and David* (in the Mauritshuis), one seems directly to feel the powerful influence of Puritan emotions. The excellent analysis of Dutch cultural influences in Carl Neumann's *Rembrandt* probably gives everything that for the time being we can know about how far ascetic Protestantism may be credited with a positive fructifying influence on art.

72. The most complex causes, into which we cannot go here, were responsible for the relatively smaller extent to which the Calvinistic ethic penetrated practical life there. The ascetic spirit began to weaken in Holland as early as the beginning of the seventeenth century (the English Congregationalists who fled to Holland in 1608 were disturbed by the lack of respect for the Sabbath there), but especially under the Stadtholder Frederick Henry. Moreover, Dutch Puritanism had in general much less expansive power than English. The reasons for it lay in part in the political constitution (particularistic confederation of towns and provinces) and in the far smaller degree of military force (the War of Independence was soon fought principally with the money of Amsterdam and mercenary armies. English preachers illustrated the Babylonian confusion of tongues by reference

to the Dutch Army). Thus the burden of the war of religion was to a large extent passed on to others, but at the same time a part of their political power was lost. On the other hand, Cromwell's army, even though it was partly conscripted, felt that it was an army of citizens. It was, to be sure, all the more characteristic that just this army adopted the abolition of conscription in its programme, because one could fight justly only for the glory of God in a cause hallowed by conscience, but not at the whim of a sovereign. The constitution of the British Army, so immoral to traditional German ideas, had its historical origin in very moral motives, and was an attainment of soldiers who had never been beaten. Only after the Restoration was it placed in the service of the interests of the Crown.

The Dutch *schutterijen* [militia], the champions of Calvinism in the period of the Great War, only half a generation after the Synod of Dordrecht, do not look in the least ascetic in the pictures of Hals. Protests of the Synods against their conduct occur frequently. The Dutch concept of *Deftigkeit* [solemnity, gravity] is a mixture of bourgeois-rational honesty and patrician consciousness of status. The division of church pews according to classes in the Dutch churches shows the aristocratic character of this religion even today. The continuance of the town economy hampered industry. It prospered almost alone through refugees, and hence only sporadically. Nevertheless, the worldly asceticism of Calvinism and Pietism was an important influence in Holland in the same direction as elsewhere. Also in the sense to be referred to presently of ascetic compulsion to save, as Groen van Prinsterer shows in the passage cited below, note 92).

Moreover, the almost complete lack of *belles lettres* [belletristic] in Calvinistic Holland is of course no accident (see for instance Busken-Huet, *Het Land van Rembrandt*). The significance of Dutch religion as ascetic compulsion to save appears clearly even in the eighteenth century in the writings of Albertus Haller. For the characteristic peculiarities of the Dutch attitude toward art and its motives, compare for example the autobiographical remarks of Constantine Huyghens (written in 1629–31) in *Oud Holland*, 1891. The work of Groen van Prinsterer, *La Hollande et l'influence de Calvin*, 1864, already referred to, offers nothing important for our problems. The New Netherlands colony in America was socially a half-feudal settlement of *patroons* [patrons] merchants who advanced capital, and, unlike New England, it was difficult to persuade small people to settle there.

73. We may recall that the Puritan town government closed the theatre at Stratford-on-Avon while Shakespeare was still alive and residing there in his last years. Shakespeare's hatred and contempt of the Puritans appear on every occasion. As late as 1777 the City of Birmingham refused to license a theatre because it was conducive to slothfulness, and hence unfavourable to trade (Ashley, *Birmingham Trade and Commerce*, 1913).

74. Here also it was of decisive importance that for the Puritan there was only the alternative of divine will or earthly vanity. Hence for him there could be no *adiaphora* [indifferent from a religious viewpoint]. As we have already pointed out, Calvin's own view was different in this respect. What one eats, wears, etc., as long as there is no enslavement of the soul to earthly desire as a result, is indifferent. Freedom from the world should be expressed, as for the Jesuits, in indifference, which for Calvin meant an indifferent, uncovetous use of whatever goods the earth offered (pp. 409 ff. of the original edition of the *Instit. Christ*).

75. The Quaker attitude in this respect is well known. But as early as the beginning of the seventeenth century the heaviest storms shook the pious congregation of exiles in Amsterdam for a decade over the fashionable hats and dresses of a preacher's wife (charmingly described in Dexter's *Congregationalism of the Last Three Hundred Years*). Sanford (*op. cit.*) has pointed out that the present-day male hair-cut is that of the ridiculous Roundheads, and the equally ridiculous (for the time) male clothing of the Puritans is at least in principle fundamentally the same as that of to-day.

76. On this point again see Veblen's *Theory of Business Enterprise*.

77. Again and again we come back to this attitude. It explains statements like the following: "Every penny which is paid upon yourselves and children and friends must be done as by God's own appointment and to serve and please Him. Watch narrowly, or else that thievish, carnal self will leave God nothing" (Baxter, *op. cit.*, I, p. 108). This is decisive; what is expended for personal ends is withdrawn from the service of God's glory.

78. Quite rightly it is customary to recall (Dowden, *op. cit.*) that Cromwell saved Raphael's drawings and Mantegna's *Triumph of Cæsar* from destruction, while Charles II tried to sell them. Moreover, the society of the Restoration was distinctly cool or even hostile to English national literature. In fact the influence of Versailles was all-powerful at courts everywhere. A detailed analysis of the influence of the unfavourable atmosphere for the spontaneous enjoyment of everyday life on the spirit of the higher types of Puritan, and the men who went through the schooling of Puritanism, is a task which cannot be undertaken within the limits of this sketch. Washington Irving (*Bracebridge Hall*) formulates it in the usual English terms thus : "It [he says political freedom, we should say Puritanism] evinces less play of the fancy, but more power of the imagination." It is only necessary to think of the place of the Scotch in science, literature, and technical invention,

as well as in the business life of Great Britain, to be convinced that this remark approaches the truth, even though put somewhat too narrowly. We cannot speak here of its significance for the development of technique and the empirical sciences. The relation itself is always appearing in everyday life. For the Quakers, for instance, the recreations which are permissible (according to Barclay) are: visiting of friends, reading of historical works, mathematical and physical experiments, gardening, discussion of business and other occurrences in the world, etc. The reason is that pointed out above.

79. Already very finely analysed in Carl Neumann's *Rembrandt*, which should be compared with the above remarks in general.

80. Thus Baxter in the passage cited above, I, p. 108, and below.

81. Compare the well-known description, of Colonel Hutchinson (often quoted, for instance, in Sanford, *op. cit.*, p. 57) in the biography written by his widow. After describing all his chivalrous virtues and his cheerful, joyous nature, it goes, on: "He was wonderfully neat, cleanly, and genteel in his habit, and had a very good fancy in it; but he left off very early the wearing of anything that was costly." Quite similar is the ideal of the educated and highly civilized Puritan woman who, however, is penurious of two things: (1) time, and (2) expenditure for pomp and pleasure, as drawn in Baxter's funeral oration for Mary Hammer (*Works of the Puritan Divines*, p. 533).

82. I think, among many other examples, especially of a manufacturer unusually successful in his business ventures, and in his later years very wealthy, who, when for the treatment of a troublesome digestive disorder the doctor prescribed a few oysters a day, could only be brought to comply with difficulty. Very considerable gifts for philanthropic purposes which he made during his lifetime and a certain openhandedness showed, on the other hand, that it was simply a survival of that ascetic feeling which looks upon enjoyment of wealth for one self as morally reprehensible, but has nothing whatever to do with avarice.

83. The separation of workshop, office, of business in general and the private dwelling, of firm and name, of business capital and private wealth, the tendency to make of the business a *corpus mysticum* (at least in the case of corporate property) all lay in this direction. On this, see my *Handelsgesellschaften im Mittelalter* [*The History of Commercial Partnerships in the Middle Ages*] (*Gesammelte Aufsätze zur Sozial- und Wirtschafts geschichte*, pp. 312 ff.).

84. Sombart in his *Kapitalismus* (first edition) has already well pointed out this characteristic phenomenon. It must, however, be noted that the accumulation of wealth springs from two quite distinct psychological sources. One reaches into the dimmest antiquity and is expressed in foundations, family fortunes, and trusts, as well as much more purely and clearly in the desire to die weighted down with a great burden of material goods; above all to insure the continuation of a business even at the cost of the personal interests of the majority of one's children. In such cases it is, besides the desire to give one's own creation an ideal life beyond one's death, and thus to maintain the *splendor familiæ* [splendor and rank of the family] and extend the personality of the founder, a question of, so to speak, fundamentally egocentric motives. That is not the case with that bourgeois motive with which we are here dealing. There the motto of asceticism is "Entsagen sollst du, sollst entsagen" [you should renounce, you must renounce] in the positive capitalistic sense of "Erwerben sollst du, sollst erwerben" [you should earn, you must earn]. In its pure and simple non-rationality it is a sort of categorical imperative. Only the glory of God and one's own duty, not human vanity, is the motive for the Puritans; and to-day only the duty to one's calling. If it pleases anyone to illustrate an idea by its extreme consequences, we may recall the theory of certain American millionaires, that their millions should not be left to their children, so that they will not be deprived of the good moral effects of the necessity of working and earning for themselves. To-day that idea is certainly no more than a theoretical soap-bubble.

85. This is, as must continually be emphasized, the final decisive religious motive (along with the purely ascetic desire to mortify the flesh). It is especially clear in the Quakers.

86. Baxter (*Saints' Everlasting Rest*, p. 12) repudiates this with precisely the same reasoning as the Jesuits: the body must have what it needs, otherwise one becomes a slave to it.

87. This ideal is clearly present, especially for Quakerism, in the first period of its development, as has already been shown in important points by Weingarten in his *Englische Revolution-skirchen*. Also Barclay's thorough discussion (*op. cit.*, pp. 519 ff., 533) shows it very clearly. To be avoided are: (1) Worldly vanity; thus all ostentation, frivolity, and use of things having no practical purpose, or which are valuable only for their scarcity (i.e. for vanity's sake). (2) Any unconscientious use of wealth, such as excessive expenditure for not very urgent needs above necessary provision for the real needs of life and for the future. The Quaker was, so to speak, a living law of marginal utility. "Moderate use of the creature" is definitely permissible, but in particular one might pay attention to the quality and durability of materials so long as it did not lead to vanity. On all this compare *Morgenblatt für gebildete Leser*, 1846, pp. 216 ff. Especially on comfort and solidity among the Quakers, compare Schneckenburger, *Vorlesungen*, pp. 96 f.

88. Adapted by Weber from Faust, Act I. Goethe there depicts Mephistopheles as "Die Kraft, die stets das Böse will, und stets das Gute schafft" [The power that always intends evil and always creates the good].—TRANSLATOR'S NOTE.

89. It has already been remarked that we cannot here enter into the question of the class relations of these religious movements (see the essays on the *Wirtschaftsethik der Weltreligionen*) [*The Economic Ethics of the World Religions*]. In order to see, however, that for example Baxter, of whom we make so much use in this study, did not see things solely as a bourgeois of his time, it will suffice to recall that even for him in the order of the religious value of callings, after the learned professions comes the husband-man, and only then mariners, clothiers, booksellers, tailors, etc. Also, under mariners (characteristically enough) he probably thinks at least as often of fishermen as of shipowners. In this regard several things in the *Talmud* are in a different class. Compare, for instance, in Wünsche, *Babyl Talmud*, II, pp. 20, 21, the sayings of Rabbi Eleasar, which though not unchallenged, all contend in effect that business is better than agriculture. In between see II, 2, p. 68, on the wise investment of capital: one-third in land, one-third in merchandise, and one-third in cash.

  For those to whom no causal explanation is adequate without an economic (or materialistic as it is unfortunately still called) interpretation, it may be remarked that I consider the influence of economic development on the fate of religious ideas to be very important and shall later attempt to show how in our case the process of mutual adaptation of the two took place. On the other hand, those religious ideas themselves simply cannot be deduced from economic circumstances. They are in themselves, that is beyond doubt, the most powerful plastic elements of national character, and contain a law of development and a compelling force entirely their own. Moreover, the most important differences, so far as non-religious factors play a part, are, as with Lutheranism and Calvinism, the result of political circumstances, not economic.

90. That is what Eduard Bernstein means to express when he says, in the essay referred to above (pp. 625, 681), "Asceticism is a bourgeois virtue." His discussion is the first which has suggested these important relationships. But the connection is a much wider one than he suspected. For not only the accumulation of capital, but the ascetic rationalization of the whole of economic life was involved.

  For the American Colonies, the difference between the Puritan North, where, on account of the ascetic compulsion to save, capital in search of investment was always available, from the conditions in the South has already been clearly brought out by Doyle.

91. Doyle, *The English in America*, II, chap. i. The existence of ironworks (1643), weaving for the market (1659), and also the high development of the handicrafts in New England in the first generation after the foundation of the colonies are, from a purely economic view-point, astounding. They are in striking contrast to the conditions in the South, as well as the non-Calvinistic Rhode Island with its complete freedom of conscience. There, in spite of the excellent harbour, the report of the Governor and Council of 1686 said: "The great obstruction concerning trade is the want of merchants and men of considerable estates amongst us" (Arnold, *History of the State of Rhode Island*, p. 490). It can in fact hardly be doubted that the compulsion continually to reinvest savings, which the Puritan curtailment of consumption exercised, played a part. In addition there was the part of Church discipline which cannot be discussed here.

92. That, however, these circles rapidly diminished in the Netherlands is shown by Busken-Huet's discussion (*op. cit.*, II, chaps. iii and iv). Nevertheless, Groen van Prinsterer says (*Handb. der Gesch. van het Vaderland*, third edition, par. 303, note, p. 254), "De Nederlanders verkoopen veel en verbruiken wenig" [The Dutch sell much and need little], even of the time after the Peace of Westphalia.

93. For England, for instance, a petition of an aristocratic Royalist (quoted in Ranke, *Engl. Geschichte*, IV, p. 197) presented after the entry of Charles II into London, advocated a legal prohibition of the acquisition of landed estates by bourgeois capital, which should thereby be forced to find employment in trade. The class of Dutch regents was distinguished as an estate from the bourgeois patricians of the cities by the purchase of landed estates. See the complaints, cited by Fruin, *Tien jaren uit den tachtigjarigen oorlog*, of the year 1652, that the regents have become landlords and are no longer merchants. To be sure these circles had never been at bottom strictly Calvinistic. And the notorious scramble for membership in the nobility and titles in large parts of the Dutch middle class in the second half of the seventeenth century in itself shows that at least for this period the contrast between English and Dutch conditions must be accepted with caution. In this case the power of hereditary moneyed property broke through the ascetic spirit.

94. Upon the strong movement for bourgeois capital to buy English landed estates followed the great period of prosperity of English agriculture.

95. Even down into this century Anglican landlords have often refused to accept Nonconformists as tenants. At the present time the two parties of the Church are of approximately equal numbers, while in earlier times the Nonconformists were always in the minority.

96. H. Levy (article in *Archiv für Sozialwissenschaft* and *Sozialpolitik*, XLVI, p. 605) rightly notes that according to the native character of the English people, as seen from numerous of its traits, they were, if anything, less disposed to welcome an ascetic ethic and the middle-class virtues than other peoples. A hearty and unrestrained enjoyment of life was, and is, one of their fundamental traits. The power of Puritan asceticism at the time of its predominance is shown most strikingly in the astonishing degree to which this trait of character was brought under discipline among its adherents.

97. This contrast recurs continually in Doyle's presentation. In the attitude of the Puritan to everything the religious motive always played an important part (not always, of course, the sole important one). The colony (under Winthrop's leadership) was inclined to permit the settlement of gentlemen in Massachusetts, even an upper house with a hereditary nobility, if only the gentlemen would adhere to the Church. The colony remained closed for the sake of Church discipline. The colonization of New Hampshire and Maine was carried out by large Anglican merchants, who laid out large stock-raising plantations. Between them and the Puritans there was very little social connection. There were complaints over the strong greed for profits of the New Englanders as early as 1632 (see Weeden's *Economic and Social History of New England*, I, p. 125).

98. This is noted by Petty (*Pol. Arith.*), and all the contemporary sources without exception speak in particular of the Puritan sectarians, Baptists, Quakers, Mennonites, etc., as belonging partly to a propertyless class, partly to one of small capitalists, and contrast them both with the great merchant aristocracy and the financial adventurers. But it was from just this small capitalist class, and not from the great financial magnates, monopolists, Government contractors, great lenders to the King, colonial entrepreneurs, promoters, etc., that there originated what was characteristic of Occidental capitalism : the middle-class organization of industrial labour on the basis of private property (see Unwin, *Industrial Organization in the Sixteenth and Seventeenth Centuries*, London, 1914, pp. 196 ff.). To see that this difference was fully known even to contemporaries, compare Parker's *Discourse Concerning Puritans* of 1641, where the contrast to promoters and courtiers is also emphasized.

99. Those in possession of salvation [*Editor*].

100. On the way in which this was expressed in the politics of Pennsylvania in the eighteenth century, especially during the War of Independence, see Sharpless, *A Quaker Experiment in Government*, Philadelphia, 1902.

101. Quoted in Southey, *Life of Wesley*, chap. xxix (second American edition, II, p. 308). For the reference, which I did not know, I am indebted to a letter from Professor Ashley (1913). Ernst Troeltsch, to whom I communicated it for the purpose, has already made use of it.

102. The reading of this passage may be recommended to all those who consider themselves to-day better informed on these matters than the leaders and contemporaries of the movements themselves. As we see, they knew very well what they were doing and what dangers they faced. It is really inexcusable to contest so lightly, as some of my critics have done, facts which are quite beyond dispute, and have hitherto never been disputed by anyone. All I have done is to investigate their underlying motives somewhat more carefully. No one in the seventeenth century doubted the existence of these relationships (compare Manley, *Usury of 6 per Cent. Examined*, 1669, p. 137). Besides the modern writers already noted, poets like Heine and Keats, as well as historians like Macaulay, Cunningham, Rogers, or an essayist such as Matthew Arnold, have assumed them as obvious. From the most recent literature see Ashley, *Birmingham Industry and Commerce* (1913). He has also expressed his complete agreement with me in correspondence. On the whole problem now compare the study by H. Levy referred to above, note 96.

103. Weber's italics.

104. That exactly the same things were obvious to the Puritans of the classical era cannot perhaps be more clearly shown than by the fact that in Bunyan Mr. Money-Love argues that one may become religious in order to get rich, for instance to attract customers. For why one has become religious makes no difference (see p. 114, Tauchnitz edition).

105. Defoe was a zealous Nonconformist.

106. A merchant can hardly ever please God [*Editor*].

107. Spener also (*Theologische Bedenken*, pp. 426, 429, 432 ff.), although he holds that the merchant's calling is full of temptations and pitfalls, nevertheless declares in answer to a question: "I am glad to see, so far as trade is concerned, that my dear friend knows no scruples, but takes it as an art of life, which it is, in which much good may be done for the human race, and God's will may be carried out through love." This is more fully justified in other passages by mercantilist arguments. Spener, at times in a purely Lutheran strain, designates the desire to become rich as the main pitfall, following 1 Tim. vi, viii, and ix, and referring to Jesus Sirach (see above), and hence rigidly to be condemned. But, on the other hand, he takes some of it back by referring to the prosperous sectarians who yet live righteously (see above, note 43). As the result of industrious work

wealth is not objectionable to him either. But on account of the Lutheran influence his standpoint is less consistent than that of Baxter.

108. Baxter, *op cit.*, II, p. 16, warns against the employment of "heavy, flegmatic, sluggish, fleshly, slothful persons" as servants, and recommends preference for godly servants, not only because ungodly servants would be mere eye-servants, but above all because "a truly godly servant will do all your service in obedience to God, as if God Himself had bid him do it". Others, on the other hand, are inclined "to make no great matter of conscience of it". However, the criterion of saintliness of the workman is not for him the external confession of faith, but the "conscience to do their duty". It appears here that the interests of God and of the employers are curiously harmonious. Spener also (*Theologische Bedenken*, III, p. 272), who otherwise strongly urges taking time to think of God, assumes it to be obvious that workers must be satisfied with the extreme minimum of leisure time (even on Sundays). English writers have rightly called the Protestant immigrants the pioneers of skilled labour. See also proofs in H. Levy, *Die Grundlagen des ökonomischen Liberalimus in der Geschichte der englischen Volkswirtschaft*, p. 53.

109. The analogy between the unjust (according to human standards) predestination of only a few and the equally unjust, but equally divinely ordained, distribution of wealth, was too obvious to be escaped. See for example Hoornbeek, *op. cit.*, I, p. 153. Furthermore, as for Baxter, *op. cit.*, I, p. 380, poverty is very often a symptom of sinful slothfulness.

110. Thomas Adams (*Works of the Puritan Divines*, p. 158) thinks that God probably allows so many people to remain poor because He knows that they would not be able to withstand the temptations that go with wealth. For wealth all too often draws men away from religion.

111. See above, note 49, and the study of H. Levy referred to there. The same is noted in all the discussions (thus by Manley for the Huguenots).

112. *Charisma* is a sociological term coined by Weber himself. It refers to the quality of leadership which appeals to non-rational motives. See *Wirtschaft und Gesellschaft*, pp. 140 ff. [*Economy and Society*, pp. 241–71].—TRANSLATOR'S NOTE.

113. Similar things were not lacking in England. There was, for example, that Pietism which, starting from Law's *Serious Call* (1728), preached poverty, chastity, and, originally, isolation from the world.

114. Baxter's activity in Kidderminster, a community absolutely debauched when he arrived, which was almost unique in the history of the ministry for its success, is at the same time a typical example of how asceticism educated the masses to labour, or, in Marxian terms, to the production of surplus value, and thereby for the first time made their employment in the capitalistic labour relation (putting-out industry, weaving, etc.) possible at all. That is very generally the causal relationship. From Baxter's own view-point he accepted the employment of his charges in capitalistic production for the sake of his religious and ethical interests. From the standpoint of the development of capitalism these latter were brought into the service of the development of the spirit of capitalism.

115. Furthermore, one may well doubt to what extent the joy of the mediæval craftsman in his creation, which is so commonly appealed to, was effective as a psychological motive force. Nevertheless, there is undoubtedly something in that thesis. But in any case asceticism certainly deprived all labour of this worldly attractiveness, to-day for ever destroyed by capitalism, and oriented it to the beyond. Labour in a calling as such is willed by God. The impersonality of present-day labour, what, from the standpoint of the individual, is its joyless lack of meaning, still has a religious justification here. Capitalism at the time of its development needed labourers who were available for economic exploitation for conscience' sake. To-day it is in the saddle, and hence able to force people to labour without transcendental sanctions.

116. Petty, *Political Arithmetick, Works*, edited by Hull, I, p. 262.

117. On these conflicts and developments see H. Levy in the book cited above. The very powerful hostility of public opinion to monopolies, which is characteristic of England, originated historically in a combination of the political struggle for power against the Crown—the Long Parliament excluded monopolists from its membership—with the ethical motives of Puritanism; and the economic interests of the small bourgeois and moderate-scale capitalists against the financial magnates in the seventeenth century. The Declaration of the Army of August 2, 1652, as well the Petition of the Levellers of January 28, 1653, demand, besides the abolition of excises, tariffs, and indirect taxes, and the introduction of a single tax on estates, above all free trade, i.e. the abolition of the monopolistic barriers to trade at home and abroad, as a violation of the natural rights of man.

118. Compare H. Levy, *Die Grundlagen des ökonomischen Liberalismus in des Geschichte des englischen Volkswirtschaft*, pp. 51 f.

119. That those other elements, which have here not yet been traced to their religious roots, especially the idea that honesty is the best policy (Franklin's discussion of credit), are also of Puritan origin, must be proved in a somewhat different connection (see the following essay [not translated here]). Here I shall limit myself to repeating the following

remark of J. A. Rowntree (*Quakerism, Past and Present*, pp. 95–6), to which E. Bernstein has called my attention : "Is it merely a coincidence, or is it a consequence, that the lofty profession of spirituality made by the Friends has gone hand in hand with shrewdness and tact in the transaction of mundane affairs? Real piety favours the success of a trader by insuring his integrity and fostering habits of prudence and forethought, important items in obtaining that standing and credit in the commercial world, which are requisites for the steady accumulation of wealth" (see the following essay). "Honest as a Huguenot" was as proverbial in the seventeenth century as the respect for law of the Dutch which Sir W. Temple admired, and, a century later, that of the English as compared with those Continental peoples that had not been through this ethical schooling.

120. *Wilhelm Meister's Years of Travel* (1829) [*Editor*].

121. Well analysed in Bielschowsky's *Goethe*, II, chap. xviii. For the development of the scientific cosmos Windelband, at the end of his *Blütezeit der deutschen Philosophie* (Vol. II of the *Gesch. d. Neueren Philosophie*), has expressed a similar idea.

122. *Saints' Everlasting Rest*, chap. xii.

123. Talcott Parsons famously translated "*stahlhartes Gehäuse*" or "steel-hard casing" (or "a shell as hard as steel") as "iron cage" [*Editor*].

124. "Couldn't the old man be satisfied with his $75,000 a year and rest? No! The frontage of the store must be widened to 400 feet. Why? That beats everything, he says. In the evening when his wife and daughter read together, he wants to go to bed. Sundays he looks at the clock every five minutes to see when the day will be over—what a futile life!" In these terms the son-in-law (who had emigrated from Germany) of the leading dry-goods man of an Ohio city expressed his judgment of the latter, a judgment which would undoubtedly have seemed simply incomprehensible to the old man. A symptom of German lack of energy.

125. This remark alone (unchanged since his criticism) might have shown Brentano (*op. cit.*) that I have never doubted its independent significance. That humanism was also not pure rationalism has lately again been strongly emphasized by Borinski in the *Abhandl. der Münchener Akad. der Wiss.*, 1919.

126. The academic oration of v. Below, *Die Ursachen der Reformation* (Freiburg, 1916), is not concerned with this problem, but with that of the Reformation in general, especially Luther. For the question dealt with here, especially the controversies which have grown out of this study, I may refer finally to the work of Hermelink, *Reformation und Gegenreformation*, which, however, is also primarily concerned with other problems.

127. For the above sketch has deliberately taken up only the relations in which an influence of religious ideas on the material culture is really beyond doubt. It would have been easy to proceed beyond that to a regular construction which logically deduced everything characteristic of modern culture from Protestant rationalism. But that sort of thing may be left to the type of dilettante who believes in the unity of the group mind and its reducibility to a single formula. Let it be remarked only that the period of capitalistic development lying before that which we have studied was everywhere in part determined by religious influences, both hindering and helping. Of what sort these were belongs in another chapter. Furthermore, whether, of the broader problems sketched above, one or another can be dealt with in the limits of this Journal [the essay first appeared in the *Archiv für Sozialwissenschaft und Sozialpolitik*—TRANSLATOR'S NOTE] is not certain in view of the problems to which it is devoted. On the other hand, to write heavy tomes, as thick as they would have to be in this case, and dependent on the work of others (theologians and historians), I have no great inclination (I have left these sentences unchanged).

For the tension between ideals and reality in early capitalistic times before the Reformation, see now Strieder, *Studien zur Geschichte der kapit. Organizationsformen*, 1914, Book II. (Also as against the work of Keller, cited above, which was utilized by Sombart.)

128. I should have thought that this sentence and the remarks and notes immediately preceding it would have sufficed to prevent any misunderstanding of what this study was meant to accomplish, and I find no occasion for adding anything. Instead of following up with an immediate continuation in terms of the above programme, I have, partly for fortuitous reasons, especially the appearance of Troeltsch's *Die Soziallehren der christlichen Kirchen und Gruppen*, which disposed of many things I should have had to investigate in a way in which I, not being a theologian, could not have done it; but partly also in order to correct the isolation of this study and to place it in relation to the whole of cultural development, determined, first, to write down some comparative studies of the general historical relationship of religion and society. These follow. Before them is placed only a short essay in order to clear up the concept of sect used above, and at the same time to show the significance of the Puritan conception of the Church for the capitalistic spirit of modern times.

# CONTEXTS

# OLA AGEVALL

# A Science of Unique Events: Max Weber's Methodology of the Cultural Sciences[†]

Max Weber's articles on the protestant ethic and the spirit of capitalism belong to the corpus that all sociologists are supposed to have read, or at least read about. They have attracted a considerable amount of commentary over the years, ranging from fierce critique to devout hagiography.[1] In this literature, the issues at stake are often referred to as the "Weber-thesis" (Green 1973; Eisenstadt 1968). Yet, what exactly is this thesis? In the most general formulation, it is tantamount to the claim that there is some relationship between Protestantism and capitalism.[2]

---

[†] This text is entitled "The Protestant Ethic and the Spirit of Capitalism" and constitutes Ch. 9 in the author's *A Science of Unique Events: Max Weber's Methodology of the Cultural Sciences*, Ph.D. thesis, Department of Sociology, Uppsala University, 1999. Reprinted by permission of the author.

1. For a review of the literature on Weber's essays, confer P. Besnard's *Protestantisme et capitalisme, La controverse post-Weberienne* (1970) and the bibliographic appendix in Weber (1995: 395–429).

2. In the secondary literature, not many authors take the stance that there is absolutely no such link in any form. This position, however, is taken by the Swedish economic historian Kurt Samuelsson – "l'un des adversaires les plus acharnés, sinon les plus perspicaces", as Annette Disselkamp puts it (Disselkamp 1994: 11). Other critics have focused their critique on a wide range of specific points, trying to undermine the evidence put forward by Weber. It suffices to give some examples. It has been argued that the data presented in the first part of the essay, compiled by Paul Honigsheim and quoted by Weber, suffers from serious flaws, and that Honigsheim even computed the percentage rates wrong. Richard Hamilton is critical of his use of evidence generally (Jorrat 1994). Hanyu (1993) criticizes his interpretation of theological sources with reference to the concept of "calling," arguing that the pieces of evidence Weber uses could not be so used for historical reasons. And Eduard Baumgarten (1936; cf. also Roth 1995: 16–20) has a go at Weber's interpretation of Benjamin Franklin's maxims, from which Weber reconstructed the capitalist spirit, arguing that Weber was blind to the irony and roguishness of the works he quotes (i.e. *Advice to a Young Tradesman* 1748 and *Necessary Hints to Those That Would Be Rich* 1736).
   On these matters I will have nothing to say. I am out of my depth concerning many of the areas where Weber has been criticised. Most certainly I am at a loss when it comes to evaluating Weber's use of theological sources. Yet this chapter is not intended as a defence of any specific empirical thesis put forward by Weber. For all I know, his argument might or might not be empirically false, I employ the same technique as Weber himself so often used when discussing methodological issues: I put questions of empirical validity aside. To the extent that I try to undermine the arguments of Max Weber's critics, it is solely from the point of view that they have misunderstood Weber from a *methodological* point of view, typically by imputing *validity claims* to his argument which are at odds with his methodology.

Now, a modern student is easily led to believe that the *novelty* in Weber's essays was the claim that there is or was some form of link between protestant ethic and the spirit of capitalism. This, however, is misleading. The idea that there is a bond linking Protestantism and capitalism was by no means novel in Weber's days.

We may take our cue from Reinhardt Bendix, stating that ". . . Weber himself considered these notions a commonplace in the literature," (Bendix 1980: 299). It is worth while to linger on this topic for a while. Annette Disselkamp concludes that Weber's thesis continues a long tradition. In the 18th century it was commonplace, and in the 19th century it was part of the dogma of the protestant bourgeois propaganda. As examples she cites Charles de Villers' *Essai sur l'esprit et l'influence de la Réformation de Luther* from 1804 as well as Francois Guizot's *Histoire de la civilisation en Europe* from 1828 (Disselkamp 1994: 13). Paul Münch goes further, and identifies a whole series of authors that held the view as early as the 17th century (Münch 1995).

Weber actually *quotes* several authors—economists and historians as well as practitioners and laymen—which clearly held the view that Protestantism is connected to capitalism. The Belgian economist Émile de Lavaleye is one example. He was the "author of a textbook in economics which was widely used in the eighties and nineties of the last century. In a chapter entitled 'Influence of Philosophical and Religious Doctrines on the Productiveness of Labor' he specifically linked evangelical Christianity with the economic prosperity of countries, noting that the equalitarianism and the simple life-style of Protestants favored economic progress while intolerance was harmful to it. Lavaleye also mentioned Voltaire's observation that there were no poor to be found among the Quakers in England and the Mennonites in Holland. In addition, he published a pamphlet comparing Protestantism and Catholicism in their relation to freedom and prosperity obviously intended as a partisan argument in the religious conflicts of his country" (Bendix 1980: 300). This is only one example of many of authors referred to by Weber who held the "thesis" in some form or other. Matthew Arnold is also mentioned, along with poet John Keats, and so is, the historian Henry Thomas Buckle's work *Civilization in England*. So predominant was the belief in a connection between Protestantism and capitalism that Werner Sombart, two years before the publication of Weber's articles, wrote: "That Protestantism, particularly in its Calvinist and Quaker varieties has materially advanced the development of capitalism . . . is a too well-known fact, in no need of further substantiation" (Sombart 1902: 381).

Let us stop here. We clearly see that not only had previous and contemporary authors suggested the "thesis", but Weber was also very much aware of not being original in this respect.[3] Yet, what was the purpose of writing his essays, if the "thesis" was so well known as to be commonplace?

A preliminary answer to this question is that Weber sought to establish a different kind of relationship between Protestantism, or rather Puritanism, and capitalism. As a matter of fact, the essays on the protestant ethic and the spirit of capitalism must have appeared to be a fine laboratory for testing his methodological ideas. I will suggest that this is what he actually did. This is not to say that the investigation was not undertaken for other, independent reasons, only that it provided a nice practical case to see his principles work in practice. Why this is so will become clearer as we go along. We begin, however, with some notes on the publication history of Weber's articles. The version available in English is a translation of a somewhat revised edition, included in the three-volume work *Gesammelte Aufsätze zur Religionssoziologie* (1920/1988: 17–206). The English translation is supplanted with a "preface". This "preface", however, is a preface to the entire *Gesammelte Aufsätze zur Religionssoziologie* and not specifically to the essays on the Protestant Ethic. It might therefore be misleading to read it as a declaration of intent for the latter work. Originally, the work had been published fifteen years earlier, in 1904–1905, as a two piece article in *Archiv für Sozialwissenschaft und Sozialpolitik*. This means that it was written in the same period, and simultaneously with, the essays in the *Wissenschaftslehre*. This shows in the *Wissenschaftslehre* itself, for it contains several references to issues relating to problems raised in the Protestant Ethic. (Weber 1922/1985: 23, 32, 33, 197, 198). Some of these are merely statements of fact or hypotheses, probably things that sprang to mind since he was working on these problems in any case. But Weber also quotes the problems of Protestantism as especially neat and clear-cut examples of the methodological principles he is propounding. Also, as Stephen Turner has remarked, Weber "discussed the methodological problems of explaining capitalism" in the essay on 'Objectivity' in social research and social policy, and that he seemed to indicate there how he regarded the explanation in 'The Protestant Ethic' " (Turner 1985: 171).

3. It is obvious that the lack of originality of Weber's thesis, thus stated, is not common knowledge to sociologists, despite the work of Günther Roth and others. Murray Davis, writing on the phenomenology and rhetoric of the classics, asks what makes a social scientific text "interesting." His answer is that theorists regarded as interesting if they "denied various commonly held audience assumptions" (Davis 1986: 287). He quotes Max Weber's study of the protestant ethic and the spirit of capitalism as an example. "Weber's assertion that the Protestant Ethic produced capitalism denied the then commonly held assumption that religion is either unrelated to the economy or (for Marxists) derived from it" (Davis 1986: 287). This is plainly mistaken. Whatever Weber did in asserting a relation between religion and capitalism, it was certainly not unfamiliar to the audience of his day. At least Davis' contention that the thesis went against a "*then* commonly held assumption" is simply false. It is still possible, of course, that the thesis works this way on the audience of today, and that this makes it interesting to us. It is plausible that the force Weber's thesis has on students derives from the fact that it is at odds with audience assumptions.

Considering that Weber wrote the methodological essays and the essays on the Protestant Ethic virtually simultaneously, it would be surprising if he did not think in terms of this methodology in this substantial work. As a matter of fact we *do* find the language of Weber's *Wissenschaftslehre* in the study on the Protestant ethic. Historical individual, ideal type, and adequacy are all there, and so is much of the notions accompanying them.[4] In this chapter, we shall therefore interpret the Protestant Ethic from the point of view of Max Weber's *Wissenschaftslehre*. In doing so, I will rearrange Weber's argument somewhat, in order to bring out the methodological aspects.

### The "Capitalist Spirit" as a Historical Individual

If something is to be explained in the historical sciences, the first step must be to constitute the explanandum, and an explanandum in the historical sciences can only be a *primary historical individual*. We need to select the significant characteristics from the inexhaustible manifold of reality, and distinguish them from the insignificant (Weber 1904/1993: 10). In contrast to the natural sciences, the "significant characteristics" are not significant because they are instances under a law. They are significant precisely because they are *culturally* significant, i.e. because they are significant to members of society. We are to look for what makes the object so constituted unique and individual, rather than focusing on what it has in common with all other

---

4. The ideas to this chapter derive in part from Stephen Turner's work. Turner too believes that the Protestant Ethic must be read from the point of view of Weber's methodological writings, although his focus is more narrowly concentrated on the theory of adequate cause. Yet, Turner believes that von Kries' terminology is nowhere to be found in Weber's study: "*Weber did not make explicit appeals to von Kriesian language or considerations in the body of the essay 'The Protestant Ethic.*' The primary evidence in Weber's own writings for connections between the thesis of the Protestant ethic essay and the methodological essays comes from the methodological essays themselves" (Turner 1985: 171). This is not quite true. There *are* references to adequacy in the Protestant Ethic, e.g. on pages 24 and 29 in Weber 1904/1993. (The same passages are found on pages 49 and 56 in the revised edition in *Gesammelte Aufsätze zur Religionssoziologie* 1920/1988.) However, these references to adequacy disappear in Talcott Parsons' English translation. The preface to the *Gesammelte Aufsätze zur Religionssoziologie* also contains a reference to "objective possibility" (Weber 1920/1988: 4). As we have already said above, the preface is not written for the Protestant Ethic, but in this context, this only makes it more interesting. The preface was written in 1919, which means that Weber continued to refer to the theory of adequate cause until the time of his death. Turner is right, however, that Weber is far from explicit on these points in the main text of the Protestant Ethic. Also, these references to adequacy do not concern the main points of the argument. Yet, I think that Turner's thesis is further corroborated by the, admittedly sparse, references to adequacy Weber actually makes. Turner's view is strengthened even more if we look at the debate that followed upon the publication of the Protestant Ethic. The articles attracted two critics, Karl Fischer and Felix Rachfahl. Both launched criticisms against Weber's thesis, and in the replies to his critics, Weber kept insisting that his *sole* objective was to establish adequacy. We shall treat this debate in more detail further on in this chapter.

phenomena of a certain class. This is exactly what Max Weber does: "In the title of this study is used the somewhat pretentious phrase, the '*spirit* of capitalism'? If any object can be found to which this term can be applied with any understandable meaning, it can only be an historical individual, i.e. a complex of elements associated in historical reality which we unite into a conceptual whole from the standpoint of their cultural significance. Such a historical concept, however, since it refers in its content to a phenomenon significant for its unique *individuality*, can't be defined . . . according to the formula genus proximum, differentia specifica, but it must be gradually *composed* out of the individual parts which are taken from historical reality to make it up. Thus the final and definitive concept can't stand at the beginning of the investigation, but must come at the *end*. We must, in other words, work out in the course of the discussion, as its most important result, the best conceptual formulation of what we here understand by the spirit of capitalism of what we here understand by the spirit of capitalism, that is the most adequate from the point of view *which interests us here*" (Weber 1904/1993: 11).

This description fits neatly with Weber's proclamations in the *Wissenschaftslehre*. The elements from which to form historical individuals are *already* significant in the world of the actors, and a cultural science is to take heed of this pre-established significance. "Capitalism" no doubt has cultural significance in this sense. No matter whether we think of capitalism as good or evil, as curse or boon, it will hardly be denied that it influences aspects of our lives which are relevant from the point of view of values.

But "capitalism" is still completely amorphous and unspecified. The spectrum is narrowed down by the specification that what Max Weber is interested in is what he calls the "*spirit* of capitalism". But then again we have no very specific idea what this "spirit" is supposed to be. The first task must be to work out a concept of this spirit. There is, as Weber said, a complication here, due to the fact that the elements making up the material are already significant to the actors themselves. These elements can't be defined beforehand, prior to empirical investigation. They can only be established empirically, in the course of the investigation, since it can only be determined empirically what was "significant" to the actors themselves. Hence Weber does not start out by stating in full the point of view that interests him, i.e. the *reason* why the "spirit of capitalism" is constituted as the primary historical individual. Rather, he starts out by recounting the elements of the spirit of capitalism, leaving the "point of view" implicit in the background. Since most sociologists today are familiar with the elements Weber presents as parts of the spirit of capitalism, we can safely begin our exposition from the other end.

What interests Max Weber is a particular *mode of conduct* (*Lebens-führung*) adequate for capitalism.[5] It has nothing to do with greed, nor with the behaviour found among economic adventurers or robber barons. Like phenomena are not specific to modern capitalism. They existed long before capitalism was established, and are not even well suited for a capitalist economy. The mode of conduct particularly adequate for capitalism is rather a methodical and calculating behaviour: carefully supervising all aspects of business, working *continually*, and *reinvesting* the returns in the company. Or as Gordon Marshall summarises the maxims for everyday conduct Weber takes to be constitutive of the "capitalist spirit": "be prudent, diligent, and ever about your business; do not idle, for time is money; cultivate your creditworthiness and put it to good use, for credit is money; be punctual and just in the repayment of loans and debts, for to become a person of known-credit-worthiness is to be master of other people's purses; be vigilant in keeping accounts; be frugal in consumption and do not waste money on inessentials; and, finally, do not let money lie idle, for the smallest sum soundly invested can earn a profit, and the profits reinvested soon multiply in ever-increasing amounts" (Marshall 1993: 18).

In our days, as well as in Weber's, the question does not arise *why* this mode of conduct is called for. Acting against it is rewarded by elimination from the market. "The capitalistic economy of the present day is an immense cosmos into which the individual is born, and which presents itself to him, at least as an individual, as an unalterable order of things in which he must live. It forces the individual, in so far as he is involved in the system of market relationships, to conform to capitalistic rules of action. The manufacturer who in the long run acts counter to these norms, will just as inevitably be eliminated from the economic scene as the worker who can not or will not adapt himself to them will be thrown into the streets without a job" (Weber 1904/1993: 17). As Weber continues to say, "capitalism of today, as it has become dominant in economic life, fosters and creates the economic subjects it needs – industrialists and workers – by means of an 'economic *selection*'" (Weber 1904/1993: 17). There is thus a natural selection operating on the economic subjects: the choice for an economic subject is between complying with this mode of conduct and being thrown out of the market. No special "mentality" is needed to uphold this mode of conduct, this *Lebensführung*. Indeed, the economic subjects could have the most diverse motives for complying with it – purposively rational, value rational, traditional – but since

5. "Lebensführung" figures prominently in Wolfgang Schluchter's interpretation of Max Weber's works (Schluchter 1991). Schluchter makes "Lebensführung" the key category in Weber's writings, an interpretation we shall not discuss further here.

compliance is a necessity for staying alive on the market, we may hypothesise that purposively rational motives predominate.

However, it is just this *Lebensführung* that constitute the "spirit of capitalism" as Max Weber construes it. *This* is the "primary historical individual" and the explanandum of the Protestant Ethic (Marshall 1993: 18). What is to be explained is not capitalism itself, conceived as an economic form or as a system. It is the "spirit", the mode of conduct uniquely appropriate to capitalism. For this "spirit", Weber claims, was alien, even incomprehensible, to pre-capitalist society. The task he set himself was to explain its naissance.

It won't do to explain the origin of this mode of conduct by reference to the concept of economic "selection". Weber grants it that arguments from selection can explain why this *Lebensführung* emerged as the victor once it had appeared on the scene. But saying that it would prove to be the "fittest" if it would enter the scene does nothing to explain how and why it *did* enter the scene. "For this form of *Lebensführung* and conception of "calling", adapted, to the unique individuality of capitalism, to be "selected" and win over other *Lebensführungen*, it must first *come into existence*. Moreover, it must emerge not only among a few isolated individuals, but as an outlook on the world borne by *groups* of people" (Weber 1904/1993: 17).

### The Ideal Type "Protestant Ethic" and Its Uses

The argument so far is only concerned with establishing the explanandum. It remains to be seen how the emergence of this *Lebensführung* can be explained. This brings us to the theory of adequate causation. Now, since the amount of causal factors leading up to a concrete event is always infinite, it is impossible in principle to recount them all. Explanations of concrete historical events are thus always one-sided. Yet, even though we can't consider *all* causes, *every* condition could be a cause. That is to say, there are no a priori restrictions on what could cause. Events in nature can have historically significant consequences no less than human action; "materialistic" or "economic" causes are no less possible than "idealistic" ones. Whether or not a certain condition was the cause of a certain event can't be adjudicated on a priori grounds. The only way to determine whether a certain condition caused an event was to establish whether it raised the objective possibility for that event, thereby making it an adequate cause.

Now, in order to make this kind of explanation, both the cause and the effect must be *isolated* and *generalised*. Only then can it be established whether or not, according to *nomological* knowledge (or *Erfahrungsregeln* as Weber prefers to say), the (generalised) cause would in *general* lead to the (generalised) effect. These are the argumentative steps involved in establishing objective possibility and adequate causation. One more thing needs to be added, however. As we have seen earlier in this study, however, Max Weber did not believe that the purported "laws" of economics are actually laws in the sense of the natural sciences. He prefers to refer to them as "ideal types", and so the explanans we are looking for, the secondary historical individual, is to be framed as an ideal type. What we should expect, then, is that Weber tries to establish an ideal type, such that we can ask whether, in general, it would lead to a *Lebensführung* of the kind he describes. "Although Weber did not say so explicitly, presumably the ideal-type presented in 'The Protestant Ethic' is genetic, and hence to be understood as an objective possibility construction. Presumably he also believed that the cause he identified increases the probability of the outcome sufficiently to be considered an adequate cause" (Turner 1985: 172).

Considering that ". . . speculation on the possible relationships between religion and the rise of capitalism had a long and distinguished pedigree", which Max Weber also recognises, it was rather natural for Weber to look for an explanans in Protestantism (Marshall 1993: 19). But it is one thing to note a relationship between Protestantism and capitalism, and another to explain it. Weber adds in the revised edition from 1920 that the existence of a relationship between the two "is not a 'novelty'. Lavaleye, Matthew Arnold, and others already perceived it. . . . Our task here is to explain the relation" (Weber 1920/1988: 28). One explanation is in fact frequently suggested in the literature. It holds that the ban on usury, asceticism in the cloisters etc, in the Catholic church had hampered economic development, and that Protestantism had relaxed the religious command of economy sufficiently to let economic development loose. This is not at all what Max Weber has in mind. The explanation works on the assumption that religious sentiment and power was basically a hindrance. It also assumes that as soon as this hindrance is removed, economic behaviour will be allowed to develop "normally". No longer fettered by religious prejudice, the individual will develop a "spirit of capitalism."

Weber's thesis is the exact opposite: a "capitalist spirit" did not develop because religious sentiments were weakened, but because they were exceptionally strong. The "spirit of capitalism" is not natural to man. Left to his own devices, he will not develop it as a matter of course. On the contrary, Weber claims, the basic attitude towards economic affairs is "traditionalism". Man does not wish to earn as much as possible, but to lead the life he is already leading. As a consequence it is common that workers do not perform more but *less* when their salaries increase. They can maintain their current standard while working less. To explain why they would subject themselves under the harsh and methodical regiment of the spirit of capitalism, it is not satisfactory to say that a hindrance has been lifted. What must be found is rather a *positive* force, something compelling enough for the economic subjects to take on a radically different view of economic matters and of work.

Max Weber, as is well known, purports to find this in the very doctrine of some varieties of Puritanism. Thus, it is from this doctrine that the ideal type "protestant ethic" is to be construed. We must be aware here that logically, if not practically, there are three different steps involved in working with "ideal types". Each step can be subjected to criticism. The first involves constructing the pure type. It is the ideal type in this sense that we see expressed in the set of characteristics used to constitute it. Yet, as Weber says, the ideal type considered for itself is a product of sheer imagination, and taken as it stands it need not be a valuable means of attaining knowledge. The question whether it is valuable, whether it is something other than a mind game, can only be decided if it is related to how it is *used*. If the ideal type, if conceived as the explicit propositions that make it up, it is not an hypothesis, but it can be *used* as an hypothesis. Now, there are two senses of "using the ideal type as an hypothesis". It must, of course, be possible to place the ideal type in the empirical context we are interested in – either by finding it approximated in the empirical material or by drawing on the way in which the actual empirical material deviates from the ideal type. In the case of the Protestant Ethic it is the former that is sought for. It is hypothesised that the constructed ideal type is also found in the empirical material. The hypothesis involved is that the ideal type approximates the secondary historical individual. But the ideal type is also a hypothesis in relation to the explanandum. If the ideal type is actually found in the empirical material, does it increase the objective possibility for the effect that we have in mind? This is presumably the sense Weber refers to when he says that the ideal type is not a hypothesis but that it can be used as one.

When constructing ideal types, these three steps are not separated. The reason we construe it in the first place is that we believe that it increases the objective possibility of the effect. We also wouldn't bother to construe it if we did not believe that it could be found approximated in reality. Logically, however, these three steps must be kept apart.

To illustrate, we shall make a short detour. We use an example from *Economy and Society* which, as we shall see, is related to the argument in the Protestant Ethic (cf. Weber 1921/1990: 4 *et seq.*). We take as our point of departure Weber's four famous ideal types of actions. Weber distinguishes between purposive rational (*Zweckrational*), value rational (*Wertrational*), traditional, and affective action. These ideal types are introduced in connection with the notion of understanding, as examples of explanatory understanding. This latter category is contrasted with a more immediate form of understanding. We understand, Weber says, what is going on when we see someone reaching for the doorknob, opening a window, aiming with a rifle, or chopping wood. What we don't observe directly is what motive prompted the person to perform that action. The man chopping wood could be doing so out of purposively rational motives, in which case he is chopping wood because this action, according to his experience and his expectations, will bring him closer to his goal – in this case to get some good firewood into the house. Or he could be doing so for affectual reasons. Let us say he had a row with his wife, and that he is chopping wood in order to unleash and work out piled up frustration. It would seem a bit far-fetched to imagine the man chopping wood for "value rational" or "traditional" reasons. This is nevertheless what we shall do here. First, however, we will alter the example somewhat.

Ever since Alfred Schütz' book on *Der sinnhafte Aufbau der Welt* (1934), commentaries have primarily focused on the theoretical problems associated with the definitions of "motives", "actions", "rationality" and with the obviously troublesome relation between the four ideal types. In these commentaries, the onus is placed on one single action and the examples and counterexamples used are typically of one single action or a short sequence of actions and omissions. I do not wish to contest the value of this kind of argument. They are no doubt important in their own right. On the other hand, I don't believe them to be particularly illuminating from the point of view of Weber research. We recall that Max Weber said that the key problem in economics, methodologically as well as substantially, is how to explain "the origin and continued existence of economic institutions, which have not been created purposively by a collectivity, but which nevertheless . . . function appropriately" for our needs (Weber 1903/1985: 29). In other words: the theoretical challenge for economics is how to explain the emergence and continued existence of economic institutions from the *unintended consequences* of action. Classical economics and the marginalists had excelled in this kind of explanation. They had, however, limited themselves to studies of how the unintended consequences of *purposively rational* actions can explain certain outcomes. Moreover, they had portrayed their explanations as proceeding from "laws" on a par with the laws of nature – thus turning purposively rational action into a "psychological law", an "axiom", an "a priori" or the like. Max Weber, as we have seen, disagreed with this self-description. The mode of explanation, however, suited him fine. But why limit this mode of explanation to explanation from *purposively* rational action? If the *homo oeconomicus* is no longer conceived

as a psychological law but as an ideal type, nothing stands in the way
of constructing, for example, value rational ideal types in order to see
how the unintended consequences of such action can explain the
emergence and continued existence of economic (or other) institutions and phenomena. I suggest that this is what Max Weber does in
the Protestant Ethic, and that this study provided Weber with a laboratory to work out his ideas in practice: the mode of explanation he
used there appeared to be unprecedented in the literature.[6] What is
important here is how the ideal types of actions are *used*. The primary
use Max Weber makes of them is not to explain one particular action,
performed by a particular person, by saying that "she acted out of
purposively rational motives" or "she acted out of value rational
motives". From the point of view of economics, this would seem to be
a rather uninteresting kind of explanation. Of course it is possible that
a certain economic phenomenon was brought about by the decision
of a single person. We can't rule out any kind of cause apriori, and it
must be allowed that the actions or omissions of one single person
could be an adequate cause of a certain economic event. And perhaps
it is meaningful to say that this person acted in accordance with the
ideal type of value rational action, although I very much doubt it.
Why not just say that she had ethical motives for performing her
action? Focusing on the verbal formulation of the ideal type and not
on its uses seems to lead astray, for, as Weber said, the knowledge-
value of an ideal type can only be determined from how it is *used*. And
whatever uses Weber made of the ideal types of action, he did not use
them merely as a classification of the actions of particular individuals.
Having said this, we can return to the example of the man chopping
wood.

Let us alter this example, so that it is no longer about observing a
man chopping wood at a particular occasion. Let us say instead that
we observe the man going out into his backyard *every day* to chop wood.
What we are observing, then, is not a particular event, but the way
he continually leads his life, i.e. his *Lebensführung*. We still understand his acts "directly", recognising it as the act of chopping wood.
We also observe that his behaviour is repeated continually, so that we,
"according to *Erfahrungsregeln*" can "count on it". We know what this
man is doing, and we also know that there is a recurring pattern. But
we do not yet know the motives for his actions, and we do not know

6. The marginalists were debarred from this sort of reasoning to the extent that they believed
the *homo oeconomicus* to be a psychological law or an innate disposition of all human
beings. And even if they didn't believe so, they did nothing to work out explanations other
than those on purposive rationality. The older generation of the historical school of economics, on the other hand, could not contribute either, because of their conflation of laws
and causality. This conflation worked in two ways to prevent the kind of explanations
Weber was looking for. According to Weber, these views are only possible from an emanatist
and organicist point of view.

the reasons why he has adopted this perennial behaviour as his *Lebensführung*. Let us first assume that his motives are purposively rational. We could be dealing with a very prudent man, who acts on the expectation (correct or mistaken) that it will be a very cold winter, and that it is more efficient and secure to chop a small amount of wood each time, distributing the required work over the entire year. Or he could be *employed* to chop wood. In both cases we have found the motives behind his actions, and the reasons for their perennial recurrence. Yet, what is important is that the *Lebensführung* remains the *same* in both cases. The motivations for keeping with the *Lebensführung* are different (although we are, arguably, dealing with purposively rational action in both cases[7]), and yet the *Lebensführung* is the same.

Let us now make a thought experiment, and construct another kind of ideal type for the motives behind the perennial conduct of the wood-chopping man. This time we construct it on the basis of *value rationality*. We assume that he is a religious man, and that the religion he adheres to has a set of articles of belief. It proclaims a doctrine of predestination. It is determined beforehand who will come to heaven and who will not, and no good deeds can change this preordained order. Yet even though there is nothing the believer can do to influence his state in grace, he can, and no doubt will, try to find out whether he is among the *electi*, the chosen ones. The anxious and haunted believer will desperately seek *certitudo salutis*. And, according to the religious doctrine, there are *signs* of being chosen. If God lets you lead a life in accordance with his commands, and not fraught with doubts, this is a sign of being among the *electi*. Now, according to the religion our wood-chopping man believes in, God demands that every day, you get up early in the morning and chop wood – this is what it means to work in ones calling. It is also considered a grave sin to unnecessarily waste the wood by burning it. Such luxury is unbecoming and sinful. Giving the wood away to the Church – so that the wood could be used as ornament in the churches – is also against the commands of God, for his church is simple and chaste and will know no adornments. The wood-chopping man obeys these commands meticulously. He rises early every day to go into his backyard and chop wood that he never spends. Oversleeping and not doing a good days work is a sin. Yet it is not a lapse that can be put

---

7. This is not necessarily so. The act of going to work is perhaps most often an example of "traditional" action. Normally, the worker presumably does not reflect upon whether his act of "going to work" is the best means, according to *Erfahrungsregeln*, of achieving some end. It *is* of course the best means of keeping the job. But this is hardly a consideration he normally reflects upon before going to work. However, the case can be construed in such a way that it is an example of purposively rational action. We could assume, for example, that this particular worker has been threatened with dismissal if he doesn't show up. In that case purposively rational motives *are* in play.

right through confession or good deeds. His lapsus is not one that can be made up for, for there is nothing you can do to influence your state in grace. The failure to live up to these commands is interpreted in another way: God didn't let me lead my life in accordance with his wishes. He has let me succumb to temptations, to stray from his path – a sign that I am not among the *electi*. Hence there is a very methodical streak in the behaviour of the wood-chopping man. One single day of absence from the axe, or one single log unnecessarily spent, would be a sign that he is condemned, which will naturally cause anxiety. These, in sum, are the *value rational motives* impelling our man to methodically and continually chop away, whilst the pile of wood ever increases. It is the "ethic" that motivates his *Lebensführung*.

This brings us back to where we started this detour: the three different steps involved in forming an ideal type. We have no doubt constructed an ideal type here. *If* a man believed in this religion, *then* this would increase the objective possibility for the existence of a quite impressive woodpile. Considering the definition of the ideal type, we would thus have to concede that this is indeed an ideal type.

Of course, constructing such an ideal type would be an "idle game", to quote Weber. There is no religion that decrees perennial wood chopping or a ban on burning logs. So the ideal type is useless in the sense that there is nothing in the real world to correspond to it or approximate it. Nor can we get anything useful out of empirical behaviour "deviating" from this norm. But suppose we did find a sect that believes in this religion. Could it then be used as an ideal type? The answer to this question must still be negative. To be sure, we could take a scientific interest in the sect. Yet, in that case it would most certainly be as a *primary historical individual*. We would be interested in explaining how this belief system came into being. At no point, however, is our scientific interest in the sect motivated by an interest in the resulting woodpiles. Even though we might have a scientific interest in the sect, it would not be as an explanans, and so there would still be no point in constructing a generic ideal type from the beliefs of the sect.

It is clear, then, that there are several steps involved in forming an ideal type, and that it can only be measured according to how it is used, not as it is formulated. Let us now once again consider the ideal type we constructed of the religious beliefs of the wood-chopping man. If we just change it slightly, we have a formulation Max Weber gives of the "protestant ethic". The only elements we need replace are those which refer to the act of "chopping wood". It is not logs that are not to be spent, but money; and the "calling" is not specifically concerned with chopping wood but with work in general. This time the constructed ideal type is not an "idle game". It is constructed from

an actually existing religious doctrine – and the lion's share of the
Protestant Ethic is an attempt to show how this doctrine gradually
emerged. Before we make some brief remarks on how Weber does
this, however, we should ask whether it can serve as a genetic ideal
type, i.e, whether the existence of people believing in the doctrine
would increase the objective possibility for the existence of the primary historical individual we are interested in. We recall that the historical individual we are interested in is a particular *Lebensführung*
adequate to capitalism. The maxims corresponding to this *Lebensführung* [were] summarised as: "be prudent, diligent, and ever about
your business; do not idle, for time is money; cultivate your credit-
worthiness and put it to good use, for credit is money; be punctual
and just in the repayment of loans and debts, for to become a person
of known credit-worthiness is to be master of other people's purses;
be vigilant in keeping accounts; be frugal in consumption and do not
waste money on inessentials; and, finally, do not let money lie idle,
for the smallest sum soundly invested can earn a profit, and the profits reinvested soon multiply in ever-increasing amounts" (Marshall
1993: 18). It was granted that this *Lebensführung*, once it has come
into existence, would typically lead to economic advantages. Once it
is there, others can imitate it. Weber conceded that in our days, those
who are unwilling or unable to organise their business according to
this *Lebensführung* would be eliminated from the market; no special
mentality is needed to keep it going. But he added that this does
nothing to explain why and how it came into being in the first place.
The protestant ethic, such as it appears in the ideal type that we construed, does seem to provide one explanation to how this *Lebensführung* originated. If there is a religion in which the believers
regulate their conduct in everyday life according to a strict work ethos,
while at the same time not spending their moneys, there is a considerable increase of the objective possibility that the believer will act in
just the way that was described as the *Lebensführung* adequate for
capitalism. He does not do so *because* he believes that this will give
him business advantages. Had this been the reason, he would have
acted out of purposively rational motives, i.e. his embracing this particular *Lebensführung* would be motivated by his belief that, given his
expectations on the way things and men behave, this is the most efficient means of reaching his business goals. It turns out that it *is* in
fact an efficient means towards this end. But this was not the reason
for choosing to organise his conduct this way. The reason was *religious*,
i.e. *value rational. Hence, Weber has explained the emergence of a
Lebensführung adequate to capitalism from the unintended consequences of value rational behaviour.*

Yet, it is of course not quite true that Weber has succeeded in
[explaining] it yet. All that is established, and I am inclined to say that

the argument *so far* is on safe grounds, is that this sort of *Lebens-führung* would result *if* there was a religion in the empirical world corresponding to the ideal type. What remains to be done is to show that this ideal type is also *in fact* found in the real world. Only then will Weber have established that the *Lebensführung* in question has emerged, "not only among a few isolated individuals, but as an outlook on the world borne by *groups* of people" (Weber 1904/1993: 17). Max Weber tries to show that this was actually the case, and he attempts to demonstrate how the doctrine corresponding to the ideal type emerged gradually, one element being added after another.

This strategy of exposition had a price. It invited . . . misunderstandings. The title of the essays also contributed in the same direction, for it is in fact a misnomer. The ethic described in the ideal type is not that of Protestantism in general. The doctrines of a Martin Luther or a Philipp Melancthon do not fit the ideal type at all. Max Weber never says so either – indeed, he insists that Lutheranism has nothing at all to do with the ethos he is describing in the ideal type. Still, Weber's thesis has often been misunderstood as referring to Protestantism in general. Weber brought this on himself, even though he actually *was* explicit on this point. Partly by formulating the title the way he did, and partly because the exposition of the ideal typical "ethic" starts out with a discussion of Martin Luther.

Weber had a reason for starting with Martin Luther, however. It was, according to Weber, in Luther's translation of the bible that the concept of "calling" first took on *both* a religious and a worldly meaning. That the concept of "calling" was no longer merely a calling to God, but also contained a sense of work in this world, was a presupposition for later developments. Yet almost all the characteristics of the ideal type "protestant ethic" was missing in Luther's doctrine, and hence this variety of Protestantism did not increase the objective possibility for the *Lebensführung* to develop. For this to be the case, all of the elements recounted above must be present. It so happens that this rules out Calvin too. Calvin was so sure that he himself was among the *electi* that it never occurred to him that there was a need for other outward signs. This element of the ideal type came into being only with Calvin's followers. Neither "Protestantism" nor "Calvinism" did thus fit the description, according to Weber.

The denominations he thought matched the description were all of a later date: "It appears to Weber that a number of seventeenth century Reformed Churches subscribed to a common code of conduct according to which believers were expected to organize their daily lives. He focuses specifically on four such religious groupings: the various neo-Calvinist Churches and denominations of Western Europe and North America; Continental Pietism; Anglo-American Methodism; and the sects associated with and developing out of Anabaptism.

Collectively these movements comprise 'ascetic Protestantism'. He accepts that these labels are merely heuristic" (Marshall 1993: 70).

If we would formulate Weber's thesis, it would therefore be in the following terms. Certain denominations within the Reformed Churches were such that they, unintentionally, promoted a doctrine that was causally adequate for the rise of a *Lebensführung* identical to that of the "spirit of capitalism", i.e. a *Lebensführung* adequate to modern capitalism.

Formulated in this way, it is clear that the thesis does not rule out the possibility that this *Lebensführung* could be produced in other ways. In our days, it *is* produced in other ways. No special mentality is needed to promote it, for, with the capitalist system once established, deflectors are eliminated from the market. It does not matter what motives it is that impel the economic subjects to comply – be it purposively rational, value rational, or traditional motives. What matter is *that* they comply. The economic system selects the economic subjects it needs, and makes no distinction as to the motives responsible for making the economic subject fit, and hence of not being eliminated.

It is also compatible with Weber's thesis that other causes could bring about that same *Lebensführung* before modern capitalism had become rooted. Yet saying so doesn't make it so. If someone wishes to propound a thesis to this effect, it would have to be demonstrated in the same way as Weber purported to demonstrate the influence of the "Protestant ethic".

## Max Weber and His Critics

Considering that Max Weber's thesis in *The Protestant Ethic and the Spirit of Capitalism* must be specified in this way, there is a stark contrast to how the thesis has often been discussed in sociology and related areas. As Wilhelm Hennis says, "seldom has anyone had such bad fortune in the avoidance of misunderstanding. The libraries written on the 'Weber-thesis' would otherwise never ever haven been written" (Hennis 1988: 27). For one thing, as Hennis notes, "the 'Weber-thesis' has long been misunderstood as a causal hypothesis on the origin of capitalism", adding that "this no longer happens among German scholars" (Hennis 1988: 26). There are various degrees of misrepresentations in the literature. Unfortunately a rather large portion of the literature on the "Weber-thesis" is working on the assumption that it simply says that Protestantism "caused capitalism". These studies also take it that "causing" should be read either as "being a necessary condition", as "being a sufficient condition", or as "being a necessary and sufficient condition". Proceeding from these assumptions, scholars have then set out to show that there are non-capitalist protestant countries or to show that there are non-protestant capitalist countries. This way of putting the issue finds a clear expression in Kurt Samuelsson's famous book *Religion and Economic Action*: "Was it religion, the doctrines of Protestantism, that impelled men to economic achievement? Were the Protestant states more successful economically [than] the Catholic and, if so, does religion provide the explanation and cause of this difference? Would 'capitalism', that powerful economic advance which surged across northern and Western Europe and later America, never have come into being had it not been for the doctrines of Protestantism? Weber asserted strenuously that such causal links did indeed exist" (Samuelsson 1957/1993: 1–2). Samuelsson does recognise that Lutheranism does not count among the denominations expressing the "Protestant ethic" – not every scholar has done even that. To refute Weber's thesis, then, we only have to find counter examples, examples where Protestantism and capitalism do not occur together. If we can find such examples, we can congratulate ourselves to a successful refutation.

However, stating Weber's thesis as "*Protestantism caused*, i.e., was a necessary and/or sufficient condition for, *capitalism*" is wrong on all accounts. Each of the three words used in the statement gravely misrepresents Weber's argument. The historical individual to be explained is not capitalism; the explanans is not Protestantism; and if "cause" is equated with necessary and/or sufficient conditions, the use of this term, too, is based on a misunderstanding.

If we are to believe Wilhelm Hennis, the mistaken belief, that Max Weber's thesis said that Protestantism was the cause of capitalism, is no longer to be found among German scholars. That might be true. Yet, the problems of interpretation did not disappear with the demise of this mistaken view. If the thesis was not about a causal relationship between Protestantism and capitalism, then what was it about? The immediate candidate was the *spirit* of capitalism – an interpretation that found support in the title of Weber's essay. If Weber was not aiming at explaining the naissance of capitalism, then he was perhaps interested in explaining the birth of the capitalist spirit. This interpretation gave rise to a new set of problems, however. The way Weber defined the capitalist spirit, it seemed to amount to the same thing as the commands of the protestant ethic. But in that case, we would be dealing with an *internal* relationship, not a causal relationship. The protestant ethic *converges* or *congrues* with the spirit of capitalism on a set of rules. The conclusion must be, then, that causal reasoning plays no part in *The Protestant Ethic and the Spirit of Capitalism*. Rather than causality, Weber's study is about "convergence", "elective affinities", "equivalence", or "congruence".

This interpretation finds it very hard to deal with the causal reference implicit in Weber's use of "adequacy" in the texts. It is even likely that it was an obstacle to recognising the technical import of adequate cause theory. Unfortunately, the term "adequacy" appears in the very passages that the advocates of this interpretation like to quote. As a result, we find some very peculiar, and very characteristic, translations of "adequacy" in the works of these scholars – for according to their interpretation, it is out of the question that "adequacy" has anything at all to do with causality. To exemplify, we may quote Ephraim Fischoff. Fischoff rejected the view that Weber was getting at a causal link between Protestantism and capitalism: "In the light of all this Weber's thesis must be construed not according to the usual interpretation, as an effort to trace the causative influence of the Protestant ethic upon the emergence of capitalism, but as an exposition of the rich congruency of such diverse aspects of a culture as religion and economics. The essay should be considered as a stimulating project of hermeneutics, a demonstration of interesting correlations between diverse cultural factors" (Fischoff 1965: 114–115). In support of his interpretation, Fischoff turns to Max Weber's response to critical remarks from Karl Fischer. "Replying to Fischer's criticism, Weber insisted that [in] the Protestant essay he had expressed himself with utter clarity on the relationship between religion and economics generally, but he none the less admitted that misunderstanding might possibly have arisen from certain turns of phrase. Accordingly he promised to remove in a future reissue all expressions which seemed to suggest the derivation of institutions from religious motives; and he expressed his intention of clarifying the fact that it was the spirit of 'methodical' *Lebensführung* which he was deriving from Protestant asceticism, *and which is related to economic forms only through congruence (Adäquanz)*" (Fischoff 1965: 110–11, italics added).

Fischoff's translation of adequacy as "congruence" is telling enough, and he provides the most obvious example. But he is not alone in his mode of interpretation. Others have gone down the same path. We even find a suspicious looking formulation in the English edition of Wilhelm Hennis' *Max Weber. Essays in Reconstruction*, where "adequacy" is translated as "adequacy-*equivalence*" (Hennis 1988: 28–29).

The only way to get out of this impasse, and to recognise the role of causality in Weber's essays, is to take seriously Weber's assurance that what he tried to explain was a particular *Lebensführung* appropriate to capitalism. A *Lebensführung*, a mode of conduct, is outward behaviour. It can be brought about by a host of different motives. In Max Weber's terminology, we may say that we immediately understand the mode of conduct of the actors, i.e. what they are in fact doing, but that we do not know immediately what motivated their mode of conduct. The relation Weber describes is not a relationship between two systems of ideas, but between a particular belief and a collective mode of conduct. Thus interpreted, there is no problem in recognising the causal element in Weber's argument, and there is no need to rewrite "adequacy" as "congruence" or "equivalence".

It must be emphasised, however, that the misunderstandings Max Weber's argument fell prey to are not all of recent date. The thesis had bad fortunes already during Weber's own lifetime. It is therefore fitting that we conclude this chapter with a brief discussion of the critique raised against Max Weber's essays during the years following their publication. Max Weber's thesis attracted the attention of two critics, Karl H. Fischer (Fischer 1907/1995 and 1908/1995) and Felix Rachfahl (Rachfahl 1909 and 1910).

The critiques these two scholars delivered of Max Weber's essays are interesting from a methodological point of view. Rachfahl and Fischer represent two different camps in the *Methodenstreit* in history. Felix Rachfahl [as I have shown earlier in this study] participated in this debate as a partisan for the views of the historicists against Karl Lamprecht. Karl Fischer, on the other hand, stands close to Lamprecht's (and Gustav Schmoller's) position, in that he proposed that social scientific explanations must be concerned with establishing laws.

Considering that they are on opposite sides of the methodological gulf, we would expect them to differ in their descriptions and critiques of Weber's thesis. To the extent that methodological issues are brought up, moreover, we can read the comments of these two authors as an index over the difficulties involved grasping Weber's views from within the argumentative framework of the *Methodenstreit* in history. Read in this way, we can try to ascertain in what ways, if any, the argumentative structure prevented an assessment of Max Weber's argument. Needless to say, we can only provide a preliminary first step towards an understanding of these issues. Even so, that first step is well worth taking. Now, since Max Weber did not try to establish "laws", but was rather interested in explaining historically the emergence of a concrete event, we may venture to guess that a historicist such as Felix Rachfahl would have no objections of principle against Weber's project. Rachfahl's critique of Weber is directed towards empirical details, and methodological issues are not brought into the argument. Yet they do come to the fore in Karl Fischer's exposition and critique, and we shall make some comments on his argument.

Fischer starts out by stating the explanandum of Weber's study in terms of the occupational statistics in Baden reported at the outset of Weber's article. Upon Fischer's interpretation, what Weber is trying to explain is the fact that protestants, more often than Catholics, are found in management and the upper ranks of labour in modern industrial and commercial enterprises, are more often owners of capital etc. This, as we know, is by no means the explanandum in Weber's essays. Weber merely uses these figures to introduce his problem. Yet, it would not be fair to blame Fischer for getting it wrong. His interpretation is understandable enough. Given the fact that Max Weber begins his essay by recounting occupational statistics, it is not unreasonable to believe that the aim of the essay is to explain these figures. Max Weber himself must take some blame for confusing his readers.

What is more interesting from our point of view is how Karl Fischer describes Weber's mode of explanation. He sees in Max Weber an "idealist". Religion belongs to the superstructure, and explanations from the superstructure are "idealistic" as opposed to "materialistic". Now, Weber had explicitly declared that it was not his intention to replace a one-sided "materialist" causal interpretation of culture and history with an equally one-sided "spiritualistic" one. Karl Fischer recognises this and comments upon it by saying that "what matters is not what the author does or doesn't want but *what sort of procedure he actually follows in his investigation*, regardless of what the author assures us" (Fischer 1908/1995: 39). And since Max Weber's explanation was made in terms of ideas, i.e. in terms of the superstructure rather than the material basis, he is pegged as an idealist. Now, the only way to make this inference work is to assume that there are only two kinds of explanation, an "idealistic" and a "materialistic" *Tertium non datur*. The choice, then, is between two one-cause-theories, and no other alternatives are available. Either all cultural phenomena depend ultimately on "material"/economic causes, or they depend in the last instance on "ideal" causes. From what we have said so far in this book, it is clear that Max Weber doesn't fit into this grid of possible positions.

Karl Fischer thus thought that Max Weber attempted to demonstrate the viability of idealism. He is so thoroughly convinced that Weber must be an idealist in this sense that he suggests that Weber's remarks on the transformations of Baptism should perhaps be understood as a "logical development in Hegel's sense" (Fischer 1907/1995: 16). The gist of Fischer's argument is therefore to show that the facts could be interpreted materialistically, to show that it is possible that economic causes could be responsible for bringing about the result which Weber, according to Fischer, wished to explain "idealistically".

This sort of argument made no sense from Max Weber's point of view. Merely suggesting that there *could* be economic causes of the *Lebensführung* he had described proves nothing. If Fischer wants to undermine his argument by suggesting another causal scenario, *he must show that and how this happened*. It is *self-evident* that there *could* be other causes behind the events. But taking this claim to be an objection against his argument is sloppy scholarly work, unless the rival theory is proved in the same manner as Max Weber had attempted to prove his argument. Weber would be the first to admit that religious factors are not always responsible for bringing about all historical events. This idea is at the very core of his methodological outlook. Prior to the publication of Fischer's critique, Weber had written a critical article on Rudolf Stammler's book *Wirtschaft und Recht nach der materialistischen Geschichtsauffassung*. It was published in the very same journal, the *Archiv für Sozialwissenschaft und Sozialpolitik*, in which Fischer's critique of Weber appeared. Weber was quite sarcastic of Rudolf Stammler's professed belief in the necessity of monocausality. Stammler had taken over his mode of reasoning from historical materialism, but replaced "the economy" for "the law" as the factor that, in the last instance, is responsible for everything that goes on in society and history. Weber paraphrased Stammler's argument, substituting the "economic" (or "legal") interpretation of history with a mock "spiritualistic" interpretation of history. The argument then unfolds as a dialogue between the "spiritualist" and an empirical researcher – the latter being Max Weber's alter ego. The "spiritualist" rejects the counter instances produced by the empirical researcher, with the motivation that his "spiritualism" is a "methodological principle" or an "a priori" and that its truth is therefore immune against empirical refutations. The sound common sense of the empirically minded scientist, Weber adds, must treat this position as a species of *scholastic mystification*. "With the same 'logic' . . . the following 'methodological principle' could also be established. 'In the final analysis,' 'social life' is a consequence of the size of the skull, or the effects of sun spots, or indigestion" (Weber 1907/1977: 68).

Karl Fischer was obviously not aware of Max Weber's methodological writings – for he ascribes to him the very views Weber had ridiculed. As he conceived the matter, his strategy made perfectly good sense. He thought that he was undermining the claims of a scholar attempting to demonstrate the viability of idealism, and for this purpose it sufficed to show that there are other possibilities available.[8]

At this point it is fairly obvious that the communication between Fischer and Weber had broken down, and the ensuing debate is a display of impeded understanding. Fischer could not understand what Weber was really trying to do, and Weber, unable to see why he was attributed such monstrous views, became more and more irritated with his critic. Unfortunately Max Weber gave vent to his irritation by insisting on referring to Fischer as "Herr Kritiker", which must

---

8. Gross as Fischer's misunderstanding might appear, Max Weber's alleged "idealism" has been a recurring theme in some later interpretations, and not only those of a Marxist variety. As an example we may quote Paul Münch, who sees no problem in placing Max Weber in the lineage of idealist thinkers: "The essentially materialistic approach of the late eighteenth century was gradually replaced by an *idealistic* standpoint that could find a satisfactory explanation in the 'working of a spirit.' Without a doubt, Max Weber stands in this tradition as a German, a Protestant, and a representative of the educated middle classes – at best as 'a giant on the shoulders of dwarfs'" (Münch 1995: 71).

have aggravated Fischer. The tone in the debate quickly turned chilly, and in the final analysis we must conclude that it provides a further illustration that public academic controversy is no friend of subtlety.

The admissions Max Weber makes to his critic are few. The ones he [does] make are recognitions that he has perhaps not been as clear as he ought to, and that the essay could be misread as it stands. Weber thus uses his replies to Fischer to put this right by making clarifications and adjustments of his argument. "I take no responsibility for those misconceptions upon which, in my opinion, the foregoing criticism is based. I will, however, on the occasion of a separate edition of the essays (which for technical publishing reasons cannot be long postponed), try once more to remove each expression which could be understood in terms of a derivation of economic forms from religious motives – a derivation which I in fact never make – and therefore make it even clearer, if possible, that it is the spirit of a 'methodical' *Lebensführung*, which should be 'derived' from 'asceticism' in its Protestant transformation, and which even then stands in a cultural-historical relation of 'adequacy' which is important in my opinion. For this stimulus I must thank my critic" (Weber 1907/1995: 31).

In all his replies to his critics, Max Weber takes the opportunity to emphasise that the explanandum is a *Lebensführung*, a *mode of conduct*, and that he is trying to establish that puritan beliefs were an *adequate cause* of the emergence of this *Lebensführung*. "Weber resorts repeatedly, in both replies to Rachfahl, to the thesis of *Adäquanz*, as the sole epistemological objective. [ . . . ] Once again, Weber proclaims that he is only interested in the *Adäquanz* problem. As he states; in the earlier debate with Fischer he had established that 'my investigations concern only the analysis of the development of an ethical lifestyle adequate to emergent capitalism'" (Hennis 1988: 32, 34).

Yet, it is clear that neither of his critics understood what he was talking about. Max Weber's methodological outlook, propounding a selection of significant materials by means of a governing point of view and using the theory of adequate cause to conduct historical explanations, was alien to both Fischer and Rachfahl. We may indeed hypothesise that the oddity of Weber's methodological outlook from the point of view of the prevailing discourse was at least in part responsible for the lack of communication between Weber and his critics.

Before we conclude this chapter, however, we must examine the continuation of Karl Fischer's argument. Having determined Max Weber as an "idealist" and contrasted him with an economic interpretation, Fischer concludes that neither idealism nor materialism is free from objections. It might appear, then, that Fischer and Weber are in more agreement with each other than they let on. But this is a mere chimera. The solution proposed by Fischer is just as remote from Max Weber's methodological views as his description of Weber as an idealist. Fischer concludes that the problem of why people wish to earn money as an end in itself *a complex psychological problem*, and that it therefore must be answered by invoking *psychological laws or theories* (Fischer 1907/1995: 19). If we do so, we find that religion plays no part in motivating this sort of behaviour, and hence that Weber's explanation is flawed.

This argument is of the same ilk as those presented by Gustav Schmoller and Karl Lamprecht. It is based on the notion that because the material under study is of a "mental" or "psychological" nature, the only way to explain them is by means of scientific psychology. That is to say, the materials under study are thought to determine how they are to be studied. . . . this is a view that Weber had gone out of his way to combat. Weber's reply is therefore not free from sarcasm: "The knowledge produced by scientific psychology is relevant to history in exactly the same sense as that produced by astronomy, sociology, chemistry, legal dogmatics, theology, mechanical engineering, anthropology etc. It is a lay belief that history must specifically be based on scientific "psychology" because its material is made up by 'spiritual processes', i.e. because, it takes its point of departure in 'psychological presupposition' as it is believed and expressed in the vulgar language fashionable today. This belief is equally well founded as the following assumptions: Because the great deeds of 'historical personalities' today are exclusively tied to the 'medium' of sound-waves or ink, the science of acoustics or the physics of fluids must be regarded as providing the foundations of history; because history takes place on planet earth, it is astronomy which provides the foundations of history; because history is about human beings, it is anthropology which provides the foundations of history. History . . . makes 'general psychological presuppositions only in the same sense in which it makes, for example, general 'astronomical presuppositions'" (Weber 1908/1995: 51–52).

No scientific psychology is needed in order for us to understand why the puritans acted the way they did. If they believed in a doctrine of the sort that Max Weber had described ideal-typically, then there is no great mystery in why they behaved the way they did. We certainly don't need to invoke psychological laws in order to understand their mode of conduct.

However, this way of thinking was alien to Karl Fischer, who had a quite different frame of reference. It is Fischer who belongs to the majority group. Max Weber's views didn't square with the way others conceived of methodology in his day, and the debate over *The Protestant Ethic and the Spirit of Capitalism* illustrates the difficulties Weber had in conveying his message.

## References

Baumgarten, Eduard (1936). *Benjamin Franklin. Der Lehrmeister der amerikanischen Revolution*, Klostermann, Frankfurt.

Bendix, Reinhardt (1980). "The Protestant Ethic—Revisited," in Reinhardt Bendix and Guenther Roth, *Scholarship and Partisanship*, University of California Press, Berkeley.

Besnard, Philippe, ed. (1970). *Protestantisme et capitalisme. La controverse post-weberienne*, Armand Collin, Paris.

Davis, Murray (1986). "'That's Classic!' The Phenomenology and Rhetoric of Successful Social Theories," *Philosophy of Social Science*, 16:285–301.

Disselkamp, Annette (1994). *L'Éthique Protestante de Max Weber*, PUF, Paris.

Eisenstadt, Samuel, ed. (1968). *The Protestant Ethic and Modernization. A Comparative View*, Basic Books, New York.

Fischer, Karl H. (1907/1995). "Kritische Beiträge zu Professor Max Webers Abhandlung 'Die Protestantische Ethik und der Geist der Kapitalismus'," *Archiv für Sozialwissenschaft und Sozialpolitik*, Bd. 26:232–42. Reprinted in Weber 1995.

Fischoff, Ephraim (1965). "The History of a Controversy," in Robert W. Green, ed., *Protestantism, Capitalism and Social Science. The Weber Thesis Controversy*, D. C. Heath, London.

Green, Robert W., ed. (1973). *Protestantism, Capitalism and Social Science. The Weber Thesis Controversy*, D. C. Heath, London.

Hanya, Tatsuro (1993). "Max Webers Quellenbehandlung in der 'Protestantische Ethik,' Der Begriff 'Calling'," *Zeitschrift für Soziologie*, Jg. 22, Heft 1:65–75.

Hennis, Wilhelm. (1988). *Max Weber. Essays in Reconstruction*, Allen & Unwin, London.

Jorrat, Jorge Raul (1994). "Sobre Weber, Parsons y la lectura de porcentajas," *Desarollo Economico*, Vol. 34, No. 134:285–90.

Marshall, Gordon (1993). *In Search of the Spirit of Capitalism, An Essay on Weber's Protestant Ethic Thesis*, Hutschinson, London.

Münch, Paul (1995). "The Thesis Before Weber," in Hartmut Lehmann & Günther Roth, eds.: *Weber's Protestant Ethic. Origins, Evidence, Contexts*, Cambridge University Press, Washington.

Rachfal, Felix (1909). "Kalvinismus und Kapitalismus," *Internationale Wochenschrift für Wissenschaft, Kunst und Technik*, Jg. 3: 1217–38, 1249–68, 1287–1300, 1319–34, 1347–66. Reprinted in Weber 1995.

Rachfal, Felix (1910). "Nochmals Kalvinismus und Kapitalismus," *Internationale Wochenschrift für Wissenschaft, Kunst und*

*Technik*, Jg. 4: 689–702, 717–34, 755–78, 777–94. Reprinted in Weber 1995.

Roth, Günther (1995). "Introduction," in Hartmut Lehmann and Günther Roth, eds., *Weber's Protestant Ethic. Origins, Evidence, Contexts*, Cambridge University Press, Cambridge.

Samuelsson, Kurt (1957/1993). *Religion and Economic Action. The Protestant Ethic, the Rise of Capitalism, and the Abuses of Scholarship*, Toronto, University of Toronto Press.

Schluchter, Wolfgang (1991). *Religion und Lebensführung*, Bd. 1–2, Suhrkamp, Frankfurt a/M.

Schütz, Alfred (1934). *Der sinnhafte Aufbau der sozialen Welt. Eine Einleitung in der verstehende Soziologie*, Suhrkamp, Frankfurt a/M.

Sombart, Werner (1902). *Der moderne Kapitalismus*, Bd. 1–2, Duncker & Humblot, Berlin.

Turner, Stephen (1985). "Explaining Capitalism: Weber on and against Marx," in Robert Antonio and Ronald Glassman, eds., *A Weber-Marx Dialogue*, Kansas, University Press of Kansas.

Weber, Max (1903/1985). "Roscher und Knies und die logischen Probleme der historischen Nationalökonomie," *Schmollers Jahrbuch für Gesetzgebung, Verwaltung und Rechtspflege*, 27., 29., 30. Jg, Reprinted in Weber 1985.

Weber, Max (1904/1993). "Die protestantische Ethik und der 'Geist' des Kapitalismus, I.," *Archiv für Sozialwissenschaft und Sozialpolitik*, Bd. 21: 1–110. Reprinted in Weber 1993.

Weber, Max (1907/1977). "R. Stammlers 'Überwindung' der materialistischen Geschichtsauffassung," *Archiv für Sozialwissenschaft und Sozialpolitik*, Bd. 24. Reprinted in Weber 1922/1985.

Weber, Max (1907/1995). "Kritische Bemerkungen zu den vorstehenden 'Kritischen Beiträgen'," *Archiv für Sozialwissenschaft und Sozialpolitik*, Bd. 26:243–49. Reprinted in Weber 1995.

Weber, Max (1908/1995). "Bemerkungen zu den vorstehenden 'Replik'," *Archiv für Sozialwissenschaft und Sozialpolitik*, Bd. 26: 275–83. Reprinted in Weber 1995.

Weber, Max (1920/1988). *Gesammelte Aufsätze zur Religionssoziologie*, 3 Bd., J. C. B. Mohr, Tübingen.

Weber, Max (1921/1990). *Wirtschaft und Gesellschaft*, J. C. B. Mohr, Tübingen.

Weber, Max (1922/1985). *Wissenschaftslehre*. J. C. B. Mohr, Tübingen.

Weber, Max (1993). *Die protestantische Ethik and der 'Geist' des Kapitalismus*, Klaus Lichtblau und Johannes Winkelmann, eds., Athenäum, Hein.

Weber, Max (1995). "Die protestantische Ethik, II. Kvitiken und Antikritiken, edited by Johannes Winkelmann. Gütersloh: Gütersloher Verlagshaus.

# RICHARD F. HAMILTON

## Max Weber's *The Protestant Ethic*: A Commentary on the Thesis and on Its Reception in the Academic Community†

This paper assesses the major claims of Max Weber's *Protestant Ethic and the Spirit of Capitalism.*[1] It continues with a review of the treatment of "the Weber thesis" in subsequent scholarly literature. Only a brief summary of that assessment is possible here. The conclusions, as presented here, are essentially a "backdrop" to the review of that subsequent literature. The review will consider the treatment of "the Weber thesis" in four fields—religious studies; general history, particularly that of Europe from the sixteenth to eighteenth centuries; economic history; and sociology.

### Weber's Thesis

Weber's argument in *The Protestant Ethic* may be treated as involving twelve steps, each of which requires independent analysis, investigation, and assessment. An assessment of claims may yield four possible outcomes: support or confirmation (evidence that sustains the original hypothesis); rejection or disconfirmation (evidence that goes against the original hypothesis); non- support (evidence on the point is unavailable, or so fragmentary as to allow neither confirmation nor rejection); mixed results (contingent findings; or, another possibility, the association is confirmed but the causal argument questioned).

The twelve claims and assessments follow:

*1. Martin Luther expounded a new and distinctive religious doctrine: the concept of "the calling," secular occupations were invested with God-given purpose.*

Supported but with an important qualification. Luther did give a special meaning to this term, one that was important in his theology. Weber, however, provided a miscue on this point. He focused on economic roles and gave a very individualistic reading to the prescribed

† This paper was presented at a seminar held at the *Center for Advanced Study in the Social Sciences* of the Juan March Institute in Madrid on May 18, 1995. It was published in the Center's working paper series. Reprinted by permission of the author. See in this context also the author's *The Social Misconstruction of Reality: Validity and Verification in the Scholarly Community*, New Haven: Yale University Press, 1996.

1. Max Weber, *The Protestant Ethic and the Spirit of Capitalism*, Talcott Parsons, translator. The work first appeared in 1905. Weber's revision, published in 1920, was the basis for Parsons' translation. All references here are to the Norton Critical Edition.

activity. But the term had much more general application and the activity was guided by a corporatist rationale. This was not an irrational effort as Weber argued. It was work for the collective good. Whether Luther's use of the term was unique, one appearing in no other major language or tradition, is best viewed as an open question, one in need of confirmation.

2. *Transmission of the new doctrine to followers: The calling.*

Supported, but with an important qualification: Luther's concept, not Weber's reading of the term, was built into Lutheran pastoral literature and widely communicated.

3. *Calvin and his followers expound the doctrine of predestination.*

Supported, but with an important qualification: The doctrine was central to "Calvinism" in all of its manifestations. As opposed to Weber's declaration that it was a doctrine of "magnificent consistency," an opposite conclusion, magnificent complexity, seems more appropriate. At all points the theological specialists had to grapple with an insoluble contradiction. The reconciliation of the eternal decree on the one hand, and free will, repentence, and God's grace on the other, brought diverse, and ever-changing solutions.

4. *Transmission of the doctrine to followers: Predestination.*

Supported, but with important qualifications: This was an important Calvinist doctrine, but there is some question as to its temporal and spatial extension. Weber portrays it as important in seventeenth-century England and suggests some continuity even into the eighteenth century. But the claims of extension are open to question. The use of Richard Baxter as the exemplary representative was inappropriate. Weber's use of the Westminster Confession was seriously misleading. The predestination doctrine was being replaced by covenant theology even before the Civil War. The "collapse," it seems, proceeded rapidly after the fall of the Commonwealth. Calvinism, at its strongest, had a limited presence in western Europe. Weber later, for good reasons, discounted its importance in the Netherlands. He presented no clear evidence as to its incidence in England or in the American colonies.

5. *Among Calvinists, the predestination doctrine produced extreme salvation anxieties which were experienced in profound "inner isolation."*

Not adequately supported by Weber; rejected in subsequent research. Kaspar von Greyerz's review of the limited evidence available for seventeenth-century England showed predestination playing a "relatively minor role." Claims about the psychological outlooks of "the masses" in previous centuries, on the whole, are close to untestable. To assess Weber's claim, for example, one needs information on the "anxiety levels" of Puritans and those of some appropriate control groups. Confirmation or disconfirmation of such claims, therefore, is extremely difficult, a problem clearly indicated in Greyerz's sample of diaries and autobiographies.[2]

6. *Calvinists were told that "intense worldly activity" may be taken as a sign of salvation.*

Not supported by Weber; he presented no documentary evidence on this point. A recent review of relevant Dutch materials found no support for the claim thus providing grounds for rejection. Unlike the question of salvation anxieties, it should be noted, this is a testable claim: if valid, one should be able to cite the documentary evidence.

7. *To gain that assurance, Calvinists engaged in remarkably disciplined economic activity.*

Not supported: For this, one would have to establish, for example, that Puritans worked significantly harder than equivalent Anglicans. Such "outcome" differences are central to the validation of the entire Weber thesis. No evidence is presented to support this claim.

8. *Calvinists accumulated considerable amounts of capital which, following religious strictures, were reinvested.*

Not supported: The argument assumes capital accumulation and reinvestment (as opposed to other uses, such as hoarding, tithing, philanthropy). No evidence is presented on these questions. This conclusion depends on deduction; it is an inference following from the strictures against self-indulgence. No serious evidence is presented to support the point.

9. *The ethic and the later spirit cause substantial economic growth in Protestant nations, specifically in those influenced by Calvinism and its derivatives.*

Not supported. The most frequently presented correlations are, to say the least, somewhat crude. That the Netherlands and England showed outstanding economic performance does not establish "Protestantism" as the cause. A more detailed examination shows an unexpected relationship in the Netherlands (Catholicism in the higher ranks of Amsterdam; Calvinism in the lower classes or off on the Friesian fringes). The linkage of Puritanism (or Dissent) and economic takeoff in England is not demonstrated.

10. *Sometime later, the original attitudes were transformed; the religious ethic disappeared and was replaced by the secular capitalist spirit.*

Not supported. The support for this claim is extremely weak: one must assume that a few fragments taken from Benjamin Franklin's extensive writings do in fact represent "the spirit of capitalism" as defined by Weber. One must assume, furthermore, that the "spirit" is derived from Calvinist antecedents.

2. Kaspar von Greyerz, "Biographical Evidence on Predestination, Covenant, and Special Providence," Ch. 12 of Hartmut Lehmann and Guenther Roth, eds., *Weber's 'Protestant Ethic'—Origins, Evidence, Contexts*, Washington, DC: German Historical Institute/Cambridge University Press, 1993.

*11. The argument of extension or of diffusion: the "spirit of capitalism"
spreads out from the early centers and, later, has sweeping, general effects.*

On the generalization of the spirit, on the Iron Cage, this too is
unsupported. No evidence is presented to demonstrate the universal
presence of the compelling work ethic. No evidence is presented to
demonstrate the diffusion of that ethic in prior decades or centuries
to those previously untouched by ascetic Protestantism.

*12. Late in the nineteenth century, one finds substantial differences in
the economic and occupational standing of Protestants and Catholics, this
resulting from "the permanent intrinsic character of their religious beliefs."*

The claim of significant Protestant-Catholic differences of achievement in the late nineteenth century was not adequately supported.
The support "found" in the Baden school attendance figures involved
a copying error and a causal argument that proved to be spurious.[3]

Weber's argument, in short, appears to be badly flawed. The two
claims about doctrinal innovation are supported but with important
qualifications. The same, supported but with qualifications, holds
with respect to the two claims about their transmission. The remain-
ing eight propositions are not adequately supported, at least not in
Weber's text. These conclusions accord with Gordon Marshall's summary judgment based on his earlier review. Weber's case, he wrote,
"is empirically so thin that the only reasonable verdict for the moment
would be one of 'not proven'."[4] Not proven is not the same as wrong.
Most of the main points of Weber's argument are, in principle, empirically testable. But for some, notably for the claims about psychological reactions, the possibilities for testing have long since disappeared.[5]
The best available evidence for a test of the thesis would involve
ecological correlation, a demonstration of significant economic growth

---

3. Kurt Samuelsson, *Religion and Economic Action: A Critique of Max Weber*, E. Geoffrey
   French, translator, New York: Basic Books, 1961, p. 140.
4. Gordon Marshall, *In Search of the Spirit of Capitalism: An Essay on Max Weber's Protestant
   Ethic Thesis*, London: Hutchinson, 1982, p. 13. Jacob Viner, author of another outstanding critique, concludes as follows: "I cannot find any reference in Weber to Calvinist correspondence and autobiographies, and neither my examination of a small sample of the
   available literature nor the writings of Weber's followers offer any persuasive indication
   that this literature would give significant support to Weber's thesis. Weber, like his followers, generalized freely about the actual economic behavior of Calvinists or 'Puritans' in the
   seventeenth century; but he seems to rely on common knowledge and gives no detailed historical evidence." From "Protestantism and the Rise of Capitalism," Ch. 3 of his *Religious
   Thought and Economic Society*, Durham: Duke University Press, 1978, p. 156.
5. Viner notes also that even the grammatical form of Weber's argument signals a problem:
   "In common with some of his most important followers Weber relies heavily on the results
   which particular beliefs 'might have had' on practice. This device entails the use of what
   has been called 'the conjectural preterite'; i.e., what a writer might 'logically' have gone on
   to say if he had extended his remarks or, as applied to behavior, what a person might have
   done if he had acted out the 'logical' conclusion of his beliefs. It is a species of argument
   from ignorance which is extremely difficult to answer except by drawing attention to its
   inherent subjectivity or by asking why the historian should have found it necessary to have
   recourse to such methods" (Viner, p. 156).

in areas having a specific "Calvinist" presence as compared with some appropriate control cases. Without such systematic tests, the case remains an unsupported hypothesis.

The Protestant Ethic thesis appears to be a social misconstruction, that is, a widespread agreement about facts or interpretation which is mistaken. In a footnote, Weber refers to his argument as a "sketch," a term which seems entirely appropriate. But in the text, in many confident statements, Weber moves far beyond that indication of the tentative or of the hypothetical and treats the thesis as a well-documented conclusion. This misconstruction, the transformation of the hypothetical into a well-confirmed conclusion, is found also in the work of subsequent scholarly (and not-so-scholarly) writers, the tendency being most pronounced among sociologists. Weber and his supporters have invested the *hypothesis* with validity and have accorded world-historical significance to "the Protestant ethic."

More than scholarly analysis is operating in such misconstruction. Scholarly analysis would mean criticism, analysis, and further research on the hypothesis. It would entail some cumulation, a drawing of lessons out of the long history of controversy. A scholarly analysis would recognize, cite, and deal with important criticisms. The complexities of the Dutch case, for example, should be indicated, especially the problematic relationship there of "religious affiliation and social stratification." The complexities of the English case ought to be noted and its outright rejection in Rubinstein's research should be reported.[6] But this, by and large, has not been the case. The criticisms, as will be seen immediately, have been neglected.

## The Reception of the Weber Thesis

Gordon Marshall's work opens with a play on a famous Crane Brinton sentence: "Who now reads *The Protestant Ethic and the Spirit of Capitalism*?" Marshall's answer: "Almost everyone it seems." The continuing controversy, he reports, is "one of the longest running and most vociferous in the social sciences. . . . Most students of sociological theory, the sociologies of religion, industry, and development, of theology, and of the economic and social history of industrialization in the West are required, at some juncture, to assess the relative strengths and weaknesses of Weber's case."[7]

To some academics, that conclusion will seem entirely plausible but others will know there are grounds for doubt. The attention paid

---

6. W. D. Rubinstein, *Men of Property: The Very Wealthy in Britain since the Industrial Revolution*, New Brunswick: Rutgers University Press, 1981, pp. 145–163.

7. Marshall, *Search*, p. 9. Rubinstein writes along the same lines: "It is safe to say that virtually every economic and social historian of Britain writing in the last 30 years has accepted that there is at least some merit to the Weber Thesis in its post-1760 British context," *Men of Property*, p. 145. Both statements, those of Marshall and of Rubinstein, as will be seen immediately, are mistaken.

the Weber thesis by specialists in religious studies may be seen in an appropriate citation index, *Religion Index One*, which covers approximately 500 journals throughout the world. The four volumes for 1989–1992 contain a grand total of 32 citations of Max Weber, twelve of which, judging by titles, appear to deal in some way with the Protestant ethic. Under "Capitalism and Christianity" there were nine references that, again judging by titles, appeared to be on the Protestant ethic question, five of these repeating citations under Weber. In the four year period then, some sixteen articles were cited under those two headings. By this rule-of-thumb measure, the interest shown in the Weber thesis by the world's religion specialists amounts to about four articles a year.[8]

Philip Benedict has reviewed the treatment of the Weber thesis in the general historical literature. His conclusion reads:

> "Weber's ideas have provoked a considerable amount of comment and criticism from historians of Calvinism ever since they first appeared. A substantial literature has grown up around certain questions growing out of the Weber thesis debate. Nonetheless, when one surveys the broad range of writings devoted to the subject of early modern Calvinism, what is most striking of all is that the thesis in its broadest form has had remarkably little influence in stimulating and directing the main stream of research on the subject, except in England. Since the Weber thesis would seem to confer great importance on the history of Calvinism by suggesting that it played a particularly crucial role in moving European society down the road to modernity, this may seem surprising indeed. It points up the extreme compartmentalization of knowledge in the twentieth century and the considerable gulf between the concerns and training of those who have written about Calvinism, on the one hand, and those of Weber and of latter-day Weberians housed generally in departments of sociology, on the other."

The English exception, Benedict indicates, is due to the influence of R. H. Tawney, whose *Religion and the Rise of Capitalism* gave rise to an influential school.[9]

8. *Religion Index One: Periodicals*, Evanston, Illinois: American Theological Library Association, Volumes 21–24, 1989 to 1992. One of the sixteen references was to an article in a sociology journal, one appeared in a general history journal.

   The index to a collection of articles by Reformation historians, a collection focused on social history, contains one reference to Weber and that to a fugitive, non-substantive comment, see Lawrence P. Buck and Jonathan W. Zophy, *The Social History of the Reformation*, Columbus: Ohio State University Press, 1972, p. 31.

9. Philip Benedict, "The Historiography of Continental Calvinism," Ch. 15 of Lehmann and Roth, *Weber*. The passage quoted is from p. 306. An important history published in 1954, Benedict writes, gave six pages (of 454) to discussion of Weber's argument. Some thirty years later, a collective volume written by specialist historians gave more pages, but less favor, to Weber's ideas, suggesting that they have "become more marginal yet." The two books (with the relevant page references) are: John T. McNeill, *History and Character of Calvinism*, New York: Oxford University Press, 1954, pp. 221–223, 418–421; and Menna Prestwich, ed., *International Calvinism, 1541–1715*, Oxford: Clarendon, 1985, pp. 9–10, 269, 369–390 (a chapter by Herbert Lüthy based on a 1965 work).

The Weber thesis is generally neglected also in works of economic history. Many leading sources on the "history of industrialization" make no reference at all to "the Weber thesis." Phyllis Deane's comprehensive study of Britain's industrial revolution has no index reference to Max Weber, to Protestantism, or to religion. Her chapters, incidentally, review and document the importance of a wide range of other factors, ones neglected in most of the sociological literature. There is no reference to Weber in an older classic, in J. H. Clapham's study of French and German economic development. T. S. Ashton's brief popular account of the industrial revolution, another of the older classics, contains no reference to Weber. A later scholarly work by Ashton makes passing reference to the religious factor, touching on the Wesleyans, for example, but made no reference to Weber. Another noted economic historian, John Ulrich Nef, had little positive to say about the thesis; in a summary work on the industrial revolution, he reviewed Weber's claims but, for the most part, rejected them. Kindleberger's study of France and Britain in the century after 1850 gives four pages to "religion" and there makes passing references to Weber and Tawney. His brief account is balanced (reviewing Samuelsson, for example) and is well documented. His last comment is negative: he has been "able to reject the hypothesis that changes in religious belief and practice played a major role in the course of British or French economic development after 1850." William H. McNeill's comprehensive study, The Rise of the West has only one index reference to Weber, that to a footnote on p. 590. There one finds a single noncommittal comment on the "famous thesis." Paul Kennedy's comprehensive study of economic change and military conflict from 1500 to 2000, The Rise and Fall of the Great Powers, contains no reference to Max Weber or to the famous thesis. Of the authors reviewed to this point David Landes provides the most favorable judgment but even there the Protestant ethic thesis is given little attention, at best a few pages, in his 550 page history.[1]

1. The works discussed are: Phyllis Deane, The First Industrial Revolution, second edition, Cambridge: Cambridge University Press, 1979; J. H. Clapham, The Economic Development of France and Germany, 1815–1914, fourth edition, Cambridge: The University Press, 1936; T. S. Ashton, The Industrial Revolution, 1760–1830, London: Oxford University Press, 1948, and, also by Ashton, An Economic History of England: The 18th Century, London: Methuen, 1955; John Ulrich Nef, The Conquest of the Material World, Chicago: University of Chicago Press, 1964, Ch. 5; Charles P. Kindleberger, Economic Growth in France and Britain, 1851–1950, Cambridge: Harvard University Press, 1964, pp. 94–97; William H. McNeill, The Rise of the West: A History of the Human Community, Chicago: University of Chicago Press, 1963, p. 590n.; Paul Kennedy, The Rise and Fall of the Great Powers: Economic Change and Military Conflict from 1500 to 2000, New York: Random House, 1987; and David S. Landes, The Unbound Prometheus: Technological Change and Industrial Development in Western Europe from 1750 to the Present, Cambridge: Cambridge University Press, 1969, pp. 31–23, 160.

The following works of economic history contain no index references to Max Weber: Roderick Floud and Donald McCloskey, eds., The Economic History of Britain since 1700, 2 vols., Cambridge: Cambridge University Press, 1981. R. M. Hartwell, ed., The Causes of

Carlo Cipolla, another leading economic historian, has edited an important collection of essays on developments in sixteenth- and seventeenth-century Europe. I found no reference to Weber in this nearly 600-page work. The closest to a confirmation is a brief passage in a chapter by Hermann Kellebenz which tells of "a more thrifty attitude on the part of those of the nobility who had turned Protestant and had been influenced by the teachings of the Reformation." Some instances in which there is "exceptionally clear evidence" on the linkage of religion and technical innovation are provided. Several pages later Kellebenz reviews the secularization of Catholic church properties, noting one of the consequences—the classes that benefited "used their increased purchasing power, which in fact they often exceeded by obtaining credit, to demonstrate their new status by building houses and adopting a modern style of living worthy of them." A few pages later one learns that the social changes "brought about by the Reformation, especially secularisation, also stimulated consumer activity, as did fashion, particularly the vogue of the *nouvelle draperie*, Spanish fashions and, starting in the 1630s, the growing demand for French Fashions." No reference to Weber appears in his bibliography.

Another article in the Cipolla volume, this by Aldo De Maddalena, touches briefly on the Dutch experience. It too tells of the parcelling-out of land that followed the Reformation, much of it coming into the hands of "the rich bourgeoisie." Modern and remunerative methods

---

the *Industrial Revolution in England*, London: Methuen, 1967; Peter Mathias, *The First Industrial Nation: An Economic History of Britain, 1700–1914*, London: Methuen 1969; Joel Mokyr, ed., *The Economics of the Industrial Revolution*, Totowa, NJ: Rowman & Allanheld, 1985; E. A. Wrigley, *Continuity, Chance and Change*, New York: Cambridge University Press, 1988; and Rondo Cameron, *A Concise Economic History of the World: From Paleolithic Times to the Present*, second edition, New York: Oxford University Press, 1993. The latter is a leading economic history textbook.

Mathias has two brief discussions of the role of religion, neither of them making explicit reference to Weber (pp. 160, 164). The first of these does however contain an oblique denigrating comment. A fugitive mention of Weber appears in Mokyr. It reads, in its entirety, as follows: "A well-known and highly controversial theory of entrepreneurship is the one somehow linking businessmen to religion. Originally proposed by Weber, the argument is more successful in explaining the differences between Western Christianity and the rest of the world than in explaining differences within the West" (p. 17). No references to Weber appear in Cameron's extensive annotated bibliography; it does contain a reference to Robertson's critique of Weber and his school (p. 415).

Three index references to Weber appear in Peter Kriedte, *Peasants, Landlords and Merchant Capitalists: Europe and the World Economy, 1500–1800*, translated from the German by V. R. Berghahn, Leamington Spa, UK: Berg, 1983. None of those references touch on the Protestant ethic thesis. The thesis is reviewed and discussed in Nathan Rosenberg and L. E. Birdzell, Jr., *How the West Grew Rich: The Economic Transformation of the Industrial World*, New York: Basic Books, 1986, pp. 129–134. These authors note it has been "hotly debated" since first publication and they review some of the major arguments. Reference is made to a wide range of commentators including Robertson, Tawney, Nef, and Landes. E. L. Jones's, *The European Miracle: Environments, Economies, and Geopolitics in the History of Europe and Asia*, Cambridge: Cambridge University Press, 1981, contains an index reference to Weber, to a fugitive reference on the role of refugees in economic development. The bibliography refers only to the *General Economic History*.

of farm management followed along with short-term leases which allowed easier adaptation to changing economic conditions. As opposed to asceticism, one learns that numerous "villas and gardens also grew up around the towns, representing not only a sop to their owners' social ambitions, but also a sensible policy of investment and agronomic innovation."[2]

The most positive reception of the Weber thesis, by a considerable margin, is found in sociology. Most introductory sociology texts are generous in their commendation of Weber, the man and the scholar. Most texts in the field review the thesis and give it credence. Some, to be sure, are noncommittal, providing only a report of its major claims. Neil J. Smelser's text, for example, introduces Weber as the "great German sociologist [who] used historical research to throw light on the link between religion and social change." Later, in a biographical profile, the student is told that Weber was "a prodigious scholar" who "profoundly influenced" modern sociology. A brief account of the Protestant ethic thesis follows. Weber, it is said, "showed that values can be a powerful force for social change." This was followed by statements about Calvinists and their work habits. The principal exposition of the thesis appears several pages later where a single long paragraph reviews the Calvinism-predestination-work ethic linkage. The initial statement is a simple report: "Weber believed this ethic had a major influence on the growth of capitalism." A shorter second paragraph reports that Weber "noted other factors," specifically mentioning "the military budget and high consumer demand." Smelser's final statement is an unambiguous confirmation: "Still, the Protestant Reformation changed not only the economic structure but also a variety of institutions, including science, law, and education. The changes brought about by Calvinism combined to transform the social order." Not a single reference is provided to document the claim. There is not a single indication of any controversy about the thesis. And, clearly, there is no reference to any of the critics, none for example to Samuelsson or to Marshall.[3]

---

2. Carlo M. Cipolla, ed., *The Fontana Economic History of Europe: The Sixteenth and Seventeenth Centuries*, Glascow: Collins, 1974, pp. 240, 247, 260, and 296.

3. From Neil J. Smelser, *Sociology*, fourth edition, Englewood Cliffs: Prentice-Hall, 1991, pp. 14, 294, 300, and 309. Smelser's text has been singled out for attention because he is one of the most eminent of all current authors of introductory sociology texts. He has written many wide-ranging works, several of them dealing with economic history and economic sociology. He has edited a comprehensive review volume, *Handbook of Sociology*, Newbury Park: Sage, 1988. He would then, more than most such authors, be conversant with the entire Weber controversy. He is also the author of a relevant scholarly monograph, *Social Change in the Industrial Revolution: An Application of Theory to the British Cotton Industry*, Chicago: University of Chicago Press, 1959. Weber is given very little attention in this 400-page scholarly work. The thesis is discussed on pp. 67–77.

A review of fifteen current sociology texts revealed that all of them provided brief summary accounts of "the thesis." Some authors accepted the basic claims, commending the argument to their readers. Others gave neutral descriptive accounts, saying that Weber had argued the Calvinist impact but offering nothing on the validity of the claims. None of those texts reviewed the problems with Weber's evidence. None report the inadequacy of Offenbacher's data or the copying error; none report the misrepresentation of Franklin and Fugger; none report the difficulties involved in the Dutch case. All of these problems, it will be noted, were signaled in the Samuelsson critique published some thirty years ago. Only eight of the fifteen texts indicate some controversy over the thesis. A couple of these are at best "trace" mentions; some others indicate unambiguous vindication for the thesis. Only three texts provided references to the book-length critical studies by Samuelsson and Marshall. Two of these citations proved to be inadequate. One made reference to "Marshall, 1982" but did not list the book among the references. One made reference to "Samuelsson, 1961," saying only that it was the source for a quotation, but not indicating that it provided a major critique; the critic's name in this case was misspelled in the references. Vander Zanden's text signaled approval, Weber "marshalled evidence," but also cited Samuelsson accurately and listed four other critical studies. Those five citations were more than appeared in all of the other fourteen texts.

Many of those textbooks introduced the possibility of an opposite causal direction—that the rise of capitalism stimulated the appearance of Protestantism. In some of them the counter-thesis was given full credence even though no serious evidence was provided in its support. The documented account by Lewis A. Spitz makes this option implausible.[4] The movement was led by theologians and clergy (that is, by intellectuals); their main support was from "the populace down below."

These university-level textbooks, in short, showed a near-complete indifference to evidence, both with regard to the original thesis and to this ad hoc alternative. Instead, glossing over the criticisms, most of the texts provided either enthusiastic approval or a brief unevaluated summary of what Weber said. For much of the 1980s decade, the best-selling sociology textbook in the United States was the work of Ian Robertson. He is a professional writer, not a professional sociologist. His is the only textbook that signals doubt; he suggests that the Weber thesis is "probably unverifiable."[5]

---

4. Lewis W. Spitz, *The Protestant Reformation, 1517–1559*, New York: Harper & Row, 1985, pp. 164–165, and 180–191.
5. In addition to Smelser, the introductory sociology textbooks reviewed were:
   Brinkerhoff, David B., and Lynn K. White, *Sociology*, third edition, St. Paul: West, 1991.

Samuelsson's work contained many telling criticisms of the Weber thesis. It also, to be sure, contained some serious errors. But for the general social science audience the work has been lost from view. It has long since been out of print. In 1976 Anthony Giddens wrote an Introduction to *The Protestant Ethic* which appears both in the Scribner's and in the later Routledge editions. His four-page review of "The Controversy" contains a brief mention of Weber's use of "a study of the economic activities of Catholics and Protestants in Baden in 1895," this accompanied by an agnostic comment—"and the accuracy even of these figures had been questioned." Samuelsson is referenced at that point but few readers would be moved by that laconic statement to search out the source. Giddens could have easily pointed out the inaccuracy in the key row of percentages which add to 109%.[6]

Evidence showing the "disappearance" of Samuelsson's work may be gained from the *Social Science Citation Index* which covers a vast range of relevant literature. In the four years, 1989 to 1992, three articles referred to Samuelsson's critique. None of the three citations was accurate. All three misspelled the man's name; one, in addition, gave the English title but the date of the Swedish publication. Three references to Samuelsson appeared in the *Arts and Humanities Citation Index* in those same years. One article was listed in both sources, which means the grand total for both literatures comes to five citations. Only one of these citations, that in a specialized sociology of religion journal, was accurate. Both

DiRenzo, Gordon J., *Human Social Behavior: Concepts and Principles of Sociology*, Fort Worth: Holt, Rinehart, and Winston.

Farley, John E., *Sociology*, second edition, Englewood Cliffs: Prentice-Hall, 1992.

Inciardi, James A., and Robert A. Rothman, *Sociology: Principles and Applications*, San Diego: Harcourt Brace Jovanovich, 1990.

Johnson, Allan G., *Human Arrangements: An Introduction to Sociology*, San Diego: Harcourt Brace Jovanovich, 1989.

Kammeyer, Kenneth C. W., George Ritzer, and Norman R. Yetman, *Sociology: Experiencing Changing Societies*, fifth edition, Boston: Allyn and Bacon, 1992.

Light, Donald, Suzanne Keller, and Craig Calhoun, *Sociology*, fifth edition, New York: Knopf, 1989.

Macionis, John J., *Sociology*, third edition, Englewood Cliffs: Prentice Hall, 1991.

Popenoe, David, *Sociology*, eighth edition, Englewood Cliffs: Prentice Hall, 1991.

Robertson, Ian, *Sociology*, third edition, New York: Worth, 1987.

Schaefer, Richard T., and Robert P. Lamm, *Sociology*, New York: McGraw-Hill, 1992.

Stark, Rodney, *Sociology*, fourth edition, Belmont: Wadsworth, 1992.

Theodorson, George and Lucille, *Sociology: Principles and Applications*, St. Paul: West, 1990.

Vander Zanden, James W., *The Social Experience: An Introduction to Sociology*, second edition, New York: McGraw-Hill, 1990.

None of the texts refer to Jacob Viner's chapter. Marshall's critique is mentioned (without the citation) in Light, Keller, and Calhoun, p. 529. The inadequate citation of Samuelsson is in Farley, p. 453. Smelser's text, incidentally, does not include *The Protestant Ethic* in its listing of references; it was also omitted in the third edition.

6. Giddens, "Introduction," to Weber, *Protestant Ethic*, London: Routledge, 1992, p. xxiv.

indexes in those same years list many references to *The Protestant Ethic*.

Marshall's critique fared somewhat better in the same period: a total of 21 citations were reported in the two indexes for the same four years. Five of these were repeated references, which means Marshall was cited in sixteen articles. None of those citations appeared in the three leading American sociology journals. One lesson is easy: the readers of social science and humanities literature are frequently told of "the Weber thesis." It is regularly commended but only rarely are they provided with references to works that challenge it.[7]

Those readers, typically, are told that Weber's many critics were mistaken, having failed to appreciate the basic argument, or have missed the "larger picture," or are attending to inessential details. In another academic setting, however, a student of religious history might read the following: "The imaginative hypotheses of Weber and Troeltsch have been undermined by a winding procession of revisionist scholars: Sombart, Lujo Brentano, Tawney, Henri Hauser, Henri See, H. M. Robertson, Albert Hyma, George Harkness, Conrad Moehlmann, and Andre Sayous, not to mention the more recent contributors."[8]

There is, clearly, a serious disparity in the treatments of the Weber thesis. It is highly commended in sociology but is given little attention in the two fields most likely to have expert knowledge of the subject, Reformation history and economic history. This disparity points to a problem stemming from compartmentalization within the universities. The non-specialist sociologists do not know what the specialists have said and done. The sociologists, accordingly, present the thesis as well-founded despite its remarkably "hypothetical" character. Weber's "sketch" remains a sketch some 90 years after its first exposition. The transformation of the hypothetical into the confirmed and the presentation of the argument in bold disregard of historical evidence (that generated by two readily accessible groups of academic specialists) points to the operation of some extra-intellectual factors or processes.

The operation of the extra-intellectual may be seen in use of "saving" devices, of arguments to protect the theory from challenge. One of these points to Weber's larger enterprise. *The Protestant Ethic* is only a part of his world-historical project, one that reviewed the religions

7.  Both citation indexes are from Philadelphia: The Institute for Scientific Information. The social sciences index covers approximately 2,800 journals. The arts and humanities index covers approximately 1,800.
8.  John F. H. New, *Anglican and Puritan: The Basis of Their Opposition, 1558–1640*, Stanford: Stanford University Press, 1964, p. 96.

of China, of India, and of ancient Judaism. The suggestion is that one cannot assess the Protestant ethic "part" without consideration of those other components. But the argument is inappropriate; it is an obvious non sequitur. Claims about Luther's teachings, about Calvinism, or about Puritanism do not in any way require inquiry (or assessment) of claims about Taoism or Confucianism. Each part must stand on its own logic and evidence. Marshall reviews this line of defense and offers an appropriate conclusion: "Sociologists simply cannot escape the problems of historical counter-evidence, or more accurately . . . of the lack of substantiating evidence, by pleading for 'the big picture'."[9]

A second saving procedure is to set stringent requirements for the testing of the thesis. If evidence on the psychological responses to specific doctrines were required, any test is effectively precluded, at least for historical experience. It is easy to locate centers of "Protestantism." But one cannot know with any certainty if predestination was accepted there, whether adherents felt a profound "inner isolation," whether they desperately sought a sign of their *certitudo salutis*, whether they, as a consequence, devoted themselves to their economic tasks, and whether they diligently accumulated and reinvested. The appropriate response, in the face of that historical problem, would be a conclusion of "not proven" or, more precisely, not known (or perhaps, hardly likely to ever be known). But here, in a remarkable declaration of faith, many sociologists, authors of sociology texts for example, have treated the hypotheses, all of them, as proven.[1]

Some years ago a flurry of research activity designed to "test Weber" occurred, this through use of survey data from various American contexts. Most of those studies came up with negative findings. Those results were so persistently negative that one commentator, Andrew Greeley, appropriately, called for a moratorium. Some of Weber's defenders objected to the entire operation, this again on the basis of the stringent requirements. Instead "of examining the impact of specific beliefs," one commentator argued, "the researchers merely compared the members of two religious categories." Those researchers, it was said, had not "made the proper Weberian analytical distinctions among types of Protestants." They did not check, for example, whether those Protestants "believed in predestination [or] viewed their jobs as a calling." Those studies, accordingly, are judged to be

---

9. Marshall, *Search*, p. 140.
1. Jonathan Turner, a sociologist, has indicated some understandable concern about those who "genuflect at the sacred works of St. Marx, St. Durkheim, and St. Weber." See his *Herbert Spencer: A Renewed Appreciation*, Beverly Hills: Sage, 1985, p. 7.

"poor-quality research." They did not "take seriously the rich analytical detail" of Weber's argument.[2]

This "defense" involves a double standard since those later sociological studies are identical in form to the procedure Weber used in the opening pages of the monograph, that is, in his use of Offenbacher and others. He was examining behavioral correlates of religious affiliation, of Protestants and Catholics with no investigation of "specific beliefs." Having established, to his satisfaction, a strong association between the two, Weber then *read in* his conclusion: "Thus the principal explanation of this difference must be sought in the permanent intrinsic character of their religious beliefs" (p. 18). Weber, in short, is allowed an easy standard; his critics are held to a much more stringent requirement.

If an hypothesis is subjected to repeated test and not confirmed, a moratorium is one appropriate conclusion. If one argues that the tests are flawed, then more carefully designed tests are in order. But the common standard requires a recognition of the failed Weber-Offenbacher test. It requires recognition of Weber's persistent failure to take seriously the implications of the "rich analytical detail" of his own argument. It was, and is, necessary to control for the many factors that could affect the religion-work ethic relationship. Without that necessary investigation of the relationship with *ceteris paribus*, one cannot be sure there is any "Protestant ethic" effect at all, let alone one that is "important." And that means, until Weber's defenders work through those implications, the thesis will remain "not proven." A third defense involves the claim of a termination date: the Protestant ethic was an important factor earlier, but later it no longer had any distinctive influence. Marshall argues this point: "By the eighteenth century, Weber maintains, the new capitalist mentality has . . . become wholly independent of its religious origins." Some supporting passages appear in Weber's original, the most compelling of which announces that "today . . . any relationship between religious beliefs and conduct is generally absent." One must, however, reconcile that

2. Andrew M. Greeley, "The Protestant Ethic: Time for a Moratorium," *Sociological Analysis*, 25 (1964) 20–33. The other quotations are from Gary D. Bouma, "Beyond Lenski: A Critical Review of Recent Protestant Ethic' Research," *Journal for the Scientific Study of Religion*, 12 (1973) 141–156. Marshall, *Search*, pp. 165–66, and Zaret, in Lehmann and Roth, *Weber*, p. 245, also argue along these lines.

In a rare investigation of the sort Bouma recommends, Harold B. Barclay studied an ascetic Protestant sect, the Holdeman Mennonites, and found their beliefs impeded capitalist development. See his "The Protestant Ethic versus the Spirit of Capitalism," *Review of Religious Research* 10 (1969) 151–58. Another insightful case study is provided by Randall G. Stokes. Afrikaner Calvinism, he reports, was "theologically identical to European Calvinism of the 18th century" but had "a highly conservative impact on economic action." His explanation: this group dealt with the predestination doctrine and the resulting anxieties in a very different way. See his "Afrikaner Calvinism and Economic Action: The Weberian Thesis in South Africa," *American Journal of Sociology*, 81 (1975): 62–81.

pronouncement with his opening claim, that of "overwhelming" differences in Baden and elsewhere in the late nineteenth century.[3] Again a double standard is involved. Where later evidence appears to support the thesis, it is allowed and accepted. Otherwise, the possibility is excluded a priori.

If Protestant and Catholic work efforts were substantially different prior to the eighteenth century, that point needs to be established. If a subsequent "conversion" occurred, with Catholics forced to assimilate and adopt the more demanding Protestant standard, that process too needs to be demonstrated. Otherwise, the claim is merely an "easy out." One avoids a difficult problem, lack of support, by declaring a conversion, this without any indication of when or where it happened, and without any provision of supporting evidence.

Criticism is a normal feature of scholarly work. Where problems, or outright errors, are discovered, they should be signaled in subsequent comments and discussion. But that, as seen, has not been the case with "the Weber thesis." The work itself is canonized: it has become "a classic." And in a parallel procedure, the author is described as a "prodigious scholar." Here too one sees the double standard. That adjective, prodigious, says something about quantity or extent. But something ought to be said also about the quality of that scholarship, about the erratic relationship between text and notes, about the implications of one-person "samples" for the depiction of world-historical movements, and about the absence of systematic evidence linking religion and economic development.[4]

3. Marshall, Search, p. 129; Weber, Protestant Ethic, pp. 25–26 and, for the quotation, p. 34.
4. Another argument has appeared in recent sociological literature. This direction, not a defense mechanism, points to a later Weber formulation. One may always provide an improved or extended framework; it is a routine expectation in scientific work. If the later version is the "real" or "final" Weber position, then it is that case that should be presented, beginning with the sociology texts, not the flawed, or preliminary version of The Protestant Ethic. See Randall Collins, "Weber's Last Theory of Capitalism," Ch. 2 of his Weberian Sociological Theory, Cambridge: Cambridge University Press, 1986. The chapter originally appeared in the American Sociological Review, 45 (1980): 925–942. The key text in this connection is Weber's General Economic History, translated by Frank H. Knight, New York: Collier, 1961 [original, 1927]. The work was out of print for many years but was reissued in 1981 by Transaction Books. Few of the sociology texts reviewed here make reference to this "later theory" option; few of them cite the General Economic History.
It is not possible to cover all of the many arguments dealing with "the Weber thesis" in a brief comment. Those interested in the earlier controversies, ones involving Brentano, Hyma, Pirenne, Rachfahl, Robertson, Fanfani, Tawney, and many others, might begin with Ephraim Fischoff's review, "The Protestant Ethic and the Spirit of Capitalism—The History of a Controversy," Social Research, 11 (1944):53–77.
Another strand of the controversy has focused on scientific and technological innovations, this in the British context, the emphasis typically being on the dissenting churches. Much of this literature in this area has been quick to invoke Weber and "the Protestant ethic," but that conflates two distinct subject matters, a general work ethic and scientific aptitudes. Again, typically, much of that work has been indifferent to the ceteris paribus requirement and, accordingly, has failed to explore other possibilities, e.g. discrimination, disabilities due to the Test Act, and the simple matters of geography. For a brief discussion of this problem, see Rubinstein, Men of Property, pp. 146–149. For more detail, see the important study by George Becker, "Pietism and Science: A Critique of Robert K. Merton's

## Alternative Hypotheses

Marshall's summary conclusion, that the only reasonable verdict is "not proven," seems entirely appropriate. The implication for Weber's defenders is easy: provide the necessary proof. In the process, the serious researcher should also consider (and, if possible, test) alternative hypotheses to account for the "rise of the West." Several alternatives will be reviewed here. All of these have appeared somewhere in previous literature. They do not ordinarily appear in discussions of "the Weber thesis."

Carlo Cipolla, the noted economic historian, argued the importance of two technological innovations. England and the Netherlands developed better ships, ones that were larger and more seaworthy. They also developed superior cannons. The combination of the two gave those nations a distinctive advantage. The large ship became a movable gun platform, one allowing the concentration of unusual firepower on targets that could be approached by sea. Nations facing the Atlantic adopted the innovations (with varying success and effectiveness). The two innovations made possible the "outreach program" known as the Age of Discovery. At the same time, however, Cipolla indicated, the new age began with a decisive defeat for "the West." The expansion of the Ottoman Turks disrupted the age-old trade routes to Asia thus, in part at least, stimulating the search for the Atlantic alternatives. The Turks moved into the Balkans, up the Danube, and into the heart of Europe, a movement that was not halted until the siege of Vienna in 1683. The technological advantages, the large ships and their guns, were of no use there.[5]

The Age of Discovery and the Turkish advances occurred simultaneously with the Reformation. Charles V, the Holy Roman Emperor (and king of Spain), dealt with the conquest of the New World, with the Turks, and with Martin Luther. The New World provided a rich source of income for the Spanish treasury. But the large and complicated Empire had to pay heavy costs to maintain its hegemony. The bullion that, with intelligent direction, might have gone into economic development, went instead to the creation and provisioning of armies and to the construction of ships in Dutch shipyards.[6]

---

Hypothesis," *American Journal of Sociology*, 89 (1984): 1065–1090. Merton's reply (same issue, pp. 1091–1121), does not address the issues raised. For further relevant detail and discussion, see Becker's response in a later issue, 91 (1986): 1203–1218. For another important contribution, see Becker's article, "The Merton Thesis: Oetinger and German Pietism, A Significant Negative Case, "*Sociological Forum*, 7 (1992): 641–660. On science in Geneva under Calvin and afterwards, see Viner, "Protestantism," pp. 186–187.

5. Carlo M. Cipolla, *Guns, Sails, and Empires: Technological Innovation and the Early Phases of European Expansion* (New York: Minerva Press, 1965).

6. For some sense of the difficulties facing the Hapsburgs, see Geoffrey Parker, "Spain, Her Enemies and the Revolt of the Netherlands 1559–1648," *Past and Present*, 49 (1970): 73–95.

A peculiarity of the entire Weber controversy is an unwillingness to face up to basic economic facts. A nation with major expansionist ambitions, such as Spain (and later, France), would have greater costs because of its sizable military establishment. Major continental powers, even if defensive in orientation, will ordinarily have more costly military requirements than nations on the periphery or those located behind natural barriers. Nations deriving much of their income through the sale of military services, mercenary nations, such as the German states, would also have high-cost government. The taxes required for the support of the military means a diversion of resources from other purposes, one of which could be investment for routine economic growth. Quite apart from the budgetary costs, it should be noted, men in the military are not producing goods. They are not developing productive skills. Officers are not learning entrepreneurial skills, at least not those required for economic development.

England (and later the United Kingdom), because of its insular setting, had distinctly lower military costs. Its army was ordinarily smaller, both in absolute numbers and in per capita terms, than those of its chief continental rivals. The naval costs were clearly greater but still, on balance, total costs were lower thus, for the average citizen, "freeing" a larger portion of household revenues for other purposes, either consumption or investment. Some tens or hundreds of thousands of men, moreover, were "freed" for productive economic activities (as compared to, for example, the many hours of infantry drill). Given England's island location, surplus population could be "exported" to underdeveloped colonies where they could perform productive economic activities (versus idleness at home). England exported hundreds of thousands; France, with its different concerns and incentives, kept men at home to fill those military needs. As of 1759, the date of Montcalm's defeat at Quebec, British North America had a population of 1.6 million, most of it of English, Scotch, or Scotch-Irish origin. New France, in contrast, had roughly 60,000. Those figures take on even greater significance when one recognizes the imbalance in the populations of the home countries, the United Kingdom having roughly 7.5 million and France roughly 23 million. The English colonies had a sizable, growing, and diversified trade with the United Kingdom, a trade that continued to grow even after American independence.[7]

7. For a summary overview of army and navy expenditures, see John Brewer, *The Sinews of Power: War, Money and the English State, 1688–1783* (Cambridge: Harvard University Press, 1990), Chap. 2.

　　The figures on population, all rounded off, are from: A. Goodwin, ed., *The New Cambridge Modern History*, Vol. 8, *The American and French Revolutions 1763–93* (Cambridge: The University Press, 1965), 714; Evarts B. Greene, *American Population Before the Federal Census of 1790* (New York: Columbia University Press, 1932), 6; and C. P.

Thus far, the discussion of the economic implications of military and geographic circumstances has treated only the "static" peacetime condition. But costs escalate dramatically in wartime. The outcomes also have economic implications. At the beginning of the seventeenth century, the Netherlands was part of the Spanish empire. But, in a long and stubbornly fought struggle, the northern provinces gained their independence. After paying heavy wartime costs, Spain lost the Netherlands, its flourishing commercial center. The Dutch were also Europe's leading shipbuilders, a decisive fact for the outcome of the struggle. Because of the continued need for ships, Spanish silver continued to flow to Amsterdam even after independence.

The long military struggle in the Spanish Netherlands, according to one standard reading, stemmed from the underlying religious differences. Another reading was reported by Samuelsson. The Dutch historian Pieter Geyl, in 1955, argued the case for military determinants in the Netherlands outcome. The struggle with Spain did not involve an opposition of Dutch Protestants and Belgian Catholics. At the outset, according to Samuelsson's report, "the Protestants were no more numerous in the north than in the south." That geographic division was a result of the conflict, not a precipitating cause. The rivers that held up Field Marshall Montgomery's advance for months in 1944 had the same impact centuries earlier. The rivers, it was argued, "enabled the rebellion to entrench itself in the North provinces while Spain recovered those situated on the wrong side of the strategic barrier." Later, two large migrations occurred; Catholics moved south and Protestants moved north.

In the first half of the sixteenth century, Antwerp was the leading port city in the region, English merchants having chosen it as their major port of entry. The city "enjoyed a centrality in the economic activity of Europe that was nearly unique in history." But economic and political catastrophes followed. The settlement of the War of Liberation gave the Dutch control over the Rhine allowing access into the interior. The settlement blocked the mouth of the Scheldt, Antwerp's river, that city now being part of the Spanish Netherlands. That political fact "set the stage for" the subsequent advance of "Protestant" Amsterdam.[8]

A later major conflict began when Frederick of Prussia took Silesia from Maria Theresa of Austria. Tax revenues from that territory (with

---

Stacey, *Quebec, 1759: The Seige and the Battle* (London: Pan Books, 1973), xviii–xix. The climate and soil conditions in New France, to be sure, were not such as to encourage migration. For the problems of settlement, development, and defense, see Mason Wade, *The French Canadians, 1760–1967* (Toronto: Macmillan of Canada, 1968), Vol. 1, Chap. 1.

8. Samuelsson, *Religion*, 106. He was drawing from the essay "National State and the Writers of Netherlands History," Chap. 9 of Pieter Geyl, *Debates with Historians* (The Hague: Nijhoff, 1955), especially pp. 182–184. On Antwerp, see Spitz, *Protestant Reformation*, 28–30; and Cameron, *Concise Economic History*, 97.

a largely Catholic population) then flowed into the treasury of a "Protestant" nation. A series of wars followed, these culminating in the Seven Years War in which Catholic Austria and Catholic France were defeated by Protestant Prussia and Protestant Britain. Britain acquired the entirety of New France. In 1763, France was left with a heavy debt burden, one which had far-reaching implications for the nation's economy and political stability.

Another key consideration, one rarely given adequate attention, involves public finance. In the early sixteenth century, Spain looked to have a promising future. But a series of disastrous government decisions effectively destroyed any possibilty of a "take-off," producing instead four centuries of backwardness. Spain had the highest tax rates in Europe. A series of mistaken policies destroyed a flourishing woolen industry and ended some success in foodstuffs. France was favored with a large population, fertile lands, a central regime, and a powerful military establishment. But the government could not, or rather, did not successfully organize its finances. The sale of offices was inefficient, costly, and socially corrosive. The system of tax farming had similar consequences. By contrast, the Netherlands and England had low-cost and efficient tax arrangements. While still problematic from the perspective of modern economics, those two nations, through trial and error, made unusual progress. Rondo Cameron traces this to differences in the respective polities. The absolute monarchs of the age had little understanding of their developing economies; and they had unchecked power to implement their policies. The greater pluralism in the Netherlands and in England, especially after 1688–1689, meant more effective input from people with a knowledge of business and commerce. The creation of the Bank of England made government borrowing easier and less costly than was the case in France or Spain. The lower interest rates that resulted also aided English commerce.[9]

Religions all have some kind of institutional apparatus which, depending on the size, could represent a significant or a modest charge for the supporting economy. Jacob Viner quoted Christopher Hill on this question: "The fact that Protestantism was a cheaper religion than Catholicism became a seventeenth-century commonplace." Viner noted that the observation "remained a commonplace in the eighteenth and nineteenth centuries." But Weber, he added, avoiding an obvious economic fact, "makes no reference to this theme in his explanation of . . . the relative economic backwardness of Catholic countries."[1]

---

9. See Rondo Cameron, *Concise Economic History*, Chap. 6.
1. Viner, "Protestantism," 164. Several eighteenth-century authors commented on the number of holidays—"Because Catholics had 120 per year and Protestants only 60, the latter were thus able to record a profit from the extra 60 work days." See Paul Münch, "The Thesis before Weber: An Archaeology," in Lehmann and Roth, *Weber*, Chap. 2, especially, pp. 64–65.

Sociologists influenced by the Weber thesis have frequently noted the link of Protestantism and cities and, making unwarranted translation, think automatically of "the bourgeoisie." But Spitz pointed up another option: "The clergy constituted a significant part of the population, in many cities, such as Worms, comprising at least 10 percent of the population." Six thousand of Cologne's 40,000 population were clerics. Hamburg had 450 parish priests for a population of 12,000[2] The total population figures, it will be noted, would include children, hence the clerical presence among adults must have been much greater than even these figures suggest. With the Reformation and a dramatic shift of clergy into economically productive occupations, one would expect significant changes in economic growth, that quite independent of callings and predestination.

The confiscation and sale of church properties generated immense amounts of capital which, presumably, was put to more "productive" use than was previously the case. If so, that too would have had some positive economic impact. Again one has the question: how much weight, with ceteris paribus, should be assigned the calling? The "secularization" of church properties in Germany came at a relatively late point, in the early nineteenth century, an effort stimulated by the threat of Napoleon Bonaparte. This event, the *Secularization*, figures prominently in all serious histories of the period. With church income drastically reduced, many activities had to be abandoned, among them, the Catholic universities (18 of them) and church-sponsored schools. That had impacts for the Catholic population which, four score years later, were to be seen in Offenbacher's statistics.[3]

A reform movement within an established church would continue to be supported out of public funds. The same would hold for a breakaway movement which, as with Lutheranism or the Church of England, then became the established church. But a reform movement that chose independence had to be supported by its own members. For them, independence meant a new tithe to pay for the clergy, buildings, publications, transport, missions, and so forth. Those sums, obviously, were not available for reinvestment (at least not as conventionally understood). Those choosing independence, moreover, were doubly taxed since they ordinarily were required to continue paying the costs of the established church.

The ethical teachings of any religion would also, presumably, have some impact on the use of personal or household economic resources.

---

2. Spitz, *Protestant Reformation*, 50–51.
3. See James J. Sheehan, *German History: 1770–1866* (Oxford: Clarendon Press, 1989), 243–246, 269–272, 355. The change, Sheehan reports, was "one of the greatest territorial rearrangements in all of European history" (243). See also Rudolf Morsey, "Wirtschaftliche und soziale Auswirkungen der Säkularisation in Deutschland," in Rudolf Vierhaus and Manfred Botzenhart, eds., *Dauer und Wandel der Geschichte: Aspekte europäischer Vergangenheit* (Münster: Verlag Aschendorff, 1966), 361–383.

Diligence in work, Weber's single-minded emphasis, is only one of many possible economic impacts of "religion." Daniel's discussion of Wenzeslaus Linck's activity in Nuremberg, as indicated, supports Weber on a key theme, on the importance of the calling albeit in conjunction with a notion of social responsibility. One relevant consideration in this connection is "last wills and testaments and the execution of legacies." Linck held that "gifts to the church, as endowments for the recitation of death masses . . . was an exploitation of man by the church." The suggestion by the clergy that eternal benefits would follow the generous endowment were stimulated, not by freely willed choice, but by fear of damnation. He argued an opposite course, for economic and social reasons, it was "absolutely necessary" that goods be left to one's natural heirs "so that they would not be future burdens on society." His plea for "social justice and civic responsibility" was very popular and the sermon was reprinted and given wider circulation.[4] What weight, if any, should be assigned the calling and what weight given the change in inheritance patterns?

It is easy to make the purely logical case for asceticism: less drinking, smoking, and carousing, would mean a greater "surplus" for capital investment. But have we seen a comparison of household accounts? Did the Puritans invest? Or did they hoard their money? Or did they give it to the church in regular tithing? For poor people, the choice of asceticism as against wayward living would have considerable impact on a family's well-being. But what of the wealthy? How much difference would it make for them? The rather ascetic Baptist, John D. Rockefeller, had a large Euclid Avenue home in Cleveland and, later, a large home in New York City just off Fifth Avenue. But how much difference did his—relative—asceticism make as compared, for example, to the luxury and extravagance of Episcopalian J. P. Morgan? Again, have we seen the accounts? How much of their respective fortunes went into the household and idle consumption? How much did Morgan lose economically because of his art works, the library, and his famous yacht, the Corsair? Most of these questions, it will be noted, are unanswered. Most, in fact, are unasked.[5]

Apart from the Rockefeller and Morgan comparison, the hypotheses reviewed to this point touch on events occurring in the fifteenth to the seventeenth centuries, prior to what many would count as the decisive development—the "Industrial Revolution." Most accounts, for good reason, place the first of those transformations in the United

4. Daniel, "Hard Work," 45.
5. It is not entirely certain that those luxuries should be counted as losses or as "wasteful" expenses. Morgan concluded a major business agreement on board the Corsair. "Appearances," the show of wealth or of "solidity," can have real economic consequences. Again, one should not beg questions.

Kingdom, basically in England. There is a long-standing struggle over the concept and the appropriate dates. Many focus on the period from 1750 to 1850. Most accounts focus on the cotton industry and, accordingly, on Manchester and surrounding Lancashire. If the latter limitation is accepted, an even later dating of "the Revolution" is appropriate. Cotton did not overtake woolens as the nation's leading export product until after 1800. The phenomenal growth of Manchester came in the 1830s and 1840s. This poses some problem for the Weber thesis. Almost two centuries intervened between the Puritan triumph in seventeenth-century England and this economic takeoff.[6]

Economic historians have provided a wide array of hypotheses to account for the development of "the West," only a small sample of which may be touched on here.[7] Early in the modern era England moved to eliminate internal trade barriers. Anticipating Adam Smith and the recommendations of liberal economics, a larger trade territory had been created. Geography also played a role, the island location and navigable rivers made possible a coastal trade which also meant a larger economic base. In addition, in the eighteenth century, an extended infrastructure was built to link up that territory, this with the construction of canals and highways. The industrial revolution, moreover, was preceded by a series of innovations collectively termed the agricultural revolution. That produced a healthier, longer-lived population which, other things equal, would ordinarily mean a more productive population. The demographic revolution, which began in the middle of the eighteenth century, produced a demand for food, clothing, and housing which, because of the prior innovations, could be met with reasonable success.

A series of five innovations in the cotton industry, the flying shuttle, the carding machine, the spinning-jenny, the water-frame, and the cotton gin, made possible the breakthrough that most people see as central to "the" industrial revolution. A parallel series of innovations led to the use of steam engines and coal as power sources and to the creation of the machine tool industry. The need for iron and steel, for frames in spinning and weaving, for the steam engines, and later for

6. See N. F. R. Crafts, "British Economic Growth, 1700–1831: A Review of the Evidence," *Economic History Review, Second Series,* 36:(1983): 177–199. For more detail see Crafts, *British Economic Growth during the Industrial Revolution* (New York: Oxford University Press, 1985).

7. The "new economic history" (sometimes termed the new institutionalism) focuses on the long term, on facilitating conditions developed in the centuries prior to 1800. Europe had a system of states as opposed to the empires elsewhere, those of the Ottomans, of India, and of China. Other things equal, competing states encourage innovation and some transfer of procedures follows. Private property, eventually, came to be more secure in "the West" than elsewhere. The incentive to hoard capital was reduced and interest rates fell accordingly. The European states, those on the Atlantic, built large ocean-going ships and mastered the intricacies of navigation. The empires, in contrast, "stayed home." See especially North and Thomas, *Rise of the Western World,* Jones, *European Miracle,* and Rosenberg and Birdzell, *How the West Grew Rich.*

rails, brought a third series of innovations and the development of another major industry. Some notion of the timing is useful: the flying shuttle gained wide adoption in the 1750s and 1760s; the spinning-jenny was patented in 1770; Whitney's cotton gin was introduced in the last decade of the century; use of the steam engine in textile manufacture "on a considerable scale" came only in the 1820s, 1830s, and 1840s."[8]

The explanations provided by economic historians focus on technology, on the sources of the innovations, and on social organization, the ability to adopt and use the inventions. It is striking that Phyllis Deane's account of the industrial revolution in Britain makes no mention of the Weber thesis. Rondo Cameron's economic history of the world, which of course deals with central Europe in the Reformation period and in the centuries thereafter, also makes no reference to Weber, to the calling, or to a Puritan work ethic. Deane and Cameron did not find it either necessary or useful to give so much as a paragraph to Weber's cultural and social psychological argument. David S. Landes' economic history of Western Europe from 1750 provides a close parallel to Deane's and Cameron's in that his analysis centers on innovations and organization. It does, as noted above, give some attention to the Weber thesis, providing five paragraphs of exposition and two other paragraphs that give it some credence. The supporting evidence provided is very limited and scarcely compelling. In a work of 555 pages, "the Protestant ethic" does not appear to count for much.[9]

8. On the "industrial revolution," see Deane, *First Industrial Revolution*; Cameron, *Concise Economic History*; and Landes, *Unbound Prometheus*. The expression "industrial revolution" is problematic. For the details, see Cameron, 165–167.

9. Landes provides the following: a brief exposition of the Weber thesis along with several other explanations (22–23); a paragraph-length exposition of the English experience, one giving credence to the Weber claim of a Dissent-entrepreneurialism linkage, this also accompanied by other explanations (73–74); and a paragraph discussion of the Calvinism-entrepreneurialism link in the Mulhouse region of Alsace (160). The English case is based on the crude ecological relationship ("surely no coincidence that Dissenters were more numerous in the North and Midlands") and a study that has been successfully challenged by Rubinstein. On those points, see Watts' on discussion of the frequency and location of dissent (reviewed above in the text), and Rubinstein, (p. 184). For the Mulhouse experience, see Landes, "Religion and Enterprise: The Case of the French Textile Industry," in Edward C. Carter II, Robert Forster, and Joseph N. Moody, eds., *Enterprise and Entrepreneurs in Nineteenth- and Twentieth-Century France* (Baltimore: Johns Hopkins University Press, 1976), 41–86.

Wolfgang Schivelbusch has advanced still another hypothesis, this in an important chapter entitled "Coffee and the Protestant Ethic." Prior to the seventeenth century, he reports, alcoholic beverages were standard fare for most European populations. English families began the day with a breakfast of beer soup. That was followed, in the course of the day, by the drinking of beer or ale which, on the whole, was healthier than water. The subsequent widespread use of coffee transformed a generally begrogged population, making it into a sober, alert, and active force. This change, understandably, brought about a dramatic improvement in work habits. See his *Tastes of Paradise: A Social History of Spices, Stimulants, and Intoxicants*, trans. David Jacobson, New York: Pantheon, 1992, Chap. 2.

## Weber and the "Ghost of Marx"

Many writers and commentators have portrayed the Weber thesis as an argument against Marx, a claim that seems immediately plausible. Albert Salomon, in 1945, wrote that Weber engaged "in a long and intense dialogue with the ghost of Karl Marx." That figure of speech appears frequently in the textbooks. Marshall cites five commentators who saw Weber's essay as a direct response to Marx. Marshall, however, reports an entirely different intellectual history. It developed out of themes covered in Weber's earlier work and was also a response to a controversy within the German universities, specifically between classical economics (rational self-interested calculating individuals) and the historical school (unique values associated with different training and traditions).[1]

A recent contribution supports Marshall's reading of the intellectual history and provides additional details. Friedrich Wilhelm Graf points to Weber's use of German theological sources and to his concern with issues of Protestant church politics. "This heavy dependence on the theological discussion," Graf argues, "indicates that more value judgments, and specifically denominational ideology, are present in *The Protestant Ethic* than Weber himself realized or present interpreters are aware." Weber's argument, unexpectedly, is centered on the work of the Bern theologian, Matthias Schneckenburger, who emphasized the differences between Lutheranism and Calvinism. He portrayed the former as generating passivity, the latter as generating activism. Schneckenburger also argued predestination as somehow the driving force.

Another much-cited author in Weber's monograph is Albrecht Ritschl, the "most influential German-speaking Protestant theologian of the late nineteenth century." Ritschl played down the denominational differences, arguing that Protestantism generally was "the religion of progress" and that Catholicism was both backward and inferior. For Ritschl, Luther was "a true modernizer." In Weber's notes, Graf reports, no other author is "as frequently or contentiously [criticized] as Ritschl." Both theologians, clearly, assigned major importance to the "role of ideas" in human behavior. Their dispute was over the options—which ideas? Weber adopted the Schneckenburger argument for his purposes, taking Calvinism as the aggressive, driving force. For his

---

1. The Albert Salomon quotation appeared first in an essay on "German Sociology," in Georges Gurvitch and Wilbert E. Moore, eds., *Twentieth Century Sociology* (New York: Philosophical Library, 1945), 596. Guenther Roth cites the passage, and questions it, in his account, "The Historical Relationship to Marxism," in Bendix and Roth, *Scholarship and Partisanship* (Berkeley: University of California Press, 1971), 228. References to Marx's ghost appear also in the sociology textbooks, those of Macionis, 107; Robertson, 15; and VanderZanden, 20. For Marshall's comments, see *Search*, 203, n44, and 22–40, 150.

argument about the development of capitalism, he had to focus on the English experience, on the role of Puritanism.[2]

It was the *Kulturkampf*, Bismarck's struggle against Catholicism, that provided the context for the controversy, not the *Sozialistenkampf*. Ritschl was arguing that Protestantism was a better religion than Catholicism. Along with many others, he was making a case that the social impacts of Protestantism were more desirable than those associated with Catholicism. Ritschl, who supported Bismarck in the "battle of the creeds," has been described as a National-Liberal theologian.[3] Weber carried this "battle" one step further, making a crucial distinction within the Protestant camp.

Guenther Roth introduces his discussion of this issue with an unexpected observation: "The hatred [Weber] felt for his Lutheran heritage and the German authoritarian realities was so great that he modeled his notion of ethical personality and innerworldly asceticism to a considerable extent after an idealized image of English history, especially of Puritanism." In 1906, in a letter discussing *The Protestant Ethic*, Weber wrote: "The fact that our nation never went through the school of hard asceticism, in no form whatsoever, is the source of everything that I hate about it (and about myself)." The "radical idealism" of the Protestant sects, those of England and America, had produced the modern "freedom of conscience and the most basic rights of man," values he ardently defended. But that crucial formative experience was missing in Germany. In 1911, to another correspondent, he wrote that: "A people which, as we Germans, has never dared to behead the traditionalist powers will never gain the proud self-assurance that makes the Anglo-Saxons and Latins (*Romanen*) . . . so superior to us in the world." In her biography of her husband, Marianne Weber wrote that *The Protestant Ethic* "is connected to the deepest roots of his personality and in an undefinable way bears its stamp."[4]

---

2. See Friedrich Wilhelm Graf, "The German Theological Sources and Protestant Church Politics," Chap. 1 of Lehmann and Roth, *Weber*. The quotation re Weber on Ritschl appears on p. 42. Graf writes that: "*The Protestant Ethic* demonstrated that Weber became involved in theological discourse more than any other sociologist of the century" (48–49). Two other chapters in that volume provide important information on the "theological" and political background of the monograph, those of Paul Münch, Chap. 2, "The Thesis before Weber," and Thomas Nipperdey, Chap. 3, "Max Weber, Protestantism, and the Context of the Debate around 1900."

3. On Ritschl as National-Liberal theologian, see Graf, 43.

4. Guenther Roth wrote that "Weber greatly sympathized with the Puritan and liberal traditions of England. Sometimes he sounded as if he were half English." See his "Weber the Would-Be Englishman: Anglophilia and Family History," Chap. 4 of Lehmann and Roth, *Weber*, 83. Philip Benedict commented on the extent to which "Weber's essay was a product of the confessional rivalries and prejudices of the specific time and place in which it was written, not to mention Weber's own critical attitude toward Germany's Lutheran inheritance, to which the Reformed tradition constituted in his eyes a superior alternative." From "Historiography," 325. The Marianne Weber quotation is from her *Max Weber: A Biography*, trans. Harry Zohn (New York: Wiley, 1975), 335.

The index to Marianne Weber's biography of her husband contains only six references to Marx, Marxism, or Marxists. Two of these are remarkably positive: "Weber expressed great admiration for Karl Marx's brilliant constructions and saw in the inquiry into the economic and technical causes of events an exceedingly fruitful, indeed, a specifically new heuristic principle that directed the quest for knowledge into entire areas previously unilluminated." And also: "Weber suspected all political metaphysics up to that time as a kind of mimicry by which the privileged classes protected themselves against a rearrangement of the spheres of power. In this respect he shared Karl Marx's conception of the state and its ideology."[5]

The "ghost of Marx" claim, although not entirely without foundation, seems somewhat exaggerated, an overstatement. It appears to be still another social misconstruction. For Marxists, it serves a useful purpose. That Germany's leading sociologist felt it necessary, supposedly, to mount such a challenge is proof of the importance of the Marxian theory.

# GUDMUND HERNES

## The Logic of *The Protestant Ethic*[†]

Great sociology is great literature. The appeal of an analysis lies not just in its substantive content—the findings and the results. It is the sense of drama induced as well—the way the results are arrived at and the suspense and surprise that are built into the intellectual plot.

To a great extent what gives us the thrills are the dramaturgical elements that provide the building blocks of the plot. They shape the deep structure of the analysis, but are often hidden by the flow of argument. The craft of the dramatist entails exploiting general elements in new ways and yet eclipsing them by the particulars of the story. When the building has been erected, the scaffolding is torn down. Originality consists as much in a new permutation of the familiar elements as in their application to a new set of concrete events.

In scientific papers the typical plots are of four kinds. The first is the *discovery*—a new observation, be it a startling relation between variables or the outlandish practices of some far-away tribe. A second is *the great account*—a new finding or an old anomaly cries out for

5. Marianne Weber, *Max Weber*, 335 and 587. Fischoff writes that Weber "was an admirer of the Marxian hypothesis, only objecting that it should not be made absolute and universal, a summary philosophy," in "Protestant Ethic," 67.

† Reproduced with permission from Gudmund Hernes, *The Logic of* The Protestant Ethic, copyright © 1989 by SAGE Publications, by Permission of Sage Publications Ltd. Page numbers for Weber's *The Protestant Ethic and the Spirit of Capitalism* refer to this Norton Critical Edition.

explanation. That is, puzzles or riddles have to be cracked or decoded, and this is done in terms of a general rationale. A third plot in scientific papers is the *logical Pandora's box*. The great account will have implications, that is, a potentiality of hidden meanings which are dormant in a general model, but can be awakened by sharp reasoning. Such logical upshots are especially pleasing when they provide surprises such as counterintuitive implications of reasonable assumptions. Finally, we have the *empirical ordeal*—comparing such implications with actual observations. This is how great accounts are tested: those survive having implications that can withstand the onslaught of brute fact.

Scientists can specialize in each of the four types of plots. Some cultivate *observations* by travels to strange lands, doing legwork in inner cities, or running factor analyses. Others prefer *model building*: the making of logical worlds or tendering theoretical vistas that can match the observations of the voyagers. Others again find their mission in *deriving theorems* from such models; they extend the worlds of the great model-builders: a Freud, a Marx, a Darwin, or an Einstein. Finally, we have the sworn *empiricists*—those who check whether the logical "predictions" from the models actually square with the facts, be they survey analysts crunching data or laboratory workers in white lab coats shaking test tubes.

Great scientists traverse all these categories. They make discoveries and create isomorphy between the imaginary world of models and the real world of empirical observations. Their theoretical originality consists in large part in their permutations of known elements. They dress up elementary structures in ever-new concrete outfits.

In this article I examine Max Weber's classic, *The Protestant Ethic and the Spirit of Capitalism*, to identify the logical building blocks he uses in its dramatic composition.[1] The main thesis is that we appreciate it as a distinguished work both because of the particular logical elements used and the way that Weber strings them together in the dramatic construction of the work. Among the dramaturgical techniques used are the "cunning of history," that is, causal effects of intentional action working behind the backs of the actors, and the paradoxes that arise when they set in motion forces that trap themselves. Among the logical elements are the sophisticated use of multivariate analysis, the prisoner's dilemma, and the reversal of

---

1. The concern in this article is with the logic of Weber's argument, not with its empirical validity. Neither will I take up how he later addressed this question. One such analysis is found in Randall Collins (1980).

  Hayden White (1975) has analyzed *The Historical Imagination in Nineteenth-Century Europe* from the perspective of the deep poetic structural content of narratives. I do not, however, use his metahistorical typology here.

  For an analysis of how economists use traditional means of persuasion, see Donald N. McCloskey (1986).

conditional probabilities. The dramatistic exposition of Weber's analysis can also help us to understand what Robert K. Merton (1984, 1092) has identified as the "Phoenix phenomenon":

> the continuing resiliency of theoretically derived hypotheses such as Durkheim's on suicide rates or Max Weber's on the role of ascetic Protestantism in the emergence of modern capitalism even though they have been periodically subjected to much and allegedly conclusive demolition ("falsification").

## Establishing the Case

Weber starts with a simple but startling observation: Occupational statistics in any country of mixed religious composition show that business leaders, the higher grades of skilled labor, and the higher technically and commercially trained personnel of modern enterprises are all overwhelmingly Protestant.

Several authors have pointed out that Emile Durkheim (1958) in *Suicide* is the precursor of causal analysis in the social sciences. Working in the nineteenth century he "understood the logic of multivariate analysis much as we understand it today" (Riley 1963, 414). Weber understood it equally well.[2] Actually, it is the first of the logical archetypes that he uses in *The Protestant Ethic*. Indeed, his whole first chapter, "Religious Affiliation and Social Stratification," is about little else.

In crime investigation establishing the case is mandatory for pursuing it. Merton has cautioned us that an important first element in the practice of science is "establishing the phenomenon": that it is enough of a regularity to require and allow explanation.[3] In this way pseudofacts that induce pseudoproblems are avoided. This is exactly why Weber sets out to establish his case.

Hence Weber first eliminates several possible *spurious* relationships that could account for religious differences in occupational structure. For example, the differences may be due to differences in cultural development, as illustrated in East Germany by Catholic Poles who are less embedded in a capitalist culture than are Protestant Germans. Here the effect of religion cannot be identified because it coincides with national differences in development, that is, because of multicollinearity. However, Weber eliminates the cultural development

---

2. Lazarsfeld and Oberschall (1965) show that Weber made systematic use of crosstabulation in some of his empirical studies. My main point here is that he also used the *logic* of crosstabulation in his qualitative reasoning.

3. "In the abstract, it need hardly be said that before one proceeds to explain or to interpret a phenomenon, it is advisable to establish that the phenomenon actually exists, that it is enough of a regularity to require and to allow explanation. Yet, sometimes in science as in everyday life, explanations are provided of matters that are not and never were" (Merton 1987, 21).

TABLE 1
Proportions in Modern Occupations by
Religion and Cultural Development

| CULTURAL DEVELOPMENT | Different | | Same | |
|---|---|---|---|---|
| RELIGION | Protestant | Catholic | Protestant | Catholic |
| IN MODERN OCCUPATIONS | ◯ | ○ | ◯ | ○ |

TABLE 2
Distribution Expected by an "Inheritance Theory" of the
Differences Between Protestants and Catholics

| | Inherited resources | |
|---|---|---|
| | High | Low |
| Protestants | X | |
| Catholics | | X |

explanation by checking figures for religious affiliation *within* regions where cultural development is the *same*. His argument can be represented in a trivariate table, as in Table 1, where the sizes of the rings illustrate relative sizes in proportions. The left part of the table shows the difference between the East Germans and the Poles. The right part disproves the argument about cultural development. His conclusion on this point is that the more freedom capitalism has had in altering the social distribution of the population, the more clearly the effect is shown.

The next explanation that Weber eliminates is that the differences between Protestants and Catholics are due to factors predating the Reformation:

> A number of those sections of the old Empire which were most highly developed economically and most favoured by natural resources and situation, in particular a majority of wealthy towns, went over to Protestantism in the sixteenth century. The results of that circumstance favor the Protestants even today in their struggle for economic existence. (p. 15)

Here Weber suggests an "inheritance theory" of differences between the two religious groups, illustrated in Table 2. He eliminates this explanation by looking at the educational practices of the two groups. He infers from a multivariate analysis of the type illustrated in Table

### TABLE 3
Proportion in Technical Studies by Inherited
Resources and Religion

| INHERITED DEVELOPMENT | High | | Low | |
|---|---|---|---|---|
| RELIGION | Protestant | Catholic | Protestant | Catholic |
| TECHNICAL STUDIES | ◯ | ○ | ◯ | ○ |

### TABLE 4
Business Participation by Minority Position and Religion

| MINORITY POSITION | Yes | | No | |
|---|---|---|---|---|
| RELIGION | Protestant | Catholic | Protestant | Catholic |
| BUSINESS PARTICIPATION | ◯ | ○ | ◯ | ○ |

3. Regions that vary in inherited resources are Baden, Bavaria, and Hungary. The dependent variable is the proportion of graduates in technical studies, and the sizes of the rings indicate the differences in proportions found. He repeats this analysis with a different dependent variable—the proportion of skilled laborers in industry compared with those in the crafts. The empirical distributions show the same preponderance of Protestants. Hence he concludes that the religious atmosphere of the home community has determined choice of education and occupation (p. 17).

Having eliminated extraneous factors, Weber tests the explanatory power of religion. It was a well-known finding that national and religious minorities, involuntarily excluded from positions of political influence, were driven into economic activity. Weber again carries out a multivariate analysis of the kind illustrated in Table 4. And in a beautiful statement of the outcome of a multivariate analysis, he concludes

> Both as ruling classes and as ruled, both as majority and as minority, [Protestants] have shown a special tendency to develop economic rationalism which cannot be observed to the same extent among Catholics either in the one situation or in the other. Thus the principal explanation of this difference must be sought in the permanent intrinsic character of their religious beliefs, and not only in their temporary external historico-political situations. (p. 18)

This relationship is all the more striking as it runs counter to "a tendency [about the effect of minority position] which has been observed at all times" (p. 17).

### The Smoking Gun

Having established the phenomenon, Weber sets as his task the investigation of the peculiarities of Protestant religions that might have resulted in the described behavior.

He first suggests a possible explanation that fit the popular judgments of the times, namely that the greater *otherworldliness of Catholicism* "must have brought its adherents to a greater indifference toward the good things of this world" (p. 18). To check, Weber performs yet another multivariate analysis. Protestantism is not an indicator of joy of living and Catholicism an indicator of otherworldliness. There are variations *within* the denominations, and hence denomination and otherworldliness have to be treated as two independent variables. The results of his analysis are presented in Table 5. By this analysis Weber first rejects the notion that Catholicism is synonymous with otherworldliness—to the contrary he finds that in France, Catholics in the lower ranks are "greatly interested in the enjoyment of life, whereas they in the upper are hostile to religion" (pp. 19). Second, "not all the Protestant denominations seem to have had an equally strong influence" in the direction of capitalistic culture.[4] And from this he reaches the *paradoxical conclusion*—one that creates suspense in his drama:

> The supposed conflict between other-worldliness, asceticism, and ecclesiastical piety on the one side, and participation in capitalistic acquisition on the other, might actually turn out to be an intimate relationship. (p. 19)

However, before Weber is satisfied that the relationship between capitalist acquisitiveness and otherworldliness is solid, he has to reject another possibility. To do so, he employs a different logical archetype.

The inference that business acumen is most developed in the otherworldly oriented Protestant groups may be an *ecological fallacy*. On the one hand, the most pious representatives may have sprung from commercial circles as a "sort of reaction against mammonism" (p. 19). On the other hand, the remarkable circumstance that so many capitalist entrepreneurs have come from clergymen's families might be explained as a "reaction against their ascetic upbringing" (p. 19). If

---

4. Later in his book Weber shows that where there was a strong otherworldly orientation among Catholics in monasteries, this also led to capital accumulation (for example see p. 92). However, in monasteries the economic activities were not *innerworldly*, but were withdrawn from the world.

TABLE 5
Business Participation by Otherworldliness and Religion

| OTHER-WORLDLINESS | High | | Low | |
|---|---|---|---|---|
| RELIGION | Protestant | Catholic | Protestant | Catholic |
| BUSINESS PARTICIPATION | ◯ <br> Calvinists <br> Puritans <br> Quakers <br> Mennonites | ○ | ◯ <br> Lutheran | ○ <br> French <br> Catholic |

this were so, there would be an inverse relationship between other-worldliness and acquisitiveness. However, Weber rejects this possibility by showing that the *correlation also holds at the individual level:*

> This form of explanation fails where an extraordinary capitalistic business sense is combined in the same persons and groups with the most intensive forms of a piety which penetrates and dominates their whole lives. Such cases are not isolated, but these traits are characteristic of many of the most important Churches and sects in the history of Protestantism. Especially Calvinism, wherever it has appeared, has shown this combination. (p. 19)

By this set of inferences, Weber has so to speak arrived at the "smoking gun": the source of capitalism is found in the ascetic branches of Protestantism:

> The spirit of hard work, of progress, or whatever else it may be called, the awakening of which one is inclined to ascribe to Protestantism, must not be understood, as there is a tendency to do, as joy of living nor in any other sense as connected with the Enlightenment. . . . If any inner relationship between certain expressions of the old Protestant spirit and modern capitalistic culture is to be found, we must attempt to find it, for better or worse, not in its alleged more or less materialistic or at least anti-ascetic joy of living, but in its purely religious characteristics. (p. 20–21)

The logical archetype that provides the underlying structure of Weber's plot is a set of multivariate analyses that eliminate extraneous factors to test whether his explanatory factor holds up when other variables are controlled. This is the type of analysis that Lazarsfeld later was to formalize; both Weber and Durkheim were astute in their use of it. At the same time Weber shows his awareness of the ecological fallacy and how it can be avoided. He displays his acumen by

establishing the phenomenon in a way that Merton admonishes theoretically and Lazarsfeld advises us how to carry out technically.

Weber's argument is usually not dissected in this way. When done,
we find one of the enduring entrapments of his exposition: the rules
of method ensconced in his prose—rules taught in the abstract in our
introductory courses. No doubt one of the pleasures of reading him
stems from the more or less subliminal recognition of familiar elements in an intriguing concrete analysis.

## Rounding Up the Usual Suspects

Next Weber addresses what should be understood by *the spirit of
capitalism*. He goes about it inductively, trying to arrive at the general
concept from a particularly pure example, which he finds in Benjamin
Franklin's *Necessary Hints to Those That Would Be Rich* and *Advice
to a Young Tradesman*. From this Weber identifies the spirit of capitalism as an *ethos*, an ethically colored maxim for the conduct of life,
the quintessence of which is (1) "the earning of more and more money,
combined with (2) the strict avoidance of all spontaneous enjoyment
of life" (p. 53). Such a motive—the making of money as an end in
itself—

> from the point of view of the happiness of, or utility to, the single
> individual, appears transcendental, and absolutely irrational.
> Man is dominated by the making of money, by acquisition as the
> ultimate purpose of his life. Economic acquisition is no longer
> subordinated to man as the means for the satisfaction of his
> material needs. This reversal of what we should call the natural
> relationship, so irrational from a naive point of view, is evidently
> a leading principle of capitalism as it is foreign to all peoples not
> under capitalistic influence. (p. 25)

Weber finds this feeling to be closely connected to religious ideas,
"the result and the expression of virtue and proficiency in a calling"
(p. 25), and he finds the idea of a *duty in a calling* "most characteristic
of the social ethic of capitalist culture, and in a sense the fundamental basis of it" (p. 25).

What Weber sets out to do is to explain the *origin* of this idea,
"not in isolated individuals alone, but as a way of life common to
whole groups of men" (p. 26). If one is able to identify its origin, one
will also be able to identify the origins of capitalism. Once capitalism
is established, competition forces men to conform. Hence it is not
the *reproduction* of capitalism, but its *generation* that really needs
explanation.

Weber presents two theories as suspects in the case, which he then
proceeds to eliminate by causal analysis. The first is a "naive historical materialism" that argues that ideas originate as a superstructure

TABLE 6
Modes of American Capitalism and the Spirit of Capitalism

| | | Developed capitalism | |
| | | Yes | No |
| --- | --- | --- | --- |
| Capitalistic order established before spirit of capitalism | Yes | | South |
| | No | New England | |

over economic situations. Weber shows that in the terrain of Benjamin Franklin's birth, Massachusetts, the spirit of capitalism "was present before the capitalist order," Capitalism was far less developed in the southern states, although they had been formed by large capitalists for business motives. So Weber rejects the materialistic theory by the analysis illustrated in Table 6. In New England, the *causal order* is opposite to that predicted by a naive historical materialism (the spirit came first). In the South, the *correlation* is the reverse of the predicted (structure has a weak impact on motivation). Thus Weber gives a nice example of how to test causal theories by observations: He (1) finds different values of the causal variable, (2) investigates covariation, and (3) checks causal direction.

The other suspect is avarice—*auri sacra fames*—greed for gold. He rejects this theory first because greed was well known and not "less powerful outside of bourgeois capitalism" (p. 27). Hence the assumed cause did not have a unique effect. Moreover,

> the universal reign of absolute unscrupulousness in the pursuit of selfish interests by the making of money has been a specific characteristic of precisely those countries whose bourgeois-capitalistic development, measured according to Occidental standards, has remained backward. (p. 27)

So the correlation is the opposite of what the theory predicts. What Weber again does is to carry out a causal analysis of the kind shown in Table 7. Since "*auri sacra fames* is as old as the history of man" (p. 27), it has hampered rather than promoted capitalism, and the correlation thus is the reverse of the predicted. So this explanation has to be rejected. Indeed, as Weber points out, "absolute and conscious ruthlessness in acquisition has often stood in the closest connection with the strictest conformity to tradition" (p. 28). This is important, as Weber thinks that in order to explain the origins of capitalism one must account for how *traditionalism* was overcome—the breaking-away from the status quo.

In his first chapter, Weber uses the logic of multivariate analysis to establish the nexus between Protestantism and capitalism. In his

TABLE 7
Capitalistic Development by Avarice

| | | Developed capitalism | |
| | | Yes | No |
| --- | --- | --- | --- |
| Unfettered avarice | Yes | | Adventure capitalism |
| | No | Bourgeois capitalism | |

second, he uses the logic of causal inference to eliminate both a "naive materialist" and an avaricious explanation of the origins of capitalism. That is, inlaid in Weber's arguments are logical archetypes that only much later were codified in the works of social science methodology.

## The Scene of the Crime

To explain how capitalism originated, Weber has to describe the setting in which it took place: What kinds of actors were displaced by the new breed infused with the spirit of capitalism, and in what kind of social structure were they embedded?

In constructing social theories, two types of assumptions must be made: *actor assumptions* and *structure assumptions*.

For *actors* we must specify what they *want*, what they *know*, what they *believe* and what they *can do*. This is done in microeconomics, in which the actors are consumers and producers, the former maximizing utility and the latter profit; both are fully informed and both have resources they can allocate for different uses.

For the *structure* we must specify the possible *states* the actors can be in (such as roles, positions, or choices, some of which are collective properties, for example, laws), the *correlates* of these states (such as payoffs or costs), and the *distribution* of actors over states, which is distinct from them as individuals. In microeconomic theory, the most important characteristic of the structure is the number of other actors, used to define three main types of organizational forms of the market: perfect competition, oligopoly, and monopoly.

The task of model building is to work out the logical consequences or *systemic effects* of specific actors operating within the specified structure, for example, which choices maximize producers' profits under monopoly. We modify or change a model by altering or amending the actor assumptions, the structure assumptions, or both. To use a metaphor from drama: The actor assumptions concern the *casting*

TABLE 8
Models of Social Change

|  |  | Structure changes actors | |
|---|---|---|---|
|  |  | No | Yes |
| Actors change structure | No | 1 | 2 |
|  | Yes | 3 | 4 |

of the model, the structure assumptions its *staging*, and the systemic consequences are the *plotting* that results.

For a model of social change, we have to ask two questions: (1) Do the actors change the structure? and (2) Does the structure change the actors? These questions give four combinations summarized in Table 8. In Box 1 we find *models of static equilibrium:* The actors carry out some transactions, but remain the same, as does the structure within which they act. (An example is adaptation of marginal costs to prices under pure competition.) In Box 3 we find *models of structural change:* The actors change the structure they operate in, but the principles guiding their own behavior remain unchanged. Here we can cite cobweb models of hog cycles, or models of monopolization in which competitors knock each other out of the market. In Box 2 we find—allowing a neologism—*models of actoral change:* The structure actors are placed in changes their wants, knowledge, beliefs, or capacities, as in models of socialization (for instance, of achievement motive). In Box 4 we find *dialectical models:* The actors change the structure, but react to conditions of their own making and are themselves modified by the structural changes they have produced. What characterizes dialectical models is that systemic effects generated by the actors not only feed back and change the structure, but that this in turn transforms the actors (Hernes 1976). Weber follows the logic of model building by specifying actor and structure assumptions. On this basis he constructs a dialectical model.

The key concept in Weber's explanation is *traditionalism.* Weber describes two types of traditionalistic actors: laborers and entrepreneurs.

The specific attribute of traditionalistic workers is that an increase in their rewards may not lead to an increase in their output. A peculiar difficulty has been met with surprising frequency: The opportunity to earn a high wage may not interest them in increasing their efficiency.

> Raising the piece-rate has often had the result that not more but less has been accomplished in the same time, because the worker reacted to the increase not by increasing but by decreasing the amount of his work. (p. 28)

TABLE 9
Types of Motivation and Types of Enterprise

|  |  | Capitalistic enterprise | |
|  |  | No | Yes |
|---|---|---|---|
| Spirit | Traditionalistic |  | Traditional capitalism |
|  | Capitalistic | Franklin | Modern capitalism |

Thus traditionalistic workers are characterized by the fact that beyond a certain point, a raise in the wage rate lowers their supply of labor. This is what modern economists call the "backward bending" curve of labor supply.[5] In Weber's words, "the opportunity of earning more was less attractive than that of working less" (p. 29). People do not "by nature" wish to earn more and more money, but simply to live as they are accustomed to living and to earn as much as necessary for this purpose. The traditionalistic workers adjust their supply of labor so that they can satisfy their traditional needs. This "immense stubborn resistance" is the "leading trait of precapitalist labour" (p. 29).[6]

Having portrayed traditionalistic workers, Weber moves to the other key group of actors: the traditionalistic entrepreneurs. His basic point is that economic *motivation* and economic *organization* vary independently of each other. That is, they can be crossclassified as in Table 9. Benjamin Franklin was filled with the spirit of capitalism, while "his printing business did not differ in form from any handicraft enterprise." In contrast, the putting-out system of the continental textile industry had a form of organization that was in every respect capitalistic, with use of capital, purchase of the means of production, hiring of labor, and selling of the product. The system even had the objective aspect of a rational economic process in the form of bookkeeping.

> But it was traditionalistic business, if one considers the spirit which animated the entrepreneur: the traditional manner of life, the traditional rate of profit, the traditional manner of regulat-

5. Compare Gordon Marshall (1982, 52).
6. It is interesting to note that Chayanov (1966), writing about the same period, found that this attitude was characteristic of peasant labor. The peasant balances what experience tells him are the needs of his family against his evaluation of the drudgery of his tasks. See also Weber on turning "peasants into labourers" (p. 33).

ing the relationship with labour, and the essentially traditional
circle of customers and the manner of attracting new ones. All
these dominated the conduct of business, were at the basis, one
may say, of the *ethos* of this group of business men. (p. 33)

Such then, was the orderly and tranquil scene with traditionalistic
workers and traditionalistic entrepreneurs. The former did not seek
to earn as much as possible, but only as much as was necessary to
keep their accustomed standard of living. The latter did not seek to
maximize profit, but only to stabilize it at the habituated level.

## The Transgression

Having described the tranquil social setting, Weber depicts, by a nice
piece of "synthetic history" of the putting-out system in the textile
industry, what took place. Enter the new entrepreneurs, whom Weber
characterizes in action:

> Now at some time this leisureliness was suddenly destroyed
> and often without any essential change in the form of organi-
> zation such as the transition to a unified factory, to mechani-
> cal weaving, etc. What happened was, on the contrary, often no
> more than this: some young man from one of the putting-out
> families went out into the country, carefully chose weavers for
> his employ, greatly increased the rigour of his supervision of
> their work, and thus turned them from peasants to labourers.
> On the other hand, he would begin to change his marketing
> methods by so far as possible going directly to the final con-
> sumer, would take the details into his own hands, would per-
> sonally solicit customers, visiting them every year, and above
> all would adapt the quality of the product directly to their
> needs and wishes. At the same time he began to introduce the
> principle of low prices and large turnover. There was repeated
> what everywhere and always was the result of such a process
> of rationalization: those who would not follow suit had to go
> out of business. (p. 33)

The new funds were not important, the new spirit was. The motive
force was not a question of capital sums, but

> above all, of the development of the spirit of capitalism. Where
> it appears and is able to work itself out, it produces its own cap-
> ital and monetary supplies as the means to its ends, but the
> reverse is not true. (p. 34)

Weber also argues that these first innovators, the vanguard of capitalistic conduct, had to have a particular moral constitution to face
and brave the mistrust, hatred, and moral indignation their actions
met. They had to be unusually strong characters to escape from

economic shipwreck, to command the absolutely indispensable confidence of customers and workmen, and to overcome the

> infinitely more intensive work which is demanded of the modern entrepreneur. But these are ethical qualities of a quite different sort from those adapted to the traditionalism of the past. (p. 34)

The *new entrepreneurs* saw acquisitive activity for its own sake as a calling. This calling was indeed necessary to overcome the reactions against them and their new practices from the traditionalists, who could—mistakenly—understand it only as "the product of a perverse instinct, the *auri sacra fames*" (p. 35).

Weber also argues that a *new worker* is brought forth. Discussing how traditionalistic work attitudes may reduce effort in response to higher pay, he submits that the output of labor may be increased by *lowering* wages. But he argues that the efficiency of labor decreases with a wage that is physiologically deficient. Moreover he gives three reasons why this is a poor strategy from a pure business point of view: It does not serve (1) when production requires skilled labor, (2) when production requires the use of expensive machinery, or (3) in general wherever any great amount of sharp attention or initiative is required. For advanced production a different kind of worker is indispensable: workers with (1) "a developed sense of responsibility" who are (2) "freed from continual calculations of how the customary wage may be earned with a maximum of comfort and minimum of exertion. Labor must be performed as if it were an absolute end in itself, a calling" (p. 30).

## Hardened Souls

A new type of worker with such characteristics, Weber argues, cannot be evoked by changing wages. Workers are not a product of nature, but a product of inculcation. They cannot be brought into being by changing *payoffs*, only by changing *preferences*. When more effort from the traditional actors is not procurable, new actors who obey different principles are needed. Stated differently: To explain the origins of capitalism, what is needed is a new type of actor, not a new type of structure. The actors in turn bring forth the new structure.

Such workers, Weber finds, were produced among those having a specific religious background. His example is from capitalism at his own time, showing again that he is more concerned with constructing a consistent model than buttressing it with historical evidence.[7]

---

7. Gordon Marshall also makes this point when he writes that "Weber documents his argument with an unconvincing mixture of fictitious illustrations, composite instances drawn from diverse times and places, and anecdotal empirical examples" (1982, 45). But see my comments on "the centipede of scientific inference."

Employers universally find ordinary working women unable to give up inherited work habits for more efficient ones:

> Explanations of the possibility of making work easier, above all more profitable to themselves, generally encounter a complete lack of understanding. Increases of piece-rates are without avail against the stone wall of habit. (p. 30)

In contrast ("statistical investigation confirms it") women having a Pietistic background have a better educational training, ability for mental concentration, and so on,

> as well as the absolutely essential feeling of obligation to one's job, are here most often combined with a strict economy which calculates the possibility of high earnings, and a cool self-control and frugality which enormously increases performance. This provides the most favorable foundation for the conception of labour as an end in itself, as a calling which is necessary to capitalism: the chances of overcoming traditionalism are greatest on account of religious upbringing. (p. 30)

The same religious factors were present in much the same form in the early development of capitalism, which "can be inferred from numerous facts" (p. 30), such as Methodist workmen having had their *tools* destroyed when persecuted by their comrades for working too hard.

Weber's logical metaphor is that of a culture of traditional entrepreneurs and workers set in their habits and customs, invaded by a new social agent: extraordinary persons with the capacity to suffer stress, strife, and censure. In short, a harder strain of actors emerges. The new entrepreneurs among them were men who had

> grown up in the hard school of life, calculating and daring at the same time, above all temperate and reliable, shrewd and completely devoted to their business, with strictly bourgeois opinions and principles. (p. 34)

These *new entrepreneurs* saw "money-making as an end in itself" (p. 30); the *new workmen* saw "labour as an end in itself" (p. 36).

Both variants of the new type encounter a hostile environment of traditionalists, when fellow businessmen meet their new contenders with hatred and moral indignation or when fellow workers destroy the tools of their new competitors. Both are able (p. 34) to free themselves from the common tradition and to penetrate "economic life with a new spirit" (p. 34). Both types of the new species have in common their affairs as a calling. The *Homo novus* gets nothing out of his work or his "wealth for himself, except the irrational sense of having done his job well" (p. 35).

What Weber does, therefore, is to introduce a very powerful logical archetype: a selection model. At some point a new type of actor, a social mutant infused with the spirit of capitalism, penetrates a population of traditionalists. Over time the vigorous newcomers grow in number relative to the less robust oldtimers. The intruders generate more successors. The logic of this process will be described later.

However, since we are dealing with intentional actors rather than with causally determined genetic processes, Weber must first explain two things: (1) Where did the new spirit of capitalism originate—from what source did it spring? and (2) Why did it catch on? Having described *what* the carriers of the new spirit did and *how* they did it, Weber's next task is to explain *why* they did it. From where did they get their fortitude and perseverance?

> What was the background of ideas which could account for the sort of activity apparently directed toward fit alone as a calling toward which the individual feels himself to have an ethical obligation? For it was this idea which gave the way of life of the new entrepreneur its ethical foundation and justification. (p. 37)

### The Astounding Motive

Weber starts by eliminating a possible explanation. Sombart had argued that economic rationalism was "the salient feature of modern economic life as a whole" (p. 37). And it is true, Weber says, that rationalization of technology and organization is an important ideal of modern bourgeois society. Similarly, individual enterprises are rationalized on the basis of rigorous calculation, in sharp contrast to the

> hand-to-mouth existence of the peasant, and to the privileged traditionalism of the guild craftsman and of the adventurer's capitalism, oriented to the exploitation of political opportunities and irrational speculation. (p. 38)

Hence the spirit of capitalism may best be understood as part of the development of rationalism as a whole and as a result of the crucial role that rationalism plays in problem solving. If so, Protestantism would be of interest only as a stage prior to the development of a purely rationalistic philosophy.

To reject this model, Weber takes three different forms of rationalism. Then he shows that they all correlate negatively with capitalistic development, as in Table 10. From this analysis he emphasizes that life may be rationalized from fundamentally different directions. Rationality itself is a historical concept that "covers a whole world of different things" (p. 39). Hence the task is to find out whose

> intellectual child the particular concrete form of rational thought was, from which the idea of a calling and the devotion to the labour in the calling has grown. (p. 39)

TABLE 10
Capitalist Development by Type of Rationality

| | | TYPE OF RATIONALITY | | | | |
| --- | --- | --- | --- | --- | --- | --- |
| | | Law | | Philosophy | | Practical |
| | | + | − | + | − | + | − |
| Capitalist development | High | | England | | | | |
| | Low | Rome, Southern Europe | | Roman Catholic countries | | Italy France | |

Weber formulates the astounding counter-thesis to Sombart's that he has hinted at before: Far from the idea of a calling being rational, it is *irrational* from the standpoint of purely eudaemonistic self-interest, and yet it is one of the most characteristic elements of capitalistic culture. Hence

> we are here particularly interested in the origin of precisely the irrational element which lies in this, as in every conception of a calling. (p. 39)

Weber goes on to show that the concept of a calling, both the meaning of the word and the idea it contained, was a product of the Reformation. It had not existed in antiquity nor among the predominantly Catholic peoples. Unquestionably new was the valuation and emphasis of "the fulfillment of duty in the worldly affairs as the highest form of moral activity which the individual could assume" (p. 40).

The key question is the *practical* significance of the new moral justification of worldly activity. Luther cannot be claimed for the spirit of capitalism, but his concept of calling lent itself to different interpretations, depending on the *religious* evolution in different Protestant churches.[8]

---

8. I have argued that Weber introduces a social mutant as a key feature of his model construction. The question then arises why and how the particular theological construction of Calvinism arose. Here it seems that Weber hints at a *cognitive model*, in which the working out of *internal consistence* is at the heart of the argument. Weber writes about the development of the doctrine of predestination:

> With Calvin the process was just the opposite [from that of Luther]; the significance of the doctrine for him increased, perceptibly in the course of his polemical controversies with theological opponents. It is not fully developed until the third edition of his *Institutes*, and only gained its position of central prominence after his death in the great struggles which the Synods of Dordrecht and Westminster sought to put an end to. With Calvin the *decretum horrible* is derived not, as with Luther, from religious experience, but from the logical necessity of his thought; therefore its importance increases with every increase in the logical consistency of that religious thought. (p. 51)

In Weber's specific argument there is a *model for change of actors* based on logical or cognitive consistency (that is, what actors can and do believe), and he connects the working out of consistency to a social process, namely intellectual conflict or polemics.

Luther's interpretation was traditionalistic. Individuals should remain in their preordained stations, accept things as they were, and obey authority. Thus the ethical result of Lutheranism for worldly effort was at best questionable and probably negative. Hence one must look into other forms of Protestantism where a different relation between religious motivation and practical action can be found.

Weber finds illustrated what he seeks in Milton's *Paradise Lost*, a powerful expression of the Puritan's acceptance of and attention to his life in this world as a task. But he wants to replace this literary interpretation "by a somewhat more precise logical formulation" (p 45). It is then not enough to look at the *moral practice* of other Protestant sects. Such practices must be tied to their ideas about afterlife, which overshadowed everything else. The crux here is not the official doctrine

> rather something entirely different: the influence of those psychological sanctions which originated in religious belief and the practice of religion, gave direction to practical conduct and held the individual to it. Now these sanctions were to a large extent derived from the peculiarities of the religious ideas behind them. (p. 48–9)

What Weber is after is the *psychologic*: the mental make-up that translates devotion into action. This can only be done by constructing a model or an ideal type of the religious ideas "in their most consistent and logical forms" (p. 49).

The essential difference between Calvinism and Lutheranism or Catholicism is the doctrine of predestination, which in the words of the Westminster confession of 1647 means that "some men and angels are predestinated unto everlasting life, and others foreordained to everlasting death." This God has done "out of His mere free grace and love, without any foresight of faith or good works, or perseverance in either of them" (p. 50). Hence grace and salvation are the result of God's supreme power. It cannot be attributed to or influenced by personal worth.

> God's grace is, since His decrees cannot change, as impossible for those to whom He has granted it to lose as it is unattainable for those to whom He has denied it. (p. 52)

The sacraments ordained by God must be scrupulously observed, not to attain grace, but as the external manifestation of faith. What was most important to humanity—salvation or damnation—was hence beyond the power of the church, sacraments, priests, or individuals themselves by faith or deeds. There were no magical means whatever of attaining the grace of God.

The decisive problem in the doctrine of predestination, which sooner or later "must have arisen for every true believer and have forced all other interests into the background," was the question, "Am I one of the elect?" (p. 55). According to the doctrine there were no means of certitude, either from faith or action. The elect are God's invisible church—invisible also to the elect—but this attitude was impossible for the mass of ordinary people.

> For them the *certitudo salutis* in the sense of recognizability of the state of grace necessarily became of absolutely dominant importance. So, whenever the doctrine of predestination was held, the question could not be suppressed whether there were any infallible criteria by which membership in the *electi* could be known. (p. 56)

The key question is: What could the Calvinists know, in their anguish caused by the doctrine of predestination? First, it was

> held to be an absolute duty to consider oneself of the chosen, and to combat all doubts as temptations of the devil, since lack of self-confidence is the result of insufficient faith, hence imperfect grace. (p. 56)

If we translate this into a probability statement,[9] it says that the elect were characterized by a high degree of assurance or conviction of their salvation, that is,

$$P\ [\text{Self-confidence/Elect}] = \text{Very High} \qquad (1)$$

and

$$P\ [\text{Doubt/Doomed}] = \text{Very High} \qquad (2)$$

This also had an external manifestation, in that the doomed could be identified among those not belonging to the church:

> Whoever kept away from the true Church could never belong to God's chosen band, nevertheless the membership of the external Church included the doomed. (p. 52)[1]

In other words:

$$P\ [\text{Belong to the Church/Elect}] = 1 \qquad (3)$$

and

$$P\ [\text{Belong to the Church/Doomed}] > 0 \qquad (4)$$

---

9. Weber was well aware of probability theory and used its logic on many occasions. Perhaps most well known is his definition of power as the "probability that a person is in a position to carry out his will, despite resistance," and so on (see Lazarsfeld and Oberschall 1965). I am not arguing here that Weber is explicitly using conditional probabilities, but that the *logic* of his argument is cast in these terms.
1. See also p. 54 for "the necessity of belonging to the true Church for salvation."

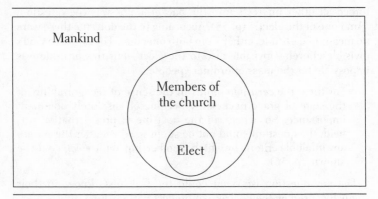

Figure 1: Venn-diagram illustrating mankind, members of the church, and the elect.

It is also known that the "world exists to serve the glorification of God and for that purpose alone" (p. 54). A member of the elect is in this world only to increase God's glory by "fulfilling His commandments to the best of his ability" (p. 54). Labor in a calling is *in majorem gloriam Dei*, not as for Luther as an expression of brotherly love (pp. 40, 54). Good works were not only willed by God, they were the works of God through the elect—and through the elect as they worked in mundane callings, not in monastic seclusion from the world.[2] God wills that *social life be organized* according to his commandments, which is secured by shared labor in a calling and expressed in the fulfillment of daily tasks and service in the interest of the rational organization of society (p. 54), and "unwillingness to work is symptomatic of the lack of grace" (p. 83). In other words:

$$P\,[\text{Ascetic worldly activity/Elect}] = 1 \tag{5}$$

and

$$P\,[\text{Unwillingness to work/Doomed}] = 1 \tag{6}$$

Weber's analysis of Calvinist doctrines thus has the logical character of a set of conditional probability statements. The crux is: How are the statements translated into a model of motivation?

---

2. Weber writes: "The only way of living acceptably to God was not to surpass worldly morality in monastic asceticism, but solely through the fulfillment of the obligations imposed upon the individual by his position in the world. That was his calling" (p. 40). Compare his remarks on monastic ascetism.

This happens by a *psychological reversal of the conditional proba-bility statements*. First, if none of the elect were outside the true church, the probability of being one of the elect would be higher if one belonged to the church. This can be illustrated by a Venn-diagram in Figure 1, or, as a probability statement:

$$P\,[\text{Elect/Church}] > P\,[\text{Elect}] \tag{7}$$

Hence belonging should give some assurance and move people to join.[3] However, for Weber the central problem is not the formation of denominational communities nor the development of the official doctrines. It was not this that gave Calvinism the power that it pos-sessed. Weber's concern is the members of the church in acute psy-chological need of a sign of grace. In practical pastoral work, the anguish caused by the doctrine of predestination had to be met. Gradually the doctrines of Calvin were modified, and a concept of proof of faith through works appeared. In the Calvinist formation of communities outside of the church organizations ordained by God, the belief that the Christian

> proved his state of grace *in majorem Dei gloriam* was decisive, and a sharp condemnation of idolatry of the flesh and of all depend-ence on personal relations to other men was bound unperceived to direct this energy into the field of objective (impersonal) activ-ity. (p. 119n, n. 34).

From the knowledge that the elect engaged in ascetic worldly activ-ity was inferred that asceticism was a sign of salvation.

> Only one of the elect really has the *fides efficax*, only he is able by virtue of his rebirth (*regeneratio*) and the resulting sanctifi-cation (*sanctificatio*) of his whole life, to augment the glory of God by real, and not merely apparent, good works. It was through the consciousness that his conduct, at least in its fundamental char-acter and constant ideal (*propositum obaedientiae*), rested on a power within himself working for the glory of God; that it is not only willed of God but rather done by God that he attained the highest good towards which this religion strove, the certainty of salvation. (p. 58)

3. Although Weber does not discuss this point much, it should have a recruitment effect for Calvinism:
> It is tempting to refer to the undoubted importance for the social character of the Reformed Christianity of the necessity for salvation, following from the Calvinist idea of incorporation into the body of Christ . . . of reception into a community of conforming to the divine prescriptions. (p. 119n, n. 34)

Good works were not a means of salvation, but a sign of election. Thus:

$$P \text{ [Elect/Ascetic worldly activity]} = \text{High} \qquad (8)$$

This is the reversal of the conditional probability statement in inequality 5 above, which gives the psychological impetus for ascetic worldly activity.

If one is to put the argument about the psychological reversal in its "most consistent and logical form"—as was Weber's explicit aim—this can be done in terms of Bayes's law:

$$P \text{ [Elect/Ascetic]} = \frac{P \text{ [Elect]} P \text{ [Ascetic/Elect]}}{P \text{ [Elect]} P \text{ [Ascetic/Elect]} + P \text{ [Doomed]} P \text{ [Ascetic/Doomed]}} \qquad (9)$$

In Bayesian terminology the P[Elect] and P[Doomed] are called the *prior* probabilities and P[Elect/Ascetic] is called the *posterior* probability. In this case it so happens that the posterior probability has a double meaning: It is the probability or confidence the Calvinists can have that they are among those attaining salvation after resurrection. And it can be shown in a Venn-diagram like the one in Figure 1 or by substituting Equation 5 into 9 that

$$P \text{ [Elect/Ascetic]} > P \text{ [Elect]} \qquad (10)$$

That this is the logic of the argument, with faith as an intervening variable, comes out clearly in the following passage:

> The community of the elect with their God could only take place and be perceptible to them in that God worked (*operatur*) through them and that they were conscious of it. That is, their action originated from the faith caused by God's grace, and this faith in turn justified itself by the quality of that action (p. 57). . . . Faith had to be proved by its objective results in order to provide a firm foundation for the *certitudo salutis*. (p. 58)

This is the psychological sanction originating in religious belief and practice that gave a direction to practical conduct and held the individuals to it. "For them the *certitudo salutis* in the sense of recognizability of the state of grace became of absolute dominant importance" (p. 56). And in practical pastoral work

> in order to attain that self-confidence intense worldly activity is recommended as the most suitable means. It and it alone disperses religious doubts and gives the certainty of grace. (p. 57)

The reversed probability is turned into a motive for moral action. The causal structure of this argument is depicted in Figure 2. Good works

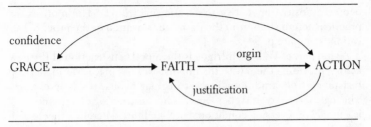

Figure 2: Causal structure of Weber's motivational argument.

were not a means of attaining salvation, but an indispensable sign that salvation was attained. At the same time this action—choosing to lead a systematically rationalized life—was under the control of individuals, and hence the *certitudo salutis* or subjective probability of salvation was something individuals could create in themselves.

> In practice this means that God helps those who help themselves. Thus the Calvinist, as it is sometimes put, himself creates his own salvation, or, as would be more correct, the conviction of it. But this creation cannot, as in Catholicism, consist in a gradual accumulation of individual good works to one's credit, but rather in a systematic self-control which at every moment stands before the inexorable alternative, chosen or damned. (p. 58)

This system of thought was very different from Catholicism, where an individual's life is seen as a succession of acts, some of which could be atoned and forgiven, whereas others could be accumulated as a sort of insurance. In contrast to such a *succession*, the Calvinists looked upon life with good works in a calling as a unified *system*. Whereas Catholicism thought in terms of a balance, Puritanism thought in terms of the definite alternative of salvation or damnation held for a life as a whole (p. 125n, n. 94). This principle implied methodological control over the whole person, and in contrast to medieval asceticism, it transformed asceticism to activity within the world (p. 61). While ascetic monasticism had driven individuals farther from everyday life, Protestant asceticism drove them into mundane activities.

Weber wanted to pinpoint the psychological sanctions for worldly activity. We have seen that the structure of the argument is that of reversing the conditional probabilities of the Calvinist doctrine (how faith and action depends on election) into conditional probabilities for salvation (how the certainty of being in the elect depends on action justifying faith). These probabilities were transformed into imperatives for a systematic life in worldly action, a "transformation of asceticism to activity within the world" (p. 61). The necessity of proving one's faith in worldly activity "gave the broader groups of religiously inclined people a positive incentive to asceticism" (p. 62). The motives for practical action stem from the desire for salvation or the proof of salvation (compare p. 94).

A vital part of Weber's intrigue is the moral construction of the new actors, providing them with the impulse to work in this world, defying resistance from traditionalists set in their habits, resisting change. The logical archetype Weber employs in constructing their psychology is a model of reversing conditional probabilities, whereby a theological cognition is inverted into a passion for action. Their understanding of the hereafter is transposed into a fervor for changing this world.

## The Accomplices

Weber explicitly rejects an approach in which the objective social institutions of the older Protestant churches and their ethical influences are used to explain the change in conduct. Rather than using authoritarian ecclesiastical regimentation that imposes external conformity, his research strategy is to study the practical results of subjective adoption of an ascetic faith and the moral discipline of voluntary submission (p. 79). That is, rather than studying the psychological impacts of institutional arrangements, he studies the institutional impacts of psychological make-ups. Change in the social structure is analyzed as the *result* of the conduct of a new type of actors.

Weber started with the Calvinists, because they provided in the purest form the idea of proof of grace as the psychological basis for a rational morality. But Calvinism influenced other ascetic movements and was imitated or used as a source of inspiration (p. 66). Its theological ideas diffused to wider groups.

Pietism did not have the iron consistency of Calvinism, nevertheless it showed "the penetration of methodically controlled and supervised, and thus of ascetic, conduct into the non-Calvinist denominations" (p. 68). Weber suggests that the greater emotionalism of Pietism led to social differentiation in religious affiliation:

> We may say that the virtues favoured by Pietism were more those on the one hand of the faithful official, clerk, labourer, or domestic worker, and on the other hand of predominantly patriarchal employer with a pious condescension. . . . Calvinism, in comparison, appears to be more closely related to the hard legalism and the active enterprise of bourgeois-capitalistic entrepreneurs. (p. 72)

Methodism also was weaker in consistency than Calvinism, but nevertheless stressed conduct as a sign of rebirth and later as a means of ascertaining true conversion.

Finally, Baptism provided a second independent source of Protestant asceticism, because it rested on a doctrine that differed in principle from the Calvinistic doctrine (p. 75). It rejected predestination, and "the peculiarly rational character of Baptist morality rested psychologically above all on the idea of expectant waiting for the Spirit to descend" (p. 77). But the signs of being reborn lay in the rationalization of one's personal life, and

> the radical elimination of magic from the world allowed no other psychological course than the practice of worldly asceticism. . . . The strict morality of the Baptists had turned in practice into the path prepared by the Calvinistic ethic. (p. 78)

The Baptist sects (including Mennonites and Quakers) also had a weaker conception of calling than did Calvinism. However, the interest in economic occupations was strengthened by the refusal to accept office in the service of the state and by the antagonism to any sort of aristocratic way of life.

The common point for all of the denominations was the conception of the religious state of grace marking its possessor "from the degradation of the flesh, from the world" (p. 80). Grace was obtained by different *means*, but *proof* was possible only by a specific type of conduct: rational planning of the whole of one's life as asceticism within this world (p. 80 f.).

This line of argument has considerable interest, as it shows that Weber was well aware that religious denominations with differences either in strength or type of doctrine could serve as *functional alternatives* (Merton 1968) in justifying and producing ascetic conduct in this world. Yet another methodological archetype was expertly put to use.

## The Prisoners of Success

Weber then worked out the social consequences of the Protestant ethic. The same method was used as before: He constructed a model from the most stylized examples, now treating Protestantism or Puritanism as a single whole.

For the Puritan, worldly activity serves to increase the glory of God, and waste of time is a sin as well as a sign of lack of grace: "every hour lost is lost to labour for the glory of God" (p. 82). It not only serves as a defense against temptations, but is the end of life. Methodological exercise in ascetic virtue is a proof of the state of grace.

Coleman (1986) has argued that the main intellectual hurdle both for empirical research and for theory that treats macrolevel relations via methodological individualism is to move from the assumptions about individuals to the resulting social structure.

That is, the main challenge is to provide an argument that shows how individuals generate a social system, or, put differently, how micromotives translate into macroeffects. Coleman argues that Weber fails on this point:

> [Weber] shows through illustration the effect of Protestant doctrine [macro level] on individual values [micro level] and, again through illustration, the effect of these values on individual orientations to economic behavior. What he fails to show is how these individual values [micro level] combined to produce the structure of economic organization that we call capitalism [macro level] (if in fact they did in combination produce this effect). (Coleman 1986, 1323)

I have argued that Weber not only demonstrates the effect of doctrine on values and their impact in turn on economic behavior: Weber constructs a model to provide the psycho-logic at the individual level.[4] I now want to show that Coleman's critique of Weber is misplaced, as Weber also carefully constructs a socio-logic whereby the ascetic Protestants jointly produce a new social structure.[5]

Weber's point of departure is not only methodological individualism, but social isolation as well. In his chapter on the religious foundations of worldly asceticism, Weber underlines the unprecedented inner loneliness of the single individual that the doctrine of predestination produced, and states that it fostered service in the interest of the rational organization of the social environment (p. 55). It entailed a break with traditionalism, but also represented a breach with traditional brotherly love. One could trust no one but God, and this spiritual isolation tended "to tear the individual away from the close ties with which he is bound to this world" (p. 54). One's neighbor's sins were not looked upon with sympathetic understanding, but with "hatred and contempt for him as an enemy of God as bearing the signs of eternal damnation" (p. 62). The argument, in short, is that the

---

4. Weber writes:

 The Calvinist faith is one of the many examples in the history of religions of the relation between the logical and the psychological consequences for the practical religious attitude to be derived from religious ideas. Fatalism is, of course, the only logical consequence of predestination. But on account of the idea of proof, the result was precisely the opposite. (p. 124, n. 486)

 The active energies of the elect, liberated by the doctrine of predestination, thus flowed into the struggle to rationalize the world.

 Later Weber also points to the "difference between mere ethical theories and the creation of psychological sanctions with a religious background for certain kinds of conduct" (p. 142, n. 435). And "the Protestant idea of the calling in effect placed the most serious enthusiasts for asceticism in the service of capitalist acquisition" (p. 143, n. 446).

 However, to make the move to the macro level, we have to account for how capitalist acquisitiveness produces a capitalist system. This is the question now to be addressed.

5. As stated before, I do not address the extent to which the model is sufficiently tested empirically—the concern here is with the chain of logical archetypes.

doctrine changed the Calvinists' orientation from social relations to detached, isolated yet devout, work in a calling.

However, the usefulness of a calling had somehow to be *measured*. God had designed the universe to serve

> the utility of the human race. This makes labour in the service of impersonal social usefulness appear to promote the glory of God and hence to be willed by Him. (p. 55)

Morally the (divine) usefulness could be measured

> in terms of the importance of the goods produced in it for the community. But a further, and, above all, in practice the most important, criterion is found in private profitableness. (p. 85)

This is a point that Weber alludes to in several places. On the one hand, one's own state of grace could be known by *comparing* the condition of one's own soul with that of the elect, for instance, the patriarchs (p. 58). But the Puritans also sought "to attain and continually to renew" self-confidence "in restless and successful work at a calling" (p. 71). For the Pietist A. H. Francke it was undeniable that "God Himself blessed His chosen ones through the success of their labours" (p. 69). And even Zinzendorf expressed the opinion that "even though man himself could not, others could know his state of grace by his conduct" (p. 70). In short, "success reveals the blessings of God" (p. 145, n. 462).

Two very important consequences follow. First, success in a calling is measured in *relative* terms: Even if one need not *care* for one's sinful neighbors, one had to *compare* oneself to them. If appraisal of grace was based on success and the elect were to gain confidence in their calling, they not only had to equal the results of ordinary people, the elect had to outdo them. Christians are to increase the glory of God by fulfilling his commandments to the best of their ability.

> But God requires *social achievement* [emphasized here] of the Christian because He wills that social life shall be organized according to His commandments, in accordance with that purpose. (pp. 91–92)

He had, so to speak, to prove that he was "holier than thou."[6]

---

6. In 1906 Weber wrote "The Protestant Sects and the Spirit of Capitalism" and included it next to *The Protestant Ethic* in the 1920 version of his collected essays in the sociology of religion. Here the comparative aspect of success comes out quite clearly, at the same time that Weber seems to stress the social embedding of the religious motivation more than in *The Protestant Ethic*:

> The member of the sect (or conventicle) had to have qualities of a certain kind in order to enter the community circle. Being endowed with these qualities was important for the development of rational modern capitalism. . . . In order to *hold his own* [italics added] in this circle, the member had to *prove* repeatedly that he was endowed with these qualities. They were constantly and continuously bred in him. For like his bliss [salvation] in the

Second, those who the doctrine of predestination had put in a position of unprecedented isolation not only had continually to assess their success relative to others, but also to do so in terms of economic achievement. Thereby the individualistic Protestants were, so to speak, connected behind their backs. Accomplishment was measured by private profitableness. The market therefore united the people whom theology had separated. They were not so much *isolates* as *rivals* in a market where they made their relative fortunes. A social and charitable relation to one's fellow person was replaced by a distributive and competitive one. Weber explains succinctly how the individual values combined to produce a new structure of economic organization, in his article "The Protestant Sects and the Spirit of Capitalism." In it, he compares medieval guilds and the Protestant sects:

> The capitalist success of a guild member undermined the spirit of the guild—as happened in England and France—and hence capitalistic success was shunned. But the capitalist success of the sect brother, if legally attained, was proof of his worth and of his state of grace, and it raised the prestige and the propaganda chances of the sect. . . . The premiums were placed on "proving" oneself before God in the sense of attaining salvation—which is found in *all* Puritan denominations—and proving oneself before men in the sense of holding one's own within the Puritan sects. (Gerth and Mills 1946, 321 ff.)[7]

---

beyond, his whole social existence in the here and now, depended on his "proving" himself. . . . According to all experience there is no stronger means of breeding traits than through the necessity of holding one's own in one's circle of associates. The continuous and unobtrusive ethical discipline of the sects was therefore, related to authoritarian church discipline as rational breeding and selection are related to ordering and forbidding. . . . The Puritan sects put the most powerful individual Interest of social self-esteem in the service of this breeding of traits. Hence *individual* motives and personal self-interests were also placed in the service of maintaining and propagating the "bourgeois" Puritan ethic, with all its ramifications. This is absolutely decisive for its penetrating and for its powerful effect. To repeat, it is not the ethical *doctrine* of a religion, but that form of ethical conduct upon which *premiums* are placed that matters. . . . The premiums were placed upon "proving" oneself before God in the sense of attaining salvation—which is found in *all* Puritan denominations—and "proving" oneself socially before men in the sense of "holding one's own within the Puritan sects." (Gerth and Mills 1946, p. 320 f.)
Gianfranco Poggi (1983, 78) summarizes Weber's argument in the following way:
As a grouping of religious *virtuosi* intent on proving themselves to one another, and on jointly witnessing their righteousness to outsiders, the sect alimented in members a strong feeling of individuality, an aversion from excessive mutual reliance. Each had to stand on his own feet, as an exemplar of the validity of the sect's distinctive moral design for a living. Each had to display his moral worth *von innen heraus*, demonstrate his piety and saintliness in his everyday activity.
7.  Weber precedes this quote by the following statement: "The guild united members of the same occupation; hence it united *competitors*. It did so in order to limit competition as well as the rational striving for profit which operated through competition. . . . The sect controlled and regulated the members' conduct *exclusively* in the sense of formal *righteousness* and methodological asceticism. It was devoid of the purpose of a material subsistence policy which handicapped an expansion of the rational striving for profit."

Hence the Protestants were caught by their own logic when it was translated into the real world: To hold their own, to keep their relative position, they forced each other to work harder. In effect they set up a prisoner's dilemma for themselves by taking not a good day's work, but the relative fruits of labor in a calling as a measure of success.

Since capital accumulated but not capital consumed can be measured, it was only logical that asceticism "turned with all its force against one thing: the spontaneous enjoyment of life and all it had to offer" (p. 87). Hence assets also could serve as a relative measure of success. Idleness, spontaneous enjoyment, and waste were the cardinal sins, not acquisition. This had the "psychological effect of freeing the acquisition of goods from the inhibitions of traditionalistic ethic" (p. 90). Acquisition was not only legalized, but directly willed by God.

The social outcome of the competitive structure imposed by the religiously based individual asceticism was capital accumulation. The double-barreled effect of ascetic Protestantism then, was to join the compulsion to work to the obligation to reinvest its output. This is illustrated in Table 11. In this respect it was the most important and only consistent influence toward rational bourgeois life (p. 91).

But the prisoner's dilemma that the Protestants established by their particular comparative ethic not only captured its creators. By their logic of relative success they had *changed the social structure* in a decisive way because it also entrapped all others:

> The Puritan wanted to work in a calling; we are forced to do so. For when asceticism was carried out of the monastic cells into everyday life, and began to dominate worldly morality, it did its part in building the tremendous cosmos of the modern economic order. This order is now bound to the technical and economic conditions of machine production which today determine the lives of all individuals who are born into this mechanism, not only those who are directly concerned with economic acquisition, with irresistible force. (p. 95–96)

TABLE 11
Capital Accumulation as a Result of Acquisitive Activity
and Limitation on Consumption

|  |  | Limitation of consumption | |
|---|---|---|---|
|  |  | Yes | No |
| Acquisitive activity | Yes | Protestant ethic → accumulation |  |
|  | No |  |  |

Indeed, Weber has an equally strong statement to the same effect in his second chapter:

> The capitalistic economy of the present day is an immense cosmos into which the individual is born, and which presents itself to him, at least as an individual, as an unalterable order of things in which he must live. It forces the individual, in so far as he is involved in the system of market relationships, to conform to capitalistic rules of action. The manufacturer who in the long run acts counter to these norms, will just as inevitably be eliminated from the economic scene as the worker who cannot or will not adapt himself to them will be thrown into the street without a job.

> Thus the capitalism of today, which has come to dominate economic life, educates and selects the economic subjects which it needs through a process of economic survival of the fittest. (p. 26)

By measuring success in relative terms, the Puritans established a prisoner's dilemma in which they not only ambushed themselves and ensnared non-Puritans. In addition, once it had been socially established, it in turn liberated capitalism from its connection to the Puritans' special *Weltanschauung*. It no longer needed the support of any religious forces:

> Whoever does not adapt his manner of life to the conditions of capitalistic success must go under. But these are phenomena of a time in which modern capitalism has become dominant and has become emancipated from its old supports. (p. 36)[8]

Having explained the generation of the capitalist system, he takes *competition to be the source of its own reproduction*. The paradox is that the religious belief that set men free from restraints on acquisitive activity in turn liberated the resulting economic system from that belief.

However, Weber goes further than employing the logical archetype of a prisoner's dilemma. He also strings together a set of logical elements that taken together provide a nice example of functional analysis.

Elster (1979, 28 f.) has criticized this mode of analysis. From Merton's classic essay on manifest and latent functions (reprinted in 1968) and Stinchcombe's (1968) formalization, Elster identifies a particular subtype as functional explanations proper. In Elster's analysis, an institution or a behavioral pattern X is explained by its function Y for a group B if and only if

8. See also footnote 115, p. 151: "Capitalism at the time of its development needed labourers who were available for economic exploitation for conscience' sake. Today it is in the saddle, and hence able to force people to labour without transcendental sanctions."

(1) Y is an *effect* of X;
(2) Y is *beneficial* for B;
(3) Y is *unintended* by the actors producing X;
(4) Y (or at least the causal relationship between X and Y) is *unrecognized* by the actors in B;
(5) Y maintains X by a *causal feedback* loop passing through B.

It should be pointed out that in the general analytical case there is another group (A) that is not mentioned by Elster. Group A consists of the actors producing X, and it may or may not be identical to B. The logic of these requirements is represented in Figure 3. It should also be added to Elster's argument that the feedback from Y to X through B has to work through A by either affecting A's *motives* or A's *options*. If we transpose Weber's argument into this structure, we get Figure 4. Not only can Weber's argument be transposed into these terms, but it appears that this is the way he actually thought.

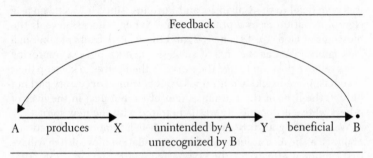

Figure 3: The logical structure of functional analysis.

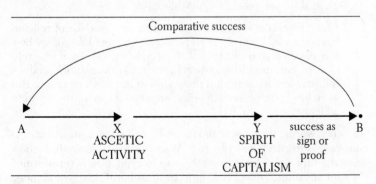

Figure 4: The functional structure of Weber's argument.

By a psychological reversal, the doctrine of predestination made the Calvinists seek a calling in ascetic worldly activity. Unintended and unrecognized by the Calvinists, this produced the spirit of capitalism.

> But it is not to be understood that we expect to find any of the founders or representatives of these religious movements [Calvinists and Puritan sects] considering the promotion of what we have called the spirit of capitalism as in any sense the end of his life-work. . . . The salvation of the soul and that alone was at the center of their life and work. Their ethical ideals and the practical results of their doctrines were all based on that alone, and were the consequence of purely religious motives. We shall thus have to admit that the cultural consequences of the Reformation were to a great extent, perhaps in the particular aspects we are dealing predominantly, unforeseen and even unwished for results of the labours of the reformers. They were often far removed from or even in contradiction to all that they themselves thought to attain. (p. 45)

But the wealth that asceticism and the spirit of capitalism generated was beneficial to the Calvinists and Puritans, since it was taken as a sign of salvation or as a proof of grace. When "success reveals the blessings of God" (p. 145, n. 462) and the relative fruits of labor in a calling are taken as the sign of success, then keeping or improving one's relative position forced the Puritans themselves to keep up their asceticism (feedback). Continuous work became a necessary part not only in the lives of the Puritans themselves, but also in the lives of others whose economic life was penetrated with the new spirit.

Weber even goes further than Elster's delimitation of functional analysis, as he also argues that the accumulation of wealth may have dysfunctional effects for the system (compare Merton 1968, 105) The "Puritanical ideals tended to give way under pressure from the temptations of wealth, as the Puritans themselves knew very well" (p. 92). And Weber quotes John Wesley:

> I fear, wherever riches have increased, the essence of religion has decreased in the same proportion. Therefore I do not see how it is possible, in the nature of things, for any revival of true religion to continue long. For religion must necessarily produce industry and frugality, but these cannot but produce riches. But as riches increase, so will pride, anger, and love of the world in all its branches. (p. 92)

In other words, the effects produced by the system undermine its sources, as illustrated in Figure 5. Weber uses this analysis to show how the Protestant ethic that gives rise to capitalism is transformed by capitalism into sober economic virtue and utilitarian worldliness, the "spirit of capitalism."

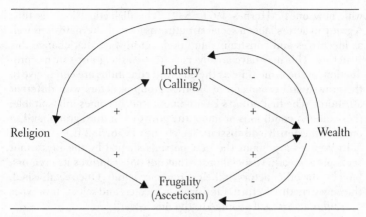

Figure 5: The dysfunctional effects of wealth.

The new structure transforms the original innovators, and they are superseded by new bourgeoisie and later by modern workers. Here Weber provides a nice example of *ideology analysis:* Those parts of the religious doctrine that can justify the social practice and legitimate the economic result are selected, retained, and propagated because they are useful for the new bourgeoisie. That is, instead of religion motivating the actions, it provides a utilitarian rationalization for the actions of the ruling group. Rather than spurring labor in the service of God, it sanctifies actions in the service of self. Ascetic literature is saturated with the idea of faithful labor, an idea that in secularized form entered theories of the productivity associated with low wages. Protestant asceticism provided a new force of decisive effectiveness for both of the new types of actors, modern workers and entrepreneurs:

> the psychological sanction of it through the conception of this labour as a calling, as the best, and often in the last analysis the only means of attaining certainty of grace. And on the other hand it legalized the exploitation of this specific willingness to work, in that it also interpreted the employer's business activity as a calling. . . . The treatment of labour as a calling became as characteristic of the modern worker as the corresponding attitude towards acquisition of the business man. (p. 94)

In this way the spirit of capitalism and rational conduct in a calling was born from the Protestant ethic (compare p. 95).

Hence the structure of Weber's argument also is *dialectical* in the sense of "systems which while they destroy themselves are pregnant

with new ones" (Hernes 1976, 532). The dialectical logic is this:
A group of actors faces a social structure as a set of alternatives as well
as incentives and constraints and then act in ways that change this
structure. This may have an adverse effect on the group's own reproduction, at the same time as the changed conditions are conducive to
the growth and expansion of another group of actors with different
attributes. The first group's environment thus becomes inhospitable;
these altered conditions promote the growth of a third group, and so
on (for an extensive discussion, see Hernes 1976, 532 ff.).

In Weber's argument the new persons shaped by the Protestant
sects produce a new social order that not only captures its creators,
but also the other actors in their economic vicinity. Once established,
the new structure in turn transforms, educates, and selects new types
of *secular* actors well adapted to the new order.

## The Argument and the Evidence

Throughout Weber's exposition, one is struck by the tenuousness of
the empirical evidence he provides. He darts from country to country,
from century to century, and does not at all try to follow the spread
of capitalism from its source. He sometimes quotes historical records,
sometimes current statistics, and even resorts to synthetic history to
make his argument plausible.

Given the uneven nature of his evidence, it is not surprising that
*The Protestant Ethic* has been demolished time after time. Yet it rises
from the ashes for another cycle of fresh intellectual attraction, what
Merton (1984) has identified as the "Phoenix phenomenon".

The question is why this happens, why resilience in the face of de-
molition? Merton has provided one answer. He argues that a part of
what he calls "the fallacy of the latest word . . . holds that a hypothesis or underlying theory is obviously to be abandoned as soon as it
appears to have been empirically falsified" (1984, 1108). Quoting
Imre Lakatos's distinction between "sophisticated" and "naive falsification," Merton argues that a theory is acceptable for sophisticated
falsification

> only if it has corroborated excess empirical evidence over its pre-
> decessor (or rival), that is, only if it leads to the discovery of new
> facts. . . . Contrary to naive falsificationism, *no experiment,
> experimental report, observation statement or well-corroborated
> low-level falsifying hypothesis alone can lead to falsification. There
> is no falsification before the emergence of a better theory.* (Merton
> 1984, 1109)

However, there may be another reason for the Phoenix phenomenon
found in the *two-tier logic of complex sociological and historical
explanations*.

The first is the *logic of argument*. Here the crucial point is that a complex sociological or historical explanation consists in the *sequencing of models*. That is, the explanation consists in linking a succession of more elementary models. This implies making specific assumptions about the types of actors involved, how they act and bring about change in the structure within which they move, and how this in turn affects them. Weber uses a wide range of such models, from different models of humanity to the selection effects of a prisoner's dilemma. He allows for men to be both ennobled and corrupted by the social structure and for the social structure to be both coercive and permissive of certain actions. Thus *in complex explanations elementary models serve as analytical modules*, sequenced together like a string of logical pearls. An explanation can be attacked or altered at this level, for example, by arguing that one can substitute a module with an alternative (for example, that Calvinism and Baptism, though doctrines differ in principle, produce the same effect on asceticism).

The second tier is *the logic of facts*. Here one must check whether each of the elementary models in the chain of argument holds empirically. In principle each logical module can be held against facts independent of the others, as when Weber takes as evidence of an ascetic ethic the attitudes of working women of his own time, or Milton's *Paradise Lost* as a powerful expression of the Puritan's stern attention to his afterlife in this world.

Jointly the two tiers can be depicted as "the centipede of scientific inference": The levels of explanation are the segments of elementary models logically linked together, and the levels of evidence are the tests of each segment by its empirical legs.

The main point is that a complex, logically sound explanation may stay very much alive even if it lacks or loses an empirical leg. Indeed, it may stand up even if many are lacerated or torn as long as the body of logical segments remains unscathed.

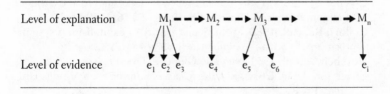

Figure 6: The "centipede of scientific inference." The Ms represent elementary models, the Es bits of evidence.

## The Verdict

The portrait of a Calvinist in *The Protestant Ethic* has much the same structure as the hero in a Greek drama: A new actor enters the scene, driven by irrational motives. He is a character under stress, potentially doomed to eternal damnation, searching for cues to salvation. This drives him to ascetic, rational actions as his proof of being among the elect, but the proof can only be obtained by performing relatively better than others.

From this flows the paradoxical systemic effects: The rational organization of society is the by-product of an irrational motive; material accumulation is the unintended result of ascetic efforts; liberated from traditionalism the actors are caught in a prisoner's dilemma; the creators are captured and in the end transformed by their own success when the religiously motivated actions generate wealth that corrupts their souls; and the system of motivation is delivered from the purposes that generated it. Behind the back of the actors, the cunning of history is at work.

It is not this overall design of the drama that provides the sole attraction of the work, but the particular dramatic devices that Weber deftly orchestrates in the argument as well. As in all drama we know them well as prototypes, but it is only when they are embodied in concrete persons caught in a surprising permutation of elementary events that they gain their dramatic appeal. In science the archetypes are logical metaphors with which we are familiar. Precisely for this reason they provide surprise and suspense when they are juxtaposed in original ways and implanted in concrete progressions. They constitute the driving motive forces connecting the sequence of events that transform the stage of action. The enduring allure of the story told in *The Protestant Ethic* lies in Weber's masterly command of the overall plot and the logical links among actions, outcomes, repercussions, and responses.

## References

Chayanov, A. V. 1966. *The theory of peasant economy*. Eds. Daniel Thorner, B. Kerblay, and R. E. F. Smith. Homewood, IL: Irwin.

Coleman, James S. 1986. Social theory, social research, and a theory of action. *American Journal of Sociology* 91 (6): 1309–35.

Collins, Randall. 1980. Weber's last theory of capitalism: A systematization. *American Sociological Review* 45 (6): 925–42.

Durkheim, Emil. 1951. *Suicide*. Glencoe: Free Press.

Elster, Jon. 1979. *Ulysses and the sirens*. Cambridge: Cambridge University Press.

Gerth, H. H., and C. Wright Mills. 1946. *From Max Weber: Essays in sociology*. Oxford: Oxford University Press.

Hernes, Gudmund. 1976. Structural change in social processes. *Journal of Sociology* 82 (3): 513–47.

Lazarsfeld, Paul, and Anthony R. Oberchall. 1965. Max Weber and empirical social research. *American Sociological Review* 30 (2): 185–99.

Marshall, Gordon. 1982. *In search of the spirit of capitalism*. London: Hutchinson.

McCloskey, Donald M. 1986. *The rhetoric of economics*. Madison, WI: Harvester Press.

Merton, Robert R. 1968. *Social theory and social structure*. Enlarged 3rd ed. Glencoe: Free Press.

———. 1984. The fallacy of the latest word: The case of "Pietism and science." *American Journal of Sociology* 89 (5): 1091–1121.

———. 1987. Three fragments from a sociologist's notebooks: Establishing the phenomenon, specified ignorance, and strategic research materials. *Annual Review of Sociology* 13: 1–28.

Poggi, Gianfranco. 1983. *Calvinism and the capitalist spirit*. Amherst: University of Massachusetts Press.

Riley, Mathilda. 1963. *Sociological research*. New York: Harcourt, Brace and World.

Stinchcombe, Arthur L. 1968. *Constructing social theories*. New York: Harcourt, Brace and World.

Weber, Max. 2008. *The Protestant ethic and the spirit of capitalism*, translated by Talcott Parsons. New York: Norton.

White, Hayden. 1975. *Metahistory. The historical imagination in nineteenth-century Europe*. Baltimore: Johns Hopkins Press.

# PETER BREINER

## Weber's *The Protestant Ethic* as Hypothetical Narrative of Original Accumulation[†]

This article addresses the 'hypothetical', 'self-referential' and 'constructed' nature of Weber's *The Protestant Ethic and the 'Spirit' of Capitalism*. In particular, I want to argue that the complaints of commentators that his account lacks empirical verification (Marshall, 1983: 66, 95, 115, 119) are misplaced. Weber's narrative in *The Protestant Ethic* does not function as an historical explanation of the origins of capitalism that can be tested against a body of facts.[1]

---

[†] Reproduced with permission from Peter Breiner, *Weber's* The Protestant Ethic *as Hypothetical Narrative of Original Accumulation*, copyright © 2005 by SAGE Publications, by permission of sage Publications Ltd.

[1]. Of course, the originality of *The Protestant Ethic* lies not in inquiring into the origins of capitalism, a mainstay of the Historical School of Economics (Hennis, 1988b; Loader, 2001;

Rather, it seeks to give a plausible account of how modern capitalism *could have* arisen, or, more accurately, how an agent motivated to rationally accumulate capital *could have* arisen so as to launch, as a byproduct of that agent's activity, a system of social relations that can accumulate capital without requiring an entrepreneurial type to move it along.[2] I also argue that the self-referential nature of Weber's concepts, especially of the Calvinist ethic and the capitalist 'spirit', is a strength, not a weakness of his account. Indeed, my argument here is that Weber saw the strength of his thesis to be precisely in its hypothetical and self-referential nature. To understand why one might read *The Protestant Ethic* in this way, I would like to read his work against two other hypothetical accounts of capitalist accumulation: that of Adam Smith and that of marginal utility theory, both of which will prove inadequate when compared to Weber's account.

## The Distinction between Genetic and Generic Concepts

Weber's *The Protestant Ethic* is perhaps the greatest example of how genetic concepts might show the inadequacies of generic concepts in political economy. Writing this work at virtually the same time as his famous 'Objectivity' essay, Weber uses it to demonstrate precisely the force of his ideal-typical approach to social inquiry in general and his defense of genetic historical concepts in particular (Poggi, 1983: 75). Indeed, so seamless is the overlap between his methodological strictures on the ideal type in the 'Objectivity' essay and those in *The Protestant Ethic* that one can say with some confidence that the latter is in part meant to carry out the program of the former.[3]

At the center of Weber's famous defense of the ideal-type is his criticism of the use of general concepts, especially in deductive theories of economics as practiced by marginal utility theory. Without going into a full discussion of this knotty question in Weber, I want merely to point to his strategy of argument for why deductive theories of economics fail should they claim to provide generic concepts and general laws applicable to all economies. Weber does not directly challenge the goal of deducing economic behavior from a simple psychological motive such as human acquisitiveness or a general maxim of conduct like the principle of marginal or final utility. Rather, he claims that such constructs are not what they purport to be. They are in fact, ideal-

---

Scaff, 1989: 21–3), but in turning historical economics into economic sociology (see Swedberg, 1998: 119–20).

2.  I rely here primarily on the 1905 version of *The Protestant Ethic* because in this version Weber puts emphasis on the 'origins' of rational capitalism while in the 1919 version he shifts his emphasis to the question of rationalization and disenchantment spawned by capitalism (see Beetham, 1987: 146). Citations are to the excellent new edition of Weber's early version translated and edited by Peter Baehr and Gordon C. Wells (Weber, 2002).

3.  In a footnote to his 'Rebuttal of the Critique of the "Spirit" of Capitalism,' Weber explicitly refers the reader to his 'Objectivity' article as clarification for why he uses ideal-type constructs such as 'capitalism' and 'spirit of capitalism' in *The Protestant Ethic* (2002: 263, 278).

types: concepts in which the distinctive features of some aspects of historical and cultural life are forged into an internally consistent construct. In producing such concepts, as Weber so famously put it, we engage in a 'one-sided accentuation' of what we take to be the unique features of a social relationship or culture so as to produce a utopia of that form in the true sense of the word: that is, this concept does not exist in reality (1949: 87–91). Nevertheless, it allows us to clarify and understand this reality in its uniqueness relative to other concepts from which we can draw similarities and contrasts. But what we find to be distinctive is itself related to the interests governing our inquiry and different interests will generate different complexes of ideal-types (1949: 91; 2002: 8–9). Not surprisingly, Weber finds marginal utility theory to be not a general theory of economic conduct, though it incorporates generic concepts like exchange, but in fact a genetic concept describing a perspective on the unique features of 'capitalist culture' and the behavior it seeks to cultivate (1949: 100, 91; 2002: 9). And this is true of all theories of political economy despite their generic claims.

Of course, we may want something more solid, susceptible to historical or empirical confirmation, when we engage in social inquiry. Weber responds with four powerful arguments for our inevitable reliance on the ideal-type. Firstly, he claims that as soon as we try to characterize any social phenomenon, make any stream of social action intelligible, we are compelled to use ideal-typical concepts. That is, whenever we seek to characterize historical or social phenomena by their common but distinctive traits, such as imperialism, capitalism, mercantilism, we consciously or not make use of such 'distorted' concepts. They are the means by which we make analytical distinctions within descriptions insofar as we want to focus attention on the distinctive differences between classes of phenomena (1949: 92).

This leads to the second claim, which seems a bit more controversial. To wit, since the ideal-type is not something that can be 'observed' in empirical reality (1949: 91), it can only provide us with a set of motivations and outcomes that are possible given already conceptually constructed antecedent conditions. Ideal-types are in effect imagined constructs of *what could have happened* to produce a certain outcome given 'these conditions': 'It is a matter of constructing relationships which our imagination accepts as plausibly motivated and hence as "objectively possible" and which appear as *adequate* from a nomological standpoint' (1949: 92). We should note the very careful vocabulary that Weber is using here: 'imagination', 'plausibly motivated', 'objectively possible' and 'adequate' with regard to law-like statements. Both the ideal-typical understanding of the self-understanding of agents or the social relations that they constitute and the explanation of their conduct are couched in a language of tentativeness. The notions of 'objectivity' and 'law-like generalizations' are connected to possibility in the sense that this is what we could plausibly expect given the internal relations between these beliefs or these social relations and these outcomes (see Weber, 2002: 122).

The reason why ideal-types must inevitably consist of imaginative constructs of possible outcomes has to do with a third claim: that the reality that these constructs capture is so intertwined that we can only grasp some small portion of this causal nexus by disentangling it through concepts and relating these concepts to one another. There is no capturing social or historical reality in its full multiplicity (Weber, 1949: 81, 84). Thus Weber's intensely contrasting types of agent and beliefs in *The Protestant Ethic* are meant to suggest possible streams of conduct within a causally intertwined reality rather than a representation of that reality itself (2002: 69).

This leads us finally to a fourth claim, which has proven perhaps to be the most controversial. Since ideal-types are utopias that synthesize distinctive features of a social phenomenon, they are not susceptible to confirmation or disconfirmation by reference to brute empirical data. They already contain the relevant data, albeit in a simplified and one-sided form. Therefore, if they fail to register some crucial feature of the historical activity being analyzed, the proper response is to point to a new set of features and relations that the previous set failed to account for and forge them into a set of ideal-types from a new perspective (Weber, 1949: 95). Thus Weber's ideal-types do not, as it were, represent a particular set of empirical facts out there. They provide possible histories.

What, then, are we to call these possible histories? In Weber's early writing on the Elbian rural laborers he refers to his work as providing 'developmental tendencies' (Scaff, 1989: 29; Weber, 1989: 158, 182), but I would like to refer to these histories as 'conceptual narratives', for what Weber provides in a work like *The Protestant Ethic* is not a history of rational capitalism, but a possible series of historical conjunctures understood as movements from one set of (ideal-typical) concepts – in this case, of justification of one's direction in life (*Lebensführung*) – to another (see Hennis, 1988a). In Weber's words, these types are 'indispensable' for 'expository purposes' (1949: 90, 94). These conceptual narratives are plausible accounts of the origins of a particular historical development or set of historical tendencies such as the formation of modern capitalism, but Weber does not argue that any one narrative is the only one possible.[4]

The advantage for Weber of narrating conceptually is that he neither has to produce a model that applies to all stated conditions of behavior, as in formal economics, nor does he need to simply give an

---

4. Even in his fiercest polemics against his opponents of *The Protestant Ethic*, such as Brentano and Sombart, he is ultimately defending the distinctions he draws in his ideal-types (2002: 344, 346–50).

historical description of a unique set of circumstances based on independent empirical evidence – as we have said, the concepts themselves already are distillations of the evidence one might use to support them. Rather, these conceptual narratives allow us – perhaps better put, ask of us – to suspend our demand for factual validation and instead give over to the stream of genetic concepts so that we might see where they take us in relating types of meaningful conduct to one another and its consequences.[5] For example, in *The Protestant Ethic*, Weber's accounts of Franklin, the first bourgeois entrepreneurs, Calvinism, Baxter and Puritanism synthesize the distinctiveness of various types that as a composite produce the rationally accumulating capitalist. But the connection among them that Weber will draw is not co-extensive with the multiple causes that might have produced Western capitalism (see Collins, 1986a). It captures instead the crucial features needed to solve a central problem in the formation of rational capitalism – its need for relentless accumulation.

### The Puzzle of 'Original' Accumulation

Weber's identification of social science with ideal-types as distorted, imaginative constructs of possible developments within a causally entangled history, and his use of them to construct conceptual narratives, is uniquely suited to solving a fundamental problem in economics whose solution evaded Adam Smith, marginal utility and, in a different way, even Marx: the famous problem of 'original' or 'primitive accumulation'. 'Original accumulation' or 'primitive accumulation' represented something of a mystery for classical political economy. For within political economy, generalizations regarding the steady (and limitless) pursuit of profits and the increased division of labor required there to be an original moment when capital would steadily be saved, invested and not consumed, and labor would be turned into a commodity to be bought for a wage. The problem for most classical political economists was that it was difficult to derive this moment from the routine functions of economic conduct. The tendential laws of political economy, especially on price formation, were not well suited to explain the conditions that had arisen to render these laws operative (see Perelman, 2000). Both Smith and marginalist economics sought to solve the problem by providing generic hypothetical accounts of 'original' accumulation. It is to the problem of these generic approaches that I would like to turn for the moment, for, as we shall see, the generic approach will lead to a rather complex form of question-begging that Weber's *Protestant Ethic* thesis, precisely

---

5. This is why Weber again and again repeats that the validity of this work and its success in capturing the influence of 'the capitalist spirit' will only be established once the investigation, that is, the conceptual narrative, is complete (2002: 7, 9, 48, 263).

because it is a provisional ideal-typical construct, can claim to resolve.

In *The Wealth of Nations*, Adam Smith offers two theories of capital accumulation (see Perelman 2000: 217–24). His first and most famous one views original accumulation of capital as flowing out of the division of labor. Smith, as is well known, claims that the division of labor generates increased wealth because, through specialization of production, the working person can produce more than she or he needs to live (1976: 5, 7, 9). But the problem for Smith is to explain where the division of labor itself comes from. Here he invokes his equally well-known 'propensity of human nature' to exchange one specialized good for another out of self-love. Thus self-interest drives the propensity to exchange one's surplus, which in turn expands the division of labor, producing a market that generates extra surplus, which in turn provides a further stimulus to advance one's own interest through exchange (1976: 17–18). The problem with this account is that the division of labor becomes a byproduct of the propensity to exchange out of self-interest, but exchange driven by self-interest in satisfying differential needs already assumes the existence of both the division of labor and an exchange economy that in tandem designate the social roles of the butcher, brewer and baker of his famous example (1976: 19). Indeed, Smith himself admits that exchange based on self-interest can only produce a steadily increasing surplus if a separate institution exists: 'the market' embedded in 'a commercial society' (1976: 19). Needless to say, the human propensity that drives the steady increase of surplus presupposes a society that will cultivate this motivation.

Smith offers a second theory that focuses specifically on capital accumulation distinct from the division of labor. Under this theory there is a class of individuals that store up a 'stock of goods between the moment of producing and selling goods'. But in an argument that seems to put the cart before the horse, Smith claims that this accumulation precedes the division of labor. The owner of this capital stock brings about the division of labor by hiring labor and machinery, and once this specialization of production and exchange is brought into being, each new surplus produced by deploying capital provides an added increment to be reinvested (1976: 291–2). By properly mixing the division of labor and machinery, the owner of capital stock can maintain a dynamic process of steady capital accumulation – expanding output with the same amount of work. But to succeed at this the owner of capital stock must constantly raise the proportion of productive labor – labor that produces added value – to unproductive labor that does not (1976: 351–2). The dilemma that the accumulator faces is that in wealthy countries, less and less of the aggregate profit goes into reinvestment and more into supporting unproductive labor

(1976: 356). So what can prevent the process of accumulation from dissipating into replacement costs and supporting unproductive labor?

To find an answer Smith must appeal to the inclination to practice parsimony: 'Capitals are increased by parsimony and diminished by prodigality and misconduct', and therefore 'parsimony, and not industry, is the immediate cause of the increase of capital' (1976: 358–9). Only the individual who saves and then invests by hiring more productive labor which in turn increases the amount of exchangeable value of productive inputs generates more capital over and against revenue that is used for immediate consumption. But, of course, this explanation for sustained capital accumulation tends to beg the question regarding the source of capital: namely why should we be inclined to accumulate, or, more precisely, where do individuals inclined to accumulate capital come from? Smith answers by positing two types of individual character: the 'frugal man' who engages in productive labor by reinvesting his gains, and the prodigal who 'pays the wages of idleness with whose funds which the frugality of his forefathers had, as it were, consecrated to the maintenance of industry' (1976: 359–60). He then proposes that the former is moved by a general tendency built into human inclinations while the latter represents a deviation: 'the principle which prompts to save, is the desire of bettering our condition, a desire which, though generally calm and dispassionate, comes with us from the womb, and never leaves us till we go into the grave' (1976: 362–3). Saving and accumulating are built into our passions. The problem with this solution is that it can only explain the lack of consistent capital accumulation by a series of blockages produced by the minority of prodigals who should indulge their passion to enjoy present advantages only for fleeting moments. Yet wherever he looks, Smith finds prodigal agents erecting barriers to the general inclination of moral psychology (1976: 363, 367). He has no satisfying explanation for this.

It would seem that under both of Smith's accounts, the moment of original accumulation would have had to occur as a condition of its occurrence. What we have, therefore, is a multiple begging of the question with regard to the motives to methodically accumulate capital.

The theory of marginal utility – so central to Weber's criticism of generic concepts in the social sciences – does even a worse job in explaining capital accumulation. Where classical political economy seeks a hypothetical, albeit generic, account of accumulation either in the division of labor or in the division of the passions between the prodigal and the thrifty classes, marginalist economics simply derives the relentless maximizing of profit as an attribute of a law governing all economic behavior: the famous law of final utility. Capital accumulation, in which the entrepreneur invests in inputs up to the last increment before s/he fails to get an increment of return, derives from consumption based on the last increment before the consumer switches to another item. So at least within the logic of the theory, there is in effect no original accumulation prior to consumption – indeed there should be no steadily rising profits at all (see Collins, 1986b; Schumpeter, 1993: 27–31). Among the marginalists with whom Weber was most intimately acquainted – in particular Carl Menger and Böhm-Bawerk of the Austrian school of marginalism – two explanations were offered for capital accumulation. Menger rejects Smith's abstinence theory of capital and instead defines capital into existence as simply command over quantities of economic goods of a higher order to be deployed in a future that is an ever more distant period of time – that is, capital goods are goods whose final increment is not exhausted in immediate consumption (Menger, 1950: 153, 155–6). Böhm-Bawerk seeks to flesh this out by invoking two disturbances in the adjustment of the marginal value of production to the marginal value of the product. The first disturbance occurs simply due to errors, accidents or laziness. However, this explains very little, because on this account profits occur haphazardly: to say unpredicted behavior may intervene to dislocate the adjustment of production to consumption is not to say very much about continuous profit. The second disturbance occurs because there is a time lag between an initial investment and the calculation of marginal profit. On this account, following Menger, the productive means in effect pay off their marginal benefit in the future and so are perceived to be of lesser utility than goods consumed in the present. Hence, the discrepancy in perceived (temporal) value between these two goods is what produces profit (Blaug, 1985: 502–4; Schumpeter, 1993: 34).

The difficulty here is that there are no grounds within the theory itself to assume that in the flow of goods between production and consumption one would regularly be inclined to value a future good less if the future benefit were greater, even if in practice such discrepant evaluations could occur. More significantly, Böhm-Bawerk's attempt to rescue a drive for profit provides no account of how relentless capital accumulation as a distinctive activity might launch the very productive apparatus in which marginalist calculation could hypothetically take place.[6] In his scheme the whole structure of production is simply given. Hence, marginalism has no explanation for original accumulation. Smith has an explanation, but given its reliance on a generic account of both the human passions and the

6. For Schumpeter all such theories of disturbances in the adjustment of the marginal utility of productive assets to the marginal utility of the product already assume that the productive apparatus has already been created; but they fail to explain how this occurred (Schumpeter, 1993: 36–8).

division of labor, it begs the question many times over (see Marx, 1977: 873–6).

Yet, if we are to explain how a system relying on capitalist accumulation could come about, something must have happened to produce a class of agents with the psychological motivation to accumulate – to save and reinvest – without dissipation of that impulse into an enjoyment of life's pleasures. Enter Weber's *The Protestant Ethic and the 'Spirit' of Capitalism*. At the core, Weber's work gives us an historical account of where and how the rational accumulating entrepreneur might have been forged. But matters are not quite that simple, for Weber's difficulty with deductive political economy is not in its use of a hypothetical account to understand capital and labor; rather, the problem lies in its attempt to use a generic notion of economic choices while smuggling in motives that require genetic concepts to make them intelligible. Thus Weber's contribution in *The Protestant Ethic*, I want to argue, is to give us at once a *hypothetical* and a *genetic* account of the rational accumulating entrepreneurial type. This enables him to give a theoretical account of original capitalist accumulation that is nonetheless historically contingent. Specifically, Weber takes the concept of the individual who accumulates capital, posited by economic theory, and breaks this concept into a series of plausible historical types all of which are made to converge so as to produce the entrepreneur (or class of entrepreneurs) as driving agent(s) of the original moment of accumulation. What I would like to do now is examine the strategy of this 'conceptual narrative', for once we do so, we can vindicate not so much the historical accuracy of Weber's account – which will always be subject to dispute – but its theoretical force.

### Narrative Structure and the Asymmetry between the Form and Spirit of Capitalism

The first thing we should notice about *The Protestant Ethic* is its odd narrative structure. Weber, as is well known, begins the book by setting up a puzzle which on the face of it has no clear answer: why in Europe and the United States Protestants rather than Catholics tend to be capitalists and skilled workers (2002: 2–3). If we assume that rational capitalism is resolutely secular, we would obviously be hard pressed to derive this odd demographic fact from the selection process of capitalist competition alone. Rejecting the notion that modern capitalism is the outgrowth of increased reason and secularism, Weber suggests that perhaps there is an 'inner affinity' between the Puritan 'conduct of life' and rational capitalist accumulation (2002: 7). He then promises to pursue relentlessly both conceptual poles of this affinity to see if by the end of his inquiry we will be able to find a hidden connection between these seemingly opposed forms of activity.

But then focusing only on the capitalist side of this relation, Weber raises an even more puzzling question, which he illustrates by providing us with two thoroughly contrasting ideal-typical pictures of the meaning of rational capitalism. He first provides a picture of an agent-less capitalism that accumulates by making all agents adapt to its imperatives:

> Today's capitalist economic order is a monstrous cosmos, in which the individual is born and in which in practice is for him, at least as an individual, simply a given, an immutable shell [*Gehäuse*] in which he is obliged to live. It forces on the individual, to the extent that he is caught up in the relationships of the 'market', the norms of its economic activity. The manufacturer who consistently defies the norms will just as surely be forced out of business as the worker who cannot or will not conform will be thrown out of work.
>
> (2002: 13)

Precisely because the capitalist market selects only for those who will adapt to the accumulation process without being moved by any one agent, Weber argues, it blinds us to its actual origins. It has effaced its origins in the very functioning of its principle of selection:

> In order that this kind of conduct of life and attitude to one's 'profession' [*'Berufs'-Auffassung*], 'adapted' as it is to the peculiar requirements of capitalism, could be 'selected' and merge victorious over others, it obviously had first to come into being and not just in individuals, but as an attitude held in common by groups of people. The origin of this attitude is therefore what needs to be explained.
>
> (2002: 13)

The puzzle then is how the involuntary selection principle of capitalism as a *form of production* could itself have been voluntarily 'selected' as a *way of life* in competition with alternative ways of living.

As a tentative first answer, Weber introduces the figure of Benjamin Franklin, who represents the polar opposite of this 'monstrous cosmos': an agent who accumulates as if there were an ethical imperative to do so – an historically located version of Adam Smith's parsimonious individual. Franklin becomes, for Weber, the embodiment of 'the capitalist spirit' as *Lebensführung*, as a consistently pursued form of life conduct. The most salient quality of Franklin is his attitude toward capital: money begets money, and so one should relentlessly invest rather than consume; and this activity is not a matter of desire or greed but of duty – and duty not merely to an ethical imperative but to one's calling in life (2002: 9–12). Implicit in this contrast is the question of how a shared 'mentality' of accumulation as an ethical obligation could produce a reified machinery of accumulation that selects its own agents. The answer to this question proves elusive for Weber, because on his account there is no law-like convergence between the 'spirit' of capitalism represented initially by Franklin and the impersonal capitalist production process:

> The 'capitalist' form of an economy and the spirit in which it is run do indeed stand in a generally *adequate* relationship to each other, but not in a relationship of mutual dependency governed by any law. We shall nevertheless provisionally use the expression 'spirit of capitalism' for that attitude which, *in the pursuit of a calling [berufsmäsig]*, strives systematically for profit for its own sake in the manner exemplified by Benjamin Franklin.
>
> (2002: 19)

We should note here that for Weber the figure of Franklin merely exemplifies but does not provide incontrovertible evidence for the capitalist spirit. But by the same token, his definition of 'the capitalist spirit' does not depend on whether Franklin truly embodies it.

In any case, there is in fact an odd asymmetry here. Franklin is the exemplification of a rational yet moral attitude toward capitalist accumulation, but by Weber's own admission he in fact was a traditional craftsperson. This asymmetry produces for Weber a further complication: specifically, just as, in the case of Franklin, the capitalist spirit might accompany a traditional form of production, a capitalist form of production could be conducted with a traditionalist spirit (2002: 20–1). Thus it would seem that there is relation between a spirit of deliberate and methodical accumulation for its own sake and the form of modern capitalist production, but the explanation of this relationship is far from self-evident. Indeed, just as with the relation of Protestantism and rational capitalism, a final accounting of the relation of capitalism as a spirit and capitalism as form of production is deferred to the very end of the book. And in its place Weber turns to the second and overriding question of his inquiry: how a figure like Franklin could be produced. And here the first puzzle regarding the relation of Protestant asceticism and the secular capitalist type comes into play, for Franklin, as Weber stylizes him, advances two claims that are not contextually intelligible and seem more like residues from a previous setting: first, Franklin argues that we are bound by some transcendent demand to increase money from money as if this stemmed from a religious duty, but no such religious justification is provided; and, second, Franklin invokes the concept of 'diligence in one's calling' in a way that at once points back to an earlier Calvinist notion of calling and forward to the modern secular idea of commitment to one's profession within the division of labor (2002: 12–13). Thus Weber is now justified in examining those doctrines and character types in the past in which these two demands made sense: the Protestant practical teaching on ascetic restraint and the Protestant concept of work in a calling. Only in the process of such an inquiry into the missing context for Franklin's doctrine will he be able ultimately to elicit a connection between 'the capitalist spirit' and the 'form' of capitalist production that at the end of the day needs no capitalist spirit to function. That is, only by filling in the variety of types of character moved by the concept of calling (*Beruf*) will the asymmetry between Franklin's utilitarian ethic of rational accumulation and his traditional mode of production be solved such that the agent of the capitalist spirit will also launch a rational form of capitalist production and accumulation.

### Constructed Affinities and Correspondences

At this point, I would like to pay special attention to the peculiar way in which Weber constructs an historical and conceptual affinity between the Calvinist as the embodiment of the Protestant ethic of calling and the entrepreneur as the embodiment of 'the spirit' of capitalism. What interests me here is not the historical validity of this relationship but rather the way in which Weber deploys this affinity to describe the historical appearance of the first rationally accumulating entrepreneurs as part of the 'unforseen and indeed *unwished for* consequences of the work of the [Calvinist and Puritan] reformers often far removed from, or even in virtual opposition to, everything they had in mind' (2002: 35). Weber is explicit that this ironic outcome is a backward construction 'from our particular point of view' (2002: 35). Hence, he will deliberately intensify the features of his types that produce the ironic outcome while diminishing those features that do not.

The Calvinist, on Weber's account, is driven to order life methodically precisely because God has set a plan for the world but will not reveal it. Weber famously claims that this doctrine encouraged in the Calvinist an irrational fear that he was not among the elect (2002: 72–3), and so to discharge this fear, he must engage in some worldly activity, but of what kind is left completely open. What this activity should be is purely formal (Poggi, 1983: 65). The substance is constituted by one's vocation or calling, which is God's purpose in this world. To prove, however, that he is one of the 'called', the serious Calvinist must devote himself unconditionally to 'the calling', whatever that calling may be. This unleashes a relentless organized energy and methodical organization of one's time based on proving one's ability to deny oneself worldly pleasures. Specifically, this means

fulfilling one's religious duties and working ceaselessly in one's calling (2002: 77–8). But this does not entail that the activity must be
aimed at accumulation of capital. Indeed, the emphasis on fulfilling
one's duties in a calling consists specifically of labor in service to the
secular life of the community and the glory of God rather than of
wealth accumulation (2002: 76).

Weber stresses the non-economic nature of Calvinism as a form of
'life conduct' for two reasons. First, this attitude toward life paradox-
ically cultivates the kind of character type needed for the accumulation of capital to occur, a character who will not dissipate the fruits
of his activity in worldly pleasures. And second, the logic of action
that corresponds to such a type may with the right background conditions unleash a set of effects that could produce in agents a drive
to increase capital as an unintended result. But all this happens subsequent to the Calvinist model of tensed activity on behalf of the
*Beruf*. Systematic capitalist accumulation can attach itself to the
concept of *Beruf* only after this form of vocational activity has been
shaped into a form of ascetic self-denial that will not compromise
with the all too reasonable demand that without any firm evidence
that there is another higher felicity in the offing, we should enjoy the
fruits of our labor in this life. The kind of figure that Adam Smith
posits as the outcome of a trans-historical psychological predisposi-
tion and that marginal utility theory locates within the process of
consumption itself depends on the appearance of a most unique historical type: the ascetic Protestant. This historical figure is driven to
rationally organize his or her life-work around the calling in order to
elicit – or, more accurately, produce – signs of salvation in a world
utterly bereft of such signs.

But as commentators have often pointed out (Poggi, 1983: 79–80,
83), Weber's construct of this historical type rests on an unprovable
imputation of psychological motive: 'The doctrine . . . engendered,
for each individual a feeling of tremendous inner loneliness' (2002:
73). It is this loneliness fed by doubt that one is among God's elect
that drives 'the tireless labor in a calling' to produce signs of grace.
Now there is no way of actually validating whether in fact the Calvinist experienced the severe doubt and was moved by the subsequent
drive, *Antrieb*, to prove himself among the elect through systematic
action in the calling. Weber, in effect, argues that such radical doubt
*must have* led to the psychological reaction to the doctrine, for we
have no way of explaining what we do know: that the Calvinist took
into the world the concept of ascetic denial through devotion to the
calling (2002: 82, 87). Here again it is necessary to impute motives
that would make seemingly 'irrational' conduct intelligible. But, of
course, the significance of the Calvinist for Weber in relation to the
first capitalist accumulators depends on imaginatively reading this

motivation into the Calvinist's conduct. To be sure, the historical evidence based on the self-descriptions of the Puritans and their views of deviants from the doctrine of predestination gives Weber grounds for ascribing these motives to them (see MacKinnon, 1993; Zarat, 1993). However, as Weber repeatedly reminds his readers, evidence in such accounts is at best suggestive: 'Calvinism *seems* to have a closer *affinity* with the tough upstanding active minds of the middle class [*bürgerlich*] capitalist entrepreneur' (2002: 95, emphases added). Thus it would seem that not any one concept but the conceptual narrative itself that validates the imputation of motive in Weber's approach.

When we turn to these first capitalist entrepreneurs, we encounter a parallel intensification of character type, but the constructed quality of this type moves from heuristic distortion to historical fiction, albeit one that is absolutely necessary when viewed against the backdrop of the problem of political economy that Weber is seeking to solve. The first entrepreneurs, the agents of original or primitive accumulation, are portrayed not as a class of acquisitive maximizers of profit exploiting a class with only their labor-power to sell, as described in Marx's account of 'primitive accumulation' (see Marx, 1977: 873–936), but as a noble caste that suffered a great deal of social condemnation in their drive to press the ascetic ideal of accumulation upon a recalcitrant economic order (Weber, 2002: 1–15, 21). In Weber's dramatization, they engage in a 'heroic struggle' with 'traditional' capitalism, whose spirit rejects ascetic devotion to the calling, detailed rational ordering of time, and formal and precise business practice (2002: 22, 77). Purifying his ideal-typical account of this first generation of 'steely hard Puritan merchants' (2002: 77), Weber rather cunningly places all of the qualities associated with the self-interest model of capitalist accumulation – the exploitation of labor, the conspicuous enjoyment of wealth – under the category of the traditional spirit of capitalism.

In a direct assault on Smith and a more indirect one on marginalism, Weber argues that it takes this new hard self-denying 'ethical type' bred by Calvinism to align the capitalist spirit – the inclination to accumulate as a duty, in direct analogy to the doing of one's work as a vocational duty – with the modern (rational) form of capitalist production (2002: 22, 14, 77, 283). Indeed, in a most remarkable – and I think overlooked – passage, Weber claims that 'this "new type of" entrepreneur' with a commitment to acquire wealth only as a matter of *Berufserfüllung* literally generates the very money capital he needs for reinvestment purely from his own activity in rationally and methodically organizing production (2002: 24, 22). Viewed as traditional forms of capitalism, neither banks nor commerce plays a role here (see Ingham, 2003; Swedberg, 2002).

But Weber's account does not stop simply with this neat and coun-terintuitive bifurcation of characteristics between the traditional entrepreneurs and heroic modern ones. As Harvey Goldman has pointed out, in his famous description of the transition from tradi-tional to entrepreneurial capitalism, Weber provides no historical examples of these first entrepreneurs of a 'new type' (1988: 34). Instead he describes their sudden emergence in a purely hypotheti-cal voice – the voice of fiction, of a constructed origin:

> At *some point* [my emphasis] this easy-going state of affairs was suddenly disturbed, often without there being any fundamental changes in the *form* [Weber's emphasis] of the organization – such as conversion to a unified business, machine operation, or the like. *What happened was* [my emphasis] often simply this. A young man from one of the putter-out families from the town moved to the country, carefully selected the weavers he needed, tightened up control over them and made them more depen-dent, thus turning peasants into workers. He also took personal charge of sales, approaching the ultimate buyers, the retail stores, as directly as possible; he gained customers personally, traveled to see them every year on a regular basis; most important, he was able to adapt the quality of the products exclusively to their needs and wishes, and to 'personalize' the products. At the same time he began to carry out the principle of 'low price, high turnover.' There was then a repetition of what invariably follows a 'rationalization' process of this kind: you either prospered or went under. Under the impact of the bitter struggle for survival that was beginning, the idyll collapsed. Considerable fortunes were made and not invested at interest but reinvested in the business. . . . Those who became involved got on; they had *no wish* [Weber's emphasis] to consume but only to make profits.
> (Weber, 2002: 21–2)

Weber then simply asserts that this change occurred not because of a build-up of money from commercial profits, but because a new spirit motivated these new rationally economizing entrepreneurs, the 'spirit' of capitalism – the jarring play on religious spirit is intentional (2002: 22).

Now, of course, one could say that the emergence of this new class of self-denying entrepreneurs in 18th-century Europe was so evident that exemplifying them historically was superfluous.[7] But given Weber's style in this book of finding distinctive examples for all the

7. Richard Swedberg (2002: 230–1) judges the appearance of the rational capitalist mental-ity out of traditionalist capitalist practice to be one of the uncontroversial features of Weber's argument compared to his controversial attempt to link ascetic Protestantism to the capitalist 'spirit'. However, the sudden turn by some unspecified agent from traditional to rational capitalist is just as mysterious, if not more so.

religious and ethical types he discusses, providing no exemplification at all does arouse some puzzlement. Could it be that Weber provides this generalized though fictional description precisely because the moment of original accumulation is not reducible to one historical event but instead must be metonymically distilled into a temporal moment, standing for a series of multiple events whose parameters elude us? Poggi has suggested that Weber's description of the purveyors of 'the capitalist spirit' was merely an 'imaginative construction' on his part that suggested a 'plausible' reason for rational capitalist accumulation but hardly proof (1983: 47). Not satisfied with such a conclusion, Gordon Marshall, one of the most acute commentators on the whole debate over the historical force of *The Protestant Ethic*, judges this hypothetical approach to be fundamentally flawed: 'his "provisional descriptions" of "economic traditionalism" and the "spirit of modern capitalism" are empirically unverified and possibly in practice unverifiable. *Homo capitalisticus* seems always to be just beyond the data which the researcher can unearth' (1982: 68; see also Swedberg, 2002: 230). And Marshall concludes that Weber may 'have defined the Protestant ethic and the spirit of modern capitalism in terms of each other and that his argument is therefore unfalsifiable' (1982: 119).

But perhaps the very fact that the first entrepreneurs moved by the capitalist spirit prove to be an imaginative construction derived from historical traces strengthens rather than weakens Weber's argument. Perhaps we should entertain the possibility that within Weber's conceptual narrative the first rationally accumulating capitalist cannot be exemplified in precisely the same way as the prior and subsequent figures contributing to the formation of 'the capitalist spirit' as *Lebensführung*, as a direction for life, because this class occupies a theoretical role within political economy quite distinct from its historical role in launching rational capitalism. Whether we can find historical exemplification or not, the very objective possibility of producing a rationally accumulating capitalism requires a class of people to have exchanged the role of the traditional capitalist, who seeks wealth for personal gain and an extravagant life, for the role of the 'modern' capitalist, who over a lifetime pursues profit only to reinvest it again at the cost of his material and personal well-being. Relying for an explanation on rival economic theories of original accumulation – Smith's and marginal utility theory – we simply cannot find a good reason why any class of people would be motivated to do this. Weber emphasizes again and again that from the vantage point of personal advantage and self-interest such conduct is entirely irrational (2002: 27–8). Some non-economic justification had to be at work if enough capital were to be generated and if a rational organization of work were to be imposed such that the modern economic order of capitalism could be brought about. Hence the oddly heroic story of a class fighting disapproval from the Catholic church, ordinary traditional commercial capitalists, adventurist and booty capitalists, and financiers to press their *Lebensführung*, their mode of life conduct, on economy and society.

I would suggest that Weber's ideal-typical description of this class, at once embodying the capitalist spirit and imposing the capitalist form of production, should be read as occupying a temporal place between an actual historical event and a hypothetical or imagined one – 'At some point' and 'what happened was', says Weber. The reason for the hypothetical voice is that the event being referred to is one that we cannot precisely identify historically because in fact it has multiple origins long since effaced; but nonetheless, from a theoretical viewpoint, this self-same description explains how a fundamental historical change has occurred. And precisely because we know that a fundamental move had to have taken place to start the accumulation process and that this act is constantly being reproduced under present conditions, the past – understood as a series of originary moments – is mirrored in the present and the present in the past.

## A Necessary Link between the Puritans and the Capitalist 'Spirit'?

But then what of the argument at the end of the book that seeks in a relatively straightforward way to historically link the Calvinist ethic to the business spirit through the Puritan redefinition of the concept of *Beruf* or calling? Here in the figure of Baxter, Weber creates a historical and conceptual transfer point between the ideal-typical Calvinist and the ideal-typical first entrepreneurs. The exchange of features that is merely suggested by the mirroring of the ideal-typical Calvinist and the ideal-typical first entrepreneur is explicitly brought about in the ideal-typical Puritan of the 17th century: specifically, we see in this agent a substitution of unrelenting vocational work for God's glory by vocational work for the steady accumulation of capital. But the construct is held together by a most slender thread – an extrapolation from the sermons of the moderate Baxter to the whole *Lebensführung* of the middle-class Puritan merchants (Parkin, 1988: 57). Again this should suggest that the narrative here seeks to capture something other than the historical causes of modern capitalism: to wit, a sociological reframing and critique of the assumptions behind Smith's theory of capital.

Weber famously notices that in Baxter's preaching there is a pragmatic interpretation of the profit-producing results of the division of labor that is similar to Smith's first theory of accumulation discussed earlier:

> Baxter elaborates on these fruits [of labor] in ways which in more than one respect recall Adam Smith's well-known apotheosis of the division of labor. Specialization in occupations, because it enables the workman to use his skill, leads to improvements in both the quantity and the quality of performance and thus serves the common best, which is identical with the good of the greatest number.
>
> (2002: 109)

But then Weber comments, as if answering Smith, that for Baxter – and other Puritan sects – mere labor is not enough for steady accumulation, but rather only systematic rational work in one's calling, that is, working systematically and rationally for God's greater glory. And this moral commitment will be judged in part by economic profitability, for it is God who creates this opportunity, and not to take advantage of it is to turn away from God (2002: 110).

What is crucial for Weber here is that the motivation, the drive (*Antrieb*), to pursue systematic profitability required more than mere submission to the division of labor; it required a moral commitment to one's profession and calling within it – a demand now, unlike the original Calvinist doctrine, that it is God's will that we systematically pursue profit as long as this is accompanied by self-denial and a sense that we view the goods we have earned as entrusted to us by God (2002: 112–13). The 'men of *business*' now know that the pursuit of profit is predetermined by God. They need merely monitor themselves so as not to begin to enjoy the fruits of their investments. Accumulation now has an ethical sanction. So the character type implied by Baxter's Puritan sermons starts to become congruent with the character type implied in Franklin's admonition that saving and investment are ethical duties.

However, Weber does not stop there. He also indirectly attacks Smith's other theory of accumulation: that capital stock exists prior to the division of labor and there automatically emerges a class of people that has this stock and is inclined to employ others within the division of labor to produce. Such a Puritan middle class, Weber insists, emerges in a specific moment, in the transition from Calvinism to Puritanism, but only under the religious belief that they are, as it were, 'a chosen people' similar to the Old Testament Jews. No longer suffering as did the Calvinists from God's belief in the sinfulness of all human beings, this class starts to form the model class of what Weber calls 'the heroic age of capitalism'. They are chosen because they will not, unlike the ordinary lot, dissipate their ascetic denial in the enjoyment of life's pleasures (2002: 112). The calling now refers to a class of rational accumulators of capital who are at once part of the division of labor – each specific calling has its worth as long as it is pursued diligently and with moral commitment – but also superior to it in the fact that God has selected them to produce fruit from their saving and investment. They are chosen to increase wealth precisely because they are not tempted by its pleasures. Only they have the strength to steer between the contradictory demands to increase wealth, on the one hand, and not pursue wealth as a goal of life, on the other (2002: 116). The upshot of this class consciousness is to produce the perfect accumulator, which Weber identifies as embodying 'the capitalist spirit': 'if that restraint on consumption is *combined with* the freedom to strive for profit, the result produced will inevitably be the *creation of capital* through the *ascetic compulsion to save*' (2002: 116–17). This is Weber's final answer to the mystery of 'original' or 'primitive' accumulation.

But Weber gives us a hint that this answer is tentative, merely registering the moment when the Calvinist ethic was transformed into the 'spirit of capitalism', that is, into a focused motivation to pursue investment capital for its own sake: 'It is of course impossible to put a precise figure on how great this effect was' (2002: 117). The congruence of the ascetic Puritan, the secular bearer of the capitalist spirit, and capitalism as a form of production lasts only for an instant before it becomes the renowned machine-driven 'iron casing', and therefore we can only construct that instant ideal—typically from the traces left by its subsequent effects.

## Conclusion

To sum matters up: does it matter that Weber provides no serious historical evidence for this new 'bourgeois' class with a hard ascetic attitude towards investment? Does it further matter that he relies largely on the internal relations between the ideal-typical Calvinist and the ideal-typical secular actor with the capitalist spirit? Does it matter that he exaggerates the Calvinist's radical doubt and loneliness and the Puritans' belief that their superior status as being among the elect is perfectly compatible with rationally organized work and systematic accumulation of capital? And, finally, does it matter that Weber constructs an historical fiction to describe the moment when the traditional capitalist crosses the threshold dividing customary cottage industry from the rational control over production and begins to produce for the sake of generating capital out of capital? If the argument made so far is plausible, the answer is no, for Weber's conceptual narrative solves a problem in economic theory as much as one in history. That is, for 'original accumulation' to occur there had to be an agent who was psychologically motivated to relentlessly over time forgo the rewards of his methodical systematic conduct in acquiring capital, and to do so without at any moment diverting his energies into enjoying the fruits of his activity. The Calvinist as ideal-type provides such a motivation, the Puritan combines asceticism and calculation of profit, and the subsequent entrepreneur with the 'capitalist spirit' engages in the actual investment activity. Hence Weber's reliance on the hypothetical yet historically specific character types, which seem to occupy a grey area between factual historical types and purely invented concepts: in the first case, a deliberate exaggeration of the unremitting doubt that drives the Calvinist to prove that he or she is one of the elect; in the second, an imagined moment when the traditional manufacturer crossed the threshold into a rational capitalist accumulation; in the third, an all too neatly constructed transfer point between the two.

This internal dynamic gives us the missing account that neither Smith, marginal utility theory, nor even Marx could adequately provide. But the force of this account at best depends on whether the logic embedded within the 'ideal-typical' reality may be found in the entangled one in which our intentional activity takes place. Or to put the matter differently, this is not something that can be verified by historical evidence but rather only within Weber's construct as it relates to the demands of capitalist political economy.

## References

Beetham, David (1987) 'Mosca, Pareto and Weber: A Historical Comparsion', in Wolfgang Mommsen and Jürgen Osterhammel (eds.) *Max Weber and His Contemporaries*. London: Allen & Unwin.

Blaug, Mark (1985) *Economic Theory in Retrospect*. Cambridge: Cambridge University Press.

Collins, Randall (1986a) 'Weber's Last Theory of Capitalism', in *Weberian Sociological Theory*. Cambridge: Cambridge University Press.

Collins, R. (1986b) 'Weber and Schumpeter: Toward a General Sociology of Capitalism', in *Weberian Sociological Theory*. Cambridge: Cambridge University Press.

Goldman, Harvey (1988) *Max Weber and Thomas Mann: Calling and the Shaping of the Self*. Berkeley: University of California Press.

Hennis, Wilhelm (1988a) 'Max Weber's Theme: "Personality and the Life Orders"', in *Max Weber: Essays in Reconstruction*. London: Allen & Unwin.

Hennis, Wilhelm (1988b) 'Max Weber and the Political Economy of the German Historical School', in *Max Weber: Essays in Reconstruction*. London: Allen & Unwin.

Ingham, Geoffrey (2003) 'Schumpeter and Weber on the Institutions of Capitalism: Solving Swedberg's "Puzzle"', *Journal of Classical Sociology* 3(3): 297–309.

Loader, Colin (2001) 'Puritans and Jews: Weber, Sombart and the Transvaluators of Modern Society', *Canadian Journal of Sociology* 26(4): 635–53.

MacKinnon, M.H. (1993). 'The Longevity of the Weber Thesis: A Critique of the Critics', in Hartmut Lehmann and Guenther Roth (eds) *Weber's Protestant Ethic: Origins, Evidence, Contexts*. Cambridge: Cambridge University Press.

Marshall, Gordon (1982) *In Search of the Spirit of Capitalism*. New York: Columbia University Press.

Marx, Karl (1977) *Capital*, trans. Ben Fowkes. New York: Random House.

Menger, Carl (1950) *Principles of Economics*, trans. James Dingwall and Bert Hoselitz. Glencoe, IL: Free Press.

Parkin, Frank (1988) *Max Weber*. London: Routledge.

Perelman, Michael (2000) *The Invention of Capitalism: Classical Political Economy and the Secret History of Primitive Accumulation*. Durham, NC: Duke University Press.

Poggi, Gianfranco (1983) *Calvinism and the Capitalist Spirit: Max Weber's Protestant Ethic*. Amherst: University of Massachusetts Press.

Scaff, Lawrence (1989) 'Weber before Weberian Sociology', in Keith Tribe (ed.) *Reading Weber*. London: Routledge.

Schumpeter, Joseph (1993) *The Theory of Economic Development*. New Brunswick, NJ: Transaction.

Smith, Adam (1976). *The Wealth of Nations*. Chicago, IL: University of Chicago Press.

Swedberg, Richard (1998) *Max Weber and the Idea of Economic Sociology*. Princeton, NJ: Princeton University Press.

Swedberg, Richard (2002) 'The Economic Sociology of Capitalism: Weber and Schumpeter', *Journal of Classical Sociology* 2(3): 227–55.

Weber, Max (1949) 'Objectivity' in Social Science and Social Policy', in *The Methodology of the Social Sciences*, trans. and ed. Edward A. Shils and Henry A. Finch. New York: Free Press.

Weber, Max (1989) 'Developmental Tendencies in the Situation of East Elbian Rural Labourers', in K. Tribe (ed.) *Reading Weber*. London: Routledge.

Weber, Max (2002) *The Protestant Ethic and the 'Spirit' of Capitalism and Other Writings*, trans., ed. and Introduction Peter Baehr and Gordon C. Wells. New York: Penguin.

Zarat, David (1993) 'The Use and Abuse of Textual Data', in H. Lehmann and G. Roth (eds) *Weber's Protestant Ethic: Origins, Evidence, Contexts*. Cambridge: Cambridge University Press.

# RICHARD SWEDBERG

## Weber on the Economy and Religion[†]

Weber was preoccupied with religious questions during much of his life, and according to his wife, his work testifies to "a permanent concern with religion."[1] A closer look at Weber's writings shows that he usually approached religion from the angle of its relationship to the economy. This is indeed true for *The Protestant Ethic and the Spirit of Capitalism*, which to many people has come to embody Weber's contribution to economic sociology. But it is also true for a number of his other writings, including the giant work entitled *The Economic Ethics of the World Religions* and the massive section on religion in *Economy and Society*. One of the main goals of this study is therefore to outline the *whole* analysis of economy and religion in Weber's work. I do this by discussing, besides *The Protestant Ethic* and the debates it has led to (in section II), Weber's general sociology of religion (in section I), and his analysis of the economic ethics of the world religions (in section III). I especially attempt to show that Weber's analysis contains—in addition to the spectacular thesis of *The Protestant Ethic*—a number of concepts and approaches that are very useful in analyzing the relationship between economy and religion from a sociological perspective. The general backdrop to this study is Weber's conception of social action as a special form of interest-driven action. What Weber says about religion, it should be added, is also applicable to nonreligious forms of ideal interests, from humanism to more politically inspired ideologies.

## I. AN INTRODUCTION TO WEBER'S ANALYSIS OF THE RELATIONSHIP BETWEEN THE ECONOMY AND RELIGION: CENTRAL THEMES AND CONCEPTS IN *ECONOMY AND SOCIETY*

Weber paints a magnificent panorama in the chapters on religion in *Economy and Society*, starting with the birth of religion and ending

---

† From Richard Swedberg, *Max Weber and the Idea of Economic Sociology* (Princeton: Princeton UP, 1998), Ch. 5. Reprinted by permission.
1. Marianne Weber, *Max Weber: A Biography* (New York: John Wiley and Sons, 1975), p. 335; emphasis in the original. It can be added that even though Weber was always interested in religion he nonetheless considered himself "unmusical" in religious matters. See Weber's famous letter to Ferdinand Tönnies, dated February 19, 1909, in Weber, *Briefe 1909–1910. Max Weber Gesamtausgabe 11/6* (Tübingen: J.C.B. Mohr, 1994), p. 65. It may also be noted that from early on Weber's interest in religion extended to its economic dimension. On this score Weber was possibly inspired by what Knies had to say about economy and religion in the course titled "Allgemeine Volkswirtschaftslehre (theoretische Nationalökonomie)" that Weber attended in the summer semester of 1883. For Knies on religion and economy, see Karl Knies, *Die politische Oekonomie vom geschichtlichen Standpunkte* (Leipzig: Hans Buske [1883] 1930), pp. 110–26.

with the five great world religions, covering along the way such phenomena as priesthood, hierocracy, prophecy, and salvation.[2] Most of
this material is not related to economic concerns and can perhaps
best be characterized as an attempt, from Weber's side, to lay a foundation for the sociological study of religion. Quite a bit, however,
does deal with the relationship between the economy and religion,
and here too Weber's analysis is rich. In what follows I have selected
what I consider to be the central themes in Weber's analysis of economy and religion, specifically:

the attitude toward riches in religion;

religious organizations and their relationship to economic affairs;

the religious propensity of certain socio-economic classes and
strata; and

different ways to approach salvation and how these may affect the
economy.

Weber also devotes quite a bit of space to two other, equally central
themes, namely attitudes toward the economy in the great world religions and the relationship between economy and religion in the
Reformation. Both of these topics are discussed later in this study, in
connection with the analysis of *The Protestant Ethic* and *The Economic Ethics of the World Religions*.

Before presenting the first of these themes in Weber's analysis of
economy and religion, something should be said about the general
point of departure for his analysis of religious phenomena and how
it is related to his concept of social action and interests. Since *Economy and Society* is a work in sociology, religious action is analyzed as
a special form of social action or action oriented to the behavior of
others. Religious social action, as well as religious action in general,
is driven by a combination of ideal interests, habits, and emotions.
Weber was furthermore concerned about eliminating value judgments from his analysis, and with this purpose in mind he looked for
a term to express what attracted people to religion that was both fairly
neutral and broad enough to encompass different types of religions.
The term he chose for the final version of *Economy and Society* was

2. It is not clear whether Weber had originally intended to include a section on religion in
his contribution to the *Grundriss*, but in the outline from 1914 he had assigned himself
the following topic: "Religious Communities: Religion as Conditioned by Class; Religions from Different Cultures and Economic Mentality." After Weber's death, a few hundred pages of writings on religion were found among his belongings, and it was decided
that these had been written for the *Grundriss*. Today these can be found in *Economy and
Society* in the form of two long chapters: "Religious Groups (The Sociology of Religion)"
(part 2, chap. 6; 236 pp.) and "Political and Hierocratic Domination" (part 2, chap. 15;
54 pp.). For religion in the different versions of the *Grundriss*, see Johannes Winkelmann, *Max Webers hinterlassenes Hauptwerk* (Tübingen: J.C.B. Mohr, 1986), pp. 151,
169.

"goods of salvation" or "*Heilsgüter*," which has deep roots in German theology and can be traced at least to the late sixteenth century.[3] Weber, however, used it to mean something closer to "*religious benefits*" (as it has been translated in *Economy and Society*) or "*religious goods.*"[4] In economic theory the term "goods" covers any item for which there is a need or preference, and "religious benefits" similarly encompasses a variety of religious desirables, as Weber uses it. More precisely, Weber argues, religious benefits can be this-worldly or other-worldly as well as material or spiritual; and religious social action is defined as a form of action that is oriented simultaneously to some religious benefit and to other actors (see figures 1 and 2). The term "religious benefits" or "religious goods" also suited Weber's purposes well in that it gives associations to religious behavior as, to a certain extent, an interest-driven process, rather than one inspired by ideas.[5] This last point was very important to Weber and is also reflected in his use of such terms as "psychological premium [on certain religious behavior]" and "ideal interests," which are discussed later.

3. Friedrich Wilhelm Graf, who kindly answered my questions about this term, has told me that he is not sure when *Heilsgüter* (goods of salvation) was first used by or by whom, but that it was mainly used in Lutheran and Calvinist theology from the late sixteenth and seventeenth centuries. "I suspect," Graf says, "Weber has taken the term from the works of Matthias Schneckenburger and Karl Bernhard Hundeshagen which he had read very carefully for his work on the protestant ethics" (letter to the author, October 7, 1996). The term is not used in today's theological discourse, at least not by Protestant theologians. For information on Schneckenburger and Hundeshagen, see Friedrich Wilhelm Graf, "The German Theological Sources and Protestant Church Politics," pp. 27–49 in Hartmut Lehmann and Guenther Roth, eds., *Weber's Protestant Ethic* (Cambridge: Cambridge University Press, 1993).

4. Parsons as well as Roth-Wittich translate *Heilsgüter* as "religious benefits," and according to Martin Risebrodt "the translation 'religious benefits' seems to express the meaning quite appropriately, although 'religious goods' would be possible too" (letter to the author, November 18, 1996). The term "religious benefits" is introduced in chapter 1 of *Economy and Society* ("§17. Political and Hierocratic Organizations"); see Weber, *Economy and Society: An Outline of Interpretive Sociology* (Berkeley: University of California Press, 1978), pp. 54–56, or *Wirtschaft und Gesellschaft. Grundriss der verstehenden Soziologie* (Tübingen: J.C.B. Mohr, 1972), pp. 29–30). The reader may recall that the term "goods" (*Güter*) is defined as part of "utility" in Weber's economic sociology, as presented in chapter 2 of *Economy and Society* and discussed in chapter 2 of this book. More precisely, Weber defines "economically oriented action" as a search for the "satisfaction of a desire for 'utilities' ('*Nutzleistungen*')"—with "'utilities'" consisting of "services" as well as of "goods" (cf. Weber, *Economy and Society*, pp. 68–69, or *Wirtschaft und Gesellschaft*, pp. 34–35). While it can be discussed whether the notion of "religious benefits" constitutes *the* key concept in Weber's sociology of religion as a whole, I would argue that it represents an interesting point of departure for his analysis of the relationship between the economy and religion.

5. See, for example, Weber's statement in "The Protestant Sects and the Spirit of Capitalism" (1920) that "it is not the ethical *doctrine* of a religion, but that form of ethical conduct upon which *premiums* are placed that matters. Such premiums operate through the form and the condition of the respective goods of salvation (*Heilsgüter*)"; Weber, "The Protestant Sects and the Spirit of Capitalism," p. 321 in Hans Gerth and C. Wright Mills, eds., *From Max Weber* (New York: Oxford University Press, 1946), or "Die protestantischen Sekten und der Geist des Kapitalismus," pp. 234–35 in Vol. 1 of *Gesammelte Aufsätze zur Religionssoziologie* (Tübingen: J.C.B. Mohr, 1988).

RELIGIOUS BENEFITS

|  | THIS-WORLDLY | OTHER-WORLDLY |
|---|---|---|
| MATERIAL | primitive religions | |
| SPIRITUAL | | advanced religions |

Figure 1: The Goal of Religious Action: "Religious Benefits" or "Religious Goods." *Source:* Max Weber, *Economy and Society* (Berkeley: University of California Press, 1978), pp. 54–56. *Comment:* Religious benefits (*Heilsgüter*) differ according to religion; they can be this-worldly or other-worldly as well as spiritual or material.

The first theme in Weber's sociology of religion in *Economy and Society—the attitude toward riches in religion—*is directly connected to his concept of religious benefits. In primitive religions, Weber points out, the benefits were typically material in nature and consisted of such things as a long life, health, and wealth.[6] This has also been true of more advanced religions, such as Hinduism, Buddhism, Islam, and Judaism. Except for ascetic movements and certain forms of Christianity, Weber says, religious benefits have tended to include material wealth. "Riches were the wages of piety," he notes in his discussion of early Judaism.[7]

Early forms of religion, Weber also says, tend to affect behavior, including economic behavior, in a "stereotyped" manner. "The first and fundamental effect of religious views upon the conduct of life and therefore upon economic activity was generally stereotyping."[8] By "stereotyping" Weber means that something gets "fixed or perpetuated

6. See, e.g., Weber, *Economy and Society,* pp. 399–400, 527, or *Wirtschaft und Gesellschaft,* pp. 245, 320. See also Weber, "The Social Psychology of the World Religions," pp. 277–78 in Gerth and Mills, eds., *From Max Weber,* or "Einleitung," p. 249 in Vol. 1 of *Gesammelte Aufsätze zur Religionssoziologie;* Weber, *Ancient Judaism* (Glencoe, Ill.: Free Press, 1952), pp. 197–98, 233, 370, or "Antike Judenthum," pp. 211, 250, 385 in Vol. 3 of *Gesammelte Aufsätze zur Religionssoziologie.*
7. Weber, *Ancient Judaism,* p. 223, or "Antike Judenthum," p. 238 in Vol. 3 of *Gesammelte Aufsätze zur Religionssoziologie.*
8. Weber, *Economy and Society,* p. 406, or *Wirtschaft und Gesellschaft,* p. 249. Early religion, magic, and hierocracy, Weber says, typically lead to a "stereotyping" of the economy. See, e.g., Weber, *Economy and Society,* pp. 129–30, 151, 405–6, 577–79, 1185, or *Wirtschaft und Gesellschaft,* pp. 72–73, 87, 249, 348–49, 708; Weber, *General Economic History* (New Brunswick, N.J.: Transaction Books, 1981), pp. 123, 361, or *Wirtschaftsgeschichte* (Berlin: Duncker and Humblot), pp. 117, 308. A number of other phenomena—such as law, patrimonialism, and political capitalism—can also lead to a stereotyping of the economy; see, e.g., Weber, *Economy and Society,* pp. 199, 254, 759, 1038, or *Wirtschaft und Gesellschaft,* pp. 117, 148, 444, 602. According to Weber, "stereotyping" also means that decisions that are seen as *not* falling under its categories can be made arbitrarily. See, e.g., Weber, *Economy and Society,* pp. 1185–86, or *Wirtschaft und Gesellschaft,* p. 708.

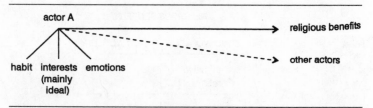

Figure 2: The Structure of Religious Social Action, according to Weber. *Source:* Max Weber, *Economy and Society* (Berkeley: University of California Press, 1978), pp. 4, 22. *Comment:* Religious social action takes place when an actor pursues religious benefits, driven mainly by ideal interests, while taking other actors into account.

in an unchanging form" (*Oxford English Dictionary*). Weber wrote around the turn of the century, before the modern concept of stereotype had come into being.[9] Using modern social science terminology, one could perhaps say that Weber's notion of stereotyping involves the labeling of a phenomenon, followed by a lock-in. A wide range of economic activities and goods can be stereotyped, according to Weber, including people's attitudes toward tools and products. The ways of stereotyping that mainly concern us here, however, are those that affect the attitude toward riches; and these include notions about acceptable types of trade and more generally, how individuals think wealth can be "honestly" acquired. When some economic activity is religiously stereotyped, Weber points out, the force of religion (that is, the incentive of religious benefits) is fused with the force of tradition (that is, the value of keeping things as they are), and the result is a formidable obstacle to economic innovation.

As history moves on, Weber says, religious stereotyping is eventually broken down, mainly through prophecy and religious rationalization. In more advanced religions, the religious benefits tend to be other-worldly and noneconomic, and religious activity itself is no longer seen exclusively in terms of ends and means, as it is in primitive religions. "The goal of religious behavior," Weber notes, "is successively 'irrationalized' until finally other-worldly non-economic goals come to represent what is distinctive about religious behavior."[1] As religious benefits become less economic and this-worldly in character, Weber adds, a general tension develops between religious

9. The modern notion of a stereotype—as a preconceived and oversimplified notion of another person—comes from Walter Lippmann's *Public Opinion* (1922). I am grateful to Robert K. Merton for setting me straight on this issue.

1. Weber, *Economy and Society,* p. 424, or *Wirtschaft und Gesellschaft,* p. 259. Weber speculates that the need for benefits in the next world would initially have been especially strong

values and the values of ordinary secular life. This tension can be resolved in a variety of ways; it usually also leads to a number of unintended consequences, which play a central role in Weber's analysis.

As religion becomes more advanced and rationalized, its attitude toward riches changes, Weber notes, especially toward riches that come from capitalist activities. At this point in his analysis Weber introduces the concept of "impersonality" ("*Unpersönlichkeit*") into his economic sociology.[2] All religions view personal relationships as central to life, he explains, and they try to regulate these relationships according to their vision of the need for *caritas* or charity toward the unfortunate. This vision draws on the old neighborhood ethic, according to which one should always try to help a brother in need.[3] But while it is possible to regulate certain economic relationships according to a religious vision of personal relationships and charity— such as the relationship between a master and his slave or between a patriarch and the members of his household—this is *not* the case, according to Weber, with most capitalist relationships. In a capitalist economy, people are typically related to one another less directly, such as a factory owner to the workers in the factory or a shareholder to the people who work for a corporation. There is also the crucial fact that if capitalist relationships were to be altered according to some notion of charity, economic difficulties would soon result. In a capitalist economy, Weber says, one must follow the rules of the market or go under—there is simply no place for *caritas*.

The second theme in *Economy and Society*—*religious organizations and their relationship to economic affairs*—is also directly connected to the notion of religious benefits or religious goods. "Hierocracy" is thus defined by Weber as the kind of organization "which enforces its

among the wealthy: "In keeping with the law of marginal utility, a certain concern for one's destiny after death would generally arise when the most essential earthly needs have been met, and thus this concern is [originally] limited primarily to the circles of the noble and the well-to-do"; see Weber, *Economy and Society*, p. 520, or *Wirtschaft und Gesellschaft*, p. 316.

2. For "impersonality," see, e.g., Gerth and Mills, eds., *From Max Weber*, p. 371; Weber, *Economy and Society*, pp. 584–85, 600, 1186–87, or *Wirtschaft und Gesellschaft*, pp. 353, 361, 708–9; Weber, "Religious Rejections of the World and Their Directions," p. 331 in Gerth and Mills, eds., *From Max Weber*, or "Zwischenbetrachtung," p. 544 in Vol. 1 of *Gesammelte Aufsätze zur Religionssoziologie*; Weber, *General Economic History*, pp. 357–58, or *Wirtschaftsgeschichte*, p. 305. Weber uses the term *Unpersönlichkeit* early on in his work, such as in his pamphlet on the stock exchange from 1894 to 1896. See, e.g., Weber, "Die Börse," pp. 267, 271 in *Gesammelte Aufsätze zur Soziologie und Sozialpolitik* (Tübingen: J.C.B. Mohr, 1988). Weber occasionally uses the term *Versachligung* as a complement to *Unpersönlichkeit*; see, e.g., Weber, *Economy and Society*, p. 585, or *Wirtschaft und Gesellschaft*, p. 353.

3. Weber, *Economy and Society*, pp. 581–85, or *Wirtschaft und Gesellschaft*, pp. 351–53. For charity, see, e.g., Weber, *Economy and Society*, pp. 579–83, or *Wirtschaft und Gesellschaft*, pp. 350–52; see also Weber, *The Religion of China* (Glencoe, Ill.: Free Press, 1951), pp. 209–10, or "Konfuzianismus und Taoismus," p. 495 in Vol. 1 of *Gesammelte Aufsätze zur Religionssoziologie*.

order through psychic coercion by distributing or denying religious benefits."[4] A "church," according to *Economy and Society*, is similar to a hierocracy, but at a later and more rational stage of development. A sect uses religious benefits and psychic coercion as well, but is less universalistic than a church or a hierocracy. One cannot be born into a sect, as one can into a church or a hierocracy; and each person has to qualify on the basis of his or her individual merits.

The final type of religious organization Weber discusses in *Economy and Society* is the monastic order. He provides no formal definition of a monastic order, but one can perhaps characterize it as a sect in which the members devote the whole day to religious activities and often also live together.

Much of Weber's discussion of hierocracy is naturally devoted to its relationship to political power. Since the strength of a hierocracy is directly related to how much power the political authorities have, Weber says, this type of organization is typically opposed to an enlargement of the treasury of the prince and his troops. The religious power also often collides with the secular power over the issue of landholdings, which both of them like to accumulate. For that reason, the landholdings of the hierocracy are a source of tension in its relationship to the aristocracy. The relationship of the hierocracy to the bourgeoisie has been considerably better throughout history than to the aristocracy, because the hierocracy tends to introduce trust and stability into commercial life, which merchants appreciate. In antiquity, for example, temples were used as depositories for money and valuables, and during the Middle Ages religious authorities often lent money, relying on their reputation and control over religious benefits to ensure repayment. But there has also been some tension between the religious powers and the commercial classes, Weber says, in particular because the monasteries have had a much cheaper labor force at their disposal than their secular competitors.

Hierocracy has definitely affected economic development, Weber says, but less through its economic activities than through its general attitude to the secular world. A hierocracy is inherently traditionalistic and tends to stereotype its surroundings, including the economy, according to Weber. As a consequence, it is suspicious of all innovations and displays "a deep antipathy toward the non-traditional power of capitalism."[5] In other words, hierocracy often encourages economic traditionalism.

4. Weber, *Economy and Society*, p. 54, or *Wirtschaft und Gesellschaft*, p. 29. A "theocracy" is a hierocracy in which a high priest is the political ruler; "caesaropapism" is the belief that the priestly power is completely subordinate to the political power. See Weber, *Economy and Society*, pp. 1159–63, or *Wirtschaft und Gesellschaft*, pp. 689–92.
5. Weber, *Economy and Society*, p. 1186, or *Wirtschaft und Gesellschaft*, p. 708.

Typically, a church develops out of a hierocracy. Although a church is a later and more rational kind of organization, Weber says, its influence on economic development has nonetheless been fairly similar to that of hierocracy. Many churches all over the world have attempted to directly influence the economy through rules about usury and the notion of a just price, for example.[6] In the West, the prohibition against usury deeply influenced legislation and also created many problems for the merchants. But they found ways of circumventing it, and the prohibition against usury never succeeded in blocking capitalism. In the seventeenth century a Calvinist produced the first theoretical justification of usury, and in the following two centuries the Catholic Church reversed its position on lending money against a market-based rate of interest.

All in all, Weber says, the Western church did not have much of an economic program. In addition, "the church did not decisively influence economic institutions" and "it did not make or unmake [economic] institutions." The church did influence people's attitudes toward the economy—but mostly in a negative manner because the economic mentality it furthered was essentially traditionalistic. The church, like hierocracy more generally, has usually encouraged a "non-capitalistic and partly anti-capitalistic [mentality]," Weber concludes.[7]

Sects have influenced the economy somewhat differently from the church, largely owing to their unique sociological structure, according to Weber. By definition, a sect chooses its members, and it can

6. Weber discusses usury quite a bit, but less so the notion of a just price. See, e.g., Weber, *Economy and Society*, pp. 562–63, 583–89, 1188–90, or *Wirtschaft und Gesellschaft*, pp. 340, 352–55, 710–11; Weber, *General Economic History*, pp. 267–71, or *Wirtschaftsgeschichte*, pp. 234–37; Weber, *The Protestant Ethic and the Spirit of Capitalism* (London: Allen and Unwin, 1930), pp. 200–201, 203–4, or "Die protestantische Ethik," pp. 56–57 in Vol. 1 of *Gesammelte Aufsätze zur Religionssoziologie*. On usury, see, e.g., Benjamin Nelson, *The Idea of Usury: From Tribal Brotherhood to Universal Other-hood* (Chicago: University of Chicago Press, 1969). Raymond De Roover, an expert on medieval finance, has charged Weber and many other economic historians with idealizing the notion of the just price; and the modern consensus is apparently that religious medieval thought was much more favorable to the idea of free competition than was earlier thought. See, e.g., Gabriel Le Bras, "Conceptions of Economy and Society," p. 563 in Vol. 3 of *The Cambridge Economic History of Europe* (Cambridge: Cambridge University Press, 1963). According to De Roover, Weber and many other economic historians closely followed Roscher's 1874 account of the theories of Henry of Langenstein the Elder (1325–1397) in their view of the just price. According to Langenstein, the producer could set his own price when the authorities failed to set a fair price, but he must not exceed what was needed to maintain his own and his family's normal lifestyle. But the ideas of Langenstein were exceptions rather than the rule during the Middle Ages, according to De Roover, and most medieval scholastic doctors simply equated the just price with the market price (with one exception: when the market failed, the authorities had the duty to step in and regulate the price). See Raymond De Roover, "Economic Thought, I: Ancient and Medieval Thought," p. 433 in Vol. 4 of David L. Sills, ed., *International Encyclopaedia of the Social Sciences* (New York: Macmillan, 1968); see also Raymond De Roover, "The Concept of the Just Price: Theory and Economic Policy," *Journal of Economic History* 18 (1958): 418–38.

7. Weber, *Economy and Society*, p. 1190, or *Wirtschaft und Gesellschaft*, pp. 711–12.

control their behavior to an extent that is not possible for a church. A sect screens candidates for honesty, good character, and the like, and maintains a high ethical standard through a continuous and mutual scrutiny by its members. Membership in a sect has thus often been used as a sign of creditworthiness by secular economic institutions. Weber also points out that it was two sects—the Quakers and the Baptists—that introduced fixed prices in the West as an alternative to haggling.[8]

The fourth type of religious organization that Weber discusses in *Economy and Society* is the monastic order, and he distinguishes between two stages in its development. Early on, a monastic movement is typically charismatic in nature and anti-economic in spirit. Its members do not work for a living but live off donations and gifts; private property is also rejected. When routinization sets in, however, some agreement is often reached with the ruling church. The hostility to economic matters is weakened, and the order typically acquires property of its own.[9]

Routinization, however, does not mean that economic behavior in the monastic order becomes identical to that in the secular world. Weber points out that in the monasteries work was used as an ascetic tool for the first time. The monks often lived and worked in a methodical and self-controlled manner. Weber also describes how religious enthusiasm—especially in combination with a methodical approach to work, as existed in the monasteries—has resulted in a number of magnificent economic accomplishments that outstrip those that are possible through ordinary labor:

> The pyramids appear preposterous unless we realize that the subjects firmly believed in the king as god incarnate. The Mormon achievements in the salt desert of Utah violate all rules of rational settlement. This is all the more typical of the monastic

8. One of the few commentators on Weber's work who has studied this issue, Stephen A. Kent, notes that the Quakers' policy on fixed prices was indeed based on their opinion that the seed of God existed in each and every person and that all customers should therefore be treated alike. He also cites a publication from 1655 by a Quaker who notes that "his business suffered from his refusal either to haggle with customers or to show them 'civil respect' by removing his hat and bowing to them when they entered his shop." See Stephen A. Kent, "The Quaker Ethic and the Fixed Price Policy: Max Weber and Beyond," *Sociological Inquiry* 53 (1983): 19; see in this context also Balwant Nevaskar, "Economic Ethic of Quakers," pp. 118–38 in *Capitalists without Capitalism* (Westport, Conn.: Greenwood, 1971). For Weber on sects, see "'Churches' and 'Sects' in North America: An Ecclesiastical Socio-Political Sketch," *Sociological Theory* 3 (Spring 1985): 7–13, or "'Kirchen' und 'Sekten' in Nordamerika," *Die christliche Welt* 20 (1906): 558–62 (which in its turn was a somewhat revised version of "'Kirchen' und 'Sekten,'" *Frankfurter Zeitung*, April 13 and 15, 1906); Weber, "The Protestant Sects and the Spirit of Capitalism," pp. 302–22 in Gerth and Mills, eds., *From Max Weber*, or "Die protestantische Sekten und der Geist des Kapitalismus," pp. 207–36 in Vol. 1 of *Gesammelte Aufsätze zur Religionssoziologie*.

9. For the monastic orders, see Weber, *Economy and Society*, pp. 1166–70, or *Wirtschaft und Gesellschaft*, pp. 694–97.

achievements, which almost always accomplish that which appears economically not feasible. In the midst of the Tibetan snow and sand deserts Lamaist monasticism produced economic and architectural wonders that in magnitude, and apparently also in quality, measure up to the largest and most famous artifacts of men: witness the *Potala* [Palace in Lhasa].[1]

In his discussion of the third major theme in *Economy and Society*— *the religious propensity of certain socio-economic classes and strata*— Weber introduces two concepts that describe the different roles that religion plays for privileged and nonprivileged groups in society: "hope for compensation," which denotes what the nonprivileged strata want from religion; and "theodicy of good fortune," which explains why privileged groups are interested in religion.[2] Privileged groups, according to Weber, are fundamentally content with their position in society, and their sense of honor and self-esteem is closely connected to their *being*. The nonprivileged, in contrast, suffer from their current position in the world and focus their sense of honor or self-esteem on what they one day might *become*. As a consequence, nonprivileged groups have a need for a religion based on an ethic of compensation or what Weber calls "hope for compensation" and which he describes as fairly calculating in nature.

Privileged and successful groups need religion for a very different purpose, namely legitimation. Their members are convinced that they deserve their good fortune and that the poor deserve their misfortune. Weber calls this "the theodicy of good fortune" and explains it in the following manner:

> When a man who is happy compares his position with that of one who is unhappy, he is not content with the fact of his happiness, but desires something more, namely his right to this happiness, the consciousness that he has earned his good fortune, in contrast to the unfortunate one who must equally have earned his misfortune. Our everyday experience proves that there exists just such a need for psychic comfort about the legitimacy or deservedness of one's happiness, whether this involves political success, superior economic status, bodily health, success in the

---

1. Weber, *Economy and Society*, p. 1169, or *Wirtschaft und Gesellschaft*, p. 696; see also Weber, *General Economic History*, pp. 364–65, or *Wirtschaftsgeschichte*, p. 311 (where Weber emphasizes asceticism—not religious enthusiasm—as the driving force behind the Tibetan achievements).
2. See, e.g., Weber, *Economy and Society*, pp. 483, 491–92, or *Wirtschaft und Gesellschaft*, pp. 294, 299–300. For the terms "theodicy of good fortune" and "theodicy of suffering," see Weber, "The Social Psychology of the World Religions," pp. 271, 273 in Gerth and Mills, eds., *From Max Weber*, or "Einleitung," pp. 242, 244 in Vol. 1 of *Gesammelte Aufsätze zur Religionssoziologie*. Weber's discussion of the relationship of privileged and nonprivileged groups to religion may well have its roots in Nietzsche's work, such as *The Genealogy of Morals* (1887). I am gratfeul to Ralph Schroeder for pointing this out to me.

game of love, or anything else. What the privileged classes require of religion, if anything at all, is this legitimation.[3]

One of the most interesting aspects of Weber's discussion of the religious propensity of socio-economic classes and strata is that he also discusses the extent to which economic forces shape religion—the opposite causal direction, in other words, from the one in *The Protestant Ethic*. Weber was very critical of the Marxist argument that religion can be explained exclusively in terms of economic forces and he publicly said so.[4] His own position was more along the lines of his 1904 essay on objectivity: that religious phenomena at the most can constitute "economically conditioned phenomena," or "behavior in non-'economic' affairs [that] is partly influenced by economic motives." In other words, the religious behavior of various socio-economic strata and classes can never be completely explained through economic forces—only "partly" so.[5]

The nobility and warrior classes, according to Weber, have historically been prevented from developing a deep religiosity both by their strong sense of honor and by their frequent exposure to the unpredictable fortunes of war. At the most they would pray for military victory and for some protection against evil magic. The gods of the nobility were strong, passionate, and not very rational. As a consequence, the religion of the nobility tended to reinforce economic traditionalism. Something similar was also true for the peasants—but their economic traditionalism was enforced by their propensity for magic rather than for a pantheon of warring and jealous gods. Their attraction to magic, Weber explains, was a result of the peasants' being so close to the organic processes and unpredictable events of nature. For peasants to become truly religious, Weber says, something very powerful has to tear them away from their normal situation in life, such as enslavement or proletarianization. The idea that peasants are very religious people is a modern notion, as he points out (see figure 3 for the relationship between religion and economy among peasants and the aristocracy).

The work circumstances of the early artisans differed from those of the peasants, and so did their religious propensity. Artisans were much less exposed to the forces of nature: they typically worked indoors; they used different muscles to perform their work; and they had more opportunity to reflect on the nature of things. Further-

---

3. Weber, *Economy and Society*, p. 491, or *Wirtschaft und Gesellschaft*, p. 299.
4. In his debate at the German Sociological Society in 1910 Weber said, for example, "We should not yield to the opinion . . . that one might view religious developments as a reflex of something else, of some economic situation. In my opinion this is unconditionally not the case." See Weber, "Max Weber on Church, Sect, and Mysticism," *Sociological Analysis* 34 (1973): 143.
5. "The nature of a stratum's religiosity has nowhere been solely determined by economic conditions"; Weber, *The Religion of China*, p. 196, or "Konfuzianismus und Taoismus," pp. 480–81 in Vol. 1 of *Gesammelte Aufsätze zur Religionssoziologie*.

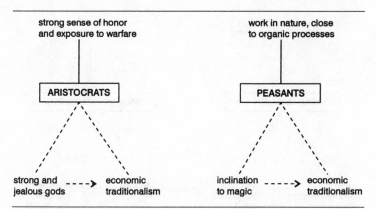

Figure 3: Religious Propensity and Attitude toward Economic Life among Aristocrats and Peasants. *Source:* Max Weber, *Economy and Society* (Berkeley: University of California Press 1978), pp. 468–76. *Comment:* Through their religious propensities, peasants as well as aristocrats tend to encourage economic traditionalism.

more, artisans often lived in the city, where blood bonds were many times replaced by new social relations. As a result, artisans tended to develop congregational and ethical types of religion, especially in the West, and these encouraged a rational lifestyle as well as a rational attitude in economic matters.

Though Weber makes clear that artisans and other petty bourgeois groups have embraced many religious experiences, from orgiasticism to mysticism, he also notes that it was from these strata that the Protestant ascetic sects would eventually emerge—and it was in these that a positive as well as a methodical religious attitude toward economic affairs would appear for the first time in history. The upper bourgeoisie, in contrast, had little interest in religion. Great merchants and early financiers had a worldly orientation to life and were skeptical toward or indifferent to religion. And while the ascetic elements in the middle classes often were positive about a rational type of capitalism, the upper strata tended to gravitate toward political capitalism, which lacked an ethical dimension (see figure 4).

Weber also discusses the religious propensity of two other groups in society: government officials and modern workers.[6] The former are sober rationalists and tend to be suspicious and distrustful of religious

---

6. For the religious propensity of these two groups, see Weber, *Economy and Society*, pp. 476–77, 484–86, or *Wirtschaft und Gesellschaft*, pp. 290–91, 295–96; Weber, "The Social Psychology of the World Religions," p. 283 in Gerth and Mills, eds., *From Max Weber*, or "Einleitung," p. 255 in Vol. 1 of *Gesammelte Aufsätze zur Religionssoziologie*.

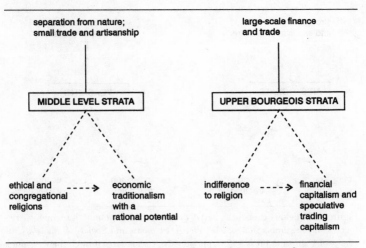

Figure 4: Religious Propensity and Attitude toward Economic Life among Some Middle-Level and Upper-Bourgeois Strata. *Source:* Max Weber, *Economy and Society* (Berkeley: University of California Press, 1978), pp. 477–84, 1178–81. *Comment:* While the ascetic elements in the middle classes often were receptive to a rational type of capitalism, the upper strata gravitated toward political capitalism, which lacked an ethical dimension.

behavior. The Confucian official exemplified this type, Weber says; he had no need for transcendence himself, but thought that magic and religion were useful to control the masses. Government officials are also ambivalent about profit-making and tend to prefer economic traditionalism. Modern workers are equally uninterested in religious questions, according to Weber, although their attitude has a different origin. The workers know from experience that they can trust their own efforts and that their fate is determined by social and economic forces, rather than natural forces of the type that govern the lives of peasants. Thus the workers reject or are indifferent to religion; and only the most desperate sections of the proletariat constitute an exception in this regard. What the workers want is "just compensation"—but of a political rather than of a religious kind. In their relationship to socialism, however, workers often display a quasi-religious attitude (see figure 5).

The fourth theme in Weber's general sociology of religion—*different ways to approach salvation and how these may affect the economy*—provides important background to his analyses in *The Protestant Ethic* and *The Economic Ethics of the World Religions*. Weber argues that the various roads to salvation may affect the economy in two different ways. First, they all entail some explicit attitudes toward economic

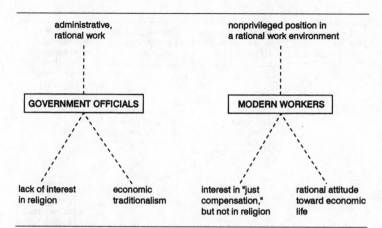

Figure 5: Religious Propensity and Attitude toward Economic Life among Government Officials and Modern Workers. *Source:* Max Weber, *Economy and Society* (Berkeley: University of California Press, 1978), pp. 476–77, 484–86. *Comment:* Workers are usually indifferent to religion and tend to have a rational attitude toward economic life. Government officials are also indifferent to religion but are ambivalent to profit-making and inclined to economic traditionalism.

life; and the more rational a religion is, the more systematic these attitudes tend to become. The mystic, for example, rejects the secular world—including work—while the Lutheran ignores the secular world and views work as a vocation. There are, however, "certain limits," Weber cautions, to the impact that this type of explicit religious attitude can have on the economy.[7]

But the different ways of seeking salvation also have a number of unintended consequences, which in certain circumstances can affect economic institutions in a profound manner. The mechanisms through which these unintended consequences influence the economy (typically in combination with intended ones) are the following. Different paths to salvation can either leave the personality of the believer intact or change it deeply and permanently. A permanent change typically entails a purification of the individual or being born again ("sanctification"). Believers whose personalities have been fundamentally changed will either withdraw from the world or attempt to change its institutions in accordance with some religious ideal. Weber says that only the efforts of the believers to change society may challenge economic traditionalism. In all other cases, the

7. Weber, *Economy and Society*, p. 528, or *Wirtschaft und Gesellschaft*, p. 321.

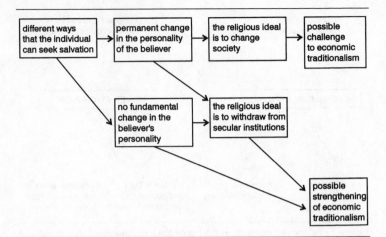

Figure 6: Different Ways of Seeking Salvation and Their Potential Influence on Economic Traditionalism. *Source:* Max Weber, *Economy and Society* (Berkeley: University of California Press, 1978), pp. 518–76. *Comment:* The various ways of reaching salvation may affect the economy in different ways. Ritualism and ecstasy, for example, do not change the believer's personality in a fundamental manner; and they tend to strengthen economic traditionalism. World-rejecting asceticism and mysticism do lead to profound personality changes but leave secular institutions intact and may inadvertently strengthen them. Only inner-worldly asceticism and fatalism have the potential to challenge economic traditionalism. The effects of the different roads to salvation are typically a combination of intended and unintended consequences.

unintended consequences of salvation efforts will probably strengthen economic traditionalism (see figure 6).

Weber analyzes a number of different ways of seeking salvation in *Economy and Society,* some of which leave the personality of the believer more or less intact and do not aim at changing social and economic institutions very much either. These include ritualism, ecstasy, doing good deeds, institutional grace, and salvation through pure faith. The impact of ritualism on the believer, Weber says, is about as superficial as that of a moving theater performance. Certain ritualistic religions also impose so many rules on the believer that only rich people can afford to follow them. Using ecstasy as a way to reach salvation has ephemeral effects and also leads in a nonrational direction. Doing good deeds has little effect on the believer's personality, especially if it is thought that bad deeds can be compensated for through good deeds.

The same is true for salvation through institutional grace and through faith alone. In the case of salvation through institutional grace, everything hinges on the institution that dispenses grace, and the individual is encouraged to obey rather than to change his or her behavior. Although the Catholic Church has a potentially powerful tool in the confession, Weber says, the way that the Church handles confessions blunts its power: sins are forgiven, and the believer is not forced to permanently change his or her behavior.[8] Salvation through faith alone—which Lutheranism offers, for example—has a similar weak effect on the behavior of the believer; it also encourages traditionalism in economic and social affairs. At the same time, Lutheranism challenges the notion of religious virtuosi in Catholicism, which restricts salvation to a minority; it furthermore proclaims ordinary secular labor to be a religious task for everyone in society (a "vocation").

There are also a few ways of seeking salvation that lead to a deep change of the believer's personality but nonetheless leave social and economic institutions intact or even strengthened. Mysticism is one of these, and here the believer sees himself or herself as a vessel to be filled by God. The mystic encourages economic traditionalism by leaving secular institutions as they are and by refusing to work. What Weber terms "world-rejecting asceticism" represents a second road to salvation that totally changes the believer's personality but again leaves the world as it is. This kind of ascetic does not want private property or a family, and he or she typically withdraws from society together with other religious virtuosi. Unlike the mystic, however, the world-rejecting ascetic works for his or her living. The fact that he or she rejects secular society in such a radical manner nonetheless tends to strengthen economic traditionalism. Since following God means withdrawing from society, economic and social institutions are automatically devalued.

According to Weber, there are only two ways of seeking salvation that change the believer's personality and may also challenge society's institutions: "inner-worldly asceticism" and predestination. The former is a very active and alert type of asceticism, which typically demands a change of society in accordance with some religious ideal.

---

8. "The psychological effect of the confessional was everywhere to relieve the individual of responsibility for his own conduct, that is why it was sought, and that weakened the rigorous consistency of the demands of asceticism"; Weber, *The Protestant Ethic,* p. 250 n. 149, or "Die protestantische Ethik und der Geist des Kapitalismus," p. 144 n. 1 in Vol. 1 of *Gesammelte Aufsätze zur Religionssoziologie.* In making this argument Weber subscribes to a psychological theory according to which a believer will change his or her behavior only if there is no other way out. He similarly points out that Egyptian religion failed to affect the behavior of its believers by allowing people to have a scarabee placed on their bodies when they were buried, thereby tricking the gods into believing that they had committed no sins. See Weber, *Ancient Judaism,* pp. 144, 199, 249, or "Antike Judenthum," pp. 156, 213, 265 in Vol. 3 of *Gesammelte Aufsätze zur Religionssoziologie.*

Some of the Protestant ascetics, for example, consciously introduced ethical-religious norms into economic life and extended their methodical approach in religious matters to money-making—two measures that would deeply affect the Western economy. That pre-destination may lead to changes in society, rather than to fatalism, may seem counterintuitive, Weber says. Nonetheless, predestination can make the believer feel that he or she is an instrument of God and that God's will must be carried out in a methodical manner. When the forces of inner-worldly asceticism and predestination are com-bined, their influence becomes particularly powerful, as I show in the next section.

## II. HISTORICAL STUDIES OF ECONOMY AND RELIGION (PART I): *THE PROTESTANT ETHIC AND THE SPIRIT OF CAPITALISM*

*The Protestant Ethic* is Weber's most celebrated study and has led to a debate that is still going on today, nearly a century after its publication. Though the main thesis—that ascetic Protestantism helped form the mentality of modern, rational capitalism—was conceived in 1898, Weber wrote the work itself a few years later, in 1903–4.[9] At the time, Weber was much concerned with methodological issues as well as with religious questions. The first part of *The Protestant Ethic*, for example, appeared in 1904, or the same year as his essay on "'Objectivity' in Social Science and Social Policy." From the terminology of the latter essay, it is clear that *The Protestant Ethic* primarily deals with an "eco-nomically relevant phenomenon" or a phenomenon that is itself noneconomic (ascetic Protestantism) but has important economic consequences (it encouraged the emergence of new type of capitalist mentality). *The Protestant Ethic* also illustrates other methodological principles, which are discussed in the essay on objectivity, and con-tains an analysis of various religious phenomena, especially Christian

9. That Weber first lectured on the main thesis of *The Protestant Ethic* in 1898 is important because it is often argued that Weber got his ideas on this score from Werner Sombart's *Der moderne Kapitalismus* (1902). According to an authority on Weber's sociology of religion, "there are at present no legitimate grounds for doubting this [that in 1898 Weber lectured on the main thesis of *The Protestant Ethic*]." See Friedrich Wilhelm Graf, "Friendship between Experts: Notes on Weber and Troeltsch," p. 223 in W. J. Mommsen and Jürgen Osterhammel, eds., *Max Weber and His Contemporaries* (London: Unwin Hyman, 1987). For Weber's own assertion of having lectured on the main thesis in *The Protestant Ethic* in 1898, see "Antikritisches zum 'Geist' des Kapitalismus," p. 150 in Max Weber, *Die protestantische Ethik II* (Gütersloh: Gütersloher Verlagshaus Mohn, 1978). A much more important source of inspiration than *Der moderne Kapitalismus* was a small work by Weber's friend and col-league Georg Jellinek, who argued that human rights had their origin in Puritan ideas and not in political thought. See Georg Jellinek, *The Declaration of the Rights of Man and of Cit-izens* (New York: Henry Holt, [1895] 1901). For different views of the relationship of Weber to Sombart as it concerns *The Protestant Ethic*, see Michael Appel, *Werner Sombart* (Mar-burg: Metropolis Verlag, 1992), pp. 121–27; Hartmut Lehmann, "The Rise of Capitalism: Weber versus Sombart," pp. 195–208 in Lehmann and Roth, eds., *Weber's Protestant Ethic*; and Friedrich Lenger, *Werner Sombart 1863–1941* (Munich: C. II. Beck, 1994), pp. 129–35.

churches and sects. In this discussion of *The Protestant Ethic*, however, I highlight its contributions to economic sociology rather than to the sociology of religion or the methodology of the social sciences. With this purpose in mind, I proceed to a presentation of the content of *The Protestant Ethic* that follows its main argument closely, but also pays special attention to economic phenomena. I then say something about the writings of Weber that complement *The Protestant Ethic* and about the debate it has generated.

*The Protestant Ethic* appeared in two installments in 1904–5 in *Archiv für Sozialwissenschaft und Sozialpolitik*. Part 1, or the first installment, is entitled "The Problem" and consists of three short chapters in which Weber presents the problem to be studied, how to study it, and in which direction a solution is to be sought. In Part 2, which appeared about half a year later, Weber presents the solution to his problem. Its title is "The Ethics of Vocation in Ascetic Protestantism," and it is about twice as long as Part 1, although it consists of only two chapters. Weber revised the whole text in 1919 for its inclusion in a multivolume set entitled *Collected Essays in the Sociology of Religion*. He added a sentence here and there and some footnotes, but changed nothing in the main argument.

Weber starts *The Protestant Ethic* with a general discussion of why Protestants seems to be much more economically successful than Catholics (chap. 1, "Religious Affiliation and Social Stratification"). The purpose of this chapter is not so much to analyze the stratification of Catholics in relation to Protestants in Weber's day as to slowly guide the reader into a more precise understanding of the problem and the terminology. In countries where there are both Catholics and Protestants, Weber notes (reproducing a statistical error in the process),[1] there are proportionally more Protestants than Catholics among managers and capital owners as well as among technically and administratively skilled workers. With this problem in mind, Weber proceeds to a discussion of several theories that had been suggested at the time as possible solutions. He also touches on the role of minorities in economic life and on the powerful effect that migration can have on economic attitudes.[2] Weber rejects all of the suggested

---

1. As part of his argument Weber also discusses the educational achievements of Catholic and Protestant students, in the course of which he cites some figures that contain a numerical error, as pointed out by Kurt Samuelsson. Weber uses a study by Martin Offenbacher, and "through a typographical or arithmetical error, Offenbacher . . . made the proportion of Protestants in the *Realgymnasien* 69% instead of 59%; Weber later took over and used this incorrect figure [in the table on page 189 in *The Protestant Ethic*]." See Kurt Samuelsson, *Religion and Economic Action* (London: Heinemann, 1961), p. 140.

2. Weber, *The Protestant Ethic*, pp. 39–40 n. 20, p. 191, or "Die protestantische Ethik," pp. 22–23, 27–28 n. 3 in Vol. 1 of *Gesammelte Aufsätze zur Religionssoziologie*. Weber argues (1) that politically excluded minorities tend to compensate by advancing in the economic sphere (e.g., the Huguenots in France or the Jews in all countries); and (2) that migrant workers typically break with their earlier traditionalism when they begin to work in different surroundings.

solutions, however, either because they are outright wrong or because they use such clumsy concepts that they fail to get a handle on the problem. To produce a successful solution, Weber notes in chapter 1, the problem must be formulated much more precisely and better concepts introduced. In the next chapter Weber moves away from his initial and rather general discussion of the relationship between religious affiliation and stratification, and states what he intends to look at in his study (chap. 2, "The Spirit of Capitalism"). What is central to modern capitalism, he says, is the tendency to view work (including money-making) as a vocation or an end in itself, and it is the origin of *this* attitude that needs to be established. It is not possible, Weber argues, that this specific approach to work is somehow the invention of a single individual; it has to originate in the collective lifestyle of a group of people. He also points out—and this is an important part of the argument in *The Protestant Ethic*—that today, when the capitalist system is safely established, there is less of a need that everybody accepts the notion of a vocation with an explicitly ethical dimension because people have to work in a systematic and restless manner anyway if they are to survive economically. At one time, however, systematic money-making and work for its own sake were looked down on in religion and hence in society at large—and the original concept of vocation consequently had to have a strong ethical component if it were to successfully establish itself.

To illustrate what he calls "the spirit of (modern) capitalism"[3]—of which vocation constitutes the central part—Weber cites some of the writings of Benjamin Franklin (1706–90). According to Franklin, the individual should work constantly, not only when he needs money or feels like it: "He that idly loses five shillings' worth of time, loses five shillings, and might as prudently throw five shillings into the sea." To not use one's capital is equally wrong because money begets money: "He that kills a breeding-sow, destroys all her offspring to the thousandth generation. He that murders (!) a crown, destroys all that it might have produced, even scores of pounds." At one point in his autobiography Franklin also quotes a passage from the Bible that his Calvinist father had often repeated to him: "Seest thou a Man diligent in his Calling? He shall stand before Kings."[4] Weber summarizes the section on Franklin by saying that this type of attitude toward work and money-making is truly novel in human history: every per-

---

3. Weber, *The Protestant Ethic*, p. 64, or "Die protestantische Ethik," p. 49 in Vol. 1 of *Gesammelte Aufsätze zur Religionssoziologie*. The German original reads: "*Geist des (modernen) Kapitalismus.*"
4. Quoted in Weber, *The Protestant Ethic*, pp. 50, 49, 53, or "Die protestantische Ethik," pp. 32, 31, 36 in Vol. 1 of *Gesammelte Aufsätze zur Religionssoziologie*. The exclamation mark was added by Weber. For the correct wording of the quotation about "a Man diligent in his Calling," see Benjamin Franklin, *The Autobiography of Benjamin Franklin* (New Haven, Conn.: Yale University Press, 1964), p. 144.

son has an ethical duty to work and make money as methodically and diligently as possible.

This ethical component clearly differentiates the spirit of modern capitalism from "the instinct of acquisition," which according to Weber can be found in all ages since the dawn of history. Weber was suspicious of this concept, which he later would criticize sharply and which has since fallen into well-deserved oblivion.[5] Weber also points out that one can find examples of the instinct of acquisition in acts that are characterized by ruthless acquisition and bound by no ethical rules whatsoever. The unethical type of capitalism that results from this type of acquisitive activity Weber labels "adventurers' capitalism," and describes as follows:

> Capitalist acquisition as an adventure has been at home in all types of economic society which have known trade with the use of money and which have offered it opportunities, through *commenda*, farming of taxes, State loans, financing of wars, ducal courts and officeholders. Likewise the inner attitude of the adventurer, which laughs at all ethical limitations, has been universal. Absolute and conscious ruthlessness in acquisition has often stood in the closest connection with the strictest conformity to tradition.[6]

The concept of adventurers' capitalism cuts across two of the categories that Weber uses in his discussion of the different types of capitalism in *Economy and Society*, namely political capitalism and

---

5. The German term for "the instinct of acquisition" or "impulse to acquisition" is *Erwerbstrieb*, and it was used, for example, by Schmoller in *Grundriss der Allgemeinen Volkswirtschaftslehre* (1900–1904) and by Sombart in *Der moderne Kapitalismus* (1902). Both Schmoller and Sombart were critical of using this concept biologically, as some economists did, and insisted that the *Erwerbstrieb* changed with social and historical circumstances. According to Weber, writing in the mid-1910s on *Economy and Society*, *Erwerbstrieb* was nonetheless "a concept . . . which is wholly imprecise and better not used at all"; see Weber, *Economy and Society*, pp. 1190–91, or *Wirtschaft und Gesellschaft*, p. 712. Weber also directs harsh criticism at the idea that the instinct of acquisition had led to the creation of capitalism ("it should be taught in the kindergarten of cultural history that this naive idea of capitalism must be given up once and for all"; Weber, *The Protestant Ethic*, p. 17, or "Vorbemerkung," p. 4 in Vol. 1 of *Gesammelte Aufsätze zur Religionssoziologie*). Nonetheless, Weber occasionally uses the term himself, roughly in the sense of a biological impulse or drive that can be formed by the resistance it meets in a personality (see Weber, *Economy and Society*, pp. 617–18, or *Wirtschaft und Gesellschaft*, p. 371; Weber, *General Economic History*, p. 356, or *Wirtschaftsgeschichte*, p. 303). I have been unable to trace the history of the concept of *Erwerbstrieb*. One possible origin may have been German psychology, another Adam Smith's famous quip about "the propensity" or "the disposition" to "truck, barter, and exchange" in *The Wealth of Nations*. See Gustav von Schmoller, "Der Erwerbstrieb und die wirtschaftlichen Tugenden," pp. 33–41 in Vol. 1 of *Grundriss der Allgemeinen Volkswirtschaftslehre* (Leipzig: Duncker und Humblot, 1900); Werner Sombart, "Das Erwachsen des kapitalistischen Geistes," pp. 378–90 in Vol. 1 of *Der moderne Kapitalismus* (Leipzig: Duncker und Humblot, 1902); and Adam Smith, *An Inquiry into the Nature and Causes of the Wealth of Nations* (Oxford: Oxford University Press, 1976), pp. 25, 30.

6. Weber, *The Protestant Ethic*, p. 58, or "Die protestantische Ethik," p. 43 in Vol. 1 of *Gesammelte Aufsätze zur Religionssoziologie*. See also *The Protestant Ethic*, pp. 69, 76, or "Die protestantische Ethik," pp. 53–54, 61.

traditional commercial capitalism.[7] The term "adventurers' capitalism" is not used in the theoretical chapter on economic sociology in *Economy and Society;* and Weber presumably introduced it in *The Protestant Ethic* in order to get a good contrast to the moral type of capitalism that ascetic Protestantism helped to create.

Weber is also careful to distinguish the spirit of modern capitalism from what he calls "the traditionalist spirit" in capitalism.[8] Unlike adventurers' capitalism, the traditionalist spirit does have an ethical component. It is, for example, held to be wrong to work in any but a traditional manner, to invest in any but a traditional manner, and so on. Weber uses an example from the textile industry in the mid-nineteenth century to illustrate the difference between the modern capitalist spirit and the traditionalist spirit of capitalism, and also to make the important point that "the capitalist form" can remain the same even if the economic spirit that animates it changes. There is naturally a tendency for a certain "form" and a certain "spirit" to go together, Weber says, but this is by no means always the case.[9] Benjamin Franklin's printing business, for example, had a traditional "form" but was animated by a nontraditional "spirit."

Weber's example of the textile industry in the mid-nineteenth century fills in some important details in his argument. Around this time in continental Europe, Weber says, a textile manufacturer typically managed a putting-out system, with some local peasants producing the cloth. The manufacturer bought the cloth from the peasants at a traditional price and then sold it from his warehouses, making a moderate profit in the process. The working day lasted some five or six hours for the owner, so there was plenty of time for leisure and rest. Capital accounting was used in this type of business, Weber notes, but things nonetheless went on in a fairly tranquil and traditional manner. One day, however, an entrepreneur would appear, with a similar type ("form") of economic organization, but with a different idea about how things should be done ("spirit"). This newly arrived entrepreneur might choose his suppliers among the peasants more carefully; he might personally approach his customers; or he might introduce a higher volume

---

7. Weber used the concept of adventurers' capitalism in the early 1900s, when *The Protestant Ethic* was published, but also some ten or fifteen years later, around the time that he wrote chapter 2 of *Economy and Society.* See Weber, *The Protestant Ethic,* pp. 20, 25, or "Vorbemerkung," pp. 7, 11 in Vol. 1 of *Gesammelte Aufsätze zur Religionssoziologie;* Weber, "Parliament and Government in Germany under a New Political Order," p. 148 in *Political Writings,* or "Parlament und Regierung im neugeordneten Deutschland," p. 323 in *Gesammelte Politische Schriften* (Tübingen: J.C.B. Mohr, 1988). For Weber's typology of capitalism in §31 in chapter 2, see Weber, *Economy and Society,* pp. 164–66, or *Wirtschaft und Gesellschaft,* pp. 95–97.

8. Weber alternatively uses the term "traditionalism." See, e.g., Weber, *The Protestant Ethic,* pp. 58–60, 65, or "Die protestantische Ethik," pp. 43–44, 50 in Vol. 1 of *Gesammelte Aufsätze zur Religionssoziologie.*

9. Weber, *The Protestant Ethic,* pp. 64, 67, or "Die protestantische Ethik," pp. 50, 51 in Vol. 1 of *Gesammelte Aufsätze zur Religionssoziologie.*

of production in combination with a lower price. Similar to Schumpeter, Weber argues that this new and innovative entrepreneur would have had to be very strong overcome all the mistrust and indignation he was apt to encounter. In contrast to Schumpeter, however, Weber says that his strength would have had to be of a moral kind.[1]

Weber discusses both the new type of entrepreneur and the new type of worker. When offered a higher wage, traditional workers will accept it—but also reduce their hours of work because their traditional needs can now be more easily satisfied. In other words, the supply curve for this type of labor is backward-sloping. In addition, the traditional workers attach no special value to work itself. On both accounts, the new workers differ: even if their wages are raised, they will continue to work the same number of hours, and they will invest more of their own character in the work because they regard it as an end in itself.

In the last chapter of Part 1 of *The Protestant Ethic*, Weber moves from the nineteenth century to the sixteenth century to look at the concept of vocation (chap. 3, "Luther's Concept of the Calling: Task of the Investigation"). The idea that one has a religious duty to properly carry out one's worldly activity, Weber says, can be traced directly to Luther's translation of the Bible. This was the first time in the history of religion, he emphasizes, that ordinary labor was infused with a positive religious meaning—and not just the activities of a small religious elite, as in the monasteries and nunneries. And from Luther the notion of vocation (*Beruf*) spread to the everyday language of all the Protestant countries. To Luther, however, work constitutes a lot to be accepted, unlike a task set by God in which one should strive to excel. As a consequence of this, Weber says, Luther's role in the development of the modern capitalist spirit was to be minor.

Calvinism and some of the Protestant sects took a more active approach to vocation than Lutheranism and were in many ways closer in spirit to modern capitalism than to the economic traditionalism of Luther. Weber notes that numerous Calvinists and members of ascetic Protestant sects had been extremely successful in their economic dealings. But exactly how to analyze the relationship between the non-Lutheran types of Protestantism and capitalism raises some difficult questions, according to Weber. One cannot find an explicit argument

1. In his famous description of what drives the entrepreneur, Schumpeter mentions "the dream and the will to found a private kingdom, . . . the will to conquer, [and] finally, there is the joy of creating, of getting things done or simply of exercising one's energy and ingenuity." Schumpeter also states that being an entrepreneur cannot be a "vocation" because it is not of a routine character. To this should be added that although Schumpeter is talking about the entrepreneur in a modern capitalist system in general, Weber is discussing the entrepreneur in the transition to such a system. See Joseph A. Schumpeter, *The Theory of Economic Development* (Cambridge, Mass.: Harvard University Press, 1934), pp. 77, 92–94. Schumpeter's work on the entrepreneur, *Theorie der wirtschaftichen Entwicklung,* appeared a few years after *The Protestant Ethic* (1904–5) in 1911; Weber's personal, annotated copy of Schumpeter's work still exists.

in favor of a new capitalist spirit in the statements of Calvin and other important Protestant leaders. The primary concern of these leaders was always with the salvation of the soul, Weber emphasizes, and not with money-making and capitalism. Some other way to investigate the relationship between religion and economy had therefore to be found. Only if this were done would it become possible to determine—and now Weber states the main task of his study—how the Protestant ethic has contributed to "*the qualitative formation and quantitative expansion*" of the modern capitalist spirit (see figure 7 for the diffusion of Protestantism).[2]

Weber provides the solution to this problem in two steps in Part 2 of *The Protestant Ethic*: he first explicates the general mechanism (chap. 4), and then applies it to the economy (chap. 5). In chapter 4 ("The Religious Foundations of Worldly Asceticism") Weber states that he is not interested in tracing the influence of either theological ideas on the individual or the teachings of the Church. Instead, he says, he will take the adoption of a certain religious faith by the individual as his point of departure in the analysis. The mechanism through which the adoption of a religious faith translates into practical behavior, he suggests, is the following one: religious benefits set "psychological premiums" on specific types of behavior, and in certain circumstances these may then lead to the formation of novel "psychological impulses."[3] Ascetic behavior, to use Weber's terminology, is the product of a religion that directs practical behavior in such a manner that impulses toward systematic and self-denying behavior are produced. Calvinism, Weber also points out, is the most consistent example of such an ascetic religion.

Calvinism had a very somber vision of humanity, in which predestination played a key role. No one but God knew who the elect were, and there was absolutely nothing that the individual could do to change his or her preordained fate. This, one might have thought, would have led to fatalism and resignation, but such was not the case. Instead, the starkness of the choice between damnation and salvation predisposed the individual to a methodical conduct in the service of God, as did the crucial fact that no forgiveness could be given for

2. Weber, *The Protestant Ethic*, p. 91, or "Das protestantische Ethik," p. 83 in Vol. 1 of *Gesammelte Aufsätze zur Religionssoziologie*. The German term for "formation" is *Prägung*; emphasis added.

3. In the first version of *The Protestant Ethic*, Weber mainly relied on the concept of "psychological impulses" (*"psychologische Antriebe"*; translated by Parsons as "religious sanctions"); in the revised edition he also used the concept of "psychological premiums"(*"psychologische Prämien"*). Around the same time that he revised *The Protestant Ethic*, Weber summarized his approach in this study in the following manner: "It is not the ethical *doctrine* of a religion that matters, but that form of ethical conduct upon which *premiums* are placed." See Weber, "The Protestant Sects and the Spirit of Capitalism," p. 321 in Gerth and Mills, eds., *From Max Weber*, or "Die protestantischen Sekten und der Geist des Kapitalismus," pp. 234–35 in Vol. 1 of *Gesammelte Aufsätze zur Religionssoziologie*. It may be added that Weber devised his own terminology with concepts such as "psychological impulses" because he did not think that there existed adequate terms in the psychology of his day.

one's sins, even if they were minor. A strong hostility to the natural state of man (*status naturalis*) and the fact that religious benefits could only be had in the next world, not in this life, operated in the same direction. Calvinism also contained a vigorous element of activism—man should serve God by changing the world in his image—and this element directed the systematic and restless activities of the believers outward, toward the existing social institutions.

Weber says that a similar ascetic and activist approach to life could also be found in Pietism, Methodism, and the Baptist sects, even though all of these started out from a somewhat different set of religious ideas than Calvinism. He also contrasts Calvinism with

Figure 7: The Diffusion of Protestantism in Europe, circa 1570. *Source*: Chris Park, *Sacred Worlds* (London: Routledge, 1996), p. 113. *Comment*: According to Weber, the spirit of modern capitalism was formed under the influence of ascetic Protestantism during the late sixteenth and the seventeenth centuries. A map of the West at the end of the seventeenth century would also show that the ideas of Calvin and the English Puritans had spread to the English colonies on the East Coast of North America. It should also be noted that by 1685, through the revocation of the Edict of Nantes, the French Protestants or Huguenots had begun their exodus to England, Holland, Prussia, and America.

Lutheranism and Catholicism in order to bring out its special character. While Lutheranism emphasizes faith and a mystical union with God, thereby weakening its ascetic and activist element, Catholicism ends up doing more or less the same, Weber argues, through the sacrament of absolution. Neither one sets a premium on the kind of behavior that can give "psychological impulses" to a consistently methodical lifestyle. Although Calvinism and the ascetic Protestant sects, as well as Lutheranism and Catholicism, all are based on the same body of thought—the Bible, which condemns the accumulation of riches as a goal in life—some of them end up encouraging economic rationalism and others economic traditionalism (see figure 8).

An ascetic lifestyle of the type that Calvinism leads to, Weber argues, influences the economy primarily through "maxims for everyday economic conduct" (chap. 5, "Asceticism and the Spirit of Capitalism").[4] According to one of these maxims, one should work hard and systematically in one's vocation. If this restless activity leads to wealth, it was imperative not to use this wealth for leisure or for the consumption of luxury items. Making a fortune was not wrong per se—as long as the riches were not used for personal indulgence. "You may labour to be rich for God, though not for the flesh and sin," as one of the authorities on Puritan ethics put it. Making plenty of money was even encouraged in Calvinism, since it was a sign that God looked upon one's labor with favor: "It is true that the usefulness of a calling, and thus its favour in the sight of God, is measured first in moral terms, and then in terms of the importance of the goods produced in it for the community. But a third criterion—which is naturally the most important one in practice—is private profitableness."[5]

That this type of Puritan ethics was very close to the nonreligious "spirit of (modern) capitalism" as propounded by Benjamin Franklin is clear. Even if the Puritans did not equate time with money, it must nonetheless not be wasted; there was also a general premium on restless activity in one's vocation (see figure 9 for Benjamin Franklin's moral bookkeeping). Because consumption of luxuries was not allowed, additional funds were constantly made available for new investments. Furthermore, the Puritans introduced a stern and honest morality into economic life. They detested the aristocracy for its idleness and luxuries, and they deeply disapproved of everything that came close to adventurers' capitalism. The hostility of the Puritans to monopolies and political capitalism undoubtedly helped a competitive and private kind of capitalism to emerge. The viewpoint that money-making and religion could very well go together also helped to legitimize capitalism:

4. Weber, *The Protestant Ethic*, p. 155, or "Die protestantische Ethik," p. 163 in Vol. 1 of *Gesammelte Aufsätze zur Religionssoziologie*.
5. Weber, *The Protestant Ethic*, p. 162, or "Die protestantische Ethik," pp. 175–76 in Vol. 1 of *Gesammelte Aufsätze zur Religionssoziologie*. The translation has been changed.

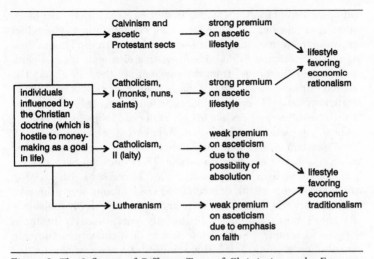

Figure 8: The Influence of Different Types of Christianity on the Economy, according to *The Protestant Ethic: Source:* See especially Max Weber, *The Protestant Ethic and the Spirit of Capitalism* (London: Allen and Unwin, 1930), pp. 197 n. 12, 259 n. 4. *Comment:* Religious benefits, according to Weber, set psychological premiums on certain forms of behavior. Some of these behaviors produce impulses toward an ascetic lifestyle and economic rationalism, while others encourage economic traditionalism.

A specifically bourgeois vocational ethic grew up. With the consciousness of standing in the fullness of God's grace and being visibly blessed by Him, the bourgeois business man could now follow his pecuniary interests as he would and feel that he was fulfilling a duty in doing so—as long as he remained within the bounds of formal correctness, as long as his moral conduct was spotless and the use to which he put his wealth was not objectionable. The power of religious asceticism provided him in addition with sober, conscientious, and unusually industrious workmen, who clung to their work as to a life and purpose willed by God.[6]

The ascetic form of the Protestant ethic, Weber says, helped to shape and to spread the spirit of modern rational capitalism. It accomplished this by breaking down the ethical disapproval surrounding traditional capitalism and by actively creating and promoting a more methodical approach to economic affairs (see Weber's whole argument in *The Protestant Ethic* as summarized in figure 10). Once this

6. Weber, *The Protestant Ethic*, pp. 176–77, or "Die protestantische Ethik," pp. 198–99 in Vol. 1 of *Gesammelte Aufsätze zur Religionssoziologie.* The translation has been changed.

had been done, however, capitalism did not need any further assistance from religion, and today's rational capitalism is a system that operates largely according to its own dynamics.[7] In the famous ending of The Protestant Ethic Weber says that economic life has hardened into an "iron cage" from the viewpoint of the individual.[8] The original Puritans are long gone, and so is their concept of vocation as a religious task. "The idea of duty in one's calling," Weber says, "prowls about in our lives like the ghost of dead religious beliefs."[9]

For a complete picture of what Weber tried to accomplish with The Protestant Ethic, some additional material needs to be taken into account. There is, first, his article "The Protestant Sects and the Spirit of Capitalism" (1st version 1906; 2d revised version 1920), which contains a wealth of interesting observations about the relationship between the ascetic sects and economic life. It is also one of Weber's most inspired and beautifully written essays. Insofar as the general argument in The Protestant Ethic is concerned, the main contribution of this article is that it indicates a new mechanism that played a role in the formation of the spirit of modern capitalism, namely the sect. According to Weber, the individual member of a sect feels compelled to always hold his or her own in the presence of other sect members. The sect, in other words, helps turn the "impulses" to engage in inner-worldly ascetic behavior into a character trait that is favorable to economic rationalism.

7. In this context see also the following statement by Weber from a few years later:
   We want to reiterate as clearly as possible that, as far as the modern industrial workforce is concerned, religion as such no longer creates differences in the way in which this seems to have been true for the bourgeoisie in the era of early capitalism. Rather, the intensity of religious influence, whether Catholic or Protestant, on conduct is important. Contemporary Catholicism, which differs so much in its thrust from medieval Catholicism, is today as useful a means of domestication as any kind of 'Protestant asceticism.' (Max Weber "Zur Psychophysik der industriellen Arbeit," pp. 239–40 n. 1 in Gesammelte Aufsätze zur Soziologie und Sozialpolitik. The translation is from Guenther Roth, "Global Capitalism and Multiethnicity: Max Weber Then and Now," unpublished paper, p. 9.)
8. In being asked by Benjamin Nelson in the mid-1970s why he had chosen to translate "ein stahlhartes Gehäuse" in The Protestant Ethic (1930) as "iron cage"—a term that has become very famous—Parsons gave the following answer:
   I cannot remember clearly just how and why I decided when more than 35 years ago I was translating Weber's Protestant Ethic essay to introduce the phrase 'iron cage.' . . . I think 'iron cage' was a case of rather free translation. I do not remember being aware at the time of the use of the phrase by John Bunyan. However, as you know, I was brought up deeply steeped in a puritan background, and whether or not I intentionally adopted the term from Bunyan seems to me probably secondary. The most likely explanation of my choice is that I thought it appropriate to the puritan background of Weber's own personal engagement in the Puritan Ethic problem.
   See the letter by Talcott Parsons to Benjamin Nelson, dated January 24, 1975, in the Harvard University Archives (HUG[FP]42.8.8, Box 10); Weber, The Protestant Ethic, p. 181, or "Die protestantische Ethik," p. 203 in Vol. 1 of Gesammelte Aufsätze zur Religionssoziologie. For Parsons's translation of The Protestant Ethic, see also Peter Ghosh, "Some Problems with Talcott Parsons' Translation of 'The Protestant Ethic,'" Archives Européennes de Sociologie 30 (1994): 104–23.
9. Weber, The Protestant Ethic, p. 182, or "Die protestantische Ethik," p. 204 in Vol. 1 of Gesammelte Aufsätze zur Religionssoziologie.

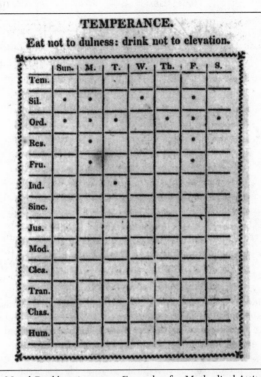

## TEMPERANCE.

### Eat not to dulness: drink not to elevation.

|       | Sun. | M. | T. | W. | Th. | F. | S. |
|-------|------|----|----|----|-----|----|----|
| Tem.  |      |    | •  |    |     |    |    |
| Sil.  | •    | •  |    | •  |     | •  |    |
| Ord.  | •    | •  | •  |    | •   | •  | •  |
| Res.  |      | •  |    |    |     | •  |    |
| Fru.  |      | •  |    |    |     | •  |    |
| Ind.  |      |    | •  |    |     |    |    |
| Sinc. |      |    |    |    |     |    |    |
| Jus.  |      |    |    |    |     |    |    |
| Mod.  |      |    |    |    |     |    |    |
| Clea. |      |    |    |    |     |    |    |
| Tran. |      |    |    |    |     |    |    |
| Chas. |      |    |    |    |     |    |    |
| Hum.  |      |    |    |    |     |    |    |

Figure 9: Moral Bookkeeping as an Example of a Methodical Attitude toward Life: Benjamin Franklin's Schedule for Developing His Character and Using Time Efficiently. *Source:* Benjamin Franklin, *Memoirs of the Life and Writings of Benjamin Franklin* (Philadelphia: T. S. Manning [1793] 1818), p. 91; cf. Max Weber, *The Protestant Ethic and the Spirit of Capitalism* (London: Allen and Unwin, 1930), pp. 124, 238 n. 100. *Explanation:* The horizontal line lists the days of the week; the vertical line lists virtues (Tem. = temperance; Sil. = silence; Ord. = order; Res. = resolution; Fru. = frugality; Ind. = industry; Sinc. = sincerity; Jus. = justice; Mod. = moderation; Clea. = cleanliness; Tran. = tranquillity; Chas. = chastity; and Hum. = humility). *Comment:* This figure reproduces one page in a booklet that Benjamin Franklin (1706–90) put together for himself in order to develop his character. Each week he focused on one virtue (in this case temperance), hoping in that manner to gradually become a better person. Weber calls Franklin's table of virtues "a classic example" of the type of methodical lifestyle that the ascetic Protestants developed, but he also points out that without sanctions, a scheme of this type would be less efficient. Weber himself received a copy of Franklin's autobiography as a Christmas gift when he was eleven years old.

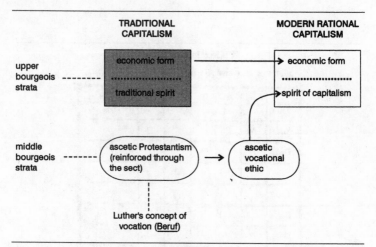

Figure 10: The Contribution of Ascetic Protestantism to the Qualitative Formation of the Modern Capitalist Spirit in the Late Sixteenth and Seventeenth Centuries, according to *The Protestant Ethic: Source:* See especially Max Weber, *The Protestant Ethic and the Spirit of Capitalism* (London: Allen and Unwin, 1930), pp. 75, 91, 220, 159, 273. *Comment:* Weber's goal in *The Protestant Ethic* was to outline and explain the contribution made by ascetic Protestantism to "the qualitative formation and the quantitative expansion" of the modern capitalist spirit. The formation of the spirit of modern capitalism started toward the end of the sixteenth century, continued during the seventeenth century, and was complete by the eighteenth century in some parts of the West. The organizational form of capitalism, however, did not undergo any changes due to religion. The shaded area in the figure represents economic activity that was considered "ethically unjustifiable or at best to be tolerated," according to the prevalent religious view. The argument about the sect's reinforcing the ideas of ascectic Protestantism was added in an article from 1906.

Weber's essay on the Protestant sects also supplies new information on the spread of the Protestant ethic. The main argument in *The Protestant Ethic*, to recall, deals not only with the formation of a new capitalist spirit but also with its diffusion. Weber's essay adds a very interesting analysis of the role played by the sects in the United States and their influence on the American social structure. Especially among the middle strata, Weber says, the sects helped to maintain and diffuse the business ethos during the nineteenth century. The reader also gets a distinct sense that the sects in the United States (as well as their secular offspring, the voluntary associations) have left an important imprint on the American national character and also contributed to the dynamism of its economic system.[1]

1. In this context see also the evocative remarks that Weber made at the 1910 meeting of the German Sociological Society: "Max Weber on Church, Sect, and Mysticism," *Sociological Analysis* 34 (1973): 140–49. In general, the influence of ascetic Protestantism on U.S.

Another place where Weber supplies complementary information on the problem in *The Protestant Ethic* is in his lecture course known as *General Economic History*.[2] Toward the end, Weber lectured on the evolution of the modern capitalist spirit, and the main thrust of what he said is more or less identical to the argument in *The Protestant Ethic*. What emerges with more clarity in the lecture series, however, is how much the Puritan business ethics differed from what Weber calls "the double ethic."[3] Earlier in history, he explains, there had been one type of ethics for one's family, clan, or community of believers, and another moral code for strangers and outsiders, which was considerably more ruthless in character. The Puritans dramatically broke with this by introducing a new type of ethics into business, according to which every individual should be treated in the same way, regardless of creed or origin.

The *General Economic History* also makes another, very important contribution to the understanding of *The Protestant Ethic*. Just by reading through Weber's account in *General Economic History*, chapter by chapter, of how modern capitalism came into being, the reader comes to realize that this was a process that took many centuries and also involved other factors than the religious ones. Modern capitalism, in other words, was not the result of some new capitalist spirit that suddenly emerged in the sixteenth and seventeenth centuries and jump-started an already existing economic organization. Weber, of course, makes this point in *The Protestant Ethic*, but he does it in a more subtle manner; and this makes it harder to understand that he is only talking about one single phase—albeit a particularly important one—in the long and difficult evolution of the modern capitalist system, namely the creation of a new capitalist spirit. Modern rational capitalism, as Weber repeatedly states in *General Economic History*, is the result of a number of events that took place *before* as well as *after* the creation of a new capitalist spirit. Among the events that took place before this event is the birth of the Western city and modern (Roman) law; and among those that came after is the factory system and the systematic use of science in production. Weber's argument on this point is particularly important to keep in mind since the consensus seems to be that *The*

society has been surprisingly neglected in social science; for an exception, see Seymour Martin Lipset's work, e.g., "Culture and Economic Behavior: A Commentary," *Journal of Labor Economics* 11 (1993): S330–47; and Seymour Martin Lipset, *American Exceptionalism: A Double-Edged Sword* (New York: W. W. Norton, 1996).

2. Two additional places are Weber's contribution to the debate surrounding *The Protestant Ethic* (discussed later in this chapter) and the section in *Economy and Society* entitled "The Reformation and Its Impact on Economic Life." See Weber, *Economy and Society*, pp. 1196–1200, or *Wirtschaft und Gesellschaft*, pp. 716–17.

3. Parsons uses the term "double ethic" (for "*Aussenmoral*") in *The Protestant Ethic*; see Weber, *The Protestant Ethic*, p. 57, or "Die protestantische Ethik," p. 43 in Vol. 1 of *Gesammelte Aufsätze zur Religionssoziologie*.

*Protestant Ethic* advocates a religious or "cultural" explanation of the birth of capitalism.[4]

The *Protestant Ethic* caused quite a bit of controversy in Weber's day, and the debate endures today, nearly a century later. Typical for the ambivalence that many social scientists apparently still feel toward Weber's study is the following statement by Barrington Moore, Jr., from the late 1970s: "It is by no means clear whether Max Weber's famous contribution in *The Protestant Ethic and the Spirit of Capitalism* constituted an important breakthrough or a blind alley."[5] To properly present the major arguments and counterarguments in the debate on Weber's thesis during the nearly one hundred years it has been going on is not possible in this work, in which I attempt instead to present Weber's sociological analysis of the economy in general. I shall therefore say only a few words about Weber's own participation in the debate, and about two recent and particularly interesting contributions from the viewpoint of economic sociology. Economists, it may be added in passing, have not shown much of an interest in Weber's thesis.[6]

Weber published four comments during 1907–10 in response to his original critics—primarily German economists and economic historians—and these articles are still worth reading since many of the criticisms directed at *The Protestant Ethic* are often repeated and based on a few misunderstandings of what Weber actually said. In his answers to the critics, Weber, for example, points out that he by no means had said that one will find the modern capitalist spirit wherever

---

4. A recent article in the *Economist* said, for example: "Perhaps the oldest school [in culture and the economy] holds that cultural values and norms equip people—and, by extension, countries—either poorly or well for economic success. The archetypal modern pronouncement of this view was Max Weber's investigation of the Protestant work ethic"; "Cultural Explanations," *Economist*, November 9, 1996, p. 26.

5. Barrington Moore, Jr., *Injustice: The Social Bases of Obedience and Revolt* (White Plains, N.Y.: M. E. Sharpe, 1978), p. 466 n. 7. Barrington Moore is referring to Weber's thesis about the origin of the work ethic.

6. I have been unable to find a single full analysis by an economist of Weber's argument in *The Protestant Ethic*. One reason for this is probably that economic theory does not address questions of this type; or, to cite Nicholas Kaldor, "economic speculation [that is, economic theory] here trespasses on the fields of sociology and social history; and the most that an economist can say is that there is nothing in economic analysis as such which would dispute the important connection, emphasised by economic historians and sociologists, between the rise of Protestant ethic and the rise of Capitalism"; Nicholas Kaldor, "The Relation of Economic Growth and Cyclical Fluctuations," *Economic Journal* 64 (1954): 67. There exist, however, some minor references to Weber's thesis in works by such well-known economists as Kenneth Boulding (positive), Albert O. Hirschman (positive), Paul Samuelson (negative), Joseph Schumpeter (negative), and Jacob Viner (negative). See Kenneth Boulding, "Religious Foundations of Economic Progress," *Public Affairs* 14 (1952): 3; Albert O. Hirschman, *The Passions and the Interests* (Princeton, N.J.: Princeton University Press, 1977), pp. 9–12; Gaston Rimlinger, "Review of Jacob Viner, *Religious Thought and Economic Society*," *Journal of Economic History* 39 (1979): 834; Paul Samuelson, *Economics* (New York: McGraw-Hill, 1970), p. 747; and Jacob Viner, *Religious Thought and Economic Society: Four Chapters of an Unfinished Work* (Durham, N.C.: Duke University Press, 1978). Schumpeter's critique of *The Protestant Ethic* is worth citing:

one finds ascetic Protestantism or that one will find capitalism wherever one finds the modern capitalist spirit.[7] This is true because other factors may intervene in the particular historical case and sometimes have done so. Weber also points out that he had never said that religion or the Reformation had somehow "caused" capitalism to emerge; his argument in *The Protestant Ethic* was rather that ascetic Protestantism had played an important role during the late sixteenth and the seventeenth centuries in the creation of a new kind of economic mentality ("the [modern] capitalist spirit") but had left the economic organization ("the economic form") unchanged.[8]

Weber furthermore says he agrees with the criticism that Calvin's opinion should not be confused with the ideas of later Calvinism—and that he had said so in *The Protestant Ethic*. He responds to his critics that a financier like Jacob Fugger (1459–1525) did not display the modern capitalist spirit at all (as defined in *The Protestant Ethic*) because Fugger lacked a sober and systematic approach to life.[9] Similarly, Sombart had been wrong to argue that the concept

---

Some economists, among whom it must suffice to mention Max Weber, have felt the need of explaining the rise of capitalism by means of a special theory. But the problem such theories have been framed to solve is wholly imaginary and owes its existence to the habit of painting unrealistic pictures of a purely feudal and a purely capitalist society, which then raises the question what it was that turned the tradition-bound individual of the one into the alert profit hunter of the other. According to Weber, it was the religious revolution that, changing humanity's attitude toward life, produced a new spirit congenial to capitalist activity. We cannot go into the historical objections that may be raised against this theory. It is more important that the reader should realize that there is no problem. (Schumpeter, "Capitalism," p. 191 in *Essays* [New Brunswick, N.J.: Transaction Books, 1989])

For a similar statement by Schumpeter, see Vol. 1, p. 228 of *Business Cycles* (New York: McGraw-Hill, 1939). A number of contemporary economists—including Kenneth Arrow, Amartya Sen, Albert O. Hirschman, and Robert Solow—also discuss their relationship to Weber in Richard Swedberg, *Economics and Sociology* (Princeton, N.J.: Princeton University Press, 1990). Recently a few articles in mainstream economic journals have argued that Weber's idea of a capitalist spirit is a useful antidote to the current notion in economic theory that wealth is only as valuable as its implied consumption. See, e.g., Gurdip S. Bakshi and Zhiwu Chen, "The Spirit of Capitalism and Stock-Market Prices," *American Economic Review* 86 (1996): 133–57; and Heng-fu Zou, "The Spirit of Capitalism and Long-Run Growth," *European Journal of Political Economy* 10 (1994): 279–93. For an attempt to model the work ethic, see Roger Congleton, "The Economic Role of a Work Ethic," *Journal of Economic Behavior and Organization* 15 (1991): 365–85. The general attitude of economists toward Weber is also discussed in section IV of the appendix, entitled "Weber's Work in Economics as Seen by Economists, Economic Historians, and Sociologists."

7. Weber, "Kritische Bemerkungen zu den vorstehenden 'Kritischen Beiträgen,'" pp. 29–31 in *Die protestantische Ethik II*. The Calvinist Afrikaners, for example, failed for a long time to develop a thriving capitalism. See, e.g., Francis Fukuyama, *Trust* (London: Penguin Books, 1995), p. 44.

8. Weber, "Kritische Bemerkungen zu den vorstehenden 'Kritischen Beiträgen,'" p. 28, in *Die protestantische Ethik II*.

9. Weber, "Kritische Bemerkungen zu den vorstehenden 'Kritischen Beiträgen,'" pp. 30, 32 in *Die protestantische Ethik II*. Jacob Fugger II, also called Jacob the Rich, was the leading figure in a banking and mercantile family that dominated Europe in the fifteenth and sixteenth centuries. For a good study of the Fuggers, which appeared in 1896 and with which Weber no doubt was familiar, see Richard Ehrenberg, *Capital and Finance in the Age of the Renaissance: A Study of the Fuggers and Their Connections* (Fairfield, N.J.: A. M. Kelley, 1985).

of the modern capitalist spirit was more or less identical to economic rationalism, since this left out its ethical dimension, which was crucial to Weber's argument.[1]

Given the enormous size of the secondary literature on *The Protestant Ethic*, one might well think that by the mid-twentieth century most of what could be said, had indeed been said.[2] However, two recent contributions to the debate are of special interest to economic sociology. One of these is James Coleman's brief comment on *The Protestant Ethic* in his famous article "Social Theory, Social Research and a Theory of Action," and the other is Gordon Marshall's effort to empirically test the main thesis in Weber's work. Coleman uses *The Protestant Ethic* as an illustration of how a sociological analysis can be improved by being carried out in accordance with the principle of methodological individualism.[3] In an ingenious

1. Weber, "Bemerkungen zu den vorstehenden 'Replik,'" p. 55 in *Die protestantische Ethik II*. Sombart had argued in *Der moderne Kapitalismus* (1902) that "the capitalist spirit" constituted "an organizational unity" of "economic rationalism" and "the instinct of acquisition." See Sombart, *Der moderne Kapitalismus*, Vol. 1, p. 391.
2. There is no current, thorough analysis of the debate on *The Protestant Ethic*. For a good introduction to the debate, however, see Gordon Marshall, *In Search of the Spirit of Capitalism: An Essay on Max Weber's Protestant Ethic Thesis* (London: Hutchinson, 1982). For an attempt to see how *The Protestant Ethic* has fared in sociology as well as in other social sciences, see the chapter devoted to *The Protestant Ethic* in Peter Hamilton, *The Social Misconstruction of Reality* (New Haven, Conn.: Yale University Press, 1996). Two good collections of texts (which, however, do not cover the developments since the early 1970s) are Philippe Besnard, ed., *Protestantisme et capitalisme. La controverse post-weberiènne* (Paris: Colin, 1970); and Robert W. Green, ed., *Protestantism, Capitalism, and Social Science: The Weber Thesis Controversy* (Lexington, Mass.: D. C. Heath, 1973). Stephen Kalberg has also recently surveyed the way *The Protestant Ethic* has fared in the U.S. debate among sociologists; see Stephen Kalberg, "On the Neglect of Weber's *Protestant Ethic* as a Theoretical Treatise: Demarcating the Parameters of Postwar American Sociological Theory," *Sociological Theory* 14 (1996): 49–70. For some recent interesting contributions to the religious side of the argument in *The Protestant Ethic*, see, e.g., the articles by Friedrich Wilhelm Graf, Kaspar von Greyerz, and Malcolm MacKinnon in Lehmann and Roth, eds., *Weber's Protestant Ethic*. Richard Hamilton also discusses the way Protestant theologians have viewed Weber's work in *The Social Misconstruction of Reality*. Unfortunately there is not enough space to mention the most important contributions to the debate of *The Protestant Ethic* or to comment on the neglected but important discussion of a Weber-derived *problematique*—namely, the structure and nature of the work ethic in Western countries and elsewhere. For two of the most interesting contributions to the post–World War II debate on *The Protestant Ethic*, see Christopher Hill, "Protestantism and the Rise of Capitalism," pp. 15–39 in F. J. Fisher, ed., *Essays in the Economic and Social History of Tudor and Stuart England* (Cambridge: Cambridge University Press, 1961); and Michael Walzer, "Puritanism as a Revolutionary Ideology," *History and Theory* 3 (1964): 59–90. For the debate on the work ethic, see, e.g., Fukuyama, *Trust*, pp. 43–8; Adrian Furnham, "The Protestant Work Ethic and Attitudes towards Unemployment," *Journal of Occupational Psychology* 55 (1982): 277–85; Ronald Inglehart, *Culture Shift* (Princeton, N.J.: Princeton University Press, 1990); Seymour Martin Lipset, "The Work Ethic, Then and Now," *Journal of Labor Research* 13 (1992): 45–54; Daniel Yankelovich and John Immerwahr, "The Work Ethic and Economic Vitality," pp. 144–70 in Michael Wachter and Susan Wachter, eds., *Removing Obstacles to Economic Growth* (Philadelphia: University of Pennsylvania Press, 1984); Daniel Yankelovich et al., *The World at Work* (New York: Octagon Books, 1985).
3. See James Coleman, "Social Theory, Social Research, and a Theory of Action," *American Journal of Sociology* 91 (1986): 1309–35; see also James Coleman, *Foundations of Social Theory* (Cambridge, Mass.: Harvard University Press, 1990), pp. 1–23.

manner Coleman reconstructs the logic in Weber's argument according to what he calls the macro-micro-macro transition. Collective religious values influence the individual believer (Step 1: macro to micro); these religious attitudes will eventually change the believer's attitude to work and profit-making (Step 2: micro to micro); and when this happens simultaneously to many individual actors, the result is a new collective attitude to economic matters (Step 3: micro to macro). For Coleman's reconstruction of Weber's argument, see figure 11.

According to Coleman, Weber starts out the analysis well enough but fails at Step 3, the micro-to-macro transition. This part is difficult to handle in any sociological analysis, Coleman says, but also the most important one since it is here that the individual actors, by taking one another into account, create a new type of social phenomenon ("the problem of transformation" in Coleman's terminology). Weber, Coleman says, failed to specify the mechanism through which the individual actors in *The Protestant Ethic* created a new social phenomenon—more precisely, the spirit of modern capitalism.

In my opinion, Coleman exaggerates Weber's failure on this point. It is perhaps true that Weber does not specify the exact mechanism at Step 3 in his analysis, but he nonetheless makes very clear that the new spirit of capitalism is the result of social interaction. More precisely, Weber emphasizes that the capitalist spirit was not the invention of a single individual but of a whole group of people, and that it should be characterized as a kind of collective "lifestyle."[4] In the article on the sects, Weber also adds a mechanism that helped the new capitalist spirit to harden into a collective mentality, namely the social

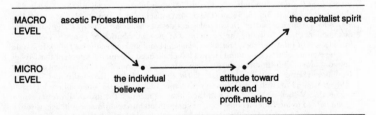

Figure 11: James Coleman's Reconstruction of the Argument in *The Protestant Ethic*. *Source:* James Coleman, "Social Theory, Social Research, and a Theory of Action," *American Journal of Sociology* 91 (1986): 1322 (the figure has been amended). *Comment:* Coleman emphasizes that the individual believer is influenced by religious beliefs (*Step 1*); how these beliefs affect his or her attitude about economic matters (*Step 2*); and how one individual's attitudes fuse with similar attitudes of other individuals into a collective lifestyle or mentality (*Step 3*).

structure of the sect. Nonetheless, Coleman's argument about "the problem of transformation" represents an original and important attempt to show how methodological individualism is at the center of Weber's argument in *The Protestant Ethic*, something that had been forgotten in the debate of this work. Coleman's own interest-based form of analysis, it may furthermore be added, displays many similarities to that of Weber.

The second important contribution to the debate of *The Protestant Ethic* that I want to highlight is that of Gordon Marshall. In a number of articles and two books—*Presbyteries and Profits* (1981) and *In Search of the Spirit of Capitalism* (1982)—Marshall argues that "the capitalist side" of the argument in *The Protestant Ethic* has been left "virtually unexplored" in the secondary literature.[5] By this he means that practically no attention has been paid in the debate on *The Protestant Ethic* to the following three central questions: (1) What exactly were the economic consequences of the ascetic Protestant ethic? (2) What would count as empirical evidence for these consequences? and (3) Is it possible to find empirical evidence for these consequences? Marshall's discussion of these questions represents, in my opinion, a very substantial contribution to the debate of *The Protestant Ethic* as well as to economic sociology more generally.

Marshall proposes several ways of establishing whether the ascetic Protestant ethic had indeed had the economic consequences that Weber claimed it did. As to the new entrepreneurs (Marshall discusses the new type of workers as well), one would expect these to be unscrupulously honest, to reinvest rather than to consume, to systematically expand their businesses, and to feel impelled to use their

---

4. Weber uses the term "lifestyle" (*"Lebensstil," "Lebensführung"*) explicitly. See Weber, *The Protestant Ethic*, pp. 52, 55, 58, or "Die protestantische Ethik," pp. 33, 37, 43 in Vol. 1 of *Gesammelte Aufsätze zur Religionssoziologie*. I discuss Coleman's interpretation of Weber at some length in "Analyzing the Economy: On the Contribution of James S. Coleman," pp. 313–28 in Jon Clark, ed., *James S. Coleman* (London: Falmer Press, 1996). It should also be mentioned that Gudmund Hernes has challenged Coleman's argument that Weber does not provide a solution to "the problem of transformation." See the excellent article by Gudmund Hernes entitled "The Logic of *The Protestant Ethic*," *Rationality and Society* 1 (1989): 123–62 (as well as the debate with James Coleman in the same volume). Hernes argues that Weber explains Step 3 in the following manner: the ascetic Protestant merchant helped to introduce a fierce form of competition into traditional capitalism through a kind of positive prisoner's dilemma. All the ascetic merchants felt that they had to outdo the other merchants in order to produce the high profits that were a sign that they were among the elect. Coleman's argument that Hernes ignores barriers to entry is countered by Hernes's argument that the ascetic Protestant merchant had the moral stamina to put up with the kind of resistance and hostility that tends to emerge when economic traditionalism is challenged.

5. Gordon Marshall, "The Dark Side of the Weber Thesis: The Case of Scotland," *British Journal of Sociology* 31 (1980): 420; see also Gordon Marshall, "The Weber Thesis and the Development of Capitalism in Scotland," *Scottish Journal of Sociology* 3 (1979): 173–211; and Gordon Marshall, "Mad Max True?," *Sociology* 17 (1983): 569–73.

time efficiently. Empirical evidence in matters of this type, Marshall continues, would include business records from the late sixteenth and seventeenth centuries. Weber had also in Marshall's opinion added another difficulty by not being consistent in his analysis of "economic form" and "economic spirit." While Weber sometimes argued as if a special form of enterprise implies a certain type of economic mentality, at other times in *The Protestant Ethic* he makes a sharp distinction between the two and insists that the spirit does not always follow the form.[6]

As to the question whether it is possible to produce empirical evidence for the main thesis in *The Protestant Ethic*, Marshall first notes that Weber himself presented no empirical evidence for the existence of a new capitalist spirit among businessmen other than some citations from Benjamin Franklin's writings. Empirically, Marshall says, the case that Weber puts forward is so thin that it can only be labeled *"not proven."*[7] He also points out that the kind of data needed to confirm or disprove the main thesis in Weber's study are rarely available for the period in question. Ideally, Marshall adds wistfully, one would have liked to interview the entrepreneurs and workers in question.

Some relevant empirical material does exist, however, and Marshall himself uses the case of Scotland to show this. His own major study, *Presbyteries and Profits*, analyzes the business records of a seventeenth-century business called the Newmills Cloth Manufactory; and according to the author this particular case largely confirms Weber's thesis.[8] Weber did not empirically prove his case in *The Protestant Ethic*, Marshall concludes, and certain parts of his argument will in all likelihood never be proven or disproven because the necessary data do not exist. But we must attempt to establish what

---

6. See the excellent discussion of this problem in Marshall's two books: Gordon Marshall, *Presbyteries and Profits: Calvinism and the Development of Capitalism in Scotland, 1560–1707* (Oxford: Oxford University Press, 1971), pp. 58–59; and Gordon Marshall, *In Search of the Spirit of Capitalism*, pp. 58–59, 64–68, 113. Weber tends to equate the two terms "economic form" ("*Form*," "*'kapitalistische' Form*") and "economic system" ("*Wirtschaftssystem*"; e.g., "*Kapitalismus als Wirtschaftssystem*"). In my mind it would have been preferable to make a distinction between the two; let "economic form" be identical to "economic organization," and let "economic system" be broader in scope and include the judicial system, labor, and the like. For Weber's use of "capitalism as an economic system" and similar expressions, see, e.g., Weber, *Die protestantische Ethik II*, pp. 28, 47, 167, 170–72; and for "economic form" and similar expressions, see, e.g., Weber, *Die protestantische Ethik II*, pp. 28, 171, and *The Protestant Ethic*, pp. 64–65, 67, or "Die protestantische Ethik," pp. 49–51 in Vol. 1 of *Gesammelte Aufsätze zur Religionssoziologie*.

7. Marshall, *In Search of the Spirit of Capitalism*, p. 13.

8. Drawing on his analysis in *Presbyteries and Profits*, Marshall concludes that both a Protestant ethic and a spirit of capitalism existed in Scotland—but that the evidence for the former's causing the latter is less strong. See Marshall, *Presbyteries and Profits*, p. 261. Marshall's other empirical examples include seventeenth-century Scottish political economists and the activities of one particular capitalist, Sir John Clerk of Penicuik (1649–1722). See Marshall, "The Weber Thesis and the Development of Capitalism in Scotland"; and Marshall, "The Dark Side of the Weber Thesis," pp. 419–40.

these parts of his arguments are, he says, and locate the relevant material for the others. If this is done in a systematic manner for Holland, New England, Scotland, and so on, Marshall speculates, it might very well turn out that Weber's thesis in *The Protestant Ethic* is largely correct.[9]

## III. HISTORICAL STUDIES OF ECONOMY AND RELIGION (PART II): *THE ECONOMIC ETHICS OF THE WORLD RELIGIONS*

Toward the end of *The Protestant Ethic* Weber says that his study is part of a larger research project focusing on ascetic rationalism in general. One of the subjects he wants to explore in the future, he says, is the role of ascetic rationalism in the history of modern science and technology; and another is the way that the formation of ascetic rationalism has been influenced by different factors, "especially economic ones."[1] But Weber decided not to proceed with these and similar questions in part because his colleague and friend Ernst Troeltsch was working along similar lines. After *The Protestant Ethic* and the essay on the sects had been completed, Weber therefore turned to other topics. He expanded his article from the late 1890s on the social and economic history of antiquity into a book-length study and also produced some work on "the psychophysics of industrial work."

Around 1911, however, he decided to resume his research project from *The Protestant Ethic*, but from a different angle. He had earlier primarily been interested in the emergence of capitalism in the West, under the influence of religious forces, but he now set out to investigate why a similar process—and again with special reference to religion—had *not* taken place anywhere else in the world. The central question became, Why had rational capitalism not emerged in China, India, Japan, and elsewhere, but only in the West? One commentator has observed that Weber "now tried to work the proof [from *The Protestant Ethic*] in reverse," and this is essentially correct.[2] As will soon be seen, however, Weber's new studies also differed in some important respects from *The Protestant Ethic*.

In his new research project, entitled *The Economic Ethics of the World Religions*, his aim was to cover all the major religions of the

9. Conversation with Marshall in Stockholm on April 29, 1996.
1. Weber, *The Protestant Ethic*, p. 183, or "Die protestantische Ethik," p. 205 in Vol. 1 of *Gesammelte Aufsätze zur Religionssoziologie*. The translation has been changed.
2. H. Stuart Hughes, *Consciousness and Society: The Reorientation of European Social Thought, 1890–1930* (New York: Vintage Books, 1958), pp. 322–23. Friedrich Tenbruck argues that it is wrong to view the studies in *The Economic Ethic of the World Religions* as "hypothesis and control evidence" for the thesis in *The Protestant Ethic* and that Weber in his later works wanted "to show . . . how and through what forces, there emerged in the world religions a dominant economic ethic"; see Friedrich Tenbruck, "The Thematic Unity in the Works of Max Weber," *British Journal of Sociology* 31 (1980): 327–28. Tenbruck, it seems to me, has a point but overdoes it by not stressing Weber's concern with rational capitalism in his studies of world religions and their economic ethics.

world.[3] Weber died before he had time to complete it, and only some of the projected studies were produced. Among those that are missing are, most important, analyses of Islam and Christianity, but Weber did complete three major studies—*The Religion of China* (1915, revised 1920), *The Religion of India* (1916–17), and *Ancient Judaism* (1917–20), plus a couple of theoretical articles. Like *The Protestant Ethic*, the three major studies address specific, historical situations, while the articles are primarily of interest for their introduction of new concepts and discussion of the theoretical implications of the empirical studies. Weber's project was primarily intended to result in a contribution to the section on the sociology of religion in *Economy and Society*, but also to "economic sociology."[4]

Of the new concepts that can be found in Weber's studies of religion during these years, three are especially important to economic sociology: "economic sphere," "ideal interests" versus "material interests," and "economic ethic." All have deep roots in Weber's work, but it was not until the 1910s—and primarily in these theoretical articles from *The Economic Ethics of the World Religions*—that Weber chose to discuss them more thoroughly and as part of his sociology.[5] The concept of "economic sphere" essentially denotes that economic activities, as history evolves, tend to become separate from other human activities and also to a certain extent to be governed by their own rules or laws ("limited autonomy" or *"Eigengesetzlichkeit,"* in Weber's terminology).[6] A certain tension is also typical for the relationship of the economic

3. As mentioned earlier, the most reliable description of Weber's proposed studies in economic ethics is an announcement from Weber's publisher for a set of books entitled *Gesammelte Aufsätze zur Religionssoziologie*, written by Weber himself and published in 1919. For a translation, see pp. 424–25 in Wolfgang Schluchter, *Rationalism, Religion, and Domination* (Berkeley: University of California Press, 1989), pp. 424–25. The collected essays in the sociology of religion were scheduled to appear in four volumes and to include a history of the European bourgeoisie in antiquity and the Middle Ages.

4. *"Wirtschafts-Soziologie."* See Weber, "Die Wirtschaftsethik der Weltreligionen," p. 237 n. 1 in Vol. 1 of *Gesammelte Aufsätze zur Religionssoziologie*. (This note was left out of the English translation; see Weber, "The Social Psychology of the World Religions," p. 267 in Gerth and Mills, eds., *From Max Weber*). Weber uses exactly the same expression and says the same thing about economic sociology in the first version of this article. See Weber, "Die Wirtschaftsethik der Weltreligionen. Religionssoziologische Skizzen. Einleitung," *Archiv für Sozialwissenschaft und Sozialpolitik* 41 (1915–16): 1 n. 1.

5. All of these concept are used in *Economy and Society* but not defined in chapter 2 on economic sociology. Weber had already spoken of "ideal" and "material needs" in his lectures on economics in the 1890s; see Weber, *Grundriss zu den Vorlesungen über Allgemeine ("theoretische") Nationalökonomie (1898)*, p. 29.

6. See the discussion of the concept of economic sphere in chapters 1 and 2 plus the section on this topic in Weber, "Religious Rejections of the World and Their Directions," pp. 331–33 in Gerth and Mills, eds., *From Max Weber*, or "Zwischenbetrachtung," pp. 544–46 in Vol. 1 of *Gesammelte Aufsätze zur Religionssoziologie*. For the concept of "Eigengesetzlichkeit," see also "Religious Rejections of the World," pp. 339, 340, or "Zwischenbetrachtung," pp. 552, 554. In translating the concept of "Eigengesetzlichkeit" as "limited autonomy," I follow Robert K. Merton. See Robert K. Merton, *Science, Technology and Society in Seventeenth Century England* (New York: Harper and Row, [1938] 1970), pp. ix–x. Weber furthermore says that each sphere has a certain "inner logic" (*"Eigenlogik,"*). (I thank Ralph Schroeder for this information.)

sphere to the other spheres in society. The economic sphere clashes, for example, with the religious sphere in capitalist society because it is very difficult to regulate rational economic actions through religious rules.

The concepts of "ideal" and "material interests" and "economic ethic" raise the issue of the role of norms in economic life. The concept of ideal interests complements the concept of material interests, which is central to the work of Marx and the Marxists. According to Weber, people are just as driven their desire for ideal interests—such as religious benefits, status honor, and so on—as they are by their desire for material interests. Indeed, to cite one of Weber's well-known formulations, it is "not ideas but material and ideal interests [that] directly govern men's conduct."[7] But even though interests propel the actions of people, Weber continues, these interests do not necessarily determine the exact direction of people's actions. In *The Protestant Ethic*, for example, Weber attempted to show how people who were driven by more or less identical interests in salvation ended up with very different attitudes toward economic life (see figure 8). In the second half of the famous formulation, just cited, about its being ideal and material interests, not ideas, that govern people's actions, Weber adds the following important qualification: "Very frequently the 'world images' that have been created by 'ideas' have, like switchmen, determined the tracks along which action has been pushed by the dynamics of interest."[8] In *The Economic Ethics of the World Religions*, Weber supplies several examples of such "world-images," including Hinduism, Buddhism and Confucianism, and shows how these have set similar ideal interests on very different "tracks."

A central concept in Weber's new studies of religion is that of "economic ethic," which is reminiscent of but not identical to what has later been called "moral economy."[9] Quite a bit of confusion, how-

7. Weber, "The Social Psychology of the World Religions," p. 280 in Gerth and Mills, eds., *From Max Weber*, or "Einleitung," p. 252 in Vol. 1 of *Gesammelte Aufsätze zur Religionssoziologie*. Little attention has been paid in the secondary literature to Weber's concepts of ideal and material interests. For an exception, see Stephen Kalberg's article on this topic; there are also scattered remarks in Wolfgang Schluchter's work. See Stephen Kalberg, "The Role of Ideal Interests in Max Weber's Comparative Historical Sociology," pp. 46–67 in Robert J. Antonio and Ronald M. Glassman, eds., *A Weber-Marx Dialogue* (Lawrence: University of Kansas Press, 1985); and, e.g., Wolfgang Schluchter, *The Rise of Western Rationalism* (Berkeley: University of California Press, 1981), pp. 25–27, 34.

8. Weber, "The Social Psychology of the World Religions," p. 280 in Gerth and Mills, eds., *From Max Weber*, or "Einleitung," p. 252 in Vol. 1 of *Gesammelte Aufsätze zur Religionssoziologie*. The term Weber uses is *"Weltbild"* (world picture).

9. The term *Wirtschaftsethik* seems to have been common in Weber's day and was used, for example, by Heinrich Dietzel in the 1890s and by Ernst Troeltsch some years later. See Heinrich Dietzel, *Theoretische Sozialökonomik* (Leipzig: Winter'sche Verlagshandlung, 1895), pp. 30–35; Ernst Troeltsch, *Die Soziallehren der christlichen Kirchen und Gruppen*, Vol. 1 of *Gesammelte Schriften* (Tübingen: J.C.B. Mohr, [1912] 1923), pp. 955–57. The term "moral economy" was introduced by E. P. Thompson in the 1970s and has often been used to make the point that people's attitudes toward their work and livelihood are not just "rational" and driven by hunger and the like, but also infused by distinct values, especially

ever, surrounds this concept, and there is little consensus on what Weber meant by it. One author, for example, equates economic ethic with Weber's notion of "practical ethics," while another argues that it is only applicable to a situation like the Middle Ages in Europe, when religion dominated everything in society, including its economy.[1] The most common interpretation, however, is the following one, which may first have been formulated by Marianne Weber: "By economic ethic he [Weber] meant, as he did in his first study [*They Protestant Ethic*], not ethical and theological theories but the practical impulses toward action that derive from religion."[2] Weber's wife, and several commentators after her, base their interpretation primarily on the following statement by Weber in one of the theoretical essays in *The Economic Ethics of the World Religions*: "The term 'economic ethic' points to the practical impulses for [economic] action which are founded in the psychological and pragmatic contexts of religions."[3] This interpretation, however, is difficult to reconcile with some other statements about economic ethic, which Weber makes in the same article from which this definition comes. Weber writes, for example, that "an economic ethic is not a simple 'function' of a form of economic organization," and that religion is "one—note this—only one of the determinants of the economic ethic."[4] These two statements make no sense if economic ethic is defined as practical impulses toward economic behavior, produced in a religious context.

Some of the difficulties surrounding Weber's notion of economic ethic disappear, however, when it is realized that when Weber speaks of "practical impulses for [economic] action which are founded in the psychological and pragmatic contexts of religions," he is not defining

---

what is fair. Weber's concept of economic ethic is, however, both broader and more differentiated than moral economy; hence, it is also, in my opinion, preferable. There is an interesting link between Weber's concept of depersonalization and his notion of economic ethic; the economic ethic of modern capitalism is extremely hard to influence from the outside. For the notion of moral economy, see especially E. P. Thompson, "The Moral Economy of the English Crowd in the Eighteenth Century," *Past and Present* 50 (1971): 76–136; see also James C. Scott, *The Moral Economy of the Peasant* (New Haven, Conn.: Yale University Press, 1976); Peter Swenson, *Fair Shares: Unions, Pay and Politics in Sweden and West Germany* (London: Adamente Press, 1989), 11 ff.; and (for a critique of the moral economy argument) Samuel Popkin, *The Rational Peasant* (Berkeley: University of California Press, 1979), pp. 1–82.

1. For the former opinion, see Charles Camic, "Weber and the Judaic Economic Ethic: A Comment on Fahey," *American Journal of Sociology* 89 (1984): 411; and for the latter opinion, see R. H. Tawney, *Religion and the Rise of Capitalism* (New York: Mentor, [1926] 1952), pp. 27, 29 ff., 39, 53. Tawney does not refer to Weber's concept of economic ethic but uses the term for his own purposes in his debate of Weber's work.

2. Marianne Weber, *Max Weber*, pp. 331–32.

3. Weber, "The Social Psychology of the World Religions," p. 267 in Gerth and Mills, eds., *From Max Weber*, or "Einleitung," p. 238 in Vol. 1 of *Gesammelte Aufsätze zur Religionssoziologie*.

4. Weber, "The Social Psychology of the World Religions," p. 268 in Gerth and Mills, eds., *From Max Weber*, or "Einleitung," p. 238 in Vol. 1 of *Gesammelte Aufsätze zur Religionssoziologie*.

economic ethics in general, but is talking exclusively about one of its subcategories, namely "the economic ethic *of a religion*."[5] In *The Protestant Ethic*, Weber similarly spoke of the "impulses" generated by ascetic Protestantism and how these under certain circumstances can turn into rational attitudes toward the economy (see figure 8). He now also says that the religious type of economic ethic comes to its fullest and most characteristic expression in one specific social stratum, which is "[the] characteristic bearer of a religion."[6]

But it should be noted that in the article from *The Economic Ethics of the World Religions*, where Weber speaks about the economic ethic of a religion, he also speaks of an economic ethic of a more general type. This latter type of economic ethic is that of a whole society, and *this* type of economic ethic is not "a simple 'function' of a form of economic organization"—a statement that reminds us of a similar argument about the capitalist spirit versus the economic form in *The Protestant Ethic*.[7] Weber also points out that an economic ethic of this second type has "a high measure of autonomy" in relation to religion, and that it is shaped just as much by "economic geography" and "history" as by religious forces.[8]

Once it is realized that Weber is using the concept of economic ethic in a few different ways in *The Economic Ethics of the World Religions*, it becomes easier to follow the complex argument in his three case studies. For China, India, and Palestine, Weber is first of all trying to track down the specific economic ethics of Confucianism, Hinduism, and Judaism and to determine in which social stratum these have come to their fullest and most characteristic expression. In the process of doing this, he also touches on the general economic ethic of these societies, as these have been formed by historical and economic-geographical conditions as well as by their religions. Weber's overarching purpose in carrying out the analysis in *The Economic Ethics of the World Religions* was to find out why rational capitalism did not emerge in non-Western societies; and just as in *The Protestant Ethic*, his answer has more to do with the spirit or mentality of the economic actors than with the

---

5. Weber writes specifically about "'Wirtschaftsethik' einer Religion," but the English translators of this text did not notice Weber's distinction between an economic ethic in general and the economic ethic of a religion. See Weber, "The Social Psychology of the World Religions," p. 267 in Gerth and Mills, eds., *From Max Weber*, or "Einleitung," p. 238 in Vol. 1 of *Gesammelte Aufsätze zur Religionssoziologie*; emphasis added.

6. Weber, "The Social Psychology of the World Religions," p. 269 in Gerth and Mills, eds., *From Max Weber*, or "Einleitung," p. 240 in Vol. 1 of *Gesammelte Aufsätze zur Religionssoziologie*.

7. Weber does not use the concept "economic ethic" (*Wirtschaftsethik*) in the first version of *The Protestant Ethic* from 1904–5, but adds it in the revised version.

8. Weber, "The Social Psychology of the World Religions," p. 268 in Gerth and Mills, eds., *From Max Weber*, or "Einleitung," in Vol. 1 of *Gesammelte Aufsätze zur Religionssoziologie*, p. 238.

concrete organization of the economy. But Weber's answer in *The Economic Ethics of the World Religions* is not limited to the economic ethics of different religions and what their characteristic bearers can tell you; he also looks at the economic ethic of the economy or society at large—and this is very different from what he does in *The Protestant Ethic*.

The characteristic features of the two types of economic ethics that Weber is referring to are summarized in figures 12 and 13, where I have also indicated what kind of practical and evaluative attitudes make up an economic ethic. Another way of expressing the whole thing is to use the term "norms" rather than "attitudes," even if it should be noted that Weber avoids this term and instead talks of actors' being oriented to a "legitimate order" in the form of a "convention" (for Weber's discussion of "legitimate order," see chapter 2). The norms that make up an economic ethic have been divided into a number of different categories, to make it easier to follow what Weber was looking for when he was writing *The Economic Ethics of the World Religions*: norms about work; norms about wealth and possessions; norms about trade, industry, and finance; norms about economic change and technical innovation; norms about giving to those without economic resources (charity); and norms about other economic actors.

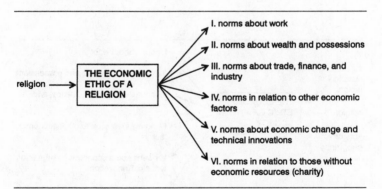

Figure 12: The Economic Ethic of a Religion, according to Weber. *Source:* See especially Max Weber, "The Social Psychology of World Religions," pp. 267–68 in Hans Gerth and C. Wright Mills, eds., *From Max Weber* (New York: Oxford University Press, 1946). *Comment:* An individual's adoption of a religious faith produces impulses to action in a variety of spheres, including the economic sphere. A number of individuals produce in this manner what Weber calls the economic ethic of a religion. Like all types of economic ethic, the economic ethic of a religion implies specific evaluative attitudes (or norms) toward work, wealth, trade, and so on. A certain stratum in society is typically central in shaping and expressing the characteristic features of a religion, and hence also its economic ethic.

Work, for example, can be viewed with contempt; it can also be viewed with indifference; and it can be viewed as a vocation. Religions often forbid certain types of work. Possessions and wealth can similarly be approved or disapproved of; and their owners may be encouraged to indulge in luxuries or told that doing so would be wrong. Usually, wealth is acceptable to other members of one's stratum only if it has been acquired in a certain way, such as through war, inheritance, or work. Most religions have disapproved of lending money for profit, and aristocrats have usually viewed trade as a form of trickery ("qui trompe-t-on?"—"who is being cheated?"—as Bismarck allegedly characterized trade).

There is also an ethical dimension to the way that people behave toward other people in economic affairs more generally. For most of history, the individual has been restrained in his or her economic dealings with people from the same tribe or family, while it has been permissible to be ruthless toward strangers and outsiders. This "double ethic," as Weber calls it, does not exist in modern society, and it is today considered "wrong" not to treat everybody the same way. Those with no economic resources have sometimes been treated with hostility, and at other times with a certain benevolence. The Puritans, for example, were against begging, while most other religions have encouraged charitable behavior toward those who are

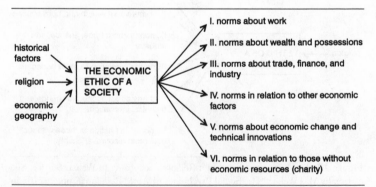

Figure 13: The Economic Ethic of a Society, according to Weber. *Source:* See especially Max Weber, "The Social Psychology of World Religions," pp. 267–68 in Hans Gerth and C. Wright Mills, eds., *From Max Weber* (New York: Oxford University Press, 1946). *Comment:* An economic ethic can be characterized as a number of evaluative attitudes (or norms) toward the different activities that make up an economy (such as work, trade, finance, and the like). The economic ethic of a society has a certain autonomy; and it is influenced by historical, religious, and economic-geographic factors.

poor and who beg. Finally, an economic ethic also entails specific attitudes toward economic change and technical innovations. Economic novelties and technical changes can be seen as something positive or as something to be feared. In China and India, for example, technical innovations were deeply feared for magical and religious reasons; there was also, as we know, a tendency to stereotype existing tools and technology.

In *The Religion of China*, which is the first study in *The Economic Ethics of the World Religions*, Weber addresses two related questions: Why did rational capitalism not emerge in China, and what impact did the economic ethic of its various religions—primarily Confucianism—have on the failure of modern capitalism to develop?[9] Weber's answer reads like one of the many lists that can be found in *General Economic History* that enumerate the factors that account for the rise of rational capitalism in the West. No bourgeoisie of the Western type emerged in China or in any independent cities. Its legal system as well as the state were patrimonial and therefore not conducive to industrial capitalism, which demands a high level of predictability and calculability from the political system. There was little rational technology, science, or accounting in China; and its economic organizations were poorly developed in comparison with the ones that could be found in the city states around the Mediterranean in the late Middle Ages. The Chinese economic mentality was thoroughly traditionalistic, and so were its various forms of religion. Weber does not single out one specific reason why rational capitalism failed to develop in China, but he notes that in more recent times there were many reasons for this failure, and that "nearly all [were] related to the structure of the state."[1] Religion, in any case, was not the decisive factor.

As in his other studies of economic ethics, Weber begins *The Religion of China* by presenting the social and political structure; next comes a detailed analysis of religion. China, Weber says, was dominated by

---

9. In the main text I follow Weber's key argument in *The Religion of China*. The passages in this work that are of particular interest to economic sociology are the following: Weber, *The Religion of China*, pp. 3–12 (money and monetary policy), 50–62 (taxation), 226–49 (Confucianism and Puritanism, including personalism and impersonality in the economy), or "Konfuzianismus und Taoismus," pp. 276–90, 335–49, 512–36 in Vol. 1 of *Gesammelte Aufsätze zur Religionssoziologie*. Weber also mentions the role of rotating credit associations in China; see *The Religion of China*, pp. 209, 292–93 n. 40, or "Konfuzianismus und Taoismus," p. 494 n. 1. Literature that evaluates Weber's analysis of China is presented later.

1. Weber, *The Religion of China*, p. 100, or "konfuzianismus und Taoismus," p. 100 in Vol. 1 of *Gesammelte Aufsätze zur Religionssoziologie*. The translation has been changed. In a letter to Robert Liefmann, dated March 9, 1920, Weber writes, "The modern economy does not only presuppose the rational . . . state but also rational technology (science) and a specific type of rational lifestyle. Why else would not capitalism have emerged in China? It had several thousands of years of time to do so!"

traditionalism in all spheres of life. The clan controlled most of what was going on at the local level, including social life and the cult of the ancestors. It also owned the land. Magic was prevalent among the peasants, and all innovations were seen as a potential threat to the spirits. Geomancy and similar types of popular magic dominated the thinking of the population and blocked any attempt to rationalize the economy. Mining, for example, was believed to disturb the spirits, and so did railways and smoke from the factories.

The literati, who were in charge of the local administration and important parts of the tax system, were firm believers in Confucianism; and the Confucian worldview was thoroughly traditionalistic in economic, social, and political matters. The Chinese state was patrimonial in nature, which meant that it was positive to substantive justice but suspicious of market forces. The state failed to rationalize the economy, to develop an economic policy, and even to control the money. The local economy was in the hands of the clans, which were bastions of economic traditionalism. The population was very hardworking and exceedingly thrifty. Individuals who were not members of one's clan were met with suspicion; and distrust permeated the economy. Economic organizations either imitated the structure of the clan or did not extend beyond the clan.

As already mentioned, Weber does not argue that a modern type of capitalism failed to emerge in China simply because Confucianism did not develop a capitalist mentality similar to the one produced in the West with the help of ascetic Protestantism. Nonetheless, Weber was particularly interested in the economic ethic of Confucianism, and the last chapter of *The Religion of China* is devoted to a comparison between Puritanism and Confucianism. These two religions differed on crucial points, Weber says, even though they were both rationalistic in spirit. Puritanism, however, wanted to radically change society, while Confucianism was reconciled to the existing order. Also their economic ethics were completely different. Puritanism viewed wealth with suspicion, whereas Confucianism valued wealth because one needed money to live like a gentleman. The Puritan regarded work as a vocation, and the Confucian shunned all types of professional specialization as contrary to the ethos of the gentleman. Successful and systematic profit-making was viewed positively in Puritanism; in Confucianism profiteering and deals in the market were viewed with disdain. In general, Weber concludes, the economic ethic of Confucianism constituted an obstacle to the emergence of a rational capitalism in China. *The Religion of China* ends with the statement that "the mentality" of Chinese society has had an autonomous influence on the economic development of the country, and that this influence has been "sharply counteractive to [modern] capitalist development."[2] Translated into the terminology of our two types of economic ethics, this means that the economic ethic of Chinese society at large helped to block the emergence of a rational type of capitalism.

Weber's second study in *The Economic Ethics of the World Religions—The Religion of India—*has a goal similar to that of *The Religion of China,* namely to determine why rational capitalism did not emerge in India and the possible role of religion—or more precisely, its economic ethic—in preventing it.[3] "Here we shall inquire," Weber says, "as to the manner in which Indian religiosity, as one factor among many other, may have prevented capitalistic development (in the occidental sense)."[4] Most of Weber's study of India is devoted to an analysis of Hinduism and the caste system, which he viewed as the most important feature of India's social structure. The Indian state varied in size: it was split into petty kingdoms at certain times and was a great empire at others. It was usually patrimonial in nature and relied heavily on the administrative skills of the Brahmans as well as on Brahmanic ideology to tame the population. The cities in India contained strong merchant groups but nonetheless failed to develop into independent sources of power. The notion of citizenship, for example, could not develop in the kind of atmosphere produced by the caste system. Pacifist sentiments of a religious origin also prevented the city merchants from developing a military power of their own; and the political rulers did not need the financial resources of the bourgeois strata as much as their counterparts in the West did. In India, Weber notes, the village was far more important than the city.

Weber defines caste as a closed status group, and he points out that it can be found in many places throughout the world, not only in

2. Weber, *The Religion of China,* p. 249, or "Konfuzianismus und Taoismus," p. 536 in Vol. 1 of *Gesammelte Aufsätze zur Religionssoziologie.*
3. In the main text I follow Weber's key argument in *The Religion of India: The Sociology of Hinduism and Buddhism* (New York: Free Press, 1958). The passages in this work that are of particular interest to economic sociology are the following: Weber, *The Religion of India,* pp. 111–17 (the caste system and the economy), 193–204 (the Jains, a sect similar in many ways to ascetic Protestantism), 216–19 (the economic ethic of Buddhism), 270–82 (capitalism and Japan), or pp. 203–17, 234–37, 295–309 in Vol. 2 of *Gesammelte Aufsätze zur Religionssoziologie.* I have chosen not to discuss the economic ethic of Buddhism in the main text because I find Weber's analysis rather sketchy (see in this context also "The Other-Worldliness of Buddhism and Its Economic Consequences," pp. 627–30 in *Economy and Society,* or *Wirtschaft und Gesellschaft,* pp. 377–78). Randall Collins claims that Weber seriously underestimated the economic role of Buddhism in China and that there existed a strong "Buddhist capitalism," particulary during the early Chinese Middle Ages and through the early T'ang. See Randall Collins, *Weberian Sociological Theory* (Cambridge: Cambridge University Press, 1986), pp. 58–73. Further literature that evaluates Weber's analysis of India is cited later. It should be noted that the translation of *The Religion of India* is poor.
4. Weber, *The Religion of India,* p. 4, or "Hinduismus und Buddhismus," p. 4 in Vol. 2 of *Gesammelte Aufsätze zur Religionssoziologie.* The translation has been changed.

India. What made the caste system in India so tremendously strong, however, was first and foremost that it had the support of a religion that advocated a very similar type of social organization, namely Hinduism; it was also supported by the kinship system. To the Hindu, in other words, it was a religious duty to uphold the caste system. The main goal in life, according to Hinduism, was to follow religious rituals strictly, thereby qualifying for a better position in the next life. An individual who did this over many lifetimes would eventually be released from "the wheel of rebirth" and enter into an eternal and dreamless sleep. Marrying the wrong kind of person, eating with the wrong kind of person, or even touching or glancing at the wrong kind of person could be ritually defiling and have fatal consequences for one's position in the next life. Different types of work were typically associated with different castes, and ritual restrictions surrounded these as well.

Historically, there have existed a bewildering number of castes, Weber notes, and it is not possible to rank them with any precision. Nonetheless, the four main castes are the Brahmans (priests), the Kshatriyas (knights), the Vaishyas (free commoners), and the Shudras (serfs). The Brahmans were originally magicians and worked as religious counselors to princes, administrators, and the like. They were paid with gifts of land; they were very greedy; and they looked down on agricultural work, money-lending, and trade. The Kshatriyas (later replaced by the Rajputs) worked as knights and soldiers for political rulers and typically got paid through prebends. Like the Brahmans, they were allowed to own land and were a privileged caste. The Vaishyas (free commoners) were mostly peasants and traders; like the Shudras (serfs), they were among the lower castes. For a variety of religious reasons the peasants were even more looked down upon in India than in the West; and to their rulers they were little but a source of taxation. The Shudras could not own land and were often craftsmen. Some Shudras worked at the royal courts; others did simple handicrafts in the villages or cities. Weber also mentions certain kinds of ritually defiling jobs, such as tanning and the handling of dead animals.

After presenting the social and political structure in the first part of *The Religion of India*, Weber attempts to show how the economic ethic of Hinduism has created obstacles to the emergence of a rational type of capitalism in India. Many ritual rules in Hinduism conflicted directly with measures that would have led to a rationalization of the economy, but Weber emphasizes that it was first and foremost the very "spirit" of the Hindu system that created problems in this regard. Since it was the religious duty of every Hindu to follow a series of ritualistic rules very closely, work tools and economic practices typically remained the same. Technical innovations were deeply feared for magical reasons; and changes from one type of work to another as well as social mobility were instinctively disapproved of. Weber notes: "A ritual law in which every change of occupation, every change in work technique, may result in ritual degradation is certainly not capable of giving birth to economic and technical revolutions from within itself, or even of facilitating the first germination of capitalism in its midst."[5]

It is true that Hinduism, according to Weber, contained some rational elements. Unlike ascetic Protestantism, however, Hinduism advocated a radical *withdrawal* from the world—and no "practical impulses" toward economic rationalism could consequently be created. Hinduism also had its magical elements, which were especially strong outside the religious and social elite. Just as in China, in India the great mass of peasants lived deeply immersed in magical thinking. All in all, rational capitalism was blocked by a number of factors in India. On the one hand, the economic ethic of Hinduism, which was most fully developed among the Brahmans, kept the rest of society in an iron grip through the caste system. And on the other hand, the patrimonial state, the kinship system, and the absence of independent cities and a powerful bourgeoisie all made it more difficult for a rational economic ethic to emerge.

Weber's third installment in *The Economic Ethics of the World Religions* is entitled *Ancient Judaism,* and it differs quite a bit from *The Religion of China* and *The Religion of India.*[6] As in the other two studies, Weber attempts to lay bare the economic ethic of Jewish religion and to establish why the Jews had failed to establish a rational type of capitalism. In addition, however, he pursues another theme, namely how Judaism made a decisive break with magic. This latter contribution of Judaism, Weber says, constitutes a true turning point in world history and was to have enormous consequences for Western society, including its economy.

*Ancient Judaism* opens with a magnificent sociological picture of early Palestine, which includes its economic geography, its major

5. Weber, *The Religion of India,* p. 112, or "Hinduismus und Buddhismus," pp. 110, 111 in Vol. 2 of *Gesammelte Aufsätze zur Religionssoziologie.*
6. In the main text I follow Weber's key argument in *Ancient Judaism.* The passages in this work that are of particular interest to economic sociology are the following: Weber, *Ancient Judaism,* pp. 28–57 (plebeian strata in early Palestine), 61–89 (social laws in Judaism), 252–54 (Egyptian and Israeli economic ethic), 255–63 (charity), 342–45 (dualistic economic ethic plus a comparison of Judaism to ascetic Protestantism), 400–403 (the economic ethic of pharisaical Judaism), pp. 406–11 (the anti-economic mentality of the Essenes), or pp. 34–66, 66–98, 269–71, 271–80, 419–21, 423–29 in Vol. 3 of *Gesammelte Aufsätze zur Religionssoziologie.* In this context see also the discussion of Jewish economic ethic in *Economy and Society;* see especially "Judaism and Capitalism," "Jewish Rationalism versus Puritan Asceticism," and "Hierocracy and Economic Ethos in Judaism," pp. 611–15, 615–23, 1200–04 in *Economy and Society,* or *Wirtschaft und Gesellschaft,* pp. 367–70, 370–74, 719–21. Literature that evaluates Weber's analysis of Judaism is cited later.

social groups, and its political and economic structure. There was little unity in Palestine at this stage, Weber says, but in times of war the different social groups came together in a confederation under the protection of Yahweh, a war god from the mountains. Yahweh was in fierce competition with Baal, a god of Phoenician and Canaanite origin with strong orgiastic and magical elements. The supporters of Yahweh fought a hard battle to eliminate Baal and rituals like "the dance around the golden calf." Yahwism was later helped in its campaign against magic by the strong emphasis in Judaism on the study of law. The prophets also helped to combat the power of magic by demanding that people follow Yahweh's commands strictly and methodically in their everyday lives. The end result of all these different forces was that Judaism, as the first religion in world history, was able to break with magic. Weber further notes that, unlike many non-Western religions, which advocated a withdrawal from the world, Judaism remained oriented to this world.

Weber's analysis of Judaism, including its economic ethic, is dominated by his portrayal of the Jews as a "pariah people," or a people ritually segregated from other peoples and in a position of political and social inferiority.[7] Many factors were involved in turning the Jews into a pariah people, Weber says, and he devotes quite a bit of attention in *Ancient Judaism* to this process. One factor that early on began to set the Jews apart from other peoples was their exclusive worship of Yahweh. Another was the notion that the Israelite peoples were unique in the sense that they—and only they—had entered into a special contract or *berith* with God. Religious rituals and rules also separated the Jews from the non-Jews, such as circumcision, the prohibition of work on the sabbath, and the rule that usury must not be practiced against other members of the Jewish faith. Under the threat of assimilation, the Jewish priesthood strengthened these rules, with full ritual segregation as a result. Political and social inferiority were later added by the Gentiles, completing the process of turning the Jewish people into a pariah people.

One important reason the Jews have been willing to put up with so much adversity and suffering throughout history, Weber says, was

---

7. In Weber's definition of pariah people in *Economy and Society*, he notes that a further characteristic is "a far-reaching distinctiveness in economic functioning." The full definition is the following:

In our usage, 'pariah people' denotes a distinctive hereditary social group lacking autonomous political organization and characterized by internal prohibitions against commensality and intermarriage originally founded upon magical, tabooistic, and ritual injunctions. Two additional traits of a pariah people are political and social disprivilege and a far-reaching distinctiveness in economic functioning. (Weber, *Economy and Society*, p. 493, or *Wirtschaft und Gesellschaft*, p. 300)

There exists a debate around Weber's concept of the Jews as a pariah people; for an introduction, see, e.g., Arnaldo Momigliano, "A Note on Max Weber's Definition of Judaism as a Pariah-Religion," *History and Theory* 19 (1980): 313–18.

that their religion contained a strong messianic element. One day, far off in time, the Jewish people believed they would reap a reward for being God's chosen people. In the meantime, however, wealth was fully appreciated by the faithful in Palestine, and so was luxury. From early on, Judaism also contained numerous rules requiring charitable behavior of the faithful toward other Jews, such as widows, the poor, and those in debt. This strong emphasis on charity was remarkable, according to Weber, because it was not so much the result of a patrimonial state (which for its own reasons often displayed an interest in the welfare of its subjects), but grew out of religious concerns. Another important feature of Jewish economic ethic was its double ethic and how it affected the issue of usury. According to Deuteronomy 23:20, "You may exact interest on a loan to a foreigner but not on a loan to a fellow-countryman." This double ethic naturally increased in strength when Judaism became the religion of a fully segregated people—and also when the Jews were met by hostility of other peoples.

According to Weber, early Judaism had strong rational elements, such as an emphasis on vigilant self-observation and self-control. But there were also decisive differences between the Jewish economic ethic and the ethic of ascetic Protestantism. While the Jewish businessman got blessed with riches for his behavior in areas other than the economy, especially the diligent study of religious law, the ascetic Protestant got rich because he worked so hard in his vocation. The double ethic also precluded the equal treatment of all economic actors, along the lines of the Baptists and the Quakers; and it allowed for a certain ethical laxity, since non-Jews could be treated in dubious ways. Whereas the Puritans despised such economic activities as usury and political capitalism, these were common among Jewish businessmen. For a variety of reasons, in other words, the Jews never developed a rational capitalist spirit; and neither did they contribute to the growth of industrial capitalism. Weber's term for the type of economic activities that the Jewish merchants excelled in was "pariah capitalism," which can be described as a form of traditional commercial capitalism.[8]

That Judaism broke so decisively with magic made it possible for rational capitalism to emerge many centuries later in Europe. As to

---

8. For Weber's polemic against Sombart's argument that it was the Jews who had created modern (rational) capitalism, see Weber, *Economy and Society*, pp. 611–15, or *Wirtschaft und Gesellschaft*, pp. 367–70; Weber, *General Economic History*, pp. 358–61, or *Wirtschaftsgeschichte*, pp. 406–11. "Pariah capitalism" is a general category and refers to more than just the Jewish people. Gary Hamilton, for example, defines it in the following manner: "The essence of pariah capitalism . . . is a structure of power asymmetry which enables an elite group to control and prey upon the wealth generated by a pariah group." See Gary Hamilton, "Pariah Capitalism: A Paradox of Power and Dependence," *Ethnic Groups* 2 (1979): 3.

the situation in Palestine itself, Weber's account in *Ancient Judaism* makes it clear that many factors besides the economic ethic of the Jews prevented the emergence of rational capitalism. One can per- haps describe Weber's two types of economic ethic—the economic ethic of a religion and the economic ethic of a whole society—in the following way. While Weber believed that for each world religion there was one particular stratum that had been "decisive in stamping the characteristic features of [its] economic ethic," this was in his opinion somewhat less the case with Judaism.[9] The reason for this is that the Jews were a pariah people in the eyes of other people and typ- ically in exile. In brief, the two economic ethics had a tendency to merge in the case of Judaism.

As mentioned earlier, Weber never had the time to carry out his studies of the economic ethic of Islam and Christianity. However, he did include a short section on the economic ethic of Islam in *Econ- omy and Society*.[1] A full study of Islam would probably have provided a detailed sociological profile of Islamic society (including its general economic ethic) as well as an analysis of the doctrine of Islam and of the emergence of the Islamic ministry. There would, no doubt, also have been a discussion of the factors that Weber saw as important to the emergence of rational capitalism: the cities and their middle strata, the political and legal machinery, and so on.[2] Weber's picture of the economic ethic of Islam, however, would probably not have been very different from the one that can be found in the section in *Economy and Society*.

Originally, Islam had a pietistic character, Weber says, and a ten- dency to withdraw from the world. Soon, however, Islam developed into the national religion of Arabic warriors with a strong feudal ethic. The goal of the holy war was to expand the political power of Islam and to supply tributes. There would be plenty of war booty, and Islam's vision of paradise, Weber notes, was one that any soldier would love. Islam also had rules against usury and gambling, and the faithful were supposed to support the poor. Weber briefly compares the Islamic economic ethic with that of the Puritans, and it is clear that the two differed on several fundamental points. The Puritan businessman, for example, rejected the notion of becoming rich

9. This is how I interpret Weber's argument in the introduction to *The Economic Ethics of the World Religions*. See Weber, "The Social Psychology of the World Religions," pp. 268–69 in Gerth and Mills, eds., *From Max Weber*, or "Einleitung," pp. 239–40 in Vol. 1 of *Gesammelte Aufsätze zur Religionssoziologie*.

1. Weber, "The This-Worldliness of Islam and Its Economic Ethics," pp. 623–27 in *Economy and Society*, or *Wirstschaft und Gesellschaft*, pp. 375–76. One can also find many impor- tant comments on Christianity—but fewer on its economic ethic.

2. For a solid introduction to the discussion of the patrimonial structure of the Islamic state, its cities, and similar issues, see Wolfgang Schluchter, "Hindrances to Modernity: Max Weber on Islam," pp. 105–78 in *Paradoxes of Modernity* (Stanford, Calif.: Stanford Uni- versity Press, 1996).

through war-related activities, especially through the acquisition of booty. He also disapproved of the sensual dimension of the feudal ethic as well as its concept of sin. According to Weber, the Islamic concept of sin was ritualistic in nature and did not reach very deeply into the soul of the believer. Also the Islamic concept of predestination failed to produce the "practical impulses" toward economic rationalism that Weber was looking for, primarily because it did not make the individual assume full and methodical control over his or her everyday life.[3] There did exist some ascetic elements in Islam—for example, fasting and a certain tendency among its warriors to live simply—but these were not very systematic, especially in comparison with the lifestyle of the Puritan middle strata. In brief, no modern capitalistic spirit was ever produced in Islam.

When Weber died, his friend and colleague Emil Lederer wrote that the studies in *The Economic Ethics of the World Religions* "mark a totally new epoch, especially in sociological research."[4] But the discussion of Weber's work has been meager, especially in comparison with the amount of writing devoted to *The Protestant Ethic*. For a long time there existed only a few scattered comments on Weber's work on economic ethics, most of which singled out one of his three studies and ignored the fact that they were part of a larger work. Some comments were also influenced by the modernization debate in the 1950s and 1960s, which was often simplistic in character.[5] In the 1980s, however, Wolfgang Schluchter edited a series of volumes about *The Economic Ethics of the World Religions*. And more recently, *The Religion of China* and *The Religion of India* have also appeared in first-rate scholarly editions as part of Weber's collected works.

Although these newer works are of high quality, most of the secondary literature on *The Economic Ethics of the World Religions* is still marred by misunderstandings of Weber's argument, just like the debate on *The Protestant Ethic*. One common error, for example, is

3. For a discussion of the concept of predestination in Islam, see Weber, *Economy and Society*, pp. 572–76, or *Wirtschaft und Gesellschaft*, pp. 346–48.

4. Emil Lederer, "Max Weber," *Archiv für Sozialwissenschaft und Sozialpolitik* 48 (1920/21): iii.

5. One of these was to lump together all non-Western countries and analyze them in terms of "traditionalism"; another to view the reasons why these countries had not followed the same course of socio-economic development as the West in social-psychological terms. Modernization theorists have also attempted to find ethics analogous to ascetic Protestantism in various countries. Some of the modernization studies that were inspired or influenced by Weber are of excellent quality, however, and represent model studies of "economic ethic." See especially Robert Bellah, *Togugawa Religion* (Glencoe, Ill.: Free Press, 1957); Robert Bellah, "Reflections on the Protestant Ethic Analogy in Asia," *Journal of Social Issues* 19 (1963): 52–60; Clifford Geertz, "Religious Belief and Economic Behavior in a Central Javanese Town," *Economic Development and Cultural Change* 4 (1956): 134–58; S. M. Lipset, "Values and Entrepreneurship in the Americas," pp. 77–140 in *Revolution and Counterrevolution* (New Brunswick, N.J.: Transaction Books, [1970] 1988). See also the fine collection of articles in S. N. Eisenstadt, ed., *The Protestant Ethic and Modernization* (New York: Basic Books, 1968).

to claim that Weber viewed countries like India and China as ill-suited for capitalist development. In fact, what Weber tried to explain was something quite different, namely why rational capitalism did not spontaneously emerge anywhere outside the West.[6] A further common error is to state that capitalism did not develop in India, China, and other places, according to Weber, because these countries, like ascetic Protestantism, lacked a religion that could create a capitalist spirit.[7] In *The Economic Ethics of the World Religions*, however, Weber argued that a number of factors other than religion also had prevented rational capitalism from emerging. These other factors, as we know from the preceding pages, include the structure of the state, the nature of the cities, the absence of a powerful bourgeoisie, and so on. In none of his three case studies did Weber attempt to establish—in the spirit of, say, John Stuart Mill's method of difference and agreement—that everything hinged on the absence of a certain type of economic religion.

Most of the high-quality contributions to the debate on *The Economic Ethics of the World Religions* have dealt with the religious side of Weber's argument. And even though Weber explicitly stated that his studies were intended as a contribution to "economic sociology," there are no attempts to establish exactly what this contribution is.[8] It seems to me, however, that three tasks are of special importance when it comes to economic sociology and *The Economic Ethics of the World Religions,* and I shall say a few words about each of them.

---

6. One commentator writes, for example, "I have imagined a number of times that the good German professor [Weber] would come back to life today, say on top of a high-rise office building in downtown Taipei, that he would take one look out the window and say, 'Well, I was wrong!'"; Peter Berger, "An East Asian Development Model?," p. 7 in Peter Berger and Hsin-Huang Michael Hsiao, eds., *In Search of an East Asian Development Model* (New Brunswick, N.J.: Transaction Books, 1988). For a similar attitude, see also Fukuyama, *Trust,* pp. 326, 350, 416–17 n. 1; and for a critique of this type of argument, see Gary Hamilton and Cheng-Shu Kao, "Max Weber and the Analysis of East Asian Industrialization," *International Sociology* 2 (1987): 289–300.

7. A version of this can be found in *The Structure of Social Action* by Parsons, but I cite one of Parsons's unpublished papers from the 1940s because it contains a more forceful and clear statement. Parsons says that the argument in *The Economic Ethics of the World Religions* is very similar to that of *The Protestant Ethic*:

Weber isolated the influence of the religious ethic by a rough, but for his broadest purposes, adequate method. What he attempted to do was to judge whether at the time preceding the emergence of the religious movement in question the general character of the social structure apart from religion was more or less 'favorable' to the development of the institutional patterns characteristic among the western world. In the two cases most fully worked out—namely, China and India—his conclusion was that at comparable stages—that is, comparable to Europe on the eve of the reformation—the situation was in all the relevant respects at least as favorable as it was in western Europe. (Weber, Paper for Barnes Symposium—unpublished, p. 19; Harvard University Archives, HUG(FP) 42.42, Box 2)

See also Talcott Parsons, *The Structure of Social Action* (Glencoe, Ill.: Free Press, 1949), pp. 539–42. For a critique of this type of reasoning as applied to China, see Gary Hamilton, "Why No Capitalism in China? Negative Questions in Historical Comparative Research," *Journal of Developing Societies* 1 (1985): 192–93.

8. Weber, "Einleitung," p. 237 n. 1 in Vol. 1 of *Gesammelte Aufsätze zur Religionssoziologie.*

The first task for economic sociology would be to confront Weber's analysis in *The Economic Ethics of the World Religions* with current findings in economic history. Not much of this has been done, except on China, where the current verdict is that Weber was wrong on several historical points.[9] Unfortunately, the secondary literature on Weber's analysis of India, Islamic society, and Jewish "pariah capitalism" is mostly polemical and ideological rather than factual in nature.[1]

9. See especially the work of Mark Elvin, Gary Hamilton, and Randall Collins in this context. Elvin both confronts Weber's thesis of why rational capitalism did not spontaneously emerge in China and evaluates Weber's research on a number of topics. Capitalism did not emerge in China, Elvin claims, because of what he calls a high-level equilibrium trap, meaning by this that a variety of noncultural factors prevented demand and supply forces from working out freely. This trap became especially strong in the early 1800s. As to Weber's opinion on separate economic topics in *The Religion of China*—such as money and monetary policy, the tax system, and the regulation of rivers—Elvin mostly finds Weber wrong or confusing. Gary Hamilton argues that Weber misunderstood the nature of Chinese patriarchal domination and also that "negative questions" such as "Why is there no capitalism in China?" invite misleading answers because they project Western experience onto China. Hamilton adds that Weber did not grasp the important role of merchants' associations in China. Randall Collins shows, among other things, with the help of the work of Joseph Needham, how Weber's view of Chinese science and technology is outmoded. For a general analysis of Chinese economic history, see Mark Elvin, *The Pattern of the Chinese Past* (London: Eyre Methuen, 1973); and for his detailed critique of Weber's *The Religion of China*, see Elvin, "Why China Failed to Create an Endogenous Industrial Capitalism: A Critique of Max Weber's Explanation," *Theory and Society* 13 (1984): 379–91. For Gary Hamilton's work on Weber and China, see especially, Gary Hamilton, "Why No Capitalism in China? Negative Questions in Historical Comparative Research," *Journal of Developing Societies* 1 (1985): 187–211; and Gary Hamilton, "Patriarchalism in Imperial China and Western Europe: A Revision of Weber's Sociology of Domination," *Theory and Society* 13 (1984): 393–425. For Collins's views, see especially Randall Collins, *Weberian Sociological Theory*, pp. 58–72; in this context see also N. Sivin, "Max Weber, Joseph Needham, Benjamin Nelson: The Question of Chinese Science," pp. 37–49 in E. V. Walter et al. eds., *Civilizations East and West: A Memorial Volume for Benjamin Nelson* (Atlantic Highlands, N.J.: Humanities Press, 1985). It is obvious that Weber was not aware of the advances in the Chinese coal and iron industry in the eleventh century, as documented by Robert Hartwell (from 1966 to 1971) and summarized by William McNeill, *The Pursuit of Power* (Chicago: University of Chicago Press, 1982). (See, however, Weber's statement in *General Economic History* that despite the "enormous armies" of China and the arms they needed, "no impulse toward a capitalistic development followed from the fact"; Weber, *General Economic History*, pp. 308–9, or *Wirtschaftsgeschichte*, pp. 265–66.)
1. The secondary literature on Weber's analyses of Islamic society, Indian society, and Jewish "pariah capitalism" is stronger on assertions than on references to current works in economic history. For two interesting general introduction to the secondary literature on *The Religion of India* (with some relevant information on economic issues), see Detlef Kantowsky, ed., *Recent Research on Max Weber's Studies of Hinduism* (Munich: Weltforum Verlag, 1986); and David Gellner, "Max Weber, Capitalism and The Religion of India," *Sociology* 16 (1982): 526–43. For some general introductions to economy and religion in Islamic society, which do not make much use of the existing literature on the economic history of Islam, see Bryan Turner, "Islam, Capitalism and the Weber Theses," *British Journal of Sociology* 25 (1974): 230–43; Bryan Turner, *Weber and Islam* (London: Routledge and Kegan Paul, 1974); Maxime Rodinson, *Islam and Capitalism* (London: Allen Lane, 1974); and Maxime Rodinson, "Islamischer Patrimonialismus—ein Hindernis für die Entwicklung des modernen Kapitalismus?," pp. 180–89 in Wolfgang Schluchter, ed., *Max Webers Sicht des Islams* (Frankfurt am Main: Suhrkamp Verlag, 1987). An innovative attempt to look at the relationship between economics and religion from the point of view of preference falsification can be found in Timur Kuran, "Islam and Underdevelopment: An Old Puzzle Revisited," *Journal of Institutional and Theoretical Economics* 153 (1997): 41–71. For an attempt to confront Weber's notion of "pariah capitalism" with findings in economic history, see Hans Liebeschütz, "Max Weber's Historical Interpretation of Judaism," *Year Book of the Leo Baeck Institute* 9 (1964): 51–52.

A second task would be to submit Weber's analysis in *The Economic Ethics of the World Religions* to the same rigor Gordon Marshall applies to *The Protestant Ethic*. There are naturally some important differences between *The Protestant Ethic* and the later studies of the world religions, but one should still be able to make some progress by addressing Marshall's three key questions: What were the economic consequences of the religion in question? What would count as empirical proof of these consequences? And can we get access to historical material on these consequences? It is true that the single studies in Weber's series on the world religions contain more references to historical material than *The Protestant Ethic* does, but one is nonetheless tempted to extend Gordon Marshall's verdict on this latter study to *The Economic Ethics of the World Religions* as well: "not proven."

The third task that deserves to be carried out has to do with the way that Weber's main argument in the individual studies in *The Economic Ethics of the World Religions* is constructed. While the general thrust of these studies is clear—to study why rational capitalism has emerged only in the West—their analytical logic is nonetheless elusive and has not been fully established. Although the reader of *The Protestant Ethic* can follow Weber's argument step by step, the the same is not true for *The Economic Ethics of the World Religions*. Wolfgang Schluchter uses the term "constellational *description*" to characterize Weber's approach in *The Economic Ethics of the World Religions*, which may well describe the current state of the art.[2] Schluchter, however, does not state why Weber would have wanted to replace a causal historical analysis with a description of this type. Even though Weber was not interested in simply imposing his series of preconditions for rational capitalism in the West onto the development in other parts of the world, these preconditions nonetheless play a significant role in the analysis in *The Economic Ethics of the World Religions*. In Weber's individual studies we also find an attempt to get some leverage by using the concept of economic ethic in two different meanings. How all of these parts fit together, however, is by no means clear.

But even if *The Economic Ethics of the World Religions* still represents something of a challenge to modern scholarship, the analysis of economy and religion that can be found in Weber's work from *The Protestant Ethic* onward is tremendously rich and filled with suggestive ideas and concepts. Weber's analysis of economy and religion is, in my mind, by far the most imaginative part of his economic sociology—even if it is obvious that Weber knew considerably less about religion than, say, about law. It was, however, far more difficult

2. Schluchter, *Rationalism, Religion, and Domination*, pp. 114–15.

and counterintuitive to show that religion had played an important role in the creation of the modern economic order than that law or politics had played such a role. Weber's linking of ascetic Protestantism with rational capitalism is particularly ingenious and represents the foremost achievement in his early work on economy and religion. Weber's second great discovery in this area, which took place some years later, has to do with his concept of economic ethic. Religion and the economy, he suggested, are always related to to each other through the moral evaluation of economic activities. Again, the concrete way in which Weber worked out the link between the economy and religion in *The Economic Ethics of the World Religions* represents a magnificent achievement in economic sociology.

# Max Weber: A Chronology

1864    Karl Emil Maximilian Weber is born in Erfurt, Thuringia, on April 21, into the wealthy household of Helene Fallenstein (1844–1919) and Max Weber (1836–1897). He is the first of eight children.

1866    Ill with meningitis.

1869    The family moves to Berlin, where the father begins a successful political career.

1871    Foundation of the German Empire.

1872    Starts attending secondary school in Charlottenburg.

1882    Graduates from secondary school and becomes a law student at the University of Heidelberg.

1883    Spends the year in Strasbourg doing military service.

1884    Moves to Berlin University.

1886    Passes the bar exam.

1888    Doctoral studies under Levin Goldschmidt, a pioneer in the history of commercial law, and military service.

1889    Successful presentation of doctoral dissertation on commercial partnerships during the Middle Ages.

1890    Bismarck is dismissed. Weber accepts an important research assignment on agrarian conditions for the *Verein für Sozialpolitik*.

1891    Presents his *Habilitation* (a second dissertation needed to teach at the university level) on the importance of Roman agrarian history to the development of law.

1892    Finishes his research for the *Verein*, begins to teach law at the University of Berlin, and becomes engaged to Marianne Schnitger (1870–1954).

1893    Accepts a position as professor in political economy at the University of Freiburg and gets married.

1894    Moves to Freiburg.

1895    Presents his inaugural lecture at Freiburg, "The National State and Economic Policy."

1896    Is appointed to a prestigious professorship in economics at the University of Heidelberg.

1897    Quarrel with father and general exhaustion lead to a nervous

breakdown, which will last for many years and force
Weber to become a private scholar.

1898        Lectures on the key thesis in *The Protestant Ethic*.

1903        Resigns his position at the University of Heidelberg
            because of his illness. Starts to work on his methodolog-
            ical essays and *The Protestant Ethic and the Spirit of Cap-
            italism*.

1904        Travels to the United States to attend the World Exhibi-
            tion in St. Louis, to visit relatives, and to gather material
            for the latter part of *The Protestant Ethic*. With two col-
            leagues, Weber assumes editorship of the journal *Archiv
            für Sozialwissenschaft und Sozialpolitik*; the first of the
            two articles that make up *The Protestant Ethic* appears in
            *Archiv*.

1905        Revolution in Russia that Weber follows closely. The sec-
            ond article of *The Protestant Ethic* appears in *Archiv*.

1906–08     Starts to identify himself as a sociologist. Publishes "The
            Protestant Sects and the Spirit of Capitalism" and
            answers critics of *The Protestant Ethic*.

1909        Helps to found the German Sociological Association.
            The final edition of *The Agrarian Sociology of Ancient
            Civilizations* is published. Weber accepts the task of
            being the editor of an enormous handbook of economics,
            in which *Economy and Society* will be published posthu-
            mously (1921–22).

1910        The Webers move to Heidelberg.

1911        Starts work on the program for future studies of reli-
            gion and the economy discussed at the end of *The
            Protestant Ethic*. *The Economic Ethics of the World
            Religions*, as this project is called, will occupy Weber
            till his death.

1913        Publishes the first version of his theoretical program for
            a radically new sociology, "Some Sociological Categories
            of Interpretive Sociology."

1914        World War I begins; Weber accepts a position to organize
            some military hospitals.

1915–17     Publishes the articles that are parts of *The Economic Ethics
            of the World Religions*, such as *The Religion of India*, *The
            Religion of China*, and *Ancient Judaism*. Writes many
            newspaper articles on the war and gives the lecture "Sci-
            ence as a Vocation."

1918        Accepts a professorship at the University of Vienna on a
            trial basis and is active in German politics.

1919    Continues political engagement. Gives the lecture "Politics as a Vocation" and accepts a chair in economics at the University of Munich.

1920    Dies from pneumonia on June 14 in Munich. The second revised edition of *The Protestant Ethic* appears in Volume 1 of Weber's *Collected Essays in the Sociology of Religion*.

# Selected Bibliography

• Indicates a work included or excerpted in this Norton Critical Edition.

• Agevall, Ola. 1999. *A Science of Unique Events: Max Weber's Methodology of the Cultural Sciences.* Ph D thesis. Department of Sociology, Uppsala: Uppsala University. An excellent introduction to Weber's methodology.

Albrow, Martin. 1990. *Max Weber's Construction of Social Theory.* London: Macmillan. A useful analysis of Weber's sociology.

Aron, Raymond. 1970. "Max Weber." Pp. 219–317 in Vol. 2 of *Main Currents in Sociological Thought.* Garden City, NY: Anchor Books. An excellent summary of Weber's work.

Barbalet, J. M. 2000. "*Beruf*, Rationality and Emotion in Max Weber's Sociology," *Archives Européennes de Sociologie* 41, 2:329–51.

Becker, George. 1997. "Replication and Reanalysis of Offenbacher's School Enrollment Study: Implications for the Weber and Merton Theses," *Journal of the Scientific Study of Religion* 36, 4:483–96.

Bourdieu, Pierre. 1987. "Legitimation and Structured Interests in Weber's Sociology of Religion." Pp. 119–36 in Scott Lash and Sam Whimster (eds.), *Max Weber, Rationality and Modernity.* London: Allen and Unwin.

• Breiner, Peter. 2005. "Weber's *The Protestant Ethic* as Hypothetical Narrative of Original Accumulation," *Journal of Classical Sociology* 5.1:11–30.

Brubaker, Rogers. 1984. *The Limits of Rationality: An Essay on the Social and Moral Thought of Max Weber.* London: Allen and Unwin. A useful introduction to Weber's concept of rationality.

Bruun, Hans Henrik. 2007. *Science, Values and Politics in Max Weber's Methodology.* 2nd expanded ed. Burlington: Ashgate. An excellent account of Weber's philosophy of science.

Carruthers, Bruce, and Wendy Nelson Espeland. 1991. "Accounting for Rationality: Double-Entry Bookkeeping and the Rhetoric of Economic Rationality," *American Journal of Sociology* 97:31–69.

Chalcraft, David. 1994. "Bringing the Text Back In: On Ways of Rendering the Iron Cage Metaphor in the Two Editions of 'The Protestant Ethic.'" Pp. 16–45 in Larry Ray and Michael Reed (eds.), *Organizing Modernity: New Weberian Perspectives on Work, Organization and Society.* London: Routledge.

Chalcraft, David, and Austin Harrington (eds.). 2001. *The Protestant Ethic Debate: Max Weber's Replies to His Critics, 1907–1910.* Liverpool: Liverpool University Press. This work contains critiques of *The Protestant Ethic* and Weber's replies to his critics.

Cohen, Jere, Lawrence Hazelrigg, and Whitney Pope. 1975. "De-Parsonizing Weber: A Critique of Parsons' Interpretation of Weber's Sociology," *American Sociological Review* 40:229–41.

Cohen, Bernard (ed.). 1990. *Puritanism and the Rise of Science: The Merton Thesis.* New Brunswick: Rutgers University Press.

Eisenstadt, S. N. (ed.). 1968. *The Protestant Ethic and Modernization: A Comparative Approach.* New York: Basic Books. A useful set of essays on *The Protestant Ethic.*

Factor, Regis. 1988. *Guide to the Archiv für Sozialwissenschaft und Sozialpolitik Group 1904–1933: A Comprehensive Bibliography*. New York: Greenwood Press.

Ghosh, Peter. 1994. "Some Problems with Talcott Parsons' Version of '*The Protestant Ethic*,'" *Archives Européennes de Sociologie* 35:104–23.

Green, Robert (ed.). 1973. *The Weber Thesis Controversy*. 2nd ed. Lexington, MA: Heath. Some key texts from the controversy over *The Protestant Ethic*.

• Hamilton, Richard. 1996. *The Social Misconstruction of Reality*. New Haven: Yale University Press. This study contains the fullest set of references to works that are part of the debate over *The Protestant Ethic*.

Hanyu, Tatsuru. 1994. "Max Webers Quellenbehandlung in der 'Protestantischen Ethik'. Der 'Berufs'-Begriff," *Archives Européennes de Sociologie* 35,1:72–103.

• Hernes, Gudmund. 1989. "The Logic of *The Protestant Ethic. Rationality and Society* 1.1:123–62.

Jellinek, Georg. 1901. *The Declaration of the Rights of Man and of Citizens: A Contribution to Modern Constitutional History.* New York: Holt. An important source of inspiration for Weber to *The Protestant Ethic*.

Käsler, Dirk. 1988. *Max Weber: An Introduction to His Life and Work*. Trans. Philippa Hurd. Cambridge, UK: Polity Press. An excellent and reliable introduction to Weber's work.

Kippenberg, Hans, and Martin Riesebrodt (eds.). 2001. *Max Webers 'Religionssystematik.'* Tübingen: Mohr.

Kivisto, Peter, and William Swatos. 1988. *Max Weber: A Bio-Bibliography*. New York: Greenwood Press. A useful but somewhat outdated reference source for Weber's work and the literature on his work.

Lehmann, Hartmut, and Guenther Roth (eds.). 1993. *Weber's Protestant Ethic: Origin, Evidence, Contexts*. Cambridge, UK: Cambridge University Press. A useful set of essays on *The Protestant Ethic*.

McKinnon, Malcolm. 1989. "Calvinism and the Infallible Assurance of Grace . . . ," *British Journal of Sociology* 39:143–210.

Marshall, Gordon. 1982. *In Search of the Spirit of Capitalism: An Essay on Max Weber's Protestant Ethic Thesis*. London: Hutchinson. An excellent study of *The Protestant Ethic*.

*Max Weber Gesamtausgabe* (Max Weber's *Collected Works*). 1984–Tübingen: Mohr.

*Max Weber Studies*. 2001. Special issue devoted to the translation of *The Protestant Ethic*. 2, 1.

*Max Weber Studies*. 2005. Special issue devoted to the centenary of *The Protestant Ethic and the Spirit of Capitalism*. 5:2.

Mitzman, Arthur. 1985. *The Iron Cage: An Historical Interpretation of Max Weber*. New Brunswick, NJ: Transaction Books. An interesting psychoanalytical biography of Max Weber.

Mommsen, Wolfgang. 2000. "Max Weber's 'Grand Sociology': The Origins and Composition of *Wirtschaft und Gesellschaft. Soziologie*," *History and Theory* 39:364–83. An important article on the coming into being of *Economy and Society*.

Mommsen, Wolfgang, and Jürgen Osterhammel (eds.). 1987. *Max Weber and His Contemporaries*. London: Unwin. This work contains useful portraits of Weber's friends, colleagues, and others connected to Weber.

Nelson, Benjamin. 1974. "Max Weber's 'Author's Introduction' (1920): A Master Clue to His Main Aims," *Sociological Inquiry* 44,4:269–78.

Parkin, Frank. 1982. *Max Weber*. London: Routledge. A useful and short introduction to Weber.

Parsons, Talcott. 1937. *The Structure of Social Action*. New York: McGraw-Hill. An important early analysis of Weber's work by the original translator of *The Protestant Ethic*.

Parsons, Talcott. 1975. "On 'De-Parsonizing Weber,'" *American Sociological Review* 40:666–70.

Poggi, Gianfranco. 1983. *Calvinism and the Capitalist Spirit: Max Weber's Protestant Ethic*. Amherst: University of Massachusetts Press. A useful, brief study of *The Protestant Ethic*.

Radkau, Joachim. 2005. *Max Weber. Die Leidenschaft des Denkens*. Munich: Verlag Carl Hanser. A recent biography of Max Weber.

Rickert, Heinrich. 1986. *The Limits of Concept Formation in Natural Science: A Logical Introduction to the Historical Sciences*. Trans. Guy Oakes. Cambridge, UK: Cambridge University Press. A key work by an important neo-Kantian philosopher whose work influenced Weber.

Roth, Guenther. 1992. "Interpreting and Translating Max Weber," *International Sociology* 7, 4:449–59.

Roth, Guenther. 2001. *Max Webers deutsch-englische Familiengeschichte 1800–1950*. Tübingen: Mohr. An important extended family portrait of the Webers.

Samuelson, Kurt. 1961. *Religion and Economic Action*. London: Heinemann. A classic in the debate of *The Protestant Ethic*.

Scaff, Lawrence. 2005. "The Creation of the Sacred Text: Talcott Parsons Translates *The Protestant Ethic and the 'Spirit' of Capitalism*," *Max Weber Studies* 5,2:205–28.

Schluchter, Wolfgang. 1989. *Rationalism, Religion and Domination: A Weberian Perspective*. Trans. Neil Salomon. Berkeley: University of California Press. A useful presentation and analysis of Weber's sociology of religion.

Schutz, Alfred. 1967. *The Phenomenology of the Social World*. Evanston, IL: Northwestern University Press. An outstanding analysis of Weber's theoretical sociology.

Sica, Alan. 2004. *Max Weber, A Comprehensive Bibliography*. New Brunswick: Transaction Publishers. The main and most up-to-date bibliography in English on Weber and the literature on Weber.

Swedberg, Richard. 1998. *Max Weber and the Idea of Economic Sociology*. Princeton: Princeton University Press.

Swedberg, Richard. 2004. *The Max Weber Dictionary*. Stanford: Stanford University Press.

Tawney, R. H. 1954. *Religion and the Rise of Capitalism*. New York: New American Library. An early and important contribution to the debate of *The Protestant Ethic*.

Tribe, Keith. 2007. "Talcott Parsons as Translator of Max Weber's Basic Sociological Categories," *History of European Ideas* 33:212–33.

Troeltsch, Ernst. 1960. *The Social Teachings of the Christian Churches*. 2 vols. New York: Harper and Brothers. An early and important study of Christianity by a friend and colleague of Weber who shared many of his ideas on the role of Protestantism.

Turner, Stephen (ed.). 2000. *The Cambridge Companion to Weber*. Cambridge, UK: Cambridge University Press.

Weber, Marianne. 1975. *Max Weber: A Biography*. Trans. Harry Zohn. New York: Wiley. The classic biography of Weber.

Weber, Max. 1930. *The Protestant Ethic and the Spirit of Capitalism*. Trans. Talcott Parsons. London: Allen and Unwin. This is the first translation into English of the second edition of *The Protestant Ethic* from 1920. It is also the text used in this Norton Critical Edition.

Weber, Max. 1946a. *From Max Weber*. Eds. and trans. Hans Gerth and C. Wright Mills. New York: Oxford University Press. An important and useful anthology of Weber's writings.

• Weber, Max. 1946b. "The Protestant Sects and the Spirit of Capitalism." Pp. 302–22 in Max Weber (eds. Hans Gerth and C. Wright Mills), *From Max Weber*. Trans. Hans Gerth and C. Wright Mills. New York: Oxford University Press. This essay from 1906 complements *The Protestant Ethic*, mainly through its analysis of the impact of the sects on their members.

Weber, Max. 1949. *Essays in the Methodology of the Social Sciences*. Trans. and ed. Edward A. Shils and Henry A. Finch. New York: Free Press. A collection of some of Weber's most important essays on the methodology of social science.

Weber, Max. 1951. *The Religion of China: Confucianism and Taoism*. Trans. Hans Gerth. New York: Free Press. A key work in Weber's sociology of religion; also a part of *The Economic Ethics of the World Religions*.

Weber, Max. 1952. *Ancient Judaism*. Trans. Hans H. Gerth and Don Martindale. New York: Free Press. A key work in Weber's sociology of religion; also a part of *The Economic Ethics of the World Religions*.

Weber, Max. 1958. *The Religion of India*. Trans. Hans Gerth and Don Martindale. New York: Free Press. A key work in Weber's sociology of religion; also a part of *The Economic Ethics of the World Religions*.

Weber, Max. 1972. *Wirtschaft und Gesellschaft. Grundriss der verstehenden Soziologie*. Ed. Johannes Winkelmann. 5th ed. Tübingen: J. C. B. Mohr.

Weber, Max. 1976. *The Agrarian Sociology of Ancient Civilizations*. Trans. R. I. Frank. London: New Left Books.

Weber, Max. 1978. *Economy and Society: An Outline of Interpretive Sociology*. Trans. Ephraim Fischoff et al. 2 vols. Berkeley: University of California Press. Weber's most important work in sociology, next to *The Protestant Ethic*.

Weber, Max. 1981. *General Economic History*. Trans. Frank Knight. New Brunswick: Transaction Books. This work, which is based on students' notes from the last course Weber ever gave, contains an important section on the role of the Protestant ethic.

Weber, Max. 1988. *Gesammelte Aufsätze zur Religionssoziologie*. 3 vols. Tübingen: Mohr. This three-volume set, in which the 1920 revised version of *The Protestant Ethic* appeared, was planned by Weber before his death.

Weber, Max. 1993. *Die protestantische Ethik und der "Geist" des Kapitalismus."* Bodenheim: Neue Wissenschaftliche Bibliothek Athenäum. This work is based on the first edition from 1904–1905 but also indicates what changes were made in the second edition from 1920.

Weber, Max. 1994. *Political Writings*. Ed. and trans. Peter Lassman and Ronald Speirs. Cambridge, UK: Cambridge University Press. A useful set of texts in Weber's political sociology.

Weber, Max. 2002a. *The Protestant Ethic and the 'Spirit' of Capitalism and Other Writings*. Trans. Peter Baehr and Gordon Wells. New York: Penguin Books. This is a translation of the first edition of *The Protestant Ethic* from 1904–05.

Weber, Max. 2002b. *The Protestant Ethic and the Spirit of Capitalism*. Trans. Stephen Kalberg. Los Angeles: Roxbury. This is a recent translation of the second edition of *The Protestant Ethic* from 1920.

Weber, Max. 2003a. *L'éthique Protestante et l'Esprit du Capitalisme*. Trans. Jean Pierre Grossein. Paris: Gallimard. This is a recent and high-quality translation of *The Protestant Ethic* into French.

Weber, Max. 2003b. *The History of Commercial Partnerships in the Middle Ages*. Trans. Lutz Kaelber. New York: Rowman and Littlefield. Weber's important first dissertation.

Weber, Max 2004. *The Essential Weber: A Reader*. Ed. Samuel Whimster. London: Routledge. An important anthology of Weber's writings, drawing mainly on new translations.

# Index